David Alstr

MY LITTLE TOWN OF CROMARTY

MY LITTLE TOWN OF CROMARTY

The History of a Northern Scottish Town

David Alston

BIRLINN

First published in 2006 by
Birlinn Limited
West Newington House
10 Newington Road
Edinburgh EH9 1QS
www.birlinn.co.uk

Hardback
ISBN 10: 1 84158 527 0
ISBN 13: 978 1 84158 527 7

Paperback
ISBN 10: 1 84158 602 1
ISBN 13: 978 1 84158 602 1

British Library Cataloguing-in-Publication Data
A catalogue record for this book is available from the British Library

Typeset by Waverley Typesetters, Fakenham, Norfolk
Printed and bound by Cromwell Press, Trowbridge

I have ... a certain harbour or bay, in goodness equal to the best in the world, adjacent to ... my little town ... of Cromarty ... which is the head town of the Shire ... the shire and the town being of one and the same name with the harbour or bay.

Sir Thomas Urquhart, *Logopandecteision*, 1653

The Northern Counties of Scotland, showing Cromarty-shire (Sir John Sinclair, a general view of the northern counties and islands of Scotland, 1795).

Contents

Part 4: After 1843

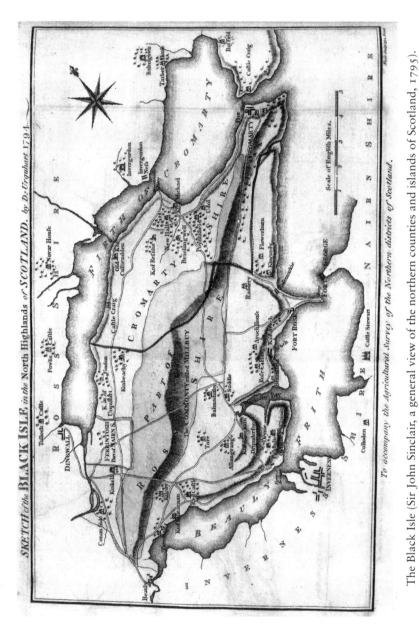

The Black Isle (Sir John Sinclair, a general view of the northern counties and islands of Scotland, 1795).

List of Plates

List of Figures and Tables

Figures

Tables

Appendix

Acknowledgements and Dedication

In 1987, at the prompting of Robin Callander, I stepped through the doors of the Scottish Record Office for the first time, to discover a wealth of archived documents relating to Cromarty. Much of the material appeared to have lain untouched for decades or, in some cases, centuries. I had moved to the town the year before and its history, indeed history as a whole, was a new interest for me. My awareness of these, apparently untapped, resources in the SRO (now the National Archives of Scotland) and the openness of the community in Cromarty to a newcomer like myself soon led to the opportunity to become involved in the establishment of a museum in the town's old courthouse, and I served as its curator from 1991 until 2003, on a part-time basis for the last four years. I am grateful to all who made that possible, especially the Courthouse trustees, chaired by Jean MacBeath MBE, and Ross & Cromarty District Council, whose museums service was then led by Graham Watson.

My first ventures into the history of Cromarty were, however, little more than the accumulation of a multitude of unrelated, and often curious, facts. But, even at this amateur level, I was struck by the patience and helpfulness of those professional historians I contacted. There were many, but the encouragement of the late Monica Clough was especially important. The Scottish Vernacular Buildings Working Group, particularly in the person of Elizabeth Beaton, was also significant as a sounding board for some of my early ideas on the town's architecture.

In the winter of 1993/4 I was rescued from the dead end of simply amassing information by Chris Whatley of the University of Dundee, who had visited the museum the previous summer. I had shown him some of my work, which he took time to read and responded with his characteristic mixture of directness and support – his comments 'badly needs to be given a focus' and 'you need to be asking the right questions', were coupled with the encouragement 'I certainly think you should do something' and the wholly unexpected suggestion that I enrol as a part-time PhD student at Dundee. I remain deeply grateful for Chris's initial interest, his act of faith in accepting a student with no previous academic background in history, and the direction he subsequently provided as academic supervisor for my research.

In the nineteen years since my first visit to the Scottish Record Office I have met with almost universal courtesy and help from all the staff in archives, libraries and national institutions. They are bodies which provide an excellent service and in which we should take great pride. Private archives have been equally helpful. I have tried, principally in the footnotes, to acknowledge the sources of all ideas and material but some contributions will inevitably have slipped through without due credit, and for this I apologise.

My final acknowledgement is to the many people in, or connected with, Cromarty and the surrounding area, who have provided information, discussed ideas, listed to talks and shown interest. I dedicate this book to all of them – but in particular:

To

Bobby Hogg
whose family have, for centuries,
lived in this town and fished these waters –
and who was one of the first to make me welcome here.

Abbreviations

NAS	National Archives of Scotland (formerly, Scottish Record Office)
NLS	National Library of Scotland
NRAS	National Register of Archives for Scotland
NSA	New Statistical Account
OSA	Old Statistical Account
SRO	Scottish Record Office

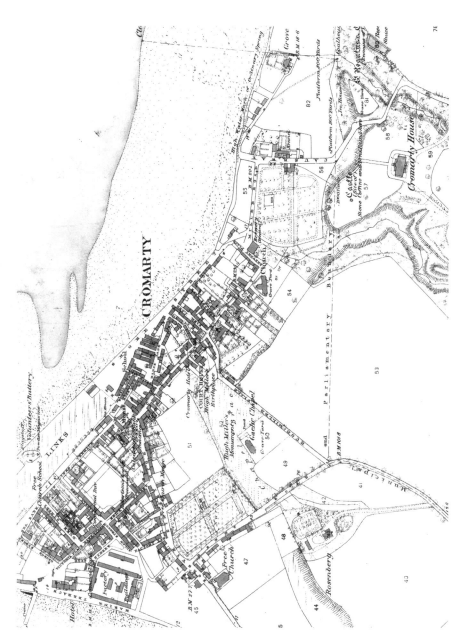

Cromarty Burgh Surveyor's map, 1870s.

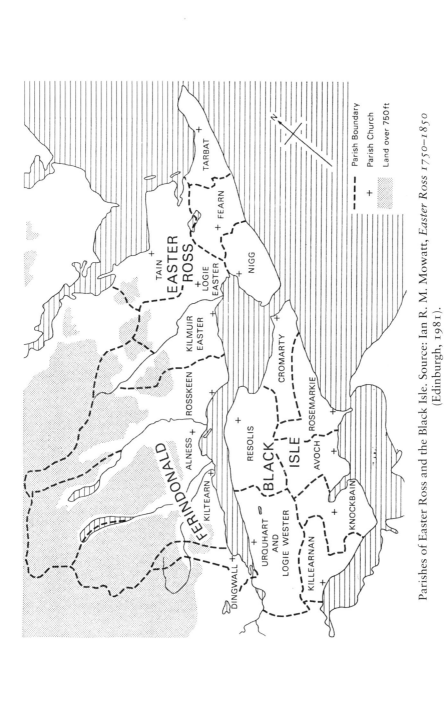

Parishes of Easter Ross and the Black Isle. Source: Ian R. M. Mowatt, *Easter Ross 1750–1850* (Edinburgh, 1981).

Introduction

This book is a history of the small town of Cromarty, north of Inverness at the tip of the Black Isle peninsula. Some are puzzled that Cromarty, with fewer than 750 inhabitants, should still, stubbornly, call itself a town, but in doing so its people show an admirable awareness of their history – of the settlement's beginnings as a royal burgh and of its days as a leading commercial centre for the northern Highlands. They are also influenced by their surroundings, by the fact that, through the accidents of history, they inhabit a place with some of the best-preserved vernacular urban architecture in Scotland. And, these influences aside, there is also a choice being made – to be a town, rather than a village, is partly a state of mind. I hope that this book will help to confirm Cromarty folk in their sense of being townspeople.

However, I hope, too, that the book has a much wider relevance because many of the people of Scotland, for much of our history, have lived in small towns, rather than in the countryside or cities, and yet we understand little of how these communities functioned. Part 1, which brings together what is known of Cromarty before 1660, contains little original material but I trust it is an accurate summary of our present knowledge of early Cromarty. The date 1660 has been chosen simply because, from this date, there are fuller records and it is possible to gain a better understanding of the social and economic circumstances of the area. There is every possibility that archaeology and other studies will greatly enhance our understanding of the earlier period. The core of the book (Parts 2 and 3) is a detailed study of Cromarty between the 1660s and the mid nineteenth century, the period when it was at its most prominent, with a population that peaked at just over 2,200 in 1831. Part 4 brings the history up to the turn of the twenty-first century.

The history of Cromarty cannot be understood in isolation from its hinterland – the farmlands of the eastern Black Isle – and the waters of the Cromarty Firth, the Moray Firth and the sea beyond. As a result there is much material in the book relevant to the more general social and economic history of the north – its agriculture, fishing, manufactures, trade, social class and population. I hope that this too will prove useful to students of the history of Scotland and the Highlands.

All visitors to modern-day Cromarty are greeted by signs that announce the little town as the 'Birthplace of Hugh Miller, Geologist and Writer'. Miller's role in nineteenth-century Scotland as a journalist, scientist, folklorist, churchman and social commentator will not be known to every reader and those looking for a detailed account of his life and work should turn to the books listed in the bibliography. I have used Miller's writings as a source in every chapter of this history but I have not used his work uncritically. One of the earliest guides to the Black Isle, published when its railway opened in 1894, was dedicated 'with reverence' to Miller, and his works were said to have 'immortalized the town and every nook and crannie in the parish'. This is a less reverential age and I hope that those who turn now to Miller will find him, as did his contemporaries, a more challenging figure.

Part 1
Before 1660

1

Before 1660

To Norroway, to Norroway,
To Norroway o'er the faem;
The king's daughter of Norroway,
Tis thou maun bring her hame.

The Ballad of Sir Patrick Spens

An Autumn journey

On 28 September 1290 Thomas de Braytoft rode into the small burgh of Cromarty. He was a 'clerk' of some importance, the medieval equivalent of a senior civil servant, ultimately responsible to Edward I of England, and he was travelling north on a mission to Orkney. A few days earlier a ship had landed in these islands carrying a young girl named Margaret, daughter of the king of Norway and granddaughter, and heir, of the last king of Scots, Alexander III. The six-year-old Margaret was more important than she could comprehend, the key to a planned union of the Crowns of Scotland and England, on more or less equal terms, through a proposed marriage to Edward's five-year-old son. It was a time of hope for many Scots. The union, already agreed in March, would end contention over succession to the Scottish throne, ease the sometimes-troubled relationship between Scotland and its more powerful southern neighbour, and preserve the Scots church, law and parliament. As he rode into the town Thomas de Braytoft could not know that Margaret, the 'Maid of Norway', had sickened during the voyage and was already dead. Thomas and his travelling companions spent the night of the 28th in Cromarty, most likely in the castle, before embarking by ferry across the waters of the Cromarty Firth. Ten days later they were back at Nigg, on the north shore, bearing the bad news.

Thomas had travelled to Cromarty by way of well-established centres of royal authority – castles under the control of the Crown, each the seat of a sheriff with legal powers over a small surrounding area, the

3

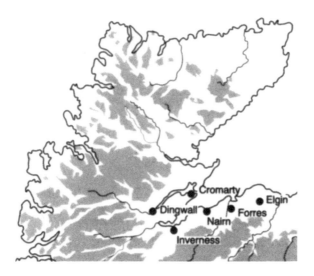

FIGURE 1.1
Royal castles around the Moray Firth.

sheriffdom, and each protecting a small settlement with the right to engage in trade, a royal burgh. In the following June, 1291, Edward of England would be appointed arbitrator of the disputed succession to the Scottish Crown and given control of thirteen such royal castles in Scotland. Six, with their sheriffdoms and burghs, were close to the shores of the Moray Firth and the adjoining Beauly and Cromarty Firths – Elgin, Forres, Nairn, Inverness, Dingwall and Cromarty – and Thomas de Braytoft would become keeper of the castles of Nairn and Cromarty. Both were probably simple constructions known as 'motte and baileys', consisting of wooden buildings within an enclosure (the bailey) on top of a natural or artificial mound (the motte). Despite its simplicity, Cromarty castle was a place of some strategic importance, since it controlled a ferry crossing on the coastal route north of Inverness.

Cromarty: a frontier post

There have been differing views as to when southern, royal authority began to be effectively exercised in the north. It was commonly held that there was no effective royal control until the reign of David I, between 1124 and 1153, when a series of royal castles and sheriffdoms were created in a line from Aberdeen to Inverness, possibly extending to Cromarty. This was then subject to an ebb and flow of influence until consolidated in the first two decades of the thirteenth century. The alternative view, now widely accepted, while not disputing the periodic insecurity of royal authority, holds that the line of control was based on a pre-existing structure of centralised power in the form of royal thanages, the most important of which, north of Inverness, appear to have been Cromarty and Dingwall. The Crown had, then, a landed presence north of Inverness from at least the eleventh century and possibly earlier.

To understand the relationship between the thanage of Cromarty and more southern centres of power, it is necessary to return to the origins of the Scottish nation. The sophisticated culture of the Picts of north Scotland is evident in the rich heritage of carved stones, not least in the Black Isle and Easter Ross. However, at some time before AD 500 another people, Scots from modern-day Antrim in the north of Ireland, had begun to settle in south-west Argyll, in what was to become the kingdom of Dalriada. They belonged to three principal tribes – the *Cenél nGábrain*, the *Cenél nOengusa* and the *Cenél Loairn*. By the middle of the ninth century Kenneth MacAlpin, king of the Scots of Dalriada, had established control over the southern Picts and, at about the same time, the territory of the northern Picts began to come into the hands of a rival Scots dynasty, of the tribe of the *Cenél Loairn*, whose power was centred in Moray. Rivalry between the two continued for almost 200 years but the superior resources of the southern dynasty and a long-running feud within the Moray-based northern dynasty gradually allowed the southern line to dominate.

While the Scots were consolidating their hold on Pictland, the west and north were coming under the influence of Scandinavians, who arrived first as raiding Vikings. Raiding was followed by settlement and during the ninth century the Norse earldom of Orkney became established, under the powerful dynasty of *Møre* from western Norway. The Earls of Orkney had considerable influence over Caithness and Sutherland, and the Norse sagas suggest two main periods of expansion south of the Oykell and the Dornoch Firth into modern-day Ross & Cromarty: first in the late ninth century by Earl Sigurd I (the Mighty) and Thorstein the Red, a Hebridean-based Viking; and second in the early eleventh century under Earl Thorfinn. There was certainly some Norse settlement along the south shore of the Cromarty Firth, revealed in the place names Culbo (*kula bol* – the farmstead on the hillock), Udale (*y-dalr* – yew dale) and Braelangwell (*langvollr* – long field), but it was Dingwall (*thingvollr* – the assembly field) at the head of the firth which was more important, probably because it controlled access to timber supplies from the valleys of the Conon and its tributaries. Cromarty, in this period, lay in the shifting frontier zone between Scots and Norse power.

Macbeth: thane of Cromarty

In 1029–30 Earl Thorfinn of Orkney pursued a campaign against the Scots *mormaer* (steward) of Moray, winning a battle at *Torfness* (Tarbatness in Easter Ross). In the *Orkneyinga Saga* the mormaer is named as Karl Hundason and this, which can be read as 'churl son-of-a-dog', is almost certainly an uncomplimentary byname for Macbeth. Macbeth was in a powerful position since, by his marriage to Gruoch, he had united the rival branches of the Moray dynasty. Moreover, because both he and his wife were descended from tenth-century kings of Scots, he presented a serious threat to the reigning Scots king, Duncan I. Duncan marched north to Moray where he was defeated and killed by Macbeth, after which, with no other adult claimant to the throne, Macbeth became king of Scotland in 1040.

There is an intriguing reference to the thanage of Cromarty in the earliest version of the story of Macbeth and the witches, as recounted by Andrew of Wyntoun in his verse *Chronicle*, written about 1420. Like Shakespeare, Wyntoun portrays Macbeth as a traitor, whose path to the kingship through the murder of Duncan begins with his encounter with the three 'weird sisters'. They appear in a dream in which, before the second and third greet him as thane of Moray and King, the first declares, 'Lo, yonder the thayne of Crombaghty'. This thanage was once dismissed by historians as 'mythical' but recent research has tended to confirm its existence – and Wyntoun is unlikely to have simply invented it.

Macbeth's power in southern Scotland was broken in 1054, when he was defeated by Duncan's son, Malcolm III (Canmore). Three years later Malcolm extended his control into the north, defeating and killing Macbeth in battle at Lumphanan, Aberdeenshire. Macbeth's stepson, Lulach, was defeated the following year. This consolidation of control by the southern-based dynasty marked a turning point in the history of the north but it was followed by almost 200 years of power struggles between the descendants of Malcolm and the remnants of the northern royal line in Moray and Ross.

Cromarty: a feudal holding

The two principal rebel families associated with Ross were the MacHeths and the MacWilliams. In 1130 Malcolm MacHeth supported a revolt against David I, led by Earl Angus of Moray (a grandson of Lulach). Angus's defeat was followed by a march north by the royal army, possibly extending into Ross. The thanages, whenever they had originated, were soon superseded by David I's network of castles linked to sheriffdoms and by the consolidation in the north of the feudal system of landholding. Under this all-embracing system of tenure, the land was deemed to belong, theoretically to God, but in effect, to the Crown, in the person of the sovereign, who might then grant holdings to his (or, rarely, her) followers. He was their feudal superior and they his vassals, who might in turn grant land to others, lower in the feudal chain. Feudal superiors exacted both services and payments from their vassals, military service being originally the more important since it allowed the king to call out armed followers to support him. David I's feudalism was to last very nearly a thousand years, for Scotland was the last country in Europe to abolish the last remnants of feudal tenure in 2002.

Although Malcolm MacHeth had been captured, on his release in 1157 he was created Earl of Ross. This was probably an attempt by the new king, Malcolm IV, to win the support of the MacHeths and was the first of a number of occasions on which the earldom would be used by the Crown to win support or reward loyalty. A more serious threat was posed in the 1170s and 1180s by rebellions launched from a power base in the northern Highlands by Donald MacWilliam, whose father was an illegitimate son of Duncan II. The danger was sufficiently serious for the king, William I, to lead an army north in 1179 and fortify two royal castles north of Inverness – at Eddirdowyr (Tarradale) on the north shore of the Beauly Firth and at Dunskaith on the north side of the entrance to the Cromarty Firth. In 1187 MacWilliam was defeated on the moor of Mam Garvia, probably north-west of Dingwall, and his severed head was presented to the king. It was, however, another ten years before the frontier of royal authority was pushed back again into Ross.

There was a further revolt involving both the MacWilliams and MacHeths in 1211 but a turning point came when the royal house gained the support of a native northern family in the person of Farquhar Mactaggart. Mactaggart, whose name means 'son of the priest', was probably associated with the sanctuary of St Duthac at Tain. He was knighted in 1215 and granted lands in Easter Ross, finally gaining the title Earl of Ross, probably c.1230 after the MacWilliams were finally crushed. Mactaggart's support for the Scottish Crown was of vital importance in the history of the area and his influence seems to have allowed an expansion of feudal settlements in the north after 1215.

All of the account above is, of course, given from the point of view of the ultimate victors, the southern dynasty of the Scots. No doubt others, in Orkney and the west Highlands, would have seen it differently but this is how it would have been regarded by the people of Cromarty living in what was, by the thirteenth century, the northern part of kingdom centred in the south. Crucially, royal authority provided the people of the burgh with security and allowed them to farm and trade.

The parish of Cromarty

The people of the burgh were also part of a well-organised national and international religious community. David I had consolidated support for the church in Scotland as a system of parishes grouped into diocese, each under the authority of a bishop appointed by the Crown, with an obligation on landowners to contribute a tenth part of the annual crop from their land for the upkeep of the local church (a *teind* in Scotland, equivalent to the English tithe). Over time teinds, also known as teind sheaves, were appropriated (diverted) to support clergy in larger religious establishments – cathedrals and monasteries – and those who received the teinds appointed poorly paid deputes (vicars) to carry out their duties in the parishes. Vicars might in turn retain the income and appoint a further, even more poorly paid, substitute – a curate. Additional income for the church was derived from the glebe – an area of land which could be farmed by the priest or rented out to provide an income – and from small teinds (also known as vicarage), which were a payment on a variety of farm produce (hay, livestock, garden and dairy produce) and, in some communities, including Cromarty, on catches of fish.[1]

Cromarty: the first records

Cromarty does not emerge into recorded history until it appears in a feudal charter granted sometime after the year 1252, and before 1272, by which William de Monte Alto (Mowat) granted a davoch of land, named Ferenes (Farness), in his holding of Crumbauthin (Cromarty), to David de Denoon, in exchange for lands in Stirling and Forfar. The castle is mentioned in the same document. Then, between 1264 and 1266, the Exchequer Rolls of Scotland record that the sheriff of Cromarty, the same William Mowat, made an annual payment of twenty-four merks (£16) for a hereditary holding from the king of six davochs of land and accounted for £7 from the burgh of Cromarty. A *davoch* (pronounced 'doch', to rhyme with 'loch') was a measure of land, probably based on its productive capacity rather than its extent. To the west of Cromarty, along the southern shore of the Cromarty Firth, lie a series of long established farmtouns, known in the mid seventeenth century as the 'four wester davochs' of Meikle Farness, Davidston, Peddieston and Little Farness. Meikle Farness has since been absorbed in Davidston and Little Farness is now simply known as Farness.

A sheriffdom of six davochs was small but typical both of earlier thanages and of similar, small sheriffdoms belonging to the early period of feudalism in eleventh-century Scotland. The sheriff held his land for a fixed payment of money which was 'less honourable or prestigious than the earlier form of feudal tenure by knight service, token payment or prayers' and seems to have first emerged during the reign of William I (1165 –1214), as a form of tenure associated with burghs or land around burghs. By an accident of history, Cromarty alone of these tiny Scottish jurisdictions survived into the early modern period, as the old sheriffdom or shire of Cromarty.[2]

There is also evidence of life in the early burgh in finds from fields around the town. Over twenty hammered silver coins dating from before 1310 have been recovered, which were either lost there or thrown out by mistake into household middens, which were then spread on the fields as manure. There are pennies and cut halfpennies, cutting a penny in two being the only way of creating a coin of lesser value. Each penny was roughly the equivalent of a day's wages for a labourer. Most are English, though there are some Scottish, Irish and continental coins, and the earliest date from 1205–10, in the reign of John I. All this tells us that by the first half of the thirteenth century there was already a sophisticated use of coin in the town and that Cromarty was part of a wider economic system which linked it with England and beyond. A further find, from the same period, is the personal seal of an English nobleman named de Castello.

Cromarty and the Wars of Independence

The news brought south by Thomas de Braytoft of the death of the Maid of Norway dashed many hopes. There was to be no amicable union of the Crowns and, as a result, Edward I had both the excuse and the opportunity to set about reducing Scotland, like Ireland, to the status of a client kingdom. He deliberately confused the issue of succession by finding eleven candidates in addition to the two front-runners, John Balliol and Robert Bruce. Eventually he came down in favour of Balliol, possibly because he was the weaker man and could be more easily manipulated. Nevertheless in 1295 the Scots parliament refused support for Edward's war in France, and instead entered into an alliance with its king, Philip IV. By 1296 Scotland and England had embarked on a series of conflicts, lasting until 1328, which would later be known as the War or Wars of Independence.

The conflict did much to forge a stronger Scottish sense of national identity, with its accompanying myths and symbolism, taken up by the Scottish poets John Barbour (c.1320–95) in The Bruce, Andrew of Wyntoun in his Chronicle and Blind Harry (fl. c.1460) in The Wallace. A later sheriff of Cromarty, Sir Thomas Urquhart (1611–c.60) recorded legends of Wallace's relief of the castle of Cromarty, after a seven and a half year siege, and of the ambush of an English army with the death of 600 of Edward's soldiers, at a spot called the Wallace Den on the

Learnie Burn, west of Cromarty. And in the early nineteenth century a young Cromarty boy, Hugh Miller, would recall that he 'first became thoroughly a Scot sometime in my tenth year' after he was 'intoxicated with the fiery narratives' of Blind Harry's *Wallace*. Miller went on to record and publish another local legend – that Wallace as a fugitive sought refuge in the 'doocot cave' on the South Sutor, the headland east of Cromarty.[3]

When Thomas de Braytoft rode into Cromarty in the late afternoon or evening of 28 September 1290, these troubles lay in the future, and Viking raids and the rebellions of the MacHeths and MacWilliams were tales from the past. He would have passed in peace by a series of flourishing farms, whose harvest was gathered in and where the threshing of grain was almost complete. And he would have entered a small, but well-established, trading town, perhaps with a few hundred inhabitants, where markets could be held in the security provided by the sheriff's castle. There was lodging for him in the wooden bailey and a parish church where he could hear mass celebrated the next morning, before crossing the ferry to the shore below the castle of Dunskaith. His expenses for the day had been one shilling and ten pence.

Lairds and sheriffs

From 1263, and possibly earlier, the sheriff of Cromarty was William de Monte Alto – William of the High Hill. The family, later known as Mowat, were in many ways typical of the mobile Anglo-Norman nobility who colonised and controlled the expanding realms of the English and Scottish kings. The family had originally settled in Mold, Flintshire, and a branch was established in Forfarshire by the twelfth century. The Mowats were long-term supporters of the Comyns, the most powerful and influential noble family in thirteenth-century Scotland, and were rewarded for this support by the grant of offices such as sheriff of Inverness and of Cromarty. The Comyns were among the leaders of resistance to Edward I of England in the 1290s and 1300s, but were opposed by a rival faction of the aristocracy, which supported the Bruces.[4]

The Cromarty sheriff – still William, although this might be a son – retained his office under Edward I in 1305 but in 1306 took part in the northern rising, which later placed Robert Bruce on the throne. In December 1315, Bruce granted the sheriffdom and burgh of Cromarty to his own brother-in-law, Hugh Ross, son of William, Earl of Ross. In March 1316, the king confirmed the grant of the burgh of Cromarty to Hugh, with an annual unspecified amount due from William Mowat, 'our sheriff'. The grant of the sheriffdom and burgh to Hugh Ross did not, it seems, remove Mowat as sheriff, but placed an intermediary between him and the king, whose officer he was. The grant was repeated when Hugh succeeded to the earldom, on his father William's death in 1323.

Earl William, although originally opposed to Bruce, had become one of his firmest supporters and his son, Hugh, having married Bruce's sister, was shown such favour that in the 1320s he became one of the most powerful magnates in the north. He held the sheriffdoms and burghs of Cromarty and Dingwall, the burgh of Nairn, estates in the Black Isle and Easter Ross, baronies and thanages in north-eastern Scotland and the Isle of Skye. Earl Hugh was killed in 1333 at the battle of Halidon Hill and was succeeded by his son William, who in 1338 granted the lands of Inchrory, near Strathpeffer, to Adam Urquhart. Urquhart was, at the time of the grant, sheriff of Cromarty. In 1358 Earl William made a grant of the burgh and sheriffdom to the same Adam Urquhart. This was done with the concurrence of Richard Mowat, son and heir of William Mowat, and was confirmed by David II in 1364. Richard was in holy orders and so could not have legitimate heirs, and thus, whatever the circumstances in which the Mowats had lost the sheriffdom, their hereditary line was at an end.

There were eight Urquhart lairds and hereditary sheriffs from this Adam Urquhart until 1600. The line of succession was Adam's son John, then his son William (d.1475), then his first son William (d.1475) and his second son Alexander, followed by Alexander's son Thomas (d.1561), his son Alexander (d.1563), and then his son Walter (d. before 1607). The land holdings of the Urquharts expanded beyond the original sheriffdom with the acquisition of the lands of Brae from the Earl of Ross in 1349, the land being held for the yearly payment of a pair of white gloves. They also held Inchrory, near Strathpeffer, which in 1608 was exchanged for lands in Cullicudden, and by shortly after 1600, with additional acquisitions of church land in the sixteenth century, the Urquharts exercised authority as hereditary sheriffs over most of what came to be known as the old shire of Cromarty.

The politics of the north

From the late fourteenth century there was a general collapse of feudalism as a force of unity in the north. The power of the state in the Moray Firth had depended on three families – the Randolphs, the Ross earls and the Morays – but all of these families died out in the senior male line in the latter part of the century. Meanwhile, in the Hebrides, the MacDonald Lordship of the Isles emerged, bringing 150 years of relative stability in the west and a flowering of Gaelic culture. The MacDonalds also extended their power eastwards, becoming one of the parties in a prolonged and complex dispute over the succession to the earldom of Ross. The Lordship was, however, perceived as a threat to the power of the Scottish Crown and the most troubled time was from 1385 to 1431, when Alexander MacDonald, Lord of the Isles, defeated an army sent north by James I, at Inverlochy, in Lochaber. From this point the politics of the Highlands changed, with the Crown seeking an accommodation, rather than confrontation, with the MacDonalds. Alexander's claim to the earldom of Ross was recognised and when he died at Dingwall in 1449 he was symbolically buried in the cathedral at Chanonry. His son John succeeded him and was soon an ally of James II in his struggles with the powerful Douglas family, earls of Moray and of Ormond, on the Black Isle.

However, John's power was gradually collapsing from within, in his western heartland. Internal feuding intensified after 1475, when a secret treaty he had made with Edward IV of England became public, and for this act of treason to the Scottish Crown the earldom of Ross was confiscated. Finally, in 1493, following raids by John's nephew in Ross, James IV declared all John's lands and titles forfeit. The ultimate beneficiaries of the fall of the MacDonalds were the Campbells in Argyll, the Gordons in Moray, and the Mackenzies in Ross.

The combination of the early breakdown of order in the Moray Firth and the power of the Lords of the Isles in the west had made the MacDonalds for a time the greatest magnates in the entire Highlands. This was a time of raids, violence and vendetta. The town of Inverness was twice burnt in the early fifteenth century, and between 1460 and 1464 a MacDonald raid on forfeited Douglas lands seized £1,500 and large stocks of grain. The recurring cycles of violence, both during this period and after the forfeiture of the Lords of the Isles, intensified the Lowland perception of Highlanders as savage and dangerous – 'wyld wykked helend-men'.

The sheriffs and their castle

Where did the sheriffdom of Cromarty stand in all this? The third Urquhart laird, William, had been engaged in raids in Sutherland and Ross, but in 1457 he received a remission from James II from any actions against him and was, at the same time, knighted. This was at a time when James, with uncharacteristic statesmanship in his granting of titles, was producing loyal adherents to the royal cause in troubled localities and by 1458 James had built up a body of loyal nobility, of which William Urquhart was a minor part. Both William and his eldest son married into Aberdeenshire families of Forbes, staunch supporters of the king.

In 1470 William was granted permission by James III to replace the old, probably wooden, castle with a stone tower on the motte hill of

Cromarty, strengthening it with gates and ditches and 'preparing its top for warlike and defensive equipment'. This grant, made in April, was shortly before James and his queen set out on a progress through the north, staying for a month in Inverness. According to William's descendant, Sir Thomas Urquhart, the tower was not completed until 1507, when it was 'contrived by a French architect' and was such that it exceeded 'any in this kingdom'. It is possible construction began shortly after 1470 and that the original stone building was later added to, possibly by the addition of a corner tower and the large walled courtyard to the south. In any event, from 1470 it ceased to be a royal holding and became the personal possession of the sheriffs. Although it was demolished c.1772, to be replaced by Cromarty House, the castle had been accurately recorded in a series of plans made in 1746. In addition, some of its features were described by Sir Thomas Urquhart in the 1650s and, relying on oral tradition, by Hugh Miller in the 1830s. It was indeed a fine piece of architecture, a 'very substantial L–plan tower bigger and more sophisticated than any surviving late medieval structure in the area'.[5] The tower was six storeys high, with its main hall on the second floor, well lit by large windows and warmed by two fireplaces. All that remains is a 'bottle' well, with a narrow entrance opening into a wider reservoir below. There is no obvious reason why the family of Urquhart, minor landowners and not major players in the feuds of the fifteenth century, should have been able to erect such an impressive building.

Cromarty was not, however, immune from attack. In 1491, as the MacDonalds attempted to regain their position, Alexander MacDonald of Lochalsh led a raid into Easter Ross before being defeated at Blar na Pairc, possibly near Dingwall. During this foray, Hutcheon Rose, son of the laird of Kilravock, and Farquhar Macintosh raided the lands of Master Alexander Urquhart of Cromarty, carrying off a considerable booty. Urquhart, seeking compensation, claimed losses from his lands of 600 cows, 100 horses, 1,000 sheep, 400 goats, 200 swine, 400 bolls of grain, £200 of household goods, and £100 for the mails (money rents) of the lands laid waste. This may have been an exaggeration. The claim amounted to over £1,100 Scots but the compensation awarded in 1493 was £528, and when this remained unpaid in 1503 a compromise was reached of the marriage of the heir of Kilravock to the sheriff's daughter, Agnes, with payment of £260 by annual instalments of £40.

By the late fifteenth century there was renewed royal interest in the north. The young King James IV took effective control of government in 1495 and from that point made frequent, almost yearly, pilgrimages to the shrine of St Duthac at Tain. These were partly in penance for the role he felt he had played in the death of his father and partly a political gesture that made it clear that royal authority extended throughout the realm. He passed through Cromarty on a number of occasions

FIGURE 1.2
Cromarty Castle showing the tower (*c.*1500) and later wing (1630s) –
computer-assisted design from plan of 1746.

– including March and October 1497, March 1499 and November
1501. Three or four boats were usually needed to ferry the king and
his retinue across the firth and in 1501 a saddle was mistakenly left
behind, for which the owner, a James Fraser, received compensation of
nine shillings. In March 1499 the king stayed overnight with the priest
in the town, probably in a house on a site later identified as the 'manse
of the vicar of Cromarty' opposite the parish church.

   In addition to the castle, there are remnants of another early building
in Cromarty, the chapel of St Regulus. A plan and sketch of the ruins
were made in 1815, showing it was a rectangular building of rough

stone, measuring *c*.45 feet by *c*.20 feet externally, oriented east–west, with a *c*.20 feet by *c*.20 feet building of dressed stone, with corner buttresses, attached to the west gable. In the floor of this was the entrance to a burial vault below. There was a single narrow window in the north wall of the chapel but the south wall had fallen away. Hugh Miller, who knew the building well, adds that the eastern gable was topped by a 'rude stone cross', the body of the chapel was lit by a range of 'narrow, slit-like windows', the roof of both parts was of 'ponderous grey slate' and that the remaining bottom course of hewn stone, in the western part, was surmounted by a Gothic moulding. In Miller's time the vault was partially filled with bones and, a few yards from the chapel, there were worn remnants of a carved, recumbent figure with hands folded on the breast. William Mackay Mackenzie, a Cromarty native and eminent twentieth-century historian, believed that it dated from the later 1300s. It seems that it was the tomb of the Urquharts. A badly worn grave-slab recovered from the floor of the parish church, carved with a cross on a stepped base, long swords and an open book, may be of the same period and there are better preserved examples of similar carved grave-slabs in other churches of the sheriffdom, four at Kirkmichael and five at Cullicudden.[6]

The burgh: early trade and commerce

Burghs played a part in the economic and social life of medieval Scotland out of proportion to their size. Some were established by royal authority, often recorded in a charter, while others were granted their privileges by powerful church authorities or secular overlords. In the north the burghs of Inverness and Dingwall have charters of 1179 and 1226 establishing, or confirming, their status. Others such as Cromarty, or the burghs of Tain and Fortrose, both associated with ecclesiastical centres, do not have clear foundation dates. Most were small and the more remote burghs, such as Cromarty, cannot have had more than a few hundred inhabitants. Their importance lay in their role in trade and in the relative freedom of their inhabitants to pursue their own commercial interests.

At the heart of the burgh stood its mercat cross, marking the place where weekly markets were held and a symbol of the royal authority that licensed its trade. Those who brought goods for sale from the surrounding countryside paid a toll, collected at the nearby tollbooth, which usually came to serve both as a meeting place for the burgh officials and as a prison. Weekly markets were supplemented by larger burgh fairs, held two or three times a year and each lasting as long as one or two weeks. Markets and fairs encouraged landward trade but Cromarty, like most east coast burghs, also had access to the sea and

FIGURE 1.3
Cocket seal of Inverness and Cromarty, late fourteenth or early fifteenth century.

the fine natural harbour of the Cromarty Firth would remain the town's greatest asset for centuries. In 1521 the historian John Major wrote in his *History of Greater Britain* that 'Scotland possesses a great many harbours of which Cromarty at the mouth of the Northern River is held to be the safest – and by measure of its good anchorage is called by sailors Sykkersand, that is safe port'. The same name is found in earlier chronicles and the Latin name with the same meaning – *Portus Salutis* – may date from the time of the third-century Greek geographer, Ptolemy.

In the nineteenth century a seal matrix, that is the metal stamp used to leave an impression in hot wax, was found on the shore near Aberdeen. It was the *cocket* or customs seal of Inverness and Cromarty and dates either from the reign of Robert II (1371–90) or from the next century. Cocket seals were issued to those burghs permitted to send staple goods overseas and were held by royal officials in the burghs known as *custumars*, who collected customs dues and issued letters of cocket, certifying that dues had been paid. In large ports there were usually two custumars, who each held half of the seal, but in some places a single person served as custumar for more than one burgh.

Customs duties were an important source of royal revenue, known as *malatout* or *maltot*. It is not clear when they were first introduced, but in 1315, when the burgh of Cromarty was granted to the earl of Ross, the *maltot* was reserved to the king, indicating that customs duties were already being levied by this date. Wool, woolfells (sheepskins) and hides were the only goods on which customs duties were paid for most of the fourteenth century and from 1364 the issue of cockets also required a *tron* (public weigh beam) for weighing wool – the tronar was usually paid a fee of 1d per sack. From 1396 there were also official enumerators of skins and hides.

Although we know nothing else of Cromarty's early trade, coin finds from around the town provide a good indicator of the burgh's economic fortunes. These are not coins from a hoard, which would in fact tell us very little, but individual coins lost over the course of centuries. As a body of evidence from such a source it has been described by Donald Bateson, a leading authority on Scottish coinage, as 'one of the most important in Scotland' giving us an insight into the economy of the town lacking in the study of almost all other burghs in Scotland. The numbers found suggest that for almost 200 years, from *c*.1200 until the late 1300s, the town was flourishing. This is then followed by a century and a half from which there is an unexpected dearth of finds and it is only after another 100 years, in the second half of the sixteenth century, that the finds once again provide evidence of a prosperous burgh.[7]

This pattern corresponds with what we know in general of the state of the Moray Firth coastlands. The troubled times from 1380 until the early sixteenth century did not favour the economy of Cromarty. However, despite the apparent downturn in trade, there was some expansion of the land under cultivation. In 1449 part of the burgh's common moor was feued to four of the burgesses to create a farm, held by them as joint tenants, which would become known as Newton of Cromarty. Such alienation of the common lands of the burgh was technically illegal but frequently done.

Fifteenth-century charters also indicate some development in the administration of the burgh. When first recorded in the late thirteenth century, the sheriff was responsible to the Crown for dues of £7 from the burgh. It was not uncommon, in early burghs, for there to be such an overlord or supervisor, usually the sheriff, assisted by officials known as *prepositi* or *ballivi*, bailies. Two *prepositi* of Cromarty are mentioned in 1263. By 1449 the burgh had its own common seal and charters were issued 'with the consent of the whole community', perhaps indicating that all the burgesses met under the authority of bailies, named here as David Moricii (Morrison) and Walter de Saint-Clair (Sinclair). There remained a close connection with the sheriff and Thomas Legat, who was a bailie in 1465, was later sheriff-depute. Other bailies named in the fifteenth century are John Donaldson (1478), John Clunes (1490) and David Denoon (1494). There is no further mention of a *prepositus* – provost – of Cromarty until the seventeenth century.

In the fifteenth century the burgh, as a lowland settlement, may well have shared the emerging negative view of its Highland neighbours as 'wyld wykked helend-men'. Over thirty named burgesses appear in documents of the fifteenth century and of twenty-seven different

surnames only one, MacVey, has a clearly Gaelic form. The others include
Sinclair, Morrison, Williamson, Donaldson, Rebayn, Urquhart, Basock,
Robertson, Gallie, Johnson, Smith, Tailor, Clunes, Gibbie and Gibson,
Nicholson, Finlayson, Reid, Denoon, Gilbert and Gilbertson. Many
would not look out of place in any burgh in the south of Scotland.

Sixteenth-century sheriffs

In 1646 Sir Thomas Urquhart, having inherited the lands of Cromarty
four years before, had an inscription carved at the entrance to the
original tower of the castle. It referred to two sculptured figures above
the entrance portraying an earlier Sir Thomas (d.1561) and his wife
Helen Abernethy. He credited the earlier laird with the building of the
castle in 1507 and his wife with the surely more impressive achievement
of bearing him twenty-five sons and eleven daughters. He 'lived more
sumptuously than any of his time, and rode pompously with a retinue
of 50 domesticks', yet built the castle, maintained his family and left his
estate unencumbered by debt. In the opinion of the later Sir Thomas,
perhaps reflecting on the debts run up by his own father, this 'man of
probity and excellence' was not to be forgotten. It was, however, Sir
Thomas's contemporary, the Cromwellian officer and enthusiastic angler
Richard Franck, who has made him truly memorable. Franck's *Northern
Memoirs*, published in 1652, records a strange ceremony devised by the
earlier Thomas. In his declining years, having lived to be more than
eighty, he began to consider himself as already dead and 'fancying his
cradle his sepulchre, wherein he was lodg'd night after night, and haul'd
by pullies to the roof of his house: approaching as near as the roof would
let him to the beautiful battlements and suburbs of heaven'. When real
rather than imagined death finally claimed him, he was succeeded by a
son Alexander, who died after only two years later and was followed by
his son, Walter, who died some time before 1607.

One of the biggest changes affecting Scottish rural society in the
sixteenth century, and benefiting them, was the feuing of kirklands to
secular tenants. This was in the form of *feuferme*, the mode of feudal
tenure by which an annual cash sum was paid for the holding. Feuing
began before, but accelerated after, the Reformation and the Urquharts
of Cromarty were amongst the principal beneficiaries. They acquired
the bishop's lands of Kirkmichael in 1564 and Kinbeachie in 1568. In
1607, the Crown gave a fresh grant to Thomas Urquhart of Cromarty of
the lands of Ardoch and of the hereditary patronage of the rectory and
vicarage of Kirkmichael, which had at some earlier date been made over
to Urquhart. The whole of the bishop's lands along the southern shore of
the Cromarty Firth also became an Urquhart possession and the tower
erected there – Castle Craig – is probably of the late sixteenth century. If

FIGURE 1.4
Castle Craig (*c.*1590) in the 1880s.

so, it was built for Thomas Urquhart of Craighouse, a younger brother
of the sheriff, Walter. It still stands, though a tottering ruin.

Other families also benefited from the feuing of kirklands. On the
south-west boundary of the sheriffdom, the Leslies of Findrassie feued
Eathie, Learnie, Craighead and Muirhead from the bishop of Ross in
1576 and 1593, with permission to build a mill. The Leslies' power
base was on the Moray coast and the old castle or mansion house of
Eathie was not required and fell into disrepair.

The sheriffs of Cromarty came to claim the position of hereditary
vice-admirals of the seas north of Inverness. The importance of this
office was that the admiralty courts they convened could declare
captured vessels to be prizes of war, in which case both the vessel and
its cargo were seized. This was a power open to abuse – neutral vessels
might conveniently be deemed to be trading with the enemy – and the
Cromarty vice-admiralty court was notoriously corrupt by the end
of the seventeenth century. The first recorded exercise of their power
is in 1524, when the *Oliver* from Flanders or Zeeland was seized at
Cromarty because it did not have a safe conduct from the king. Again,
in 1590, a vessel from Bremen bound for Orkney was detained, brought
to Cromarty and her cargo sold – presumably after she was declared a
prize by a sitting, however perfunctory, of the admiralty court.[8] These
dubious legal proceedings can only have added to the wealth of the
sheriff and the town.

The sheriff of Cromarty, with expanded land holdings, was capable
of entertaining royal visitors on his estates and in the summer of 1589
James VI went from Aberdeen 'to hunt the hart with hounds in a forest

called Cromarty'. From much the same time we have Timothy Pont's description of the settlements in the Black Isle and the distances between them. This includes a reference to the 'fair wood' of Brae-moir, some three miles long, with deer found along the burn [the Kinbeachie burn] running from there to the sea. The sheriff of Cromarty had already taken steps to protect his hunting rights here and in 1577 had accused a John Dingwall of Kildun, with sixteen others, of killing fifteen or sixteen 'great deir' with 'hagbuttis, bowis and pistols' in the Forest of Brae. And, remarkably, there is also a contemporary illustration of a hunt. A carved lintel stone from Cromarty castle, still preserved in Cromarty House, bears, in the words of Hugh Miller, 'the figures of hares and deer sorely beset by dogs, and surrounded by a thicket of grapes and tendrils. The huntsman stands in the centre, attired in a sort of loose coat that reaches to his knees, with his horn in one hand, and his hunting-spear in the other.' Miller dated it to the reign of Queen Mary (1542–67).[9]

The kirk of Cromarty

The kirk of the parish of Cromarty has been on its present site from at least the fifteenth century and probably from the creation of the parish, and there are remnants of its early structure in thick gable walls and an aumbry (cupboard) near the east gable. In addition to the parish church and the chapel of St Regulus, already described, there were other places of worship. At Navity there is evidence of two early chapels, dedicated to saints Duthac and either Bennet or, more likely, Bainan. A chaplainry of St Michael at Navity probably refers only to lands supporting a chaplain in the cathedral at Chanonry, not to a chapel site. The name Navity itself derives from *neimhidh*, meaning consecrated or holy ground, and often indicates an early Christian site, possibly superseding a pre-Christian sacred place. A well, and possibly remains of the chapel, dedicated to St Duthac survived until *c.*1800; and a burial ground, and what appears to have been a stone coffin – known as the 'fairy cradle' – survived at St Bainan's Chapel until the early 1740s. St Bainan's well, now commonly known as St Bennet's well, still flows near the shore below the chapel site.[10]

There is also a tradition of an 'Old Kirk' at Cromarty lost to coastal erosion but this must be treated with caution. The evidence for there being such a church consists of three 'productions'. First, when Bishop Pococke visited Cromarty in 1760, he noted that there were on the shore, to the east of St Regulus, the 'very imperfect remains of a church … called the Old Kirk'.[11] Second, Hugh Miller recorded the tradition that following a storm from the north-east in the mid eighteenth century, human bones were washed onto the beach 'below the town', together with 'several blocks of hewn stone', presumed to be from an old church and burial ground.[12] One piece of cornice stone could still be seen in Miller's time but the supposed site of the church was then 'covered every larger tide by about ten feet of water'.[13] And, finally, an area below high water mark is still known as the 'Kirkstanes'.

It is possible that this tradition arises from a single event c.1745 – the appearance on the shore of human bones and hewn stones after a storm. Pococke's 'very imperfect remains' could simply be these stones washed up some years before his visit, for no site 'on the shore' in 1760 was under two fathoms of water by 1835, when Miller wrote.[14] It is worth bearing in mind there was a similar, unreliable tradition in Nigg of a church below the sea, whose bells, it was said, could be heard tolling below the waves in stormy weather.

The Reformation

In 1560 the leaders of Scottish Protestants, backed by minor lairds and barons, passed legislation in the Scottish parliament, which established a radically new Protestant church, based on the Presbyterian model of Calvin's Reformed church in Geneva. However, making the new church a reality at parish level was a long process with many compromises. Chief among these was the decision in 1562 to allow the existing holders of church revenues to retain two-thirds of the income, with the other third allocated to the Crown for the support of the new church. This was, nevertheless, an improvement on the financial position of the pre-Reformation parish clergy. There was another major com-promise over lay patronage – that is, the right to appoint clergy – which the Reformers had intended to abolish. Instead patronage generally passed to the Crown, who took over the rights of the major religious institutions, and from 1587 patronage began to be granted to landowners by the Crown as a property right.

The vicar of Cromarty at the time of the Reformation, John Anderson (or Henderson), did not conform to the new religion but, as described above, retained two-thirds of the income. Only after his death in 1582 was Cromarty's first Presbyterian minister, Robert Williamson, appointed by the Crown. The initials of Williamson and his wife, with the date 1593, survive in a triangular window pediment built into the gable of an eighteenth-century house on the Causeway.

Burgh: trade and town life in the sixteenth century

In 1578 Cromarty erected a new mercat cross, which reflected a revival of the town's trade, and by 1580 Inverness was sufficiently concerned about competition from other burghs in the north to complain to the Convention of Royal Burghs about 'the usurpation' of its 'liberty, trade and traffic of merchandise of all kinds of staple goods' by other settlements including Dingwall, Chanonry, Rosemarkie, Cromarty, Dornoch and Wick. A record survives of one cargo on which Inverness may have had an eye. These were goods ordered in 1553 from John Ross of Dunskaith for shipping to Cromarty for Alexander Ross, laird of Balnagowan, and included chain mail shirts, hemp, corks, tin wash bowls, pepper, ginger, aniseed, sugar candy, a variety of drinking vessels, lead basins, linen cloth, gunpowder and 'a small canon that is right fine and shoots far'.[15]

The subsequent grant of a new charter to Cromarty in 1593, clarifying the town's rights, may have been in response to Inverness's unjustified claim to a monopoly of trade in the north. The charter acknowledged Cromarty's ancient status as a royal burgh and the extent of its lands – the eastern tip of the Black Isle peninsula, including the farms of Newton, Neilston, Bannans, Navity and the hill of Cromarty – although, in reality, much of this had already been disposed of to the principal burgess families.

Special mention is made in the charter of the harbour which had been described in an earlier report, of 1589, as 'one of the best portes in this yslande'.[16] The customs dues on staple goods were, as before,

FIGURE 1.5
Cromarty and Cromarty Castle *c.*1590 (from Pont 20).

reserved to the Crown. However, because the harbour had fallen into
ruin and the burgh had not been able to maintain it, the revenues from
three former chaplainries, of Saint Regulus in Cromarty and Saints
Duthac and Michael in Navity, were allocated to the burgh for its
repair. It seems likely that the promontory known as Maryness, with
its sandy shore to the west, was then, as now, the site of the harbour
and the grant suggests that there was some structure there, not simply
a beach on which ships could be drawn up. In addition to its weekly
markets, the burgh was granted the right to two annuals fairs, one
called St Norman's market and the other St Regulus' market, each
lasting five days. There was provision in the charter for a mercat cross
and standard weights and measures – a boll for volume, a yardstick for
length, and a tron beam for weight.

From this period we also have the first reference to Cromarty's
grammar school, in a letter to the schoolmaster from the Privy Council
telling him that funds were allocated for seven years to support Walter
Ross, son of Mr Thomas Ross, Tain, during his studies there. As the
elite of the Highlands increasingly sought education for their sons,
good schools could bring significant income to a community.[17]

In the 1580s and 1590s, as Cromarty's fortunes were reviving,
the parish minister of the Caithness parish of Dunnet, Timothy Pont
(c.1565–c.1611), travelled the country and produced a remarkable
series of hand-drawn maps, which are our earliest surviving detailed
maps of Scotland. Cromarty appears on the map of Tarbat Ness known
as *Gordon 20*, which shows the coast of the firths, from Dornoch in the
north to Eathie, just west of Cromarty. Pont's principal interest was in
recording the features of 'civil society' in the 1580s and 1590s – castles,
tower houses and towns as centres of power and the economy, together
with mills, woods and arable ground. He used a number of symbols on
his maps but, remarkably, many of his tiny drawings are not just symbols
but accurate sketches of buildings. Thus, Cromarty castle is correctly
shown as L-plan enclosed within a large courtyard. The buildings of the
burgh lie below, between the castle and the sea. Pont's sketch suggests
a street running along the line of the road at the west of Cromarty now
called the Causeway, and, from a variety of sources, we can firmly locate
the position of the mercat cross and the town's tollbooth on the east
side of this street. It is likely that the mercat cross of the earlier burgh
also stood there – a transaction in 1467 describes a Cromarty property
as 'lying between the cross of the town and the sea'. Unlike Dornoch
and Tain, which were also drawn by Pont, there is no suggestion that
Cromarty was surrounded by any form of enclosure, either a town wall
or a ditch and embankment. Pont also recorded the lost tower of Eathie,
to the west of Cromarty.

In all Scottish burghs building plots were lined out to a standard
width along the principal street and the most efficient way to erect

FIGURE 1.6
Eathie with castle and mill *c*.1590 (from Pont 20).

houses on these plots was gable-end to the street, leaving narrow lanes between the properties. The houses of Cromarty's burgesses, its mercat cross and its tollbooth all lay along its high street, but the parish kirk stood, not here as might be expected, but a little to the west. Further west still was the harbour.

A further feature of the burgh was its courthill, a mound on open ground by the shore between the harbour and the town. As the burgh expanded the courthill was surrounded by houses and finally removed in the nineteenth century, although the ground was never built on. In the 1830s Hugh Miller recorded traditions of the hereditary sheriffs holding their courts here, with the usual place of execution being the high ground further west, immediately above the harbour itself. It might also have been a place for burgh courts. The road running from the courthill back towards the town was later known as the Corpsgait (now Gordon's Lane).

Early fisheries in Cromarty

When he died in 1593, the Edinburgh merchant Ninian Lowis had seventy bolls of a prized commodity, 'great salt' – that is, sun-dried sea salt, imported from the Bay of Biscay – stored in a house in Cromarty, where he rented a cellar for £5 a year. The house was owned by Mr Thomas Urquhart, almost certainly 'of Davidston', the second of the reputed twenty-five male offspring, of the laird, Thomas Urquhart of Cromarty. Lowis also had twenty-one barrels of salmon in Rouen, in France, and was engaged in an international trade in salt salmon, which Cromarty was well placed to supply.[18]

Gordon of Straloch, writing a few decades later, described how along the Cromarty Firth 'on both shores at the low edges there are numerous wooden enclosures of great use, for when the tide ebbs and the sands are dry, fish are caught with the hand'. These were the salmon yairs or fish traps, barriers made from wooden uprights driven into the sand every twelve to eighteen inches, interwoven with branches. Out from the shore they turned back on themselves in a dogleg, creating a V-shaped trap at the juncture, into which salmon swam as they followed the tidal flow down the firth.

There were also rich fish stocks in the Moray Firth. Gordon noted that the sea yielded

> ... many kinds of cod, which are distinguished from each other by size or various marks, and turbot, skate, the fish called by the name of the dog, plaice, stingrays, mackerel, soles, angel fish, sea-eels, catfish, ugly to look at, but when skinned tender and wholesome, as well as many other kinds, even in countless numbers, which are peculiar to the north, and have not yet got their Latin names; while the river mouths and the seaside rocks teem with oysters, sea-perch, lobsters, sea-cockles, conger-eels, mussels, sea-snails, top-shell fish, scallops, and the other shellfish called by the Greeks ostracoderma.[19]

There were certainly opportunities for the development of sea fisheries at this time, emulating both the Dutch Grand Fishery, which, from 1580, had sent large fleets to the northern isles to fish for herring, and the East Fife line fishermen, who had established shore bases in the northern isles for drying cod.[20]

James Coull argues that the development of Scottish fishing settlements was in four stages: first, the emergence of specialised fishing communities in medieval towns, then, from as early as the fifteenth century, an expansion into rural coastal villages with fisher families often cultivating small plots of land, next an accelerated growth of these settlements in the seventeenth century, and, finally, a loosening of ties with the land in such communities during the eighteenth and nineteenth centuries, creating the distinct fishing communities which survived into the twentieth century.

Early fishing communities appeared in towns at river mouths where salmon and sea fisheries could be combined, with the same fishers exploiting both. Inverness and Cromarty were among the places particularly well placed to take advantage of such combined fishery because of the ease with which fish could be caught by fixed traps on the river Ness and within the Dornoch, Cromarty and Beauly Firths. Early sea fisheries in the area are confirmed by records of herring exports from Inverness in fifteenth-century Exchequer Rolls.[21]

There are three reasons for holding that Cromarty had such an early, perhaps medieval, fishing community. First, a survey of feudal tenure in the town in 1744 shows that the fishers of Cromarty, unlike most later fishing communities, held property within, rather than on the margins of, the town and held this in feu from the old burgh or in feu from one of the principal burgess families. It is likely that these holdings were once on the edge of the medieval burgh and were engulfed by the town's early expansion to the west. Second, the Cromarty fishers paid small teinds, known as vicarage, a practice associated with other early fishing settlements, such as Newhaven and Broadsea, but which had generally lapsed by the eighteenth century, when it is recorded. And third, the distinctive fisher dialect of Cromarty, and Avoch, retained some of the oldest forms of Scots, perhaps suggesting a settlement by fishers from elsewhere in Scotland. That distinct voice, like the castle of the lairds and the houses of the early burgesses, has now all but vanished.[22]

Notes

1. NRAS 0204/Bundle 160, Rental of the estate of Cromarty, 1750.
2. David Walker, *A Legal History of Scotland* (Edinburgh, 1988), ii. 561.
3. Thomas Urquhart, *Collected Works* (Edinburgh, 1834), 170; Hugh Miller, *My Schools and Schoolmaster* (Edinburgh, 1993), 38–9; Hugh Miller, *Scenes and Legends of the North of Scotland* (Edinburgh, 1994), 46–50.
4. For the Mowats see Richard D. Oram, *The Reign of Alexander II 1214–49* (Leiden, 2005) and Alan Young, *Robert the Bruce's Rivals* (East Linton, 1997).
5. Geoffrey Stell, 'Architecture and Society in Easter Ross before 1707' in John Baldwin (ed.), *Firthlands of Ross & Cromarty* (Edinburgh, 1986).
6. NLS, Huttons Shires; Hugh Miller, *Scenes and Legends*, 200–1; William Mackay Mackenzie, 'Cromarty: its old chapels and parish church' in *Scottish Ecclesiological Society* (1905); David Alston, *A Historical Guide to Ross & Cromarty* (Edinburgh, 1999).
7. Donald Bateson, *Coin Finds from Cromarty* (Cromarty, 1993).
8. NAS GD 305/1/127 no. 3.
9. Hugh Miller, *Scenes and Legends*, 79.
10. Hugh Miller, *Tales and Sketches* (Edinburgh, 1863), 265. Hugh Miller gives 'Bennet' in *Scenes and Legends*, 101. This is an unlikely dedication for what appears to be an early site. Elsewhere he gives the otherwise unknown 'Kennat' – *Sketchbook of Popular Geology* (Edinburgh, 1870) – and possibly this is simply a misprint. An older source – David Aitken's map of the Cromarty estate (Cromarty House archive) – gives the more likely 'Bainan'. Miller records that

the 'fairy cradle' was destroyed by the parish minister and elders (*Scenes and Legends*, 101). Aitken also marks the chapel of St Duthac (map reference NH 779645) and, intriguingly, a cross by the roadside to the east of Navity.

11. Richard Pococke, *Tours in Scotland 1747, 1750, 1760* (Scottish History Society, Edinburgh, 1887).

12. Hugh Miller, *Scenes and Legends*, 29.

13. Hugh Miller, *Scenes and Legends*, 101.

14. This can be confirmed by comparing David Aitken's map of the Cromarty estate made in 1764 and the first edition Ordnance Survey (1871).

15. William Macgill, *Old Ross-shire and Scotland* (Inverness, 1909), no. 673.

16. *Calendar of Scottish Papers*, 1589, 'The State of Scotland'.

17. *Register of the Secret Seal*, vii. 2505.

18. NAS, CC8/8/25.

19. Walter Macfarlane, *Geographical Collections* (Scottish History Society, 1906–08), ii.

20. William P. L. Thomson, *History of Orkney* (Edinburgh, 1987), 168.

21. James Coull, *The Sea Fisheries of Scotland* (Edinburgh, 1996), 33, 46; J. Stuart et al., *The Exchequer Rolls of Scotland* (Edinburgh, 1878–1908), 1882:231 & 1883:469.

22. For the 1744 feuars and vicarage payments, see NRAS 0204/Bundles 144 & 160. For the fisher dialect see W. Grant and D. Murison (eds), *The Scottish National Dictionary* (Edinburgh, 1931), i. page xxxvi.

2

1600–1660

I have, or at least had before I was sequestred, a certain harbour or bay, in goodness equal to the best in the world, adjacent to a place, which is the head town of the Shire; whereby I am intituled both sheriff and proprietary, the shire and the town being of one and the same name with the harbour or bay.

Sir Thomas Urquhart of Cromarty, *Logopandecteision*, 1653

Sir Thomas, elder and younger

In the early 1660s the eccentric Sir Thomas Urquhart (1611–*c*.60) – whose writings had included musings on a universal language, a translation of Rabelais' rumbustious masterpiece *Gargantua and Pantagruel* and a family tree tracing the line of the family of Urquhart, generation by generation, back to Adam and Eve – died in

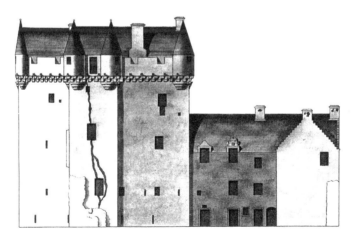

FIGURE 2.1
Cromarty Castle in 1746 showing the tower (*c*.1500) and later wing (1630s).

29

the Netherlands, reputedly in a fit of laughter brought on by news of
the restoration of Charles II. Across the sea, north of Inverness at the
eastern tip of the Black Isle peninsula, was his estate, his sheriffdom and
the royal burgh he described, both affectionately and possessively, as
'my little town of Cromarty'.

Sir Thomas's father, also Thomas (1582–1642), had inherited the
estate from his (Thomas the elder's) grandfather Walter in 1607.
Thomas (elder) was knighted in 1617 and in 1631 received permission
from the Privy Council to export 'ten chalders of bere and meal' to
Norway and to import timber from there as he was 'building a house
for his better accommodation'. This was a three-storey extension
to the castle of Cromarty, designed to provide more comfortable
accommodation than was available in a fortified tower, including an
inside kitchen, a study, dining room and private chambers. Above two
of the windows were his initials 'STV' and 'DCE' for his wife, Dame
Christian Elphinstone.

In the years before the enlargement of Urquhart's castle the firth had
been used for the embarkation of Highland troops and this activity may
have brought some benefits to the laird and the town. In September
1626 an army of 2,000 clansmen of Mackay's Regiment, recruited
in the northern Highlands, embarked from the port for service in
the forces of Christian IV of Denmark. This was a Protestant army
going to fight for the Protestant cause in Europe, with committed
Presbyterian officers including Robert Munro of Foulis, who recorded
their expedition. Two years later fewer than 400 were still alive but they
were reinforced by more recruits in 1628 and again by companies of
John Munro of Obsdale's regiment, who sailed from Cromarty in June,
July and October 1630.

By 1636, however, the elder Sir Thomas was in severe financial
difficulties and in June sold his creditors £2,000 of future annual rent
from the estate. In December of that year two of his sons, Thomas and
Alexander, imprisoned their father in a room of the castle – perhaps
to restrain him from further rash financial action. The father took the
sons to court but the matter was resolved without a formal judgement,
and he obtained royal protection from his creditors on the grounds that
his debts were the result of the 'undewtifull cariage and behaviour of
his children'. Nevertheless, the debts remained and by 1641 the lands
of Cullicudden, Culbo, Woodhead, Little Farness and Brae were all
mortgaged to Sir James Fraser, brother of Lord Lovat.

Thomas, the younger, was born in 1611, possibly in the old castle
of Cromarty, but perhaps more likely in his father house at Banff or
at Fisherie. He entered Aberdeen University at the age of eleven, left
without graduating and travelled in Europe. He was to become a
remarkable, flamboyant and eccentric man: author, mathematician,
genealogist, translator and soldier. The family were Episcopalian and

FIGURE 2.2
Sir Thomas Urquhart, drawn by George Glover, 1641.

in May 1639, with the beginning of clashes between royalists and covenanters, he took part, as a royalist, in a skirmish in Aberdeenshire, known as the 'Trot of Turriff'. Later in the same month he sailed for England with other Episcopalians and established himself at the court of Charles I, where he was knighted in 1641. He also published his first work, a dull volume of epigrams, and had a small full-length engraved portrait of himself made by George Glover. In this he stands, dressed extravagantly, receiving a laurel wreath signifying success in arts and arms.

David Stevenson has aptly summed him up saying that, in a crowd 'Sir Thomas Urquhart would be the one noticed first. He would be the one in front. He would be making extravagant gestures and talking non-stop in a loud voice. His bursting self-importance and manic elation would be as evident as his flashy, attention-attracting clothes.' A second portrait shows him surrounded by the muses who adulate him for his judgement, learning, wit, invention, sweetness and style.[1]

The elder Sir Thomas died in 1642, his son inherited and returned from London to Cromarty, to an estate encumbered by debt. He made some perfunctory attempts to recover the family's mortgaged property, but preferred to ignore the problems by travelling again in Europe, having placed the management of the estate in the hands of family friends and of his younger brother, Alexander. In December of the following year, 1643, a disturbing incident took place when three male guests at the castle were poisoned. They had eaten a meal intended for the mad, impotent John Campbell, Laird of Cawdor, who was married to Elizabeth, daughter of the old laird and sister to Thomas and Alexander. The three were found dead in their beds in the morning. There is no indication of who was behind this extreme attempt to resolve the problem of an unsatisfactory marriage.[2]

By 1644 Sir Thomas was back at court in London and preparing for publication his incomprehensible work on mathematics, *Trissotetras*, which he thoughtfully dedicated to his mother, describing it as his 'brain-babe' and consequently her grandchild. He never married and his books would be his only offspring. His brother Alexander meanwhile attached himself, prudently, to the covenanting party in Scotland. He had the title 'of Dunlugas' but Thomas, opposed to him politically, soon came to refer to him as 'Dunbugar'.

Thomas returned to Cromarty in 1645, with the library of books purchased during his travels, to an estate still, unsurprisingly, burdened by debts. One of his creditors, the ardent parliamentarian Robert Leslie of Findrassie, had had a troop of horse quartered on Sir Thomas's tenants. The billeting of troops was always an unpopular action and these had done much damage. The local ministers were also pursuing him for their unpaid stipends. In 1647, as Sir Thomas played a part in organising a Scottish army to secure the king's return to London, the estate was legally apprised (seized) by a second creditor, the Aberdeen merchant, Farquhar of Mounie – a 'lamb-devouring fox'. The combination of these with Sir James Fraser, who held the mortgages on Brae and other properties, led Sir Thomas to pen the verse:

The Scripture says that three things always crave,
The raging sea, the barren womb, and grave;
O let me debtor be to th' other three,
Free me from Farcher, Fraser, Fendrasie.

In February 1648, a decision was made by the royalists in the north to fortify Cromarty castle with feal (turf) dykes, the work to be carried out by the tenants of Fraser and Findrassie within the parishes of Cromarty, Cullicudden and Rosemarkie. No doubt this forced labour from his creditors' tenants, if it was ever exacted, would have given some pleasure. Two brass cannon were later delivered to Cromarty, a gift from John Urquhart, Sir Thomas's cousin, a colonel in the Queen of Sweden's regiment of Guards. They were later seized by English troops and taken to the Citadel of Leith. As the extremist Kirk Party took control in Scotland, Urquhart committed himself further to this hopeless local rising and, on its failure, was declared a rebel.

Charles I was executed in 1649 and by 1650 there was a new war and new alliances, as Cromwell's model army invaded Scotland. In the face of this threat, even royalists like Urquhart were accepted into the Scots army, which marched south into England the following year, only to be catastrophically defeated at Worcester in September 1651. Urquhart was imprisoned, many of the manuscripts he had taken with him were lost or destroyed, and in his absence the Cromarty estate was sequestered 'by the English and taken up by those having power from them'. Troops were quartered in the castle under the command of a Major William Bird, Governor of Cromarty, and the castle, mains farm and estate lands were 'medled with be the sequestrators and Commonwealth of England'.[3]

The estates of royalist prisoners such as Urquhart were declared forfeit unless 'their merits and services ... shall render them capable of being taken into a more favourable consideration by the Parliament'. Sir Thomas responded by offering 'the grammar and lexicon of an universal language', the full details of which were, he claimed, with his papers in Cromarty. This topic was something taken seriously by thinkers of the time and Sir Thomas was released on a five-month parole in July 1652, later extended by six weeks, to enable his return to Cromarty. Two more works were published in this year – *Pantochronochanon*, tracing his ancestry to Adam and Eve, and the chaotic *Ekskybalauron* or *The Jewel*, which included both his musings on a universal language and a 'vindication of the honour of Scotland'.

In the north Urquhart was again harassed by Findrassie, who pillaged the farm of Ardoch, but nevertheless he returned from this, his last residence in his 'little town of Cromarty', not with a worked-up scheme for the universal language but with his remarkable translation of the

FIGURE 2.3
The Cromarty Stone, carved 1651.

first three books of Rabelais' masterpiece *Gargantua and Pantagruel*. 'More Rabelesian than Rabelais', this has been deemed by some critics one of the best translations of any work of literature. The first two books were published in June 1653 and in the same year *Logopandecteision* appeared, on the face of it another introduction to his universal language but, in fact, an attack on his creditors, bankers, ministers and all those who had stood in the way of his crazy schemes to revive Cromarty and his family's fortunes. There was a further surprising work, a co-authored pamphlet defending Cromwell's dissolution of Parliament. The royalist Urquhart had become a republican propagandist, aligning himself with those in the Commonwealth who shared his fierce hatred of hard-line Presbyterians.[4]

By 1655, however, Urquhart had left Britain for the Netherlands and he never returned to Cromarty. An expression of his flamboyant spirit remained in a carved and painted stone in Cromarty castle, now known as the Cromarty Stone and displayed in the Museum of Scotland. It features harp playing mermaids, the Urquhart arms, mounted knights and the date, 1651, given according to several bizarre calendars of Sir Thomas's own devising. There is also, in Cromarty, an elaborate lectern sundial, which once stood in the grounds of the castle and may have been carved for Sir Thomas. These multi-faced dials were peculiar to seventeenth-century Scotland. Their many faces told the same time, just as Urquhart's many calendars identified the same year, and there may also have been an underlying symbolism of a single universal truth underpinning all human systems of interpretation and belief.

FIGURE 2.4
Lectern sundial (or 'star desk') probably made for Sir Thomas Urquhart.

Sir Thomas on Cromarty

Fortunately, among Sir Thomas Urquhart's maelstrom of words, it is possible to find some historical fact and intelligible comment on Cromarty and the estate. Most of this is to be found in *Logopandecteision*, with the remainder in the *Jewel*. There are welcome glimpses of the life of the ordinary people of the sheriffdom. Urquhart claimed that his tenants, although holding on unwritten five-year leases, were never removed from their holdings, passed leases from father to son, were firmly attached to their individual farmtouns and regarded leaving the home farmtoun for another as almost equivalent to going into exile. He propounded the interesting theory that this attachment to place led to small family size, a disadvantage in his view. Presumably this would have been through late marriage, although Urquhart does not say so. In any event, there is no surviving data by which to test the claim.

He portrayed the inhabitants of each farmtoun, who he refers to as a 'clan', as living lives interwoven with ancient traditions and customs, often focused on sites around the farm – 'fountains, oak-trees, little round hillocks, and great stone heaps' – to which they went at set times, to perform old rituals. He believed that, while these traditions might be foolish, they were harmless and rejected the notion that the people were engaged in witchcraft or sorcery. Such accusations could be fatal. Witch trials and burnings continued into the early eighteenth century in Scotland and there was later a tradition that a burning had taken place in Cromarty in the reign of Charles II. Urquhart wrote *Logopandecteision* shortly after a period of intensive witch-hunting in 1649 and would have been aware of earlier periods of persecution in the 1590s and 1629–30. Some of the worst was still to come in 1661–2, the most likely date for the burning in Cromarty at the 'Witch's Hole' above the harbour.

Urquhart resisted the fundamentalism and hysteria of the witch-hunters and claimed that he had 'openly purged many' individuals charged with various forms of 'communication with foul spirits' including 'peregrinations with fairies'. This was as a young man after his return from his travels on the continent, probably in the late 1620s, and he may have been sitting in judgement as depute for his father, who had a royal commission from 1611 to apprehend witches. He was aware – not surprisingly given his own character – of the power of the imagination. On one occasion he was simultaneously presented with accusations against a 22-year-old man and a 25-year-old woman. The two did not know each other, yet both had allegedly engaged in sexual intercourse with demons. He gained their trust by interviewing them informally and separately – and both openly admitted, in confidence, that the accusations were true. Urquhart, however, already sensed the sexual tensions in both of them – the man 'bashful yet prone to lasciviousness' and the women 'a sink of lust' restrained by a 'little modesty' – and did not believe them. He tested their confessions by plying them with an aphrodisiac and arranging for a footboy and a chambermaid to flirt with the two as they went to bed. The next day, in further informal interviews, both separately claimed to have been

THE WORKS OF
RABELAIS

FAITHFULLY TRANSLATED FROM THE FRENCH.

WITH VARIORUM NOTES, AND

NUMEROUS ILLUSTRATIONS BY

GUSTAVE DORÉ.

London:
CHATTO AND WINDUS, PICCADILLY.

FIGURE 2.5
Sir Thomas's translation of Rabelais embodied his opposition to hard-line
Presbyterianism. It was reprinted many times and illustrated by many artists
including D'Ore and Heath Robinson.

visited later in the night by 'foul spirits', which appeared in the form of the footboy and chambermaid and were 'entirely communicative in feats of dalliance'. It was all in the mind – in Urquhart's words 'the imagination of two had turned to a fornication of four'. His tale has a happy ending not only in their escape from charges of consorting with demons but also in the subsequent marriage of the pair to the footboy and the chambermaid.

Church affairs

Urquhart faced considerable opposition in such judgements from 'aged men of long experience', who he elsewhere describes as 'Kirkists', presumably the Presbyterian ministers and elders of the three parishes in the sheriffdom, Cromarty, Kirkmichael and Cullicudden. Urquhart had ongoing disputes with all of them. Cromarty's first Presbyterian minister, Robert Williamson, had been appointed by the Crown and remained in the parish until his death, sometime before November 1638 when William Lunan became minister. This was the year of the National Covenant – whose signatories swore to resist royal power over the church, episcopacy and innovations in worship – and, as part of this movement, there had been a riot, with burning of prayer-books, in Chanonry. Lunan's tenure was short. He was gone from Cromarty by 1641 and was later excommunicated by the Presbytery of Turriff. It may be that, like the Urquhart laird who appointed him, he had unacceptable Episcopalian sympathies.

 He was followed later in 1641 by a staunch Presbyterian, the 44-year-old Gilbert Anderson, who had served as minister at Cawdor. The other ministers were, from 1638 at Cullicudden, Charles Pape, and from 1649 at Kirkmichael, another Robert Williamson, both sons of estate tenants. During one of Sir Thomas's extended periods of absence they obtained a court decreet for an increase in stipend and had their laird, and patron, declared outlaw at the mercat cross of Cromarty should he fail to pay. Sir Thomas fulminated against them all but reserved his sharpest venom for Gilbert Anderson in a dispute over the erection of a desk (a table seat) in the church. The desk had been 'put in without his [Urquhart's] consent by a professed enemy to his House, who had plotted the ruine thereof, and one that had no land in the parish'. The point at issue here was that only heritors (principal landowners in the parish) had the right to erect seats in the church. Urquhart went on to describe how Anderson, as a consequence of this dispute 'did so rail against him and his family in the pulpit at several times ... more like a scolding tripe-seller's wife than good minister ... squirting the poison of detraction and abominable falsehood, unfit for the chaire of verity, in the eares of his tenandry, who were the only auditors'.

The offending desk may well have belonged to Urquhart's arch-enemy, Leslie of Findrassie, who had no property in the parish but owned the lands of Eathie, which, although in the parish of Rosemarkie, were close to Cromarty. Sir Thomas believed that Eathie had originally been Urquhart land, given to the church at some early date, and held by them until feued to the Leslies after the Reformation. This only served to rub salt in the wound.

Gilbert Anderson died in 1655 and was followed as minister by his son Hugh. The appointment was made by the congregation, lay patronage having been abolished in 1649 – yet another target for Urquhart wrath. All this is a vivid illustration of the bitter disputes, usually over patronage and pewing, which periodically erupted in Scottish kirks for the next 200 years.[5]

The burgh and its trade

Although Sir Thomas referred to Cromarty as 'my little town', strictly speaking this was not so. The town had received its new charter in 1593, confirming its status as an independent royal burgh. This was again confirmed in 1641, but three years later Alexander Urquhart, in his brother's absence, protested to the Scots parliament that the ratification should be without prejudice to the rights of the Urquhart family. The only record we have of burgh administration during this period is a set of accounts for its common good for a single year, 1634.[6]

There were continuing tensions with Inverness, which, despite the 1593 charter, did not fully accept Cromarty's trading rights. Sir Thomas would later accuse Inverness merchants of undermining his plans by setting about 'robbing his town of its liberties and privileges'. He appears to have had some justification, for in 1648 two Dundee merchants, George and Patrick Ruthvens, were accused of wronging the burgh of Inverness by landing goods at Tain, Dingwall and Cromarty without first offering to land them at Inverness, 'being ignorant of the toune's privelege anent breking of bulk' – that is, discharging cargo.[7]

A small outward trade in grain from Easter Ross to Aberdeen was established by the 1620s, recorded in the Aberdeen Shore Work accounts, but little of it was through Cromarty.[8] This is probably because the small vessels used could be beached close to the estate from which grain was being shipped. There were also some shipments of grain to the Firth of Forth, and the Leith Shore Accounts for 1638–9 record thirty-eight chalders of grain shipped there from Cromarty. A chalder, from the French *chaudron* (kettle), was a measure of grain equivalent to sixteen bolls. There were, too, some shipments overseas, to Holland in two Dundee vessels in 1621 and to Norway in 1631, when ten chalders of bere and meal were shipped.[9]

One limitation on export may have been the availability of suitable vessels. Most of these shipments of grain to Aberdeen were of between eight and sixteen chalders, with twelve chalders being particularly common, indicating that the boats used were of around ten tons burden. From the mid century the records suggest that larger vessels

FIGURE 2.6
Sir Thomas Urquhart surrounded by the Muses (George Glover, c.1641)
– a suitable patron for a University of Cromarty.

were commonly used, carrying a cargo of 300 to 400 bolls (fifteen to twenty tons), and larger boats would have made safer the longer journey to Leith. When the government agent, Thomas Tucker, visited the north in 1655, reporting on the ports of Scotland prior to a reform of the customs, he noted that the vessels were 'Inverness, one of 10 tonnes; Garmouth, one of 12 tonnes; Cromarty, one of 16 tonnes; Thirsoe, one of 30 tonnes'. Although Aberdeen had nine vessels, varying from twenty to eighty tons, the total capacity was still a limitation on shipping.[10]

The advantages of the harbour had been praised by Gordon of Straloch who wrote *c.*1640 of Cromarty as 'a small town at the commencement of a bay of the same name, about which one may truly say that none such is found from the Orkney Islands to Kent in England, for it is easy of access for ships, and inside is very safe and capacious, free from quicksands, shoals, and shallows, with a bottom such as sailors would desire for holding anchors, and, in short, it has all the praise of a fine harbour'. Tucker too recognised the advantages of Cromarty as a port – 'one of the delicatest harbours reputed in all Europe, the tide coming in at a great depth between two stately rocks, (called the Sooters,) through which the water passes into a large bay, where the greatest shipps of burden may ride in safety' – but he added that 'nothing comes more than a little salt to serve the countrey'.[11]

Sir Thomas, as always, had a plan – a vision for the future prosperity of Cromarty propounded in *Logopandecteision.* He echoed the assessment of Cromarty's natural advantages and with characteristic overstatement claimed of the harbour that 'ten thousand ships together may within it ride in the greatest tempest that is, as in a calm'. He further claimed to have persuaded a number of 'exceeding rich men, of five or six several nations, masters of ships and merchant adventurers' to come to settle in Cromarty, a project which was frustrated by the 'impetuosity of the usurer' – that is, by Sir Thomas's creditors seeking to be paid – and by opposition from the burgh of Inverness. The plans for the development of Cromarty were to include the expansion of fishing, the introduction of manufacturing and of new trades, mining of coal and metals, the improvement of agriculture, and the creation of what would have been, in effect, a University of Cromarty. It was magnificent stuff but all unrealised.

Agriculture

Cromarty continued to rely, not on the fanciful schemes of Sir Thomas, but on the produce of the sea and of the 'cornlands' around the burgh. The first glimpse of the detail of local agriculture is in a document from the estate of Cromarty – a rental of 'the four wester davochs' of Meikle

Farness, Davidston, Peddieston and Little Farness, for the year 1637 (Table 2.1).[12] The larger part of the rent was paid as *victual* – that is, rent paid in kind in the form of bere (the primitive form of barley grown at the time), oats, oatmeal and malt. All grain was measured in bolls, firlots, pecks and lippies – four lippies to the peck, four pecks to the firlot, four firlots to the boll. The boll, being a bowl or tub used to measure volume, varied from one part of the country to another and even from estate to estate. Later, on the Cromarty estate, it was the equivalent of nine stone (57 kg). The remainder of the rent consisted of 'custom payments' in the form of *marts* (cattle slaughtered in November at Martinmas), wedders, lambs, capons, hens, eggs, geese, peat, straw and *silver mail* (money). There was also a substantial income from the mills of Meikle Farness – a series of three mills on a water course running down to the sea, with a fourth mill at the shore. Meikle Farness also had an alehouse – a small brewery rather than an inn – and there was the 'Bogtoun of Farness', whose name suggests that it was less favourable ground brought into cultivation.

All this is common to the time. However, an interesting note is added that 'ilk oxgang of the Town has yielded, seeing they are not able to keep me in whole at one time' an additional annual victual payment. This appears to be a reference to an obligation to provide hospitality for the landowner and his household. Such obligations had once been common, especially in the Gaelic Highlands where they were known as *cuid-oidhche*, but this seems a late survival in the eastern lowlands. It appears that the hard-pressed Thomas Urquhart (elder), having spent extravagantly to enlarge the castle, was now seeking to augment this income by converting a traditional customary obligation to a firm payment of rent.

TABLE 2.1   Rental of the four wester davochs of the estate of Cromarty, 1637.

	Victual (Pecks Firlots Bolls)	Marts	Wedders	Lambs	Capons	Hens	Eggs	Geese	Loads peat	Windlins straw	Conversion of customs	Conversion of victual	Silver mail
Farness	125-2-0	1	7	4	48	48	160		364	24	£7 6s 3d	£57 10s 2d	£11 15s 6d
Bogtoun				12	12	20	6	20			15s 7d		£1 18s 10d
Mills of Farness	60-0-0		4		48	48	160	12			£2 1s 9d	£27 10s 0d	£5 11s 1d
Davidston	155-3-0	1	8	8	48	48	160		364	80	£8 4s 0d	£71 7s 8d	£12 14s 3d
Peddieston	125-2-0	1	7	4	48	48	160		364	24	£7 6s 3d	£57 10s 2d	£11 15s 6d
Little Farness	125-2-0	1	7	8	48	48	160		364	24	£7 16s 3d	£55 13s 6d	£11 15s 6d

Source: NRAS/86 & 161

Notes

1. David Stevenson, *King or Covenant? Voices from the Civil War* (East Linton, 1996), 115.
2. John Spalding, *The history of the troubles and memorable transactions in Scotland and England, from MDCXXIV to MDCXLV* (Edinburgh, 1828–9), ii. 70.
3. Thomas Urquhart, *Logopandecteision* in *Collected Works* (Maitland Club, 1834); William Macgill, *Old Ross-shire and Scotland* (Inverness, 1909), no. 571.
4. Nicholas McDowell, 'Urquhart's Rabelais: Translation, Patronage, and Cultural Politics' in *English Literary Renaissance* (Oxford, 2006).
5. Thomas Urquhart, *The Jewel* in *Collected Works* (Maitland Club, 1834), 280–1.
6. NAS E82/11/1.
7. William Mackay and Herbert Cameron Boyd (eds), *Records of Inverness*, II, (Spalding Club, Aberdeen, 1911–24), 7.
8. Louise B. Taylor, *The Aberdeen Shore Work Accounts* (Aberdeen, 1972).
9. NAS GD305/1/158/no. 121.
10. Susan Mowat, *The Port of Leith* (Edinburgh, 1994), 222.
11. Walter Macfarlane, *Geographical Collections* (Scottish History Society, 1906), ii; Thomas Urquhart, *Logopantecteision*, VI.15 in *Collected Works* (Maitland Club, 1834); Thomas Tucker in Peter Hume Brown, *Early Travellers in Scotland* (Edinburgh, 1891).
12. NRAS 0204/86 & 161.

Part 2
1660–1760s

3

Landowners and their Powers:
1660–1760s

'Father,' said she, 'you have done me wrong
For you have married me on a childe young man,
For you have married me on a childe young man,
And my bonny love is long a-growing.'

The ballad 'Young Craigston' is still sung in Aberdeenshire telling the story of the marriage of a young woman to a twelve-year-old boy – a 'childe young man'. Complaining that he was 'long a-growing', she agreed that he be sent away to 'school', which might have meant university, since students were then accepted at this young age. When she visited him, dressed in her finest green robes, he was playing at football with his fellow students, but left them to walk with her in the college park. They lingered there until darkness fell and when, in the words of the ballad, he 'lifted up her fine Holland sark' she found that she had now 'no reason to complain of his growing'. By the following year he was father of a son, but the song ends tragically with his death shortly afterwards.

FIGURE 3.1
Carved stonework from Craigston Castle.

47

The marriage was in 1632, the young woman was Elizabeth Innes of Innes and the 'childe young man' was her first cousin, John Urquhart, 'Young Craigston' of the ballad's title, who died in November 1634. There was a murky background to these events. John Urquhart's grandfather had died in November of the previous year, 1631, and his father in December. On his deathbed the father had extracted a promise from the twelve-year-old boy to care for his mother, Mary Innes, and pay all debts due by the family. Mary's brother Robert began to manipulate the situation by securing the guardianship of the boy and by marrying him to his own daughter. Then, with the excuse that Urquhart was not yet of age, Innes refused to settle debts due to the father's creditors. Those who had provided guarantees for the father's borrowings lost their money, their 'maledictions' affected the boy deeply and he was believed to have died of an illness brought on by depression. He seems to have had little pleasure from his short life, except a few games of football and his evening in the park with Elizabeth.

The inheritance that occasioned so much unhappiness consisted of the estate of the grandfather, John Urquhart of Craigston, Tutor of Cromarty (1547–1631). A 'tutor' was a legal guardian and, as a younger brother of Walter Urquhart, sheriff of Cromarty, he had become guardian of Walter's grandson, Thomas. He married three times, acquired many properties and built Craigston castle near Banff. He was said to be 'renowned over all Britain for his ... dexterity in acquiring many lands and possessions' and his castle remains as testimony to his wealth and his taste. Young Craigston had consequently been, as the ballad had it, 'a heritor of land, and likewise possessed of many bills and bonds'. This all now passed to the son conceived in the college grounds in 1632, also named John. By the 1660s he was also in control of the estate of Cromarty.

It is difficult to find anything positive to say about this fourth John Urquhart (1632–78). When he married one of the Seaforth Mackenzies in 1655, his mother's second husband, Alexander Brodie, wrote disapprovingly in his diary that 'there was much follie and looseness' at the wedding celebrations and later declared him 'so little a man to be trusted in'. As laird of Cromarty he was greedy, unscrupulous and violent. In April 1678, like his father before him, he fell into a deep depression. His daughter-in-law heard a noise from the dining room in the newer part of Cromarty castle, where she found him pacing up and down with his dressing gown pulled tightly around him. When she asked what was wrong, he replied, 'Woman, would you see?' and opened the gown to show his breast stuck with knives and forks, which had been lying on a sideboard. He died of these wounds soon afterwards.

Lairds and tenants

This chapter has begun with an account of yet another memorably odd laird of Cromarty but from the 1660s, simply because many more records survive, it becomes possible to gain a deeper understanding of the social and economic conditions within the sheriffdom. And as a result, it becomes possible to understand much more of the lives of the ordinary people on the estates and in the small burgh. Settlements such as Cromarty, with their hinterlands, are an important and relatively unexplored part of Scottish economic and social history, for even as late as 1830 two-thirds of the population still lived in the countryside or in small towns and villages.

In 1660 various branches of the Urquhart family still held the vast bulk of the lands of the old sheriffdom, albeit burdened by debt. Sir Thomas Urquhart had, however, been an absentee landlord for almost a decade and after his death c.1660 his successors would take more direct control of estate management. Scottish landowners held considerably more legal power over those who worked the land than their counterparts in most other European countries and their control over the land itself was later augmented by Acts of the pre-1707 Scottish Parliament which provided for the division of commonties (areas of land common to adjoining estates) and the abolition of runrig (portions of land reallocated among owners from time to time).

While a sense of mutual dependency between lairds and tenants, as extolled by Sir Thomas Urquhart, may have acted as a check on the exercise of these powers within a traditional, kin-based society, this was less so in lowland areas – certainly after the middle of the seventeenth century. In any event, almost all of the land in the old sheriffdom – or shire – of Cromarty passed out of the hands of the 'traditional' owners by 1700 and the opportunities for more commercial estate management, unfettered by customary ties between laird and tenant, were thus increased.

However, the successive owners exhibited a wide range of motivation in estate management and it would be a mistake to see this simply as a time of unrestrained commercialism. While a different set of values was in place by the late nineteenth century – and this included a firmly commercial approach to tenant farming – the intervening period saw landowners use their lands for a variety of social and political, as well as economic, purposes. The aim of this chapter is to outline the changes in landownership between the 1660s and the 1760s, and to indicate the general approaches of different lairds to estate management.

Under Urquhart lairds

Around 1661, after Sir Thomas's death – however and whenever that occurred – the estate passed to his brother, who was unable to keep up the property. He declined the office of sheriff but, having successfully disguised his covenanting background, received compensation in 1663 for losses during 1651–2, when it was administered by the occupying English forces. His cousin, Sir John Urquhart of Craigston, gradually took legal control and formally inherited in 1667 on Alexander's death. A wholly different style of estate management ensued. The new laird's lifestyle led him into as much, if not more, debt as his predecessors and he had therefore every reason to maximise income from his lands. In 1666, for example, both Urquhart and Sir George Mackenzie of Tarbat, with 'their ladyes and famelies', went up to York and stayed there 'till the closure of the year at a considerable cost and expense'. His association with Tarbat was, however, to prove his family's undoing, for Tarbat, acting in association with his cousin, George Mackenzie of Rosehaugh, and Alexander Brodie of Brodie, Urquhart's step-father, ensnared the Urquharts in a web of debt over a period of some twenty years.[1]

John Urquhart needed little encouragement to spend money embellishing his properties. In 1664 he was busy restoring Castle Craig, which he had apprised from his cousin Alexander, having a new hall floor laid and the interior walls parged (plastered), and, once in control in Cromarty, he created a 'great new orch-yard' below the castle and engaged an Edinburgh gardener. He also seized the burgh's common pasture along the adjoining Crook Burn, known as the Castleden, which was the site of the burgh fairs, and it is possible that this, with the creation of the orchard, closed off one of the town's streets, which had run from the kirk towards the castle.

His conflicts with the burgh increased with the enclosure of more of the common grazings, which prevented townspeople from pasturing animals or taking turf for fuel, and at a meeting of the town's council on 29 September 1669 Alexander Clunes, one of the leading burgesses, protested. Urquhart flew into a rage, swore at Clunes, beat him to the ground with his walking stick and threw away his hat and wig. The following week a clandestine meeting of the council was convened on a Saturday night in Clunes' house to appoint Thomas Lindsay as provost and Thomas Clunes and Alexander Urquhart as bailies. Of the ten present, five were named Clunes and one was Alexander Clunes' footman.

The next Tuesday a rival council of nine was produced by the laird, consisting of five Urquharts, mostly tenants of the estate, and an odd assortment including the laird's butler, a chapman (a travelling salesman) and a stranger who lived in an old barn in the town. They appointed the laird's former grieve, Henry Urquhart, as provost and chose, as bailies, the butler and Thomas McCulloch, his tenant in Farness. The only man to attend both meetings was the independent-minded Sandy Wood and, because he had voted in the Saturday election, Urquhart attacked him with equal violence, kicking him as he lay on the ground until he was 'fearfully bruised'.

The rival councils took their dispute to the Privy Council, which gave the Clunes party the opportunity to voice some of their other complaints. They alleged that the laird, as hereditary sheriff, had interfered with the jurisdiction of the burgh council by releasing and fining prisoners, thus receiving the fines instead of the burgh. He was also accused of seizing the money collected to pay the burgh's tax, with the result that the tax went unpaid and troops were quartered on the town, and of imposing a payment of *reik hens*. This tax on every occupied house – from which *reik* (smoke) issued – was the prerogative of a feudal superior and he was not superior of the burgh, whose property was held from the Crown.

The Privy Council came down firmly on the side of the laird, perhaps not surprisingly since he was a staunch royalist and had played an important role in public affairs as one of the four commissioners appointed by Charles II to determine the form of church governance in Scotland after 1661. With his 'puppet council' now firmly in place Urquhart closed in on the burgh and on 12 July 1670 a disposition was signed by the provost, two bailies, burgh treasurer and sixteen others transferring the whole property of the burgh to the laird, on the grounds that the burgh's poverty prevented it from meeting its obligations. The town lost not only its common land and other property but, subsequently, its status as a royal burgh. But whatever benefit it brought Urquhart over the next eight years, it was not enough to prevent his descent into depression and suicide.[2]

Baron, sheriff and vice-admiral

Most Scottish landowners had the right to hold baronial courts, which dealt with matters of estate management. These are described in the next chapter. More significant were the rights attaching to hereditary sheriffs, who held the power of 'pit and gallows' – that is, of execution for capital offences. There are records of these powers being exercised in Cromarty. In 1674 John Urquhart sitting as sheriff condemned Donald McFinlay to death by hanging, on a gibbet set up on the Mulbuie, where his body was left for eight days. And in 1676 Andrew Forbes, a caird or tinker, was accused of a remarkable range of crimes – stealing from corn stacks, breaking into John Urquhart's booth (market stall) in Cromarty and stealing twenty merks, stealing the communion cup from Tarbat Church, stealing timber from the shore defences at Cromarty, coining false money by putting quicksilver on coins to make them appear to be crowns, adultery with a Margaret Denune in Inverness, poisoning his own wife and, finally, perjury. He was secured in the pit (dungeon) of Cromarty castle, but on Sunday 25 May escaped by tunnelling through the stone wall, taking with him, for good measure, a blanket and a pewter cup. He was caught, taken to the gallows at the Ness, hanged and his body burned. Earlier, in 1662, Urquhart, and his depute Alexander Urquhart of Newhall, had been commissioned to try witches as part of one of the most brutal witch hunts in Scottish history – and one woman is said to have been burnt on the same spot.[3]

Urquhart also had the right to hold admiralty courts, which had the much-abused power to declare ships 'prizes of war', often on the grounds that they had been trading with the enemy, after which they could be seized and sold along with their cargo. In 1672 the *Bruce* brought two ships, the *Palmtree* and the *Patience*, into the Cromarty roads where they were declared prizes. Even by the standards of the time, the admiralty courts at Cromarty were notoriously corrupt, and the leading authority on Scots law, Viscount Stair, commented on the use of forced confessions used there in evidence. The rights to hold admiralty courts were abolished by an Act of Parliament in 1681 and all powers restored to the High Admiral of Scotland.[4]

Urquhart's authority as sheriff could easily be used to break down opposition to him and many of those who opposed him in the burgh were subsequently prosecuted. The burgh court, also in effect controlled by him from 1669, dealt with minor offences and disputes, of which there were many. In the year 1669, for example, we find a series of altercations between townsfolk – Harie Urquhart was 'daily upbraided' by a drunken fellow burgess who threatened to shoot him; Elizabeth Gordon 'reviled Agnes Williamson as a whore, thief and liar', whenever she appeared in the street; Elizabeth Gordon was also in dispute with John Reid who had retained one of four linnets sent home to her by her husband, and beat her when she went to try to retrieve it; a servant of the laird had been struck on the head with a shell, his hair pulled out and his coat torn by John Hossack; Donald Hossack in Davidston had suffered an attack by Thomas Hood who had stolen his plaid, allowed his cattle to eat Hossack's corn and taken over a patch of Hossack's grass; John Smithson complained that water from the Payhead had been diverted to run onto his property; and John Mackenzie and Sara Clunes complained that they had been unjustly treated in the quartering of soldiers on them the previous year.

Under Mackenzie lairds

Urquhart's son, Jonathon, inherited in 1678 but the knot of creditors – Tarbat, Rosehaugh and Brodie, with Hugh Dallas of St Martins as their legal agent – tightened the noose and the estate passed out of the

FIGURE 3.2
George Mackenzie, Viscount Tarbat and 1st Earl of Cromartie.

Urquharts' hands. Jonathon had observed, the year before his father's death, that 'Tarbat was a knave and a cheat' but by that time the trap was set. One of Jonathon Urquhart's last acts was to 'slight' the castle, removing anything of value and destroying as much as possible of what could not be taken. The glass in all the windows was broken; there was nothing but bare walls left in the great hall; only the doors remained in the 'Lord's chamber' and adjoining study, where there had been two beds, a cabinet, table, chairs and bookshelves; and, in the cellars, even the hooks for hanging meat had been cut out.[5]

After a number of transactions among the creditors, ownership was consolidated in two principal blocks. The lands in the westward part of the shire went to Sir Adam Gordon of Dalpholly, whose family originated from Sutherland but who had prospered as a London financier. He already held property on the north shore of the Cromarty Firth at Inverbreakie, subsequently renamed Invergordon, and later acquired more land through marriage to a daughter of Urquhart of Newhall. Much of the burgh of Cromarty and the adjoining lands was acquired by Tarbat who, when he was made an earl in 1703, took the title Earl of Cromartie. Tarbat used his considerable political influence to have an Act of Parliament passed that annexed his other lands in Ross to the old sheriffdom of Cromarty, thus giving him authority as hereditary sheriff over all his properties. This enhanced legal power must have been one of the key attractions in the acquisition of the estate.

The Cromarty estate itself had, however, been transferred to Tarbat's younger son, Sir Kenneth, before 1700. From c.1700 the distinction must be kept in mind between the Cromarty estate, which included the former royal burgh, and the Cromartie estate or estates, the property of successive earls, later administered from their seat at Castle Leod, near Strathpeffer. The difference in spelling is a later, useful convention. The Cromartie estates were forfeit to the Crown between 1746 and 1784, following the third earl's support for the 1745 Jacobite rising – the Cromarty estate was not. The town of Cromarty remained, at least in name, the administrative and judicial centre of the enlarged sheriffdom, although sheriff courts were in practice held at Milton, Tarbat's castle on the north shore of the Cromarty Firth. After hereditary jurisdictions were abolished in 1747, the sheriffdom of Cromarty was administered jointly with the sheriffdom of Ross – but it retained its own justices of peace and commissioners of supply and retained its status as a county until 1889, when it was subsumed in 'Ross & Cromarty'. Cromarty-shire also retained the right to elect a member of parliament, alternating with the larger shire of Nairn, until parliamentary reform in 1832. Thus, ownership of the small Cromarty estate carried with it, at various times, the office of sheriff and, with some manoeuvring to secure support in the enlarged sheriffdom, sufficient votes to be elected an MP.

The town of Cromarty lost its status as a royal burgh by 1684, from which date all those who had held land in feudal tenure from the burgh claimed – correctly as it turned out – to hold in their own right, directly from the Crown. This established a body of small landowners who were jealous of their independence from the laird's control as feudal superior and there were recurring disputes between these former burgess families and the lairds of Cromarty during the eighteenth century. The number of small landowners (that is, those holding land valued at less than £400 Scots) was, however, reduced by almost half by 1756 and fell even more sharply in the next fifty years. This was broadly similar to the changing pattern of landownership throughout Scotland as a whole.

There were two successive Mackenzie lairds of Cromarty in the eighteenth century: Sir Kenneth (d.1729) and Sir George (d.1748), who sold the estate in 1741. Although almost no personal or estate papers survive it is clear that the town grew significantly under Kenneth Mackenzie. Many new feus were granted and there were some moves towards improvement of agriculture. However, George Mackenzie, who inherited as the town's economy declined, lived beyond his means and descended, in style, into bankruptcy. A series of letters written between 1742 and 1748, to Gilbert Gordon, an Inverness merchant, reveal much of his character. Gordon sold cloth and Mackenzie took delight in the details of expensive clothing for his family – yellow Mantua silk for a short kilt, white silk for his wife's riding jacket, scarlet cloth to line a cloak, and chamois leather for the pockets of breeches. When a party of fellow aristocrats visited him, he declared there was 'no prince on earth as happy as I', and when Gordon himself visited Cromarty, as a church elder attending synod, Mackenzie offered him a bed, with the comment 'acquaint me whether you will choose Mr David of Tarbat, Mr John Manson or a Steuart Lass for your bedfellow and you shall be provided accordingly'. Mackenzie rode out the Jacobite rising on the basis that 'keeping snug at home is safest' and when he died in 1748, having continued to live in the same manner, his wife did not even have funds to meet the funeral expenses.[6]

The return of the Urquharts

In 1741 the estate was bought by William Urquhart of Meldrum, acting on behalf of his cousin Captain John Urquhart (1696–1756). He has been romanticised in family histories as 'the pirate' and this has obscured the reality. Urquhart supported the 1715 Jacobite rising, escaped to France and returned to London by 1717. In 1718 he went abroad again with the intention of entering 'a foreign sea service'. He received a commission as ensign in the Spanish marine in 1720, came to London in 1723 to have three ships built, with which he was to trade under licence from the Spanish Crown, and was commissioned lieutenant in 1728. By 1737 he had returned to Scotland where he settled and married. There were stable international trading conditions between 1720 and the outbreak of war between Britain and Spain in 1739. Under the Treaty of Utrecht (1713), Britain had not only gained territory but also what was known as the *Asiento*, granting the right to import slaves into Spanish America – and while this privilege created tensions, which mounted in the 1730s and culminated in the 'War of Jenkins Ear', this was not a period in which Spanish privateers were active. Contrary to the family tradition, Urquhart is likely to have made his money in transatlantic trade, possibly including the slave trade since he also owned a plantation, named Craigston, on the small Caribbean island of Carricaou.

At the age of forty-five, he had amassed enough wealth to buy two Scottish estates formerly owned by the Urquhart family – Cromarty and Craigston. Many people in Cromarty were prepared to see this as the return of the 'true' owner, who would restore the fortunes of the estate. A prophesy of the fall and rise of the Urquharts – 'a restoration to the old inheritance long looked for' – recorded by Robert Williamson, the first Presbyterian minister of the parish, was quoted with enthusiasm when news of the purchase reached the town. Williamson's father had seen a vision of a red flag with a ray of sun in it flying over the castle and interpreted this as meaning that the family of Urquhart would for a time be extinct but 'a spark would rise to enjoy it forever'. This enthusiasm was despite the fact that Urquhart was a devout Roman Catholic and it was anti-catholic legislation which had forced him to purchase the estate in the name of his Protestant cousin.[7]

Urquhart styled himself 'of Cromarty' rather than 'of Craigston', his priorities were the restoration of the castle and the landscaping of its surroundings, and he reckoned the acquisition of 'a paternal estate' among the principal blessings he had received in the course of his life. However, by 1749 local anti-catholic sentiment and a dispute over the patronage of the parish church had alienated Urquhart. His wife had been badly frightened by local antagonism and he was considering selling Cromarty. Instead he based himself at Craigston and managed Cromarty from a distance, symbolically removing to Craigston some of the carved stones from Cromarty castle. When Urquhart's son, William, came of age the estate was put on the market and the Urquharts' connection with Cromarty came to an end.

'A political job': Lord Elibank

In 1763 the Cromarty estate was advertised for sale. In addition to the attractions of being in 'good sporting country', having prospects for

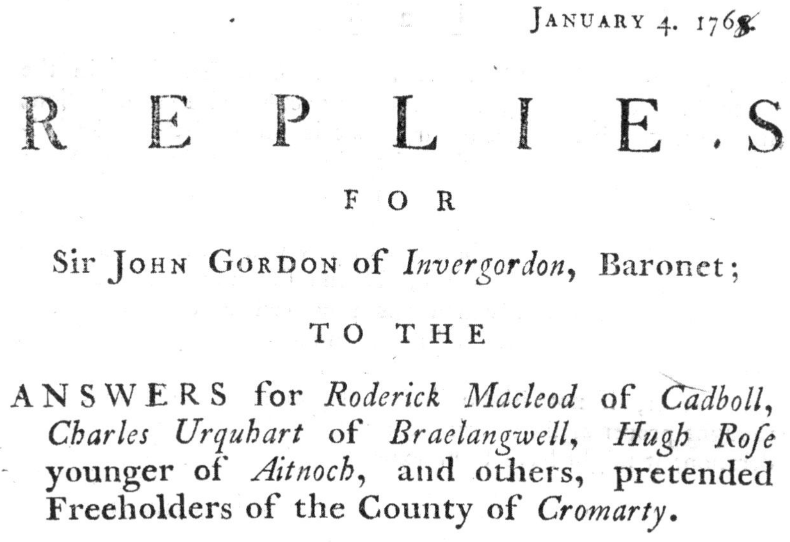

JANUARY 4. 1768

R E P L I E S

F O R

Sir JOHN GORDON of *Invergordon*, Baronet;

T O   T H E

A N S W E R S for *Roderick Macleod* of *Cadboll*, *Charles Urquhart* of *Braelangwell*, *Hugh Rose* younger of *Aitnoch*, and others, pretended Freeholders of the County of *Cromarty*.

FIGURE 3.3

The dispute between William Johnstone (later Pulteney) and Sir John Gordon over the election of an MP for Cromarty-shire in 1764 was one of the most expensive legal cases in eighteenth-century Scotland.

the development of trade and manufactures and being planted with 'an million and an half best forest trees', the advertisement indicated that the purchaser might 'with some little trouble and charge have himself elected the member of parliament for the county'.[8] The 'trouble and charge' consisted of the legal manoeuvre of granting a number of securities, known as wadsets. These wadsets were granted, not on the land itself, but on the feudal superiority of the estate. Those who held the securities, the wadsetters, by gaining a stake in the feudal superiority, gained a vote, which they could then use in support of the owner.

This manoeuvre was easier and more effective where there was a small electorate, as in Cromarty-shire. Cromarty alternated with Nairn-shire in returning a member to the House of Commons and the seat had been held since 1743, in alternate parliaments, by the Tory Sir John Gordon of Invergordon. The estate was bought in 1764 by Patrick, Lord Elibank, acting on behalf of his nephew, William Johnston – who was shortly to change his name to Pulteney, when his wife inherited the estate of Lord Bath. The purchase was made with the sole intention of having Pulteney elected as MP. This was achieved in 1768 but the election result was disputed by the losing candidate, Sir John Gordon. The ensuing court action was one of the longest, and most expensive, of the century. Elibank prevailed and the estate, having served its political purpose, was sold at a discount to his associate George Ross, who had assisted with what was called the 'political job'. Ross's improvements marked a turning point in Cromarty's development and the estate, latterly much diminished in extent, remained in the hands of the Ross family until 1976.[9]

National politics

In the century after 1660, Cromarty was, of course, affected by national politics. The restoration of Charles II to the throne in that year was followed by the imposition of episcopalian governance in the Church of Scotland, with consequent opposition from Presbyterians whose beliefs on the relationship between God, church and state had been encapsulated in the National Covenant of 1638. Hugh Anderson had succeeded his father, Gilbert, as minister of Cromarty in 1656 and, although he was a committed Presbyterian who did not accept episcopal authority in 1660, he was left undisturbed in the parish until 1662. It was only after he assisted at an illicit communion service at Obsdale, near Alness, that he was deprived of his charge by the Privy Council. Even then he appears to have remained until 1673, when he was replaced by Episcopalians – first by Thomas Urquhart and then, in 1678, by Bernard Mackenzie. Contrary to later tradition, which portrayed him as a morally weak time-server, Mackenzie was a popular and forceful character, who was prepared to champion the inhabitants of the burgh in opposition to the laird, his patron George Mackenzie of Tarbat.

Major political change came with the Union of the Parliaments in 1707. Tarbat, as first earl of Cromartie, was a staunch proponent of union with England, principally on economic grounds, believing that there would be benefits as Scotland gained trading rights in a larger market. The subsequent growth of Cromarty's trade in salt fish, described in chapter 5, initially bore out his views but there was, more generally, widespread discontent in Scotland as the promised benefits failed to materialise. Moreover, Scotland had, through the Union, moved from a 'low tax' to a relatively 'high tax' economy, within which customs and excise duties were expected to produce real returns to the Treasury. Both the Union and the ruling house of Hanover became the focus for deep anti-government resentment, with resulting connivance in smuggling, attacks on government officers and widespread support for the Jacobite cause in 1715.

Cromarty's relative prosperity in 1715 may have tempered Jacobite sentiments but they simmered after the rising failed. An unnamed brother of Alexander Urquhart of Newhall had served in the navy under Queen Anne, but refused to continue under the Hanoverian George I. For a time there was talk in Jacobite circles of Urquhart buying a ship and setting his brother up in trade as a cover for communication between Jacobites in Scotland and on the continent. The plan came to nothing when the brother entered the service of the tsar of Russia. In the same vein there were proposals in 1718 for a Jacobite invasion of Scotland. The bulk of the force was to land in the Firth of Forth but there was also to be a landing at Cromarty of '1000 foot, 50 horse, 6000 stand of arms, 6 cannon, 2 mortars and 150 bombs, in case Inverness should be garrisoned by the Usurper's troops'. Much of this was mere fancy.[10]

Support for the Jacobite cause had significantly diminished by 1745. Hugh Miller, in his 'traditional history of Cromarty' – the subtitle for his *Scenes and Legends of the North of Scotland* – claimed that there was but a single Jacobite in Cromarty, the merchant Alexander Ross, known as Silken Sawney. This was an exaggeration but there was undoubtedly little support for the cause of the house of Stuart.

More important would be the effects of Government policy after the defeat of the Jacobite force at Culloden on 16 April 1746, an event watched with enthusiasm from Cromarty Hill by a crowd from the town. The estates of the principal rebels were confiscated by the Crown and administered by the Commissioners for the Annexed Estates until 1784. The lands of the earl of Cromartie – the Cromartie estates – were forfeited, but not the smaller Cromarty estate, the property of Captain Urquhart, who despite having been out as a Jacobite in the '15 did not support the '45. This left Cromarty as the head town of the expanded shire of Cromarty, which was largely forfeit, and the Commissioners were persuaded to support some developments in Cromarty itself, including the building of its harbour in the 1780s. The Jacobite rising also led government to abolish the hereditary jurisdictions in 1748, removing the traditional authority of sheriffs and others, and replacing them with government appointed officials.

Notes

1. Alexander Brodie, *Diary of Alexander Brodie of Brodie, 1652–1680 and of his son James Brodie* (Aberdeen, 1873) and Henrietta Tayler, *The Family of Urquhart* (Aberdeen, 1946), 119 & 121. Tarbat's scheme to acquire Cromarty is described in Eric Richards and Monica Clough, *Cromartie: Highland Life: 1650–1914* (Aberdeen, 1991), 46.

2. William Mackay Mackenzie, 'The royal burgh of Cromarty and the breaking of the burgh' in *Transactions of the Gaelic Society of Inverness* (Inverness, 1927), xxxi, 374–91.

3. William Macgill, *Old Ross-shire and Scotland* (Inverness, 1909), nos 244, 245, 249.

4. David Dalrymple (Viscount Stair), *Decisions of the Court of Session between 1666 and 1671*, ii. 85; Eric Graham, 'The Scottish marine during the Dutch wars' in *Scottish Historical Review* (1982).

5. NAS GD305/20/124.

6. NAS, GD23/6/148: 34 letters from Sir George Mackenzie of Cromarty to Gilbert Gordon, Inverness.

7. NRAS 0204/Bundle 168, Letter from Lady Greenhill to Lady Pitcalnie.

8. NRAS 0204/Bundle 168.

9. William Ferguson, 'The election system in the Scottish counties before 1832' in *Miscellany II*, Stair Society (Edinburgh, 1984).

10. Historic Manuscripts Commission, *Stuart Papers*, 615.

4

Agriculture before 1760

... teaching the most profitable way, both for the manner and the
season, of tilling, digging, ditching, hedging, dunging, sowing,
harrowing, grubbing, reaping, threshing, killing, milling, baking,
brewing, batling of pasture ground, mowing, feeding of herds,
flocks, horse and cattel; making good use of the execrescence of all
of these; improving their herbages, dayries, mellificiaries, fruitages;
setting up of the most expedient agricolary instruments of wains,
carts, slades, with their several devices of wheels and axle-trees,
plows and harrows of divers sorts, feezes, winders, pullies, and all
other manner of engines fit for easing the toyl and furthering the
work; whereby one weak man, with skill, may effectuate more than
fourty strong ones without it.

Sir Thomas Urquhart of Cromarty, *Logopandecteision*, 1653

Traditional balance and nutrient traps

The economy of the town of Cromarty has depended for most of its
history on the agriculture of its hinterland. In order to understand
how farming changed over the centuries, it is important to
first appreciate the system that was in place before agricultural
'improvement' got underway. Traditional arable cultivation relied on
natural manures, principally cattle dung – but also human waste – and
lowland farming systems reflected this in the division of land into infield
and outfield. The infield, close to the farmtoun, received the bulk of
available manure and was under constant cultivation, usually with a
rotation of bere (a primitive form of barley) followed by two years
of oats. The outfield was only partially cultivated, either by grazing
cattle in temporary enclosures, known as folds, until fertility within
the fold had been increased, or simply by ploughing and planting on
unmanured ground.

In summer, cattle were grazed on commonties (areas of common
land) adjoining the farmtouns, or moved to more distant shielings

(hill pasture). However, the survival of cattle until the following year depended on the availability of winter pasture, usually consisting of small areas of permanent green pasture and the uncultivated section of the outfield. No matter how much summer grazing was available, it was winter pasture that determined the number of cattle that could be retained, the rest being slaughtered in November. Moreover it was only from winter pasture, close to the farmtoun, that manure could be gathered. The key to sustainable cultivation, and this point cannot be overemphasised, was to find a proper balance between arable and pasture. Any increase in the area of cropped land brought with it the danger of a corresponding reduction in pasture, a consequent reduction in the number of cattle and a fall in the supply of manure. It has been estimated that the optimum crop yield, in traditional systems, resulted when roughly 15 to 20 per cent of land was under arable.[1]

Demand for increased production of grain could throw this traditional farming system out of balance, as seems to have happened in southern England in the late thirteenth and early fourteenth centuries, when the area under arable increased with the pressure of population growth. Some communities were cropping up to 50 per cent of land by this time. The term 'nutrient trap' has been used to describe the inevitable fall in yields, which led to even greater pressure to expand the area under arable – with further falls in productivity. However, with improved farming methods an increase in the proportion of ground under arable could be sustained and the nutrient trap avoided.

In seventeenth-century Scotland, as lairds became less concerned with military power and more concerned with the economy of their estates, their energies were directed to increasing productivity through a variety of measures. These included rotation of crops, liming and the growth of fodder crops to feed cattle over the winter. These improvements required the consolidation of arable ground into enclosed fields and tenants were encouraged to adopt improved methods by being granted longer leases. There were also moves to do away with multiple or joint tenancies and allow a single, enterprising tenant to control a relatively large farm. Rents, which had been traditionally paid in kind, began to be converted to cash, and, to further encourage a market economy, new trading centres, known as burghs of barony, were established.

The pace of these changes in Scotland has been a matter of some debate. However, it is now generally accepted that the rural economy of late seventeenth-century Scotland was more successful than had often been assumed. Yields increased and widespread dearth occurred only in 1674–5 and, with regional variations, between 1695 and 1699. By the end of the century the standard infield/outfield ratio in lowland Scotland was around 1:2 (i.e. 33 per cent infield), with a higher ratio of 2:1 (i.e. 66 per cent infield) being achieved on improved mains farms.

Scottish agriculture, however, still lagged behind that of England. Tom Devine's study of key areas in central Scotland, *The Transformation of Rural Scotland*, shows that the decisive 'leap forward' did not take place until the three decades after 1760. Although there had been enterprise among tenants and moves to single tenancies and cash rentals before 1760, the historic pattern of cultivation – land divided into infield and outfield, with adjoining commonties – remained. It was, Devine argues, market pressures emanating from urban growth and the beginnings of industrialisation that created the opportunity for radical improvement. This was often achieved through the imposition of improving leases, which specified the farming practices to be adopted.[2]

How did farming in the area around Cromarty – and, more generally, on the fertile coastal strip around the Moray Firth – develop in the same period? The evidence can only be assessed by working back from the situation as it was described in the later eighteenth century, when consistent data on agriculture begins to be available. First, there are a number of detailed surveys of unimproved estates, made between the 1760s and the 1790s; and, second, there are two series of printed reports on the agriculture of Scottish counties, one published in the mid 1790s and another, written for the Board of Agriculture, published between 1808 and 1813. Together these show that on the fertile eastern coastal strip of Inverness, Nairn, Ross and Sutherland, the area of ground under cultivation had increased considerably by 1760, to the extent that arable ground was cultivated on a rotation system, with little distinction between infield and outfield. However, evidence of crop yields and of the limited use of manures suggests that, while both the area under cultivation and total grain production increased, yields per acre remained static or fell.

Expansion of cultivation within an open field system

After 1760 surveyors were engaged by many landowners to map their estates and assess the potential for improvement. David Aitken, one of the principal surveyors in the north, mapped the Cromarty estate in 1764. There are nine other surviving surveys by Aitken of estates on the Black Isle and Easter Ross, all carried out between the 1760s and the 1780s, each with a classification of land as arable (usually distinguishing infield and outfield), pasture, moor, wood and, in some cases, meadow. There are also surveys by Aitken of estates in Sutherland and Caithness, and, from the same period, surveys of Invergordon and east Sutherland by other surveyors.[3]

The benchmark to bear in mind in examining these is the traditional balance obtained when roughly one-third of available land was under

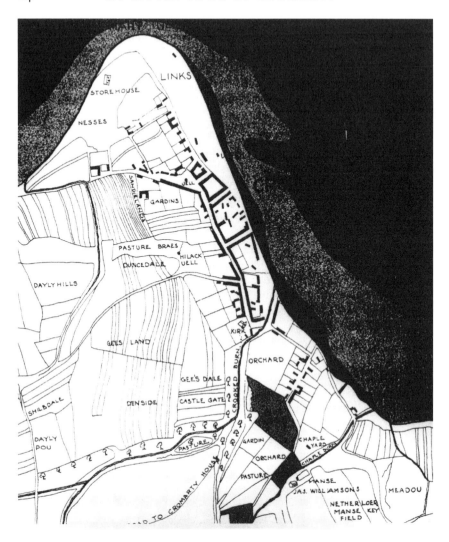

FIGURE 4.1
Cromarty and surrounding lands, redrawn from David Aitken's survey of 1764
(parts of the map showing the castle were removed when it was demolished
in 1772).

arable cultivation. In fact, the proportion of ground under permanent
arable cultivation is strikingly high – Aitken's surveys show that, by the
third quarter of the eighteenth century, it was common for over 80 per
cent of arable land to be classified as infield, that is, under permanent
arable cultivation. Across the Black Isle and Easter Ross, land use
did not, therefore, conform to the cultivation pattern that had been
common in Scotland in the seventeenth century.

In 1795 Sir John Sinclair published *A general view of the northern counties and islands of Scotland*, which began with an account of agriculture on the Black Isle, largely based on information from George Gun Munro of Poyntzfield, near Cromarty. Sinclair does not refer to a division between infield and outfield but instead describes a seven-year rotation 'generally practised in the eastern districts'. It is difficult to determine over what period the conversion from an infield–outfield system took place but there is evidence that the drive to expand arable ground began well before the end of the seventeenth century, since in 1686 there was land on Cromarty Hill which had been 'out of cultivation a long time' – indicating an earlier attempt to bring it into production.[4]

The historical development of a similar system of arable and pasture in Moray was described by William Leslie, writing in 1813.[5] Many eighteenth- and early nineteenth-century accounts of agriculture were written by enthusiastic improvers, who tended to denigrate traditional farming practices. Leslie's evidence for Moray is particularly valuable because he was both more sympathetic to the old system and more critical of some of the orthodoxies of contemporary improvers. Leslie noted, for example, traces of 'well formed, skilfully made rigs' on ground which had gone out of cultivation in the seventeenth century and argued against the 'interference' imposed on tenants under improving leases, which in his view repressed ingenuity and prevented adaptation during adverse seasons. Leslie regarded the division of land into 'croft and outfield' as an exception and believed that a rotation of bere followed by three crops of oats had been universally adopted on all arable ground 'for many centuries'. This system was, he argued, first altered by the inclusion of occasional crops of peas and had then been abandoned in favour of a rotation that incorporated grass.

The situation was, however, different in Caithness, Sutherland and inland Inverness-shire. In the early nineteenth century in Caithness and Sutherland, before major improvement, the proportion of farmland under arable cultivation was 38 per cent and 26 per cent respectively. In inland Inverness-shire the system of infield–outfield 'still prevail(ed.) over one half of the arable ground in the county'.[6]

The crucial question is: had the increase in land under cultivation along the Moray Firth, and the consequent reduction of winter pasture, led to a nutrient trap, with falling yields? There is certainly evidence of a general concern about the reduction of pasture. In Moray there was a recognised shortage and in many inland areas of the Highlands winter pasture had been reduced over the centuries by the destruction of woodland within which cattle had been grazed.[7] However, there were a number of possible 'escape routes' from the nutrient trap and if these were taken yields might be maintained. These 'escape routes' were *tathing* (i.e. the building of temporary enclosures to fold stock) on outfield or ley (fallow) ground, which addressed the problem of the loss of summer manure; use of other manures such as shell-sand, seaweed, peat, peaty soil, turf and heather; more labour-intensive cultivation, using hand tools, which improved nutrient flow within the soil; and improved crop-rotations that incorporated nitrogen-fixing plants, the most important of which was red clover.

On the Cromarty estate it is unlikely that summer tathing could have had a significant impact on yields. This was simply because so little stock was over-wintered – in 1713 tenants on the Cromarty estate over-wintered only sixty-three cattle and since the estate consisted of six principal farmtouns, each of which would have required a ploughing team of ten animals, this represents only a minimum number of animals.[8] Given the extent of the conversion of outfield, it is likely that the yields could only have been maintained through other means and by the mid eighteenth century a variety of manures were indeed in use. This included middens from the town – in 1751 the Mains farm paid 'sundries in the Town for muck being 45 loads' in September and bought '25 different dunghills from sundries being 201 cart and van loads' the following spring. Other manures included seaware and turf, the latter spread after being first used as a walling material for buildings and dykes. The use of lime could have had a significant impact on soil fertility and Captain Urquhart's improvements to the Cromarty estate in the late 1740s and early 1750s involved taking marginal ground into cultivation, some of which could not be let 'unless the master allowed lime'. Some lime was found in the form of marl (ancient shell deposits), for example from Meikle Farness where a five-year lease to Isaac Hood in 1749 reserved to the laird the 'right of carrying away white earth or limy substance'. As early as 1724 the Balnagowan estate was making payments to 'limemen' who appear to be fishers on this, or a neighbouring estate, who were predominantly employed in producing lime from shell deposits in the Cromarty Firth.[9]

A more significant source of nutrients is likely to have been the transfer of turf from the Mulbuie commonty. The reduction in green pasture and increased reliance on summer grazing on moor ground coincided with the general depletion of peat mosses on the Black Isle. Turf was a much poorer fuel and was consequently cut in larger quantities than peat, with a resulting increase in the transfer of nutrients. The increased cutting of turf across the whole of the commonty of the Mulbuie was highly labour intensive. From at least the early eighteenth century, and possibly before, until the division of the commonty in 1829, it was cut on a fifteen- to twenty-year cycle over almost the whole area. Turf and heather were cut from mid May and brought home from mid June. It took a household two months to do this, going with horses twice a day, using small carts, which carried the equivalent of 'what a fisherwoman

At Cromarty, the 11th day of September 1816 years.

In presence of the commissioner and parties, *ut antea,* James Taylor, Sheriff-clerk of Cromarty, was named clerk *pro tempore,* to whom the oath *de fideli* was administered by the commissioner; appeared the said Walter Ross, Esq. who craved to proceed in his proof under the claim for Mr Ross of Cromarty.   Whereupon

Compeared JOHN HOSSACK, residing at the Shore Miln, near Cromarty, aged 88 years, who being solemnly sworn, &c. depones, That he was born on the estate of Cromarty, and was a tenant on it from the time of his being 20 years of age, till about 15 years ago: That he always considered the road leading from Fortrose to Invergordon Ferry to be the boundary on the west, and he never knew the tenants of any other property carry away turf or heather from the east side of that road: That he knows what is called the Black Stand moss, which was used exclusively by the tenants of the estate, and a small part thereof by the tenants of Balmungy: That the lands of Poyntzfield and Udoll are the boundary at the north.   Depones, That the tenants on the estate were in use to go as far as the Chanonry moss for turf and fuel, and never were interrupted, and used also to take peats out of the moss without challenge; but it was nearly exhausted before he began to go there. Depones, That he and the other farmers on the Cromarty estate considered the whole ground lying to the north of the Black Stand moss the whole way to the outer dike of the lands of Ardoch, now Poyntzfield, and as far west as Chanonry road, to be the exclusive property of Mr Ross of Cromarty.   All which is truth, &c.

FIGURE 4.2
Evidence led in the action for the division of the Mulbuie Commonty.

could carry on her back'. While the principal reason for cutting turf was the provision of fuel, especially for drying grain, it was also gathered for turf house-walls and feal dykes. Both turf ash and old thatch and dyke material were commonly incorporated in dunghills, resulting in a transfer of nutrients from the commonty to the arable ground. Robert Dodgshon has shown the importance of such transfer in west Highland townships, where up to 70 per cent of nitrogen in the soil was provided in this way.[10]

More labour intensive cultivation is evident in the settling of *mailers* (cottars) on waste ground. The details of this will be considered in chapter 11. There is also evidence of intensive cultivation by established tenant farmers. One farmer named Robson, known as

Marcus, worked a small plot of ground at the bottom of cliffs to the east of Cromarty in the 1720s, where only hand tools could have been used but where there would have been a ready supply of seaweed as manure. He used a cave on the shore, which still bears his name, as a threshing barn.[11]

We have already seen that simple forms of crop rotation were generally in use and that the rotations show the planting of nitrogen-fixing crops of pease, albeit on a limited scale. There is no evidence of grass or clover sown by tenant farmers, although 'English clover' and grass seed were brought to Cromarty Mains in 1750,[12] confirming a point made by Devine that, in this period, significant improvements were often restricted to the mains farms.

Were these practices sufficient to prevent falling yields? The traditional expected yield was a threefold return – for each grain sown the harvest yielded one for seed, one to eat and one for rent. In 1795 it was reported that an ordinary tenant farm normally achieved a return of between two and fourfold on each boll of oats sown, and from three to fourfold on barley. In the parish of Resolis yields of 3.5 times for barley and only 2.25 times for oats and pease were reported, with a higher yield for tenants on the shore who had access to seaware.[13] Yields, then, remained static.

The calculation of the effect on overall grain production is more complex – and some readers may wish to skip this paragraph. Under a system of unimproved infield-outfield in the mid seventeenth century the total percentage of land producing a grain crop in any one year would have consisted principally of the 33 per cent that constituted the infield. A further area being cropped would be that part of the outfield under cultivation. If one fifth of the outfield were cultivated at any one time – and this would be a high proportion – this would add a further 13 per cent to the area cropped, giving a total of 46 per cent of land under cultivation. Under the system which pertained in the mid eighteenth century on the Cromarty estate this would have increased to 58 per cent – consisting of 53 per cent of arable under cultivation as infield in any one year (i.e. 75 per cent of arable ground cropped on a seven-year rotation, with two years in ley) and a further 5 per cent, being one fifth of the outfield. The change from totals of 46 to 58 per cent suggests a maximum increase in grain production, assuming static yields, of some 20 per cent on earlier levels.

Grain prices and grain exports

Since landowners received the bulk of their rent in kind, as bere and oatmeal, any business-like landowner was particularly concerned about the relative price of grain in the north and in southern urban centres to which his victual rent might be shipped and sold. A high differential was an incentive to ship grain south.

Grain prices were recorded in the yearly *fiars* – official judgements of the price of various grains, struck (set) by a fiars court assembled by the sheriff of each county and used to assess the value of a range of payments made in kind, including estate rents and ministers' stipends. The prices were assessed at Candlemas (2 February) and were referred to as the fiars for the crop of the preceding year. Thus the prices set in, say, February 1701 were the 1700 fiars. The earliest fiars in Scotland date from the mid sixteenth century and assess the price of bere and oatmeal only, but by the late seventeenth century fiars were also commonly being set for wheat, pease, malt, rye and beans. It is clear that the method of striking fiars varied considerably from county to county and that, in some counties, fiars were not always struck. Few records of fiars survive for counties north of the Great Glen before 1760 but fortunately two sources provide an almost complete series for Ross-shire for the second half of the seventeenth century and for some years in the eighteenth century. A table showing these fiars can be found at the end of the book.[14]

A comparison can then be made between the Ross-shire fiars and the Edinburgh fiars, thus identifying those years when the price differential was higher and greater profits were to be had by shipping grain to Leith (Figure 4.3). A complication is introduced by the fact that the Ross-shire fiars were set using a nine-stone boll, which was still being used in 1778. The Scottish standard measure was eight-stone and when this is taken into account the Ross-shire fiars were even lower in comparison with Edinburgh.[15]

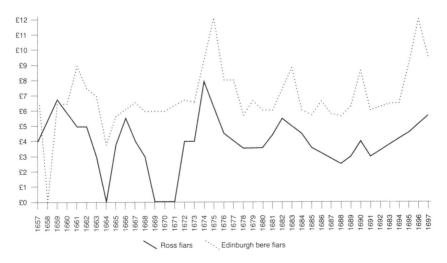

FIGURE 4.3   Ross-shire and Edinburgh fiars (£ Scots).

On the Cromarty estate Sir John Urquhart, faced with financial difficulties, responded by attempting to ship as much grain as possible – in 1663, against the advice of his agent in Edinburgh who doubted if he could honour the agreement, he contracted to supply 1,000 bolls of bere. In 1669 he did, however, supply George Anderson in Edinburgh with 500 bolls. Tarbat too regularly shipped grain to Edinburgh from his estates, including Cromarty. These exports confirm the conclusions of a study by Gibson and Smout that from at least the 1660s, if not before, Edinburgh was 'a powerful market centre ... pulling into its orbit ... the east-coast counties'.[16]

The differential in grain prices between the south and the north increased in the 1690s but Scotland as a whole returned to low grain prices with the good harvest of 1700. The next forty years witnessed a long period with few serious shortages and without many short-term fluctuations in price. During this period the Ross-shire grain price again fell in relation to the Edinburgh fiars. There was, therefore, a long period when there was a significant incentive to ship grain south and consequently an incentive to maximise production.[17]

The international market also had an influence on the north and, as in many parts of Scotland, there were significant exports of grain overseas, although these fluctuated from year to year. The Inverness customs books show exports of 8,548 bolls in 1681–2 (almost all bere and almost all shipped to Rotterdam) and 10,568 bolls in 1684–5 (80 per cent to Holland and 20 per cent to Norway) – but only 1,960 bolls in 1685–6 (all to Holland).[18] From the early eighteenth century there is a further source of evidence for overseas trade, in the corn debentures, which record bounties paid on the export of grain. Figure 4.4 shows the value of debentures for exports from the Inverness customs precinct for

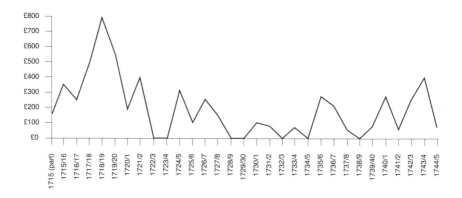

FIGURE 4.4   Corn debentures issued on exports from the Inverness customs precinct (£ sterling).

the years 1715 to 1745, showing a marked peak between 1717–18 and 1719–20. Further data from the corn debentures can be found in the tables at the end of the book.

The grain market and agricultural improvement

The key mechanisms in landlord-led improvement in lowland Scotland, both before and especially after 1760, were the implementation of changes in tenant structure, with multiple and joint tenancies replaced by single tenancies, and the use of improving leases, which specified, often in great detail, the practices to be adopted by tenants. The two mechanisms were linked, since with larger, single tenancies each tenant had full control of his land and might, at least under a long lease, benefit from improvements. Substantial improvement required not only new methods of estate management but also a sufficient number of tenants willing and able to take on such leases. This was possible because, as Devine and others have pointed out, there was more enterprise among tenants than critics in the later eighteenth century recognised. In the southern lowlands this was a result of the increased importance of local markets through which tenants could sell their crop.[19]

In the north, the differential in grain prices and the ready market in the south created an incentive for landowners to continue receiving rent in kind. They thus received not only the local value of the grain rent but the added value of the same grain sold in, say, Edinburgh. This discouraged conversion of victual rents to payment in cash, since the conversion would have been on the basis of the low local market price, available to tenants. To increase production for this underdeveloped local market, rather than for shipping south, would only have lowered the price of grain further. The view that rents paid in kind were preferable was, understandably, still held by managers of the annexed Jacobite estates after 1746.[20]

This, however, ran contrary to the preconditions for tenant participation in improved farming. A developed local market and the conversion of rents to cash were widely recognised as essential if enterprising tenants were to be engaged in the process. They would then be prepared to take on long leases, pay cash rents, invest in improved farming methods, market their grain and retain the profits. Rentals for the estate of Cromarty survive intermittently from 1637 to 1763 and show very limited conversion of victual rent to cash, with an exception of a short-lived conversion on two farms, before 1736, both of which had reverted to a victual rent by 1743.

There was some very limited participation by tenants and merchants in the export of grain. Some tenants were paying 'girnal dues' to the

Thee, Ferintosh! O sadly lost!
Scotland lament frae coast to coast!
Now colic grips, an barkin hoast
  May kill us a';
For loyal Forbes' charter'd boast
  Is taen awa!

FIGURE 4.5
Robert Burns' lament for the loss of the 'Ferintosh privilege'.

estate, which suggests that they had surplus grain stored at the *girnal* (granary), and from the 1730s the hated figure of the meal-monger or corn-factor begins to figure in local tradition, reviled because he bought up grain for export in times of shortage.[21] There was also some growth of the local market. The population of Cromarty recovered rapidly from the dearth of the late 1690s and expanded as trade in salt fish grew. This small but growing urban population required a source of food. And there were, too, sales of bere to 'the Ferintosh men' for distilling. The estate of Ferintosh, owned by Forbes of Culloden, had been granted the privilege of duty-free distilling as compensation for the destruction of Forbes' distillery by Jacobite forces in 1689 and its business expanded during the century. By 1760 Ferintosh was producing more legally distilled whisky than the rest of Scotland put together. This was mostly in small stills and when a larger distillery was built in 1782 the protests from other parts of the country led to legislation in 1786, which ended the 'Ferintosh privilege'. There are examples from the estate of Pitcalnie, Nigg, between 1734 and 1748, of grain due by tenants as victual rent being sold, on their laird's instructions, directly to Ferintosh. Any benefit of this, of course, accrued to the laird not the tenant.[22]

Yet the capacity of tenants in the north to operate within a cash economy is clear. Tenants in highland areas, dependent on trade in black cattle, paid their rent almost entirely in cash and had done so since the seventeenth century. A number of landowners held land in both the lowlands of Easter Ross and the adjoining Highlands and operated two rental systems – one based on cash, the other with payment in kind.[23]

The Cromarty estate

Improving lairds and enterprising tenants
As a result of the transactions by which George Mackenzie of Tarbat acquired the Cromarty estate, the sheriffdom of Cromarty, once

largely owned and controlled by the Urquharts, was divided by the late seventeenth century into two major blocks controlled, respectively, by Mackenzies and Gordons. Both blocks were of good arable ground ripe for improvement. The Mackenzie portion had access to the experience of Tarbat, whose estates 'were at the forefront of agricultural improvement', and Sir William Gordon was similarly praised for his improvements as early as 1727.[24] Moreover, both lairds were hereditary sheriffs-depute – a hereditary position unheard of in the rest of Scotland – giving them additional powers over their tenants.[25] Captain Urquhart, who acquired Cromarty in 1741, implemented further improving policies, as did George Munro who bought Ardoch from the Gordons in 1757. Thus, although the enthusiasm of individual owners varied, all the estates experienced sustained periods of landlord-led improvement before 1760.

The efforts of enterprising tenants can be seen in some of the small-scale improvements on the Cromarty estate.[26] In 1729 two tenants, William MacCulloch and Kenneth MacCulloch, entered into long leases under which they paid rent largely in cash. Kenneth MacCulloch became the principal improving tenant in the 1740s and 1750s, as evidenced by his new farm buildings at Allerton. William MacCulloch also improved his holding and by 1738 had taken into cultivation additional land of '10 bolls sowing' – about twelve acres. Both had opportunities for marketing grain. Kenneth MacCulloch operated the estate's only mills, to which all tenants and feuars were *thirled* (bound), and he was thus well placed to participate in the embryonic market economy. William MacCulloch was estate chamberlain and, being responsible for selling the victual rents, was in the best position of any tenant to participate in the market.

However, tenants could only pay cash rents if they could sell their crop. The immediate local market for grain would have stagnated or declined with the collapse of herring fishing after 1720. To some extent, an alternative market for bere for distilling developed at Ferintosh on the Black Isle and sales appear in many estate accounts. Nevertheless, on balance, the fact that no other tenants on the Cromarty estate entered into leases with cash rents suggests that commercial opportunities were limited by the late 1720s. Despite a landlord-led drive for improvement in the 1740s, the next partial conversion of victual rents was not until the mid 1750s.[27] There is a further indication of the underdevelopment of the local market in the rental of the neighbouring Ardoch estate. Here the customary services required from tenants were converted before the estate was sold in 1761 – but the conversion was to a payment in bere and not cash.[28]

Thus, while there were both improving lairds and enterprising tenants in the old shire of Cromarty, it is clear that the absence of local markets reduced opportunities for tenants to engage in improvement.

Landlord-led improvements

After acquiring the estate in 1741, Captain John Urquhart retained the previous factor, George Urquhart of Greenhill, until Greenhill's death in 1743. John Gorry was then appointed and from this point there appears to have been a more business-like approach to estate management. Gorry was also factor at Invergordon and more than a century later was still remembered there, probably unfairly, as 'a most cruel factor'.[29] The centrepiece of Urquhart's efforts was his proposed but unrealised plan to rebuild Cromarty castle. He did, however, make considerable progress in landscaping its policies and planted some 300 acres with 1,800,000 conifers and 60,000–70,000 hardwoods.[30]

In attempting to improve agriculture Urquhart proceeded in two ways: by taking land into his own control and by exercising greater control over his tenants. Improvements came virtually to a stop with Urquhart's death in 1756. Thus Aitken's survey of 1764 and the extant estate rental of the previous year may be taken to represent the estate at this slightly earlier date. These, together with earlier estate papers, show a number of improvements on Urquhart's own farms.[31] There had been enclosure and new building at the Mains farm which was 'well inclosed with stone dykes and hedges' with six enclosures, all with 'good, brown loamie soil'. It addition to stone dykes and hedges there was a considerable amount of wooden paling. The 'office houses of barns, kiln, stables, byre and servants houses' were in good repair, and there is evidence that some farm buildings were slated. Two new mills were built on the estate and the girnal at the Ness, vital for the storage and export of grain, was repaired and raised to two storeys. Bere and oats remained the principal crops but new varieties were being tried and grass and red clover seed were imported from England. The 'proof book' for the Mains in 1750–1 shows that some 12.5 per cent of the crop was from ground which had been fallowed and at least some lime was being used.[32] A *roup* (sale) of the contents of Cromarty castle in 1755 included equipment used in clearing fields of stones and horse-drawn ploughs – both a Yorkshire plough and a Welsh plough. There was also a 'corn fanner' for winnowing, brought from Banff in 1750.[33]

Urquhart had taken new ground into cultivation: 195 acres of moor ground at Glenurquhart was enclosed in seven parks by 1750 – thirty acres of this were planted with trees by 1752, a few acres were under crops, and the rest was used as grazing, allowing the estate to keep twenty oxen.[34] New ground was also taken in at Ardevel farm and on Cromarty Hill, where it was enclosed with fail dykes, stone dykes and paling – although some of this subsequently reverted to moor.[35]

Urquhart had, in these respects, done much that was to be expected of an improving landowner. However, his success was limited. Accounts for Cromarty Mains survive for only one year and, on the assumption that the same amounts of seed were sown in succeeding years, the yield

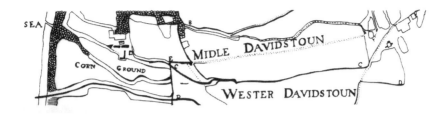

FIGURE 4.6
Part of the unimproved davoch of Davidston, redrawn from an estate plan
of 1748.

achieved was 5.2 times for bere and 5.5 times for oats.[36] This fell below
the minimum Sinclair expected from a well-conducted farm later in
the century and below the contemporary English return of 6.5–8.5
times.[37]

Tenant structure and leases

Of more lasting significance were Urquhart's policies of estate
management. On each of the 'four wester davochs' new *tacks* (leases)
issued in 1743 and 1749 reduced the number of tenants. These tacks
give some evidence of earlier joint tenancy or, at least, of communal
farming practices which were being superseded by the new leases.[38]
Further tacks of three, five and ten years were set in 1754.

Urquhart also made some use of improving leases and, from 1743,
written tacks included clauses intended to preserve the fertility of the
land. Thus no more oats or rye were to be sown in the last year of the
lease than in previous years; tenants were to protect woods; and, to
encourage planting, they were to have one third of the property of any
woods they planted during their tenancy. From 1749 tacks included
further improving clauses – ley ground under three years old was not to
be worked, and the incoming tenants were to pay for lands in grass and
ploughed land in fallow.

Devine has suggested that, in general, the reduction in the number
of tenants in the first half of the eighteenth century was piecemeal
and was not achieved by draconian means.[39] The changes in tenant
structure on the Cromarty estate in the 1740s were, as we shall see in
chapter 7, concomitant with a breakdown in relationships between the
laird and the community over patronage and religious affiliation and
were, at least in retrospect, perceived as oppressive.[40] The changes had,
furthermore, little immediate benefit. The reduction in the number of
tenants was intended to enable the creation of larger, single tenancies
– more attractive to enterprising tenants willing to enter into long,
improving leases. While some tenants took up longer leases, poorer

seasons in the mid 1750s led all of them to give up their long tacks and by 1763 it was said 'there had been no tacks worth mentioning for many years past'.⁴¹

Authority and co-operation in estate management
The implementation of Urquhart's plans required the clarification of a number of issues on which he sought legal opinion. These included the ownership of moors and commonties, thirlage of tenants to the estate mills, rights to seaware, fishings and ferry crossing, control of the harbour and the right of patronage of the parish church.⁴² Urquhart was determined to exercise his legal rights to the full and take a more aggressive approach to management, with greater reliance on law and less on custom. He began, for example, to charge interest on arrears of rent, leading his tenant Kenneth MacCulloch to point out that 'however Lawfull it may be to take % rent for Tennant arrears, it was never the practice here'.⁴³ Similarly, on completion of the enclosure at the back of the Gallowhill a proclamation was read prohibiting people going within this area to which they had had customary access.⁴⁴

Nevertheless, the principal tenants on the estate were involved, at least initially, in Urquhart's schemes. By 1746 surveys of much of the estate were complete and this was followed, around 1748, by a new division, with clearer marches and consolidated holdings. Kenneth MacCulloch, the tenant of Allerton, later claimed that he had been 'a great part of 18 months upon a new Division of all the possessions of the Estate, and gave in the rentals and marches of each' and was 'twice upon the Compriseing of all the Biggings on the Estate and gave in copies of the same'.⁴⁵ MacCulloch was not paid for this work but undertook it as a 'birlayman'.

The birlaymen were a group of respected men in a community who were trusted in arbitration and decision making in relation to boundaries, division of farms among tenants, trespass by animals, use of commonties and maintenance of dykes, etc. The birlaymen were also used as valuers of farm buildings, crops and plantings when tenancies changed hands. They might meet formally as a birlay court but it was common for them to be subsumed within the baron court. T. C. Smout has pointed out that the decline of the baron court as an institution was connected with a change in perception by landowners of their status within and relationship to the community. The baron court had evolved as a means of doing justice in the face of the community, with tenants gathered under the laird who saw himself primarily as the head of that community. With growing class-consciousness during the seventeenth century, lairds began to see themselves more in relation to other members of the land-owning class and, while still wishing to exercise authority, were less concerned to maintain this authority through consensus.⁴⁶

Urquhart's use of the birlaymen was an attempt to continue the consensual methods of the past. This was not uncommon in the north. The baron court, despite having fewer legal powers after 1747, continued to function and was still regarded, along with the birlaymen, as an integral part of estate management in the early nineteenth century in Perthshire and Inverness-shire.[47] It was also in use in Moray where improvement had been successfully introduced.[48] However, Urquhart's attempt at consensual estate management broke down in the late 1740s in a series of disputes with the community over church accommodation, patronage, the appointment of a schoolmaster, and land mortified for the poor and for the school. There were two sides to this. Urquhart antagonised many in the community by his determination to exercise his authority as laird but he also faced anti-catholic prejudice, which intensified after the Jacobite rising of 1745 – despite Urquhart's neutrality. The willingness of the congregation to oppose him was increased by a widespread evangelical revival, originating in Easter Ross in 1739.

As Urquhart's standing in the community waned, so did the authority of his court[49] and he came to rely more on his factor. The role of factors in the north was, however, becoming more difficult because principal tenants and tacksmen played a smaller role and more fell to be dealt with by the estate manager. The laird could no longer call on a body of tenants to assist him – and the estate, either through the factor or other employees, had taken on the role of dealing directly with all tenants, large and small. Urquhart's factor, John Gorry, was a busy man in charge of a number of estates, and when Urquhart moved from Cromarty to Craigston in 1749 much of the day-to-day management of Cromarty was consequently placed in the hands of two estate employees, John Urquhart and James Glen. This was far from the professional system of estate management that was to bring about improvement in the south.

Improvements on the Gordon estates

The principal Gordon property – Invergordon, on the north side of the Cromarty Firth – passed to Sir John Gordon in 1742. Newhall and Ardoch, both in the parish of Resolis, came to a second son, Charles, and to Sir John's cousin, Alexander. All three owners were enthusiastic improvers. The same factor, Gorry, was employed on Invergordon and Newhall. Invergordon, the first to be improved, might well have been the model for the other Gordon estates. The estate map of 1759 shows a 'neat grid of enclosed fields and intersecting avenues around Invergordon Castle, with a large plantation of trees'.[50] The 1756–7 accounts for the Mains farm, managed by Gorry, show that the emphasis was on cultivation of oats, hay and bere, in that order. Clover and potatoes were also grown. The enclosed fields were grass parks and the farm was buying and fattening cattle for sale.[51] There were similar enclosures at Newhall by 1755 and at Ardoch by 1757, the latter largely under grass in 1778. Bishop Pococke noted in 1760 that the owner of Newhall was 'improving his fine situation in a very good taste by planting' and by 1795 both Newhall and Ardoch were described as having 'very fine old timber'.[52] As was common, agricultural improvement was combined with other embellishments. The factor on Cromartie estate was asked to send two men from Coigach to work with a 'cassychrom' to take up whins on ground which Gordon wished to plant 'in the wilderness way'[53] – that is, with a shrubbery.

On the Newhall estate all customary services and payments had been converted to cash payments by 1755, with the exception of four tenants at the ferry who were liable for 'sea service'. Most of the farms were, however, under multiple tenancies. On Ardoch there was an emphasis on payment of rent in bere, with the fourteen tenants paying a total of 161 bolls of bere and only ten-and-a-half bolls of oats. Farms were held under multiple tenancies with some shares held on joint tacks.[54]

Gordon lairds also encountered local opposition. Between 1727 and 1733 Sir William Gordon extended his holdings on the Black Isle, planted and improved barren ground at Glenurquhart and attempted to enclose the peat moss at Blackstand. This attempt at enclosure was met by armed resistance from an estimated 500 Cromarty people.[55]

The loss of enterprising tenants

Neither the Cromarty estate, nor the Gordon estates of Newhall and Ardoch, succeeded in creating substantial farms for single tenants willing to pay cash rents and enter into improving leases. There were, therefore, few opportunities for enterprising tenants or for the area's merchants who might have engaged in agriculture as a commercial venture. The two tenants on the Cromarty estate who, in the 1730s, were willing to pay a rent wholly converted to cash were both MacCullochs and the fate of their extended family is illustrative of the wider pattern of the loss of enterprising tenants. By the 1760s they had ceased to play a role in the local economy. The former chamberlain, William MacCulloch, left Cromarty in 1744, the improving tenant Kenneth MacCulloch became bankrupt in the 1750s and the next generation of the extended family entered trade and the professions. One was a schoolmaster, another a minister and a third, possibly William's son, after failing as a wright in Cromarty, moved to London where he invented improved sea-compasses which were adopted by the navy.[56] These were the people who, in different circumstances, might have led the transformation of local agriculture.

Some local traditions, which survived in the 1820s, cast light on how the community viewed progressive farmers such as the MacCullochs. Hugh Miller recorded tales that portrayed the factor as a lawyer who introduced the law where disputes had previously been settled within the community; and the tale of MacCulloch the corn agent, set in the 1740s, told of a famished ghost haunting the deserted kirkyard of St Bennet's at Navity. This MacCulloch had had a reputation for buying up corn in good years and selling dear in times of shortage, presumably during the dearth of 1740–1. This orientation to the market economy, an integral part of agricultural improvement, marked him out in a community that had been used to a more co-operative approach in times of shortage.

'Provost' Bain

When George Ross acquired the estate of Cromarty in 1767, Alexander Bain, whose forebears had been tenants in Newton for generations, reached the age of fifty. He would become one of Ross's most trusted tenants. Bain saw himself, and men and women like him, as living symbols of the stability of rural life – perhaps even part of the 'ancient tenandrie' of which Sir Thomas Urquhart had boasted, who regarded a move from their native farmtoun as equivalent to exile to Barbados or Madagascar. Bain's parents were both from the farmtoun of Newton and had survived childhoods in the 'ill years' of the 1690s to marry in 1714. Alexander was their first child, born in January 1717.

He succeeded his father as tenant some thirty years later, by which time he was better known as 'Provost' Bain – not a civic title but a byname acquired after he travelled to Inverness with two other Cromarty men on 16 April, 1746, the day of the battle of Culloden, and the three bluffed their way into accommodation in the overcrowded town by posing as provost, bailie and doctor. Their fellow townsfolk had watched the smoke of battle from the top of Cromarty Hill.

Bain's life, like most of his neighbours, centred on the farmtoun and the wider world of the parish. Like his own parents, he married within the farmtoun, possibly on his succession to the tenancy. However, personal tragedy came during a traditional celebration at the heart of the farming year. When the last sheaf of grain was sheared it was made in to a 'straw dog' and hoisted up onto one of the farm buildings, before the 'harvest home'. There was eating and drinking, and dancing inside the large corn-drying kiln, where the 'Provost' was joined by his heavily pregnant wife. As they danced a group of lads from the neighbouring farms, hidden above on the drying floor, dropped the straw dog down among the dancers. The shock brought on premature labour, the child was stillborn and Bain's wife died a few days later. The ringleader among the boys, Thomas Keran, ran away to sea and did not return for several years.

By 1767 'Provost' Bain had married again and was the father of three sons and a daughter. His wife was none other than Thomas Keran's sister, Grace or Grizel. Thomas had come home, been forgiven, and went on to a career as a clerk in Cromarty's hemp factory. The 'Provost' would be remembered by his new family as a stoutly built, kind man, with a sense of humour. He was also a man of independent mind. He joined the Evangelical party within the church in opposing the laird's choice of minister in the 1740s – not an easy stance for a tenant of the laird to take – but he also resisted the kirk's growing puritanism, on occasion leaving home with his pockets stuffed with oatcakes for three-day binges on whisky from his own still. He distilled his whisky in Morial's Den, the gully running from Newton to the shore, up which they brought seaware as manure. The 'Provost' had a song about it.

> Ho, my Morial's Den
> And Hey my Morial's Den
> We'll drink another firlot yet –
> And Grizel winna ken.

When he died in 1797, at the age of eighty, having outlived George Ross, he used the inscription on his gravestone to make a last ironic comment, proclaiming that he had 'in the course of fifty years paid rent to five lairds of the estate of Cromarty'. Yet, despite his sense of the permanence of farmers, it was tenants like Bain who would, during the nineteenth century, be replaced by a new breed of commercial farmers.[57]

Notes

1. Robert A. Dodgshon, 'Budgeting for Survival: Nutrient Flow and Traditional Highland Farming' in S. Foster and T. C. Smout (eds), *The History of Soils and Field Systems* (Aberdeen, 1994); and *From Chiefs to Landlords* (Edinburgh, 1998), 203.
2. Thomas M. Devine, *The Transformation of Rural Scotland* (Edinburgh, 1994), 60–75.
3. Aitken surveys: Cromarty (Cromarty House archive); Tulloch (NAS, RHP 1473), Findon (NAS, RHP 3513), Newmore (NAS, RH15/44/70, no map); Novar (NAS, RHP10671); Allan (NAS, GD71/217, no map); Drynie & Kilmuir (Highland Council Archive, Inverness); Brims (NAS, RHP 1219); Pulrossie, Skelbo (NLS, Dep 313/3587); Tarradale (Highland Council Archive,

Inverness). Kirk's surveys of Kintradwell and Navidale (NLS, Dep 313/3582) and Loth (NLS, Dep 313/3583); John Hume's surveys of Golspie (NLS, Dep 313/3581) and Invergordon (in two sections: Highland Council Ross & Cromarty Area Museums Service and NAS, RH15/44/182).

4. John Sinclair, *A general view of the northern counties and islands of Scotland* (London, 1795), 19–20. This rotation comprised oats – barley on dunged ground – pease and potatoes – oats – oats – ley – ley. Ley should be distinguished from fallow. Ley grass was what grew naturally when land was left untended; land in fallow was ploughed and, usually, sown with grass seed. According to Sinclair the major part of the north Highlands practised a poorer ten-year rotation of oats – oats – oats – barley with dung – oats and a little rye or pease – oats – oats and a dunged patch of potatoes – ley – ley – ley. There is, again, no reference to infield and outfield. For the land on Cromarty Hill, see NAS GD305/1/160 no. 30.

5. William Leslie, *A General View of the Agriculture of the Counties of Moray and Nairn* (London, 1813).

6. John Henderson, *A General View of the Agriculture of the County of Sutherland* and *A General View of the Agriculture of the County of Caithness* (London, 1815); James Robertson, *A General View of the Agriculture in the County of Inverness* (London, 1808).

7. See Robert Dodgshon, *From Chiefs to Landlords*, 206 for the importance of woodland grazing in some west highland agrarian economies. Henderson noted in *General View … Sutherland* that the loss of woodland grazing in Sutherland in the first decade of the nineteenth century had led to the death of many cattle.

8. NRAS 0204/Bundle 86, Cows wintered by tenants and feuars.

9. NRAS 0204/Bundle 185, Grieve's Notebook; Bundle 86, Lease of Easter Farness; Bundle 156, Proposal for letting new ground at Leycattoch 1754. NAS, SC34/29, Balnagowan rentals (reference to the 'limemen'). Bishop Forbes confirms that it was used for manure, noting this lime deposit in the 1760s. Robert Forbes, *Journal of the Episcopal Visitation of the Right Rev. Robert Forbes M.A. of the diocese of Ross … and a memoir of Bishop R. Forbes* (London, 1886).

10. Highland Council Archive, Mackenzie of Scatwell v Magistrates of Fortrose, printed papers in the Fraser Macintosh Collection; Dodgshon, 'Budgeting for Survival', 89.

11. The 'ground where Marcus wrought' is mentioned in NRAS 0204/Bundle 156, Proposal for letting new ground at Leycattoch 1754; and its location is confirmed in Hugh Miller, *My Schools And Schoolmasters* (Edinburgh, 1994), 124.

12. NRAS 0204/John Urquhart's Account Book.

13. John Sinclair, *General view … northern counties*, 81 and *The Statistical Account of Scotland* (1791–99).

14. William Macgill, *Old Ross-shire and Scotland* (Inverness, 1909) no. 432; NAS, GD305/162/36, Fiars in Ross.

15. William Macgill, *Old Ross-shire*, no. 472.

16. A. J. Gibson and T. C. Smout, 'Regional prices and market regions: the evolution of the early Scottish grain market' in *Economic History Review*, XLVIII, 2 (1995), 278.

17. A. J. Gibson and T. C. Smout, 'Scottish food and Scottish history 1500–1800' in R. A. Houston and I. Whyte (eds), *Scottish Society, 1500–1800* (Cambridge, 1989), 64–8.

18. NAS, E72/11/1–19, Customs quarterly accounts.

19. Thomas M. Devine, *The Transformation of Rural Scotland* (Edinburgh, 1994), 68.

20. Eric Richards and Monica Clough, *Cromartie: Highland Life: 1650–1914* (Aberdeen, 1991), 41.

21. See, for example, the tack of Little Farness in 1743 (NRAS 0204/Bundle 86). The payment of girnal dues was, however, in kind rather than in cash. Hugh Miller collected these folktales in the 1820s and published them in *Scenes and Legends of the North of Scotland* in 1835. He later published an enlarged edition – Hugh Miller, *Scenes and Legends of the North of Scotland* (most recent imprint Edinburgh, 1994).

22. NAS, GD199/296 and 300.

23. Balnagowan Rentals (NAS, SC34/29) and Pitcalnie tenant books (NAS, GD199/296 and 300).

24. Clough and Richards, *Cromartie*, 43; R. Maxwell, *Select Transactions of the Honourable Society of Improvers in the Knowledge of Agriculture in Scotland* (Edinburgh, 1743).

25. The office was otherwise unknown in Scotland and its existence emerged only in evidence produced in claims for compensation following the abolition of hereditary jurisdictions in 1747. Gordon held courts in the west, while the Mackenzies did so in the east. See William Mackay Mackenzie, 'The old sheriffdom of Cromarty' in *Transactions of the Gaelic Society of Inverness*, xxx. 289–235.

26. NRAS 0204/Bundles 86 & 157. William MacCulloch took a fifteen-year tack of two oxgaits of Davidston and Kenneth MacCulloch a fifteen-year tack of two oxgaits of Meikle Farness and the five mills of Farness. NRAS 0204/Bundle 186, Fifteen year tack of five mills to Kenneth MacCulloch, 1729. NAS, GD305/163/108. The only earlier partial conversion to a cash rent was on a farm also held by a chamberlain, in the late seventeenth century – Little Farness where 12.5 per cent of the victual rent was converted to money at five merks to the boll. Harry Gordon Slade, 'The biging on Allertown: a reconstruction of an 18th century farmhouse and steading in Cromarty' in *Proceeding of the Society of Antiquaries of Scotland (1986)*, cxvi. 455–72; NRAS 0204/Bundle 186, Letter of 27 June 1738, George Urquhart to Captain John Urquhart.

27. NRAS 0204/Bundle 152.

28. NAS, RH15/44/207.

29. *Invergordon Times*, 21 Mar 1866.

30. NRAS 0204/Bundle 182.

31. NAS, GD159/32, Observations on the rental of the estate of Cromarty; NRAS 0204/Bundle 39; NRAS 0204/ John Urquhart's Account Book, 1750.

32. NRAS 0204/Bundle 182. 100 bolls were purchased in 1753, but a considerable amount of this may have been for building work on the castle and storehouse. However, in 1755 it was noted that James Glen, who then farmed the Mains, was 'inclined to put lime on'.

33. NRAS 0204/Bundle 168.

34. NRAS 0204/Bundle 36.

35. Highland Council Archive, Minutes of Freeholders of County of Cromarty, 1765, 35.

36. NAS, RH15/44/191.

37. B. A. Holderness, *Pre-Industrial Britain: Economy and Society 1500–1700* (London, 1976), 143.

38. The five-year tack of Little Farness to John Keran, Alexander McKercher and William Junor provided for the division of the farm among themselves in proportion of three quarters to Keran and McKercher and one quarter to Junor, suggesting some communal interest between Keran and McKercher. In the same year Peddieston was set to five tenants for the lifetime of one of them, Thomas Hood, perhaps indicating that he was in some way a leader of this farming community. Even leases with improving clauses might be for joint tenancies, as, for example, Wester Navity to Alexander Barkly and John McComie for five years. NRAS 0204/Bundle 86.

39. Thomas M. Devine, *The Transformation of Rural Scotland* (Edinburgh, 1994), 28.

40. The traditional local view of Urquhart was recorded by Hugh Miller, *Scenes and Legends of the North of Scotland* (Edinburgh, 1994), 330–7.

41. NRAS 0204/Bundle 182.

42. NRAS 0204/Bundle 159, Memorial and queries: Meldrum to Lord Pitfour.

43. Slade, 'The biging on Allertown', 471.

44. NRAS 0204/Bundle 36, Accounts for enclosing of Gallowhill 1756.

45. Harry Gordon Slade, 'The biging on Allertown: a reconstruction of an 18th century farmhouse and steading in Cromarty' in *Proceeding of the Society of Antiquaries of Scotland* (1986), cxvi. 455–72.

46. T. C. Smout, 'Peasant and Lord in Scotland: Institutions Controlling Scottish Rural Society, 1500–1800' in R. A. Houston and I. Whyte (eds), *Scottish Society, 1500–1800* (Cambridge, 1989).

47. James Robertson, *General View ... Inverness*, 49.

48. James Donaldson, *A General View of the Agriculture of the County of Elgin or Moray* (London, 1794), 15 and William Leslie, *A General View of the Agriculture of the Counties of Moray and Nairn* (London, 1813).

49. The decreets of the baron court might prove ineffective, as in 1750 when Gorry was attempting to recover a debt of £7 from the former estate gardener and found him unconcerned at the prospect of action in the baron court. See NRAS 0204/Bundle 181.

50. Original map held in the Highland Council Archive and date deduced from NAS, RH15/44/182. Marinell Ash, *This Noble Harbour* (Invergordon and Edinburgh, 1991), 187.

51. NAS, RH15/44/175, Invergordon Mains Accounts 1756 and 1757.

52. NAS, SC24/16/3, rental of the Newhall estate, 1755; Highland Council Archive, copy of Roy's Military Survey 1747–56; NAS, RH15/44/240a, Notes on thirlage to Newhall Miln and Newmiln; Richard Pococke, *Tours in Scotland 1747, 1750, 1760* (Scottish History Society, Edinburgh, 1887). Pococke's visit to the Black Isle was in 1760. John Sinclair, *General view ... northern counties*, 41.

53. Monica Clough, *Two Houses* (Aberdeen, 1990), 96.

54. NAS, RH15/44/199, Newhall Rent Rolls 1762, 1776, 1778; SC24/16/3, Newhall Rent Rolls 1755, 1782; NAS, RH15/44/207, Rental of Ardoch, 1764.
55. William Macgill, *Old Ross-shire and Scotland* (Inverness, 1909), no. 786.
56. *Fasti Ecclesiae Scoticanae*; NAS, CH2/66/4, Minutes of Presbytery of Chanonry, various entries in 1736 and 1737; Miller, *Scenes and Legends*, 374 & 404.
57. Cromarty Courthouse Museum, Bain ms.

5

Fishing in Cromarty and the Inner Moray Firth before 1760

I have heard of a hundred crowns given for a fresh salmon, where the (Scots) pint of wine did cost but three half pence; and of a salmon every whit as good got for six pence, where so much wine of no better kind stood you in half-a-crown, which is the proportion of twenty thousand to one. For who at Toledo, with the hundred crowns got for a salmon, supposed fresh, which at Aberdeen he bought for sixpence, did purchase four thousand pints of wine which at his return to Aberdeen yielded him two thousand crowns, hath clearly obtained twenty thousand six pences for one; or who at Aberdeen, with the two crowns got for four pints of wine which at Toledo he bought for six pence, did purchase twenty fresh salmons which at his return to Toledo yielded him two thousand crowns, hath in the same manner for one six pence obtained twenty thousand, which is a hundred to one two hundred times told.

Sir Thomas Urquhart of Cromarty, *Logopandecteision*, 1653

Early fisheries

Dutch fishing busses – the predecessors of 'factory ships' – which processed fish from smaller fishing boats, dominated commercial herring fishing in the North Sea from the sixteenth century, and Dutch fisheries in the northern isles (Orkney and Shetland) expanded until the mid seventeenth century, when the cooling of Arctic waters led to decline. Trade in the salt fish they processed was largely in the hands of Dutch merchants until their dominance of maritime trade decreased with the Anglo-Dutch Wars of 1664–7 and 1672–9. Scottish investors were anxious to exploit the opportunities created by the waning of Dutch influence and exports of fish from Scotland, which had been in decline in the 1660s, were recovering by the 1670s. Lord Tarbat, later first earl of Cromartie, was aware of the potential of the northern fisheries and in 1697 proposed that funds from the Scots Africa Company be invested in two fishing busses, each of which

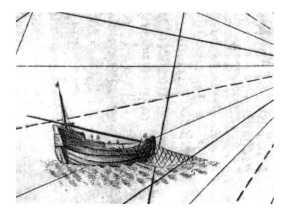

FIGURE 5.1
Herring fishing, eighteenth century.

would hold 360 barrels and would make two loadings in a season, with an estimated £6,000 profit after four years. Tarbat's scheme was not realised but there was some expansion of fishing in the north and Hugh Miller, writing in 1829, recorded the tradition that Cromarty enjoyed a flourishing trade in salt herring from some time before 1690.[1]

Scottish exports had, however, been disrupted by a French ban on imports of salt fish imposed in 1689 and, more generally, by commercial conflicts with England after 1688, which included the periodic seizure of Scottish vessels. The English market itself was not open to Scottish fish and English customs accounts show no imports of salt fish from Scotland in the three years preceding 1707.[2] When it came, the Union of the Parliaments of 1707 presented Scottish commercial interests with both threats and opportunities. Both Tarbat and his second son, Kenneth Mackenzie of Cromarty, voted for the incorporating union with England, in part motivated by the potential market in England for the grain produced on their estates. In the event, there were few grain exports to England and what emerged as a more important economic advantage was security for shipping and the use of large English vessels for shipments overseas of both grain and salt fish.

After the Union there was early lobbying from the Convention of Royal Burghs for promotion of the trade in salt fish to the Mediterranean, despite the dangers posed by the continuing War of the Spanish Succession (1701–13), which made France and Spain enemy powers. It has been commonly held that Scottish merchants were slow to respond to this opportunity and that trade with southern Europe experienced no significant development for several decades. However, the evidence of salt and fish debentures issued by the Scottish customs show that, contrary to this view, there was a significant development of

Scottish trade in salt fish in the second decade of the eighteenth century. This development was initially centred on the Inverness customs precinct, with Cromarty as the principal fish-exporting port within the precinct.

This rapid expansion in catching, processing and exporting fish had a number of causes. The movements of herring shoals were important in bringing large numbers of fish within the range of small fishing boats but the development also relied on a combination of local circumstances – a settlement pattern that maintained many estate 'fish boats' and provided an adequate supply of labour for catching and processing; an established network of trading links with Edinburgh, London and overseas; an emerging class of local merchants capable of organising the trade; and the absence of a large alternative local market for fish.

Fish and salt debentures

After 1708 a bounty was paid on exports of fish that had been cured with foreign salt, on which duty had been paid. It was claimed by means of a document, the debenture, issued by the collector of customs for the precinct. Occasionally the bounty was then paid by the collector, from cash paid on the import on salt, but more commonly it was redeemed in Edinburgh by presenting it to the Commissioners of Customs. Debentures were often endorsed by the merchant receiving them and sold on at a discount. Until 1714–15 the annual customs accounts for Scotland record the redemption of fish debentures by the name of the merchant to whom they were issued and it is only by examining the individual debentures that the customs precinct can be identified. From 1714–15 totals for each precinct were recorded but individual debentures are still the only sources of information about the kind of fish exported. From 1734–5 bounty was paid directly from salt duty and, thereafter, the annual customs accounts give no information on fish debentures. Because information from the fish debentures is not otherwise available in print there are a number of tables of data at the end of the book.

Debentures detail the quantity of fish exported – salmon in forty-two-gallon barrels, herring in thirty-two-gallon barrels and cod graded into those over eighteen inches in length and those over twenty-four inches. Barrels were sealed and branded, while cod had part of the tail cut off as they were counted. In the Inverness precinct cod were reckoned in 'long hundreds', that is, a unit of 120. The adoption of this system, which was in general disappearing by the end of the seventeenth century, suggests that the trade in salt cod was long established. There were also occasional exports of red herring, a heavily cured fish which could survive tropical temperatures. Some herring is described as 'royally cured' and at least some barrels were branded with a crown. This may indicate that the customs officers, by inspecting the cure, were providing some guarantee of quality – as was to be the case a century later with the 'crown brand' introduced in 1808. Barrels were further marked with the initials of the merchant shipping the fish. The debenture also recorded the ship, its master, port of origin and its destination.

Imported salt was cellared under the supervision of the customs officers and duty was paid only when it was removed for use. For example, in 1710 Lord Strathnaver held fifty bolls of salt in Cromarty, valued at £3 Scots per boll and with excise due at £2 Scots per boll. Since one boll was reckoned sufficient to pickle six barrels of salmon for one year and the bounty on a barrel of salmon was £10 Scots there was every reason to claim the bounty despite the need for additional payments for inspection. The system was however open to abuse by corrupt officials and in 1709 the Inverness collector was accused of falsely issuing a debenture for £196 sterling to his brother. It is also likely, given the prevalence of smuggling, that considerable amounts of salt were imported without payment of excise duty. From c.1712 there were attempts to control these abuses and the fish debentures are likely to provide a more accurate record of exports from this date.

The evidence of the debentures

For the period between the Union of Parliaments and July 1709, that is over two fishing seasons, exports were summarised by the Treasury for each Scottish customs precinct.[3] These figures show that Inverness (whose precinct included the ports of Cromarty, Fortrose, Banff and Findhorn) paid bounties on the export of 1,958 barrels of herring, 936 barrels of salmon and over 10,500 dried cod. These were relatively small amounts and the bulk of herring exports were from Kirkcaldy, Port Glasgow and Eyemouth, with most salmon shipped from Aberdeen.

From 1709–10 more detailed information on bounties is available from the customs accounts and the individual fish debentures. Figure 5.2 shows the value of debentures from Scottish exports from 1708 to 1735, from which point bounties on exported fish were no longer recorded as a separate item in the accounts. One limitation of this data is that it does not include the export of fish cured with Scottish salt. Such exports are, however, likely to have been limited because of the inherent unsuitability of the Scottish product. It is certainly clear that any attempts to market fish to the Iberian peninsula and the Mediterranean would have required higher quality imported 'Bay salt' – from the Bay of Biscay. With these provisos, it is clear that exports were highest between 1713–14 and 1719–20,[4] and the chart shows that a significant proportion of this trade was from the Inverness precinct.

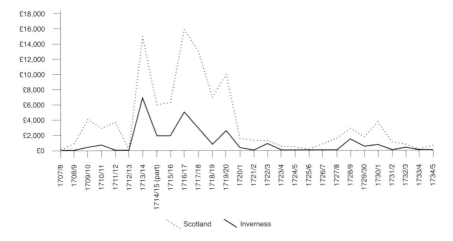

FIGURE 5.2   Fish debentures (£ sterling) issued in Scotland and the Inverness customs precinct.

Although Inverness retained its relative importance in exports over the next fifteen years, total Scottish trade in salt fish declined considerably and even in the good fishing season of 1730 exports were less than 25 per cent of their level in 1716–17. Inverness's only rival in the 'boom years' was Anstruther and the comparative performance of these ports during this period is also shown in Figure 5.3.

Further evidence of the Inverness precinct's early pre-eminence can be gained from records of salt imports. There was a marked increase in Scottish salt imports in 1712–13, in advance of the increase in salt fish exports in the following season. The duty on all imports to Scotland

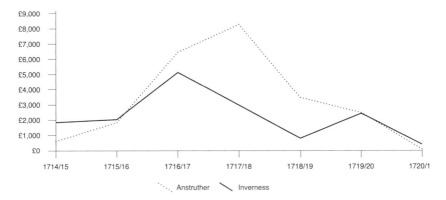

FIGURE 5.3   Fish debentures (£ sterling) issued by Inverness and Anstruther customs precinct.

was £3,584, of which £1,896 (55 per cent) was from the Inverness precinct. These figures exclude any salt which was imported without paying duty and since smuggling was rife, at least before the reform of the customs establishment in 1710, it is possible that trade in salt fish had expanded at an earlier date.

From 1712–13 to 1716–17 the fish debentures issued for the Inverness precinct identify the port from which the ship sailed and show that Cromarty was the principal exporting port within the precinct. The importance of Cromarty is also seen in the appointment in 1714 of an 'officer of salt', the only one in the precinct.[5]

The 'besom of judgement'

A century later Hugh Miller recorded the failure of fishing in Cromarty, although wrongly dating it to 'late in the reign of Queen Anne', and noted that 'for more than half a century from this time Cromarty derived scarcely any benefit from its herring fishery'. There were traditional accounts of why the shoals had left the firth – blood spilt on the water was one explanation. In another account gutters and packers, after a large catch on a Saturday, had worked through during the night and on into the Sunday evening. Since they had been unable to attend church the parish minister came to conduct a short service with them but they grew impatient. Some resumed their work, others threw fish guts at him. He ended his service abruptly with the prayer that the 'the besom (broom) of judgement would come and sweep every herring out of the firth'. Miller appreciated the story but recognised that the movement of shoals was a feature of 'the natural history of the herring'.[6]

The decline of trade in cured fish after 1720 is indicated by the fish debentures themselves and also by salt debentures, issued on salt returned to bond once it became uneconomic for merchants to hold large stocks in anticipation of catches. Salt debentures were first issued in 1719–20, to a value of £2,938, of which £2,685 related to the customs precinct of Inverness and £187 to Caithness. This represented the duty on over 200 tons of salt. During the next ten years £2,567 of debentures were issued, over 80 per cent of which were for the precinct of Anstruther. The more rapid decline of stocks in the Inverness precinct suggests that merchants were quick to withdraw from an involvement in local fishing and re-deploy their resources elsewhere. The run down of stocks in Anstruther was more gradual, despite the fact that in 1719–20 its exports of salt fish fell to a lower level than those of Inverness. A vital difference may have been the much larger local market for fresh fish from the Forth, which provided merchants with an alternative source of income and allowed them to hold stocks of salt in anticipation of future improvements.

Since the development of overseas trade in salt fish was of general interest to the Scottish mercantile community, why did the expansion of exports initially focus so strongly on the Inverness precinct – and thus on Cromarty? While one part of the answer must lie in the availability of fish stocks, it is also necessary to consider the availability of labour, both for fishing and processing, and the landowners and merchant class who were able to provide capital, co-ordinate processing and shipping, and deal with the complexities of the tax and bounty systems.

The fishing communities

A study of the fishing communities of the Black Isle and Easter Ross reveals two distinct settlements patterns, both well established by the late seventeenth century, which together created a readily available pool of labour for the development of commercial fisheries. The first settlements were early, possibly medieval, fishing communities, such as Cromarty and Avoch. Cromarty's origins have been described in chapter 1. The second form of settlement was the growth of a fishing community around an estate fish boat. The geography and history

FIGURE 5.4
A fishing boat in the Cromarty Firth, 1750s.

of the fertile coastal strip north of Inverness created a situation in which, from at least the late sixteenth century, much of the land was held in relatively small estates. Each of these had a coastline and was, by sea, within a reasonably short distance of Inverness and the port of Cromarty. Land transport, by contrast, involved circuitous routes around the heads of the firths and often dangerous river fords. It was desirable, then, for each estate to have its own boat – and it made economic sense for this to be a fish boat and for the fishers to be available as an additional source of labour within the estate. These factors led to the creation of the numerous estate fishing settlements, clustered within a small geographic area. A survey by James Skinner identifies thirteen fishing communities of this type on the Easter Ross coast, many clearly established by 1691 and others likely to have been in existence by the same date.[7]

These communities were characteristically established and maintained by the estate on which they were sited, usually being granted some arable land, which was often held in common by the fishers. The clearest examples of common land are the 'land possessed in runridge by the fishers of Pertenleich' on the Balnagowan estate and the 'Fisheris 8 acres of land which never payed a penny but given them to dwell upon for the furnishing of fishe to the place and the country upon the country's expense' identified in a rental of Fearn Abbey, 1561–6.[8]

Fishermen were regarded by some landowners as 'by the constant custom of the place tyed and obliged to the same servitude and service that coall hewers and salters are ... in the South' and in 1713 a group of lairds in Tarbat and Tain banded together in an attempt to prevent fishers moving from one master to another.[9] Fishers were also linked to their home estates by fulfilling other roles. Many provided seasonal labour to local farms and the fishers on the Balnagowan estate in the 1720s are referred to as 'limemen', producing shell lime from deposits in Nigg Bay.[10] However, their most important subsidiary role was as part of the system of transport. This is particularly clear in the Sutherland estate papers, where there are numerous references to fishers taking goods between Dunrobin and Cromarty. For example, in a letter of 19 July 1720 Lady Strathnaver asked George Urquhart in Cromarty 'to send bottles by ... Macandie one of our fishers'.[11]

Trade in salt fish: lairds and merchants

The development of fisheries in the early eighteenth century was also assisted by a pattern of established trading links. The earlier exploitation of salmon had necessitated importing high-quality salt from the Iberian Peninsula and barrel staves and hoops, usually from the Baltic. This three-way trade can be illustrated from seventeenth century records. In

1639 the *Falcon* of Leith sailed from Dingwall with a cargo of salmon and in 1613 four *lasts* (a unit of measurement of goods shipped by sea) of salmon passed through Aberdeen from Sutherland bound for Dieppe. In 1618 ten bolls of salt 'in salmond trees' were shipped from Aberdeen to Sutherland; and a cargo of salt and 'goids of iron' for barrel hoops were shipped from Aberdeen to Chanonry in 1667.[12] There was also trade in white fish and herring from a comparatively early date and a substantial trade in salt cod from the Inverness area was noted in 1769 by Thomas Pennant, who believed that it had been at its peak before the mid seventeenth century.[13]

Local lairds were actively involved in the promotion of fishing through their control of the fishing communities. Although fishers in a number of communities in the Black Isle and Easter Ross, but not in Cromarty, held small portions of land, they were clearly identified in rent rolls as fishers and not as cottars or tenants, suggesting that they were primarily dependent on fishing. The rental of boats and land differed in detail from place to place. In Cromarty, fishers held six boats from the Cromarty estate, paying both a cash rent of 7s 6d each – which was partly a conversion of an earlier payment of 'meal fish' and partly a payment of small teinds – and a payment of 'castle fish', which by 1750 had been converted to a cash payment. Most fishers held their properties in feu rather than as tenants, some holding a blench feu, that is with no feu duty. At Portleich in the 1750s the earl of Cromartie provided two fishing boats for a rent of £44 Scots each (£3 13s 4d). The fishers provided one shearer from each household to the Mains farm and assisted with haymaking and peat cutting. They were also obliged to transport goods in their boats to Dingwall and Inverness, the only payment being meal for their subsistence. They made no payment for the land they held. On the Ankerville estate in the 1770s the tenants of Shandwick and Rarichies each paid seven bolls of meal for a fish boat, the fishers themselves paid a cash rent of five shillings, and the estate was responsible for the upkeep and repair of the boats. At Portmahomack in the 1790s a new boat was provided every seven years by the laird in return for one fifth of the catch or other gains.[14]

With this degree of control, a number of lairds became actively involved in the promotion of fishing in the late seventeenth and early eighteenth centuries. In Sutherland a number of adjoining landowners formed a partnership in 1686 and in 1698 Sir William Binning of Bavelaw and Lord Tarbat agreed to set up a herring fishing station on Loch Broom. Tarbat promoted a further scheme in 1712 and, although it is not clear how this fared, it was at an end by 1721 when there was a roup of the fishing gear lying at Cromarty and Coigach.[15]

Lairds, however, came to rely more on the expertise of merchants, who might also be minor landowners, in the general management of the fishery. These merchant-landowners soon expanded their role by leasing fishing boats for one or more seasons from the larger landowners, rather than forming partnerships. Initially this seems to have been for a proportion of the catch. Thus, in March 1714 Lord Strathnaver gave a three-year tack to Munro of Newmore of his four boats at Balcoxtoun, near Golspie, with the provision that Newmore was to join his 'four boats of Balintraid' with Strathnaver's boats in the cod and herring fishing seasons. Strathnaver was to receive half the catch.[16] In Cromarty, Urquhart of Greenhill, second son of the minor landowner Urquhart of Newhall, played a similar role, but the terms of some of Urquhart's dealings with Strathnaver lacked clarity. In July 1719 Urquhart offered to hire Strathnaver's boats for the herring season 'paying as he pays others'. Subsequently it emerged that Strathnaver believed he had entered into an agreement to lease his six boats at £3 each, while Urquhart held that he was to pay, if the fishing was good, a hogshead of claret and '2od for each measured barrel of herring for the boat's part'.[17] The ambiguity in this contract is instructive since it suggests a transition from joint ventures, with shared risk, to commercial leases.

A similar transition is seen with the earls of Cromartie. The first earl's attempts to develop a fishery in Lochbroom have been noted above. The second earl had abandoned this venture by 1721 and turned to an agreement with an Inverness merchant, Thomas Robertson, by which he 'sett to the said Thomas Robertson ... his haill fishing boats for fishing of Cod, herring and other white fishes' these being boats on the west coast and at Milton, Tarbat Ness and Wilkhaven.[18] Robertson was one of the leading merchants in the salt fish trade and, in 1713–14 as trade expanded, he claimed bounty of £1,069 – over 15 per cent of the value of fish debentures issued in the precinct. His nearest rival was Munro of Newmore, who claimed just over 5 per cent.

The trade in salt fish also involved merchants from the south. In 1718 Munro of Newmore contracted with Patrick Stewart, merchant in Edinburgh, agreeing to send out his eight boats and whatever other boats he could hire in the Moray Firth to catch herring, which was to be 'delivered' on the shore at Cromarty. The details of this contract indicate the complexity of the operation and the vital role of local merchants. Munro undertook to supply storehouses for salt, vats and casks; to provide a plot of land for 'curing and manufacturing' the herring; to assist in providing 'gutters, packers, coopers and other servants ... and to cause then attend upon the said work'; and to provide a person to attend the fishing as an overseer. Stewart, who was to buy half the fish, was to pay half the premium for the extra boats; to arrange for ships to call at Cromarty by a fixed date; to pay Munro £5 15s for each last cured; and to deliver 50 lasts of new herring casks and 800 bushels of Spanish or Lisbon salt to Cromarty.[19] The increasing involvement of Edinburgh merchants was paralleled in the grain trade where

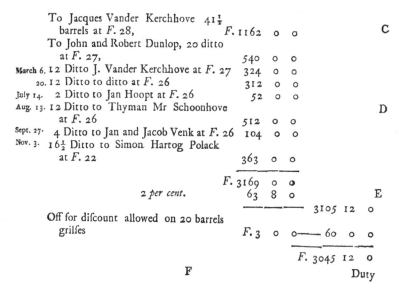

A C C O M P T fale of 120 *barrels of falmon received in December* 1750, B
by Alexander Rofs, for accompt and rifque of Meffrs Charles Brodie mer-
chant at Lethen, and Mr Gilbert Barclay merchant in Cromarty, and fold
as follows :

To Jacques Vander Kerchhove 41½ barrels at F. 28,	F. 1162	0	0	C
To John and Robert Dunlop, 20 ditto at F. 27,	540	0	0	
March 6. 12 Ditto J. Vander Kerchhove at F. 27	324	0	0	
20. 12 Ditto to ditto at F. 26	312	0	0	
July 14. 2 Ditto to Jan Hoopt at F. 26	52	0	0	
Aug. 13. 12 Ditto to Thyman Mr Schoonhove at F. 26	512	0	0	D
Sept. 27. 4 Ditto to Jan and Jacob Venk at F. 26	104	0	0	
Nov. 3. 16¼ Ditto to Simon Hartog Polack at F. 22	363	0	0	

F. 3169   0   0

2 *per cent.*   63   8   0   E

3105 12 0

Off for difcount allowed on 20 barrels grilfes   F. 3   0   0—— 60 0 0

F. 3045 12 0

F   Duty

FIGURE 5.5
Account for salt salmon shipped from Cromarty, 1759/60.

landowners moved from shipping on their own account to selling their grain to Edinburgh merchants, who took responsibility for shipping.

The marketing of salt fish led to the establishment of a wider network of contacts, with merchants in London and overseas, and created a volume of trade which justified the use of larger vessels, such as the *St George* of London which in early 1714 shipped 2,000 barrels of salt fish from Cromarty.[20] This in turn created opportunities for an increase in imports from the Mediterranean, the Iberian Peninsula and across the North Sea, enabling local merchants to supply the increasingly sophisticated tastes of the gentry.

The role of Cromarty merchants

Herring had to be processed quickly and the trade was therefore concentrated in key centres, such as Cromarty, which had coopers, supplies of salt and a pool of labour. Such centres also became

convenient points at which to gather supplies of salt cod for grading
and shipping. However, in 1713–14 Cromarty merchants themselves
held only a little more than 5 per cent of the trade in salt fish from the
Inverness precinct[21] and we should think of Cromarty as a processing
centre, whose facilities were being used by a large number of merchants
within the precinct and beyond. As such it benefited considerably from
the trade but was vulnerable in the event of a downturn.

Although the number of local merchants was small, they nevertheless
displayed a capacity for enterprise. Urquhart of Greenhill both shipped
salt fish and had his own fishing boats, and the fish debentures show
that at least nine other merchants designated as being 'of Cromarty'
were active – John Laing, Thomas Clunes, John Macleod, Andrew
Bain, Alexander Barkly, George Munro, Colin Mackenzie, William
Mackintosh, John McFerquher and John Robertson.

Population, labour supply and changes in the fishing community

The contract between Stewart and Newmore, referred to above, uses
the term 'manufacturing' to refer the processing of fish and this is
a useful reminder of the quasi-industrial nature of herring curing.
Herring had first to be caught but without bringing together other raw
materials (salt, barrel hoops and staves), organisation of labour (some
of it skilled), knowledge of markets and provision of shipping, there
was no final product in which to trade. The processing of cod involved
similar amounts of labour. Cod were caught during the spring great-line
fishing, from April until June, and the catch was salted and then dried
in the open, with women and children laying the fish out in dry weather
and collecting it together in wet. The curing took upwards of a month
to complete.[22]

The success of the herring fishery and the demand for the skilled
labour of fishers led to a weakening of the ties between fishers and lairds.
It is clear that in the early eighteenth century fishers were receiving cash
payments for fish caught and were therefore benefiting directly. The fact
that landowners felt it necessary to act in unison in 1713 to prevent
fishers moving 'from one master to another' suggests that, in practice,
there was at least some mobility, which they perceived as a threat.
There is also evidence of growing independence in Cromarty where, as
early as 1704, fishers were encouraged by a disaffected clergyman to
stop making customary payments, known as vicarage, to the laird.[23]

Malcolm Gray has noted that when fishing communities turned to
herring fishing, much of their traditional life had to change, a view
shared by Hugh Miller. Traditional white fishery necessitated the
involvement of women and children in a daily routine of baiting and

cleaning family lines, thus favouring early marriage and large families. This was unnecessary for herring fishing in which success was more a result of skill, knowledge and ingenuity, with the best crews catching twice as much as the poorer.[24] Later marriage was then an option, since a young fisherman could hope to succeed without a wife and family to assist him. Over the next 200 years, those communities which successfully retained their involvement in herring fishing had a very different history from those which came to rely principally on long-line fishing for white fish.

Notes

1. For Lord Tarbat's scheme see NAS, GD305\163 Vol. XVI nos 218, 219, and Monica Clough, 'Early Fishery and Forestry Developments on the Cromartie estate of Coigach: 1600–1746' in John Baldwin (ed.), *Peoples and Settlement in North-west Ross* (Edinburgh, 1994). For the traditions recorded by Hugh Miller see his series of articles in the *Inverness Courier* during 1829, republished as a pamphlet *Letters on the Herring Fishery* (Inverness, 1829) and subsequently in his posthumous *Tales and Sketches* (Edinburgh, 1863). There is support for this tradition in NRAS 0239, Catalogue of Dunrobin Muniments, 340–2.
2. NAS, RH4/157.
3. NAS, RH2/4.
4. The annual figures are distorted by a change in the accounting year between 1713–14 and 1714–15, such that the former annual total is inflated and the latter deflated. Nevertheless, it is clear that the period 1713–1720 was a high point for exports.
5. *Calendar of Treasury Books*, 17 Sept 1714.
6. Hugh Miller, *Scenes and Legends* (Edinburgh, 1994), 245.
7. Cromarty Courthouse Museum, survey by Dr James Skinner of fishing settlements in Easter Ross.
8. NAS, RHP 13229, Volume of Balnagowan Maps, 1808 and *Origines Parochiales, Parish of Fearn*.
9. T. C. Smout, *History of the Scottish People* (London, 1970), 169; NAS, GD199/6.
10. NAS, SC34/29.
11. For example NLS, Dep313/570.
12. Information on Leith Shore Dues from Sue Mowat (personal communication); Louise B. Taylor, *The Aberdeen Shore Work Accounts* (Aberdeen, 1972).
13. James Coull, *Sea Fisheries*, 84; Walter Macfarlane, *Geographical Collections* (Scottish History Society, 1906–8), ii. 449; Thomas Pennant, *A Tour in Scotland 1769* (London, 1790) i. 178–9.
14. For Cromarty see NRAS 0204/Bundle 160; for Portleich NAS, GD305/1/155 no. 25; for Ankerville (NAS, RH44/279); and for Portmahomack, *OSA*, Parish of Fearn.
15. NRAS, Survey 0239: Catalogue of Dunrobin Muniments, 340–2; Monica Clough, 'Early Fishery and Forestry Developments on the Cromartie estate of

Coigach: 1600–1746' in John Baldwin (ed.), *Peoples and Settlement in North-west Ross* (Edinburgh, 1994); NAS, GD305 163(XVI) nos 216 and 255.

16. NLS, Dep313.
17. NLS, Dep313/570.
18. NAS, GD305/1/155 no. 25.
19. William Macgill, *Old Ross-shire*, no. 463.
20. Information extracted from fish debentures in NAS, E508/7/6.
21. Information extracted from fish debentures in NAS, E508/7/6.
22. For cod fishery see Coull, *Sea Fisheries*, 29; for proposals for covered drying areas, NAS GD305 163(XVI) 216; for cod drying in Sutherland, NLS, Dep313.
23. NAS, GD199 no. 6; William Mackay Mackenzie, 'Cromarty: its old chapels and parish church' in *Scottish Ecclesiological Society*, 1905.
24. Malcolm Gray, *Fishing Industries of Scotland* (Aberdeen, 1978), 38; Hugh Miller, *Tales and Sketches* (Edinburgh, 1863), 194–6.

6

The Town and its Trade before 1760

This harbour, in all the Latin maps of Scotland, is called Portus
Salutis; by reason that ten thousand ships together may within it
ride in the greatest tempest that is as in a calm; by virtue of which
conveniency, some exceeding rich men, of five or six several nations,
masters of ships, and merchant adventurers, promised to bring their
best vessels and stocks for trading along with them, and dwell in that
my little town with me.

Sir Thomas Urquhart of Cromarty, *Logopandecteision*, 1653

The port of Cromarty

There was a marked contrast between the potential of the Cromarty Firth as a port and the reality of its meagre trade. In 1655 Thomas Tucker, surveying the ports of Scotland, described it as 'one of the delicatest harbours reputed in all Europe' but brought things down to earth by adding that 'nothing comes here more than a little salt to serve the countrey'. The situation was little better in 1706 when Daniel Defoe observed that the firth was 'the finest harbour, with the least business of, perhaps, any in Britain'.[1] During the eighteenth century there was a shift in the focus of Scottish trade – from east coast ports such as Cromarty, trading with the northern Europe and the Mediterranean, to increasingly dominant west coast ports, which benefited from the growing opportunities of transatlantic trade. The east coast was further disadvantaged because it suffered more than the west from the actions of French privateers and although a convoy system to protect ships operated from 1708, the weak link was the coast between Leith and Orkney, which was patrolled by only one cruiser.[2]

Nevertheless, there were successes. Exports of salt fish, described in chapter 5, were at their highest between 1710 and 1715, a period when there was both a general upsurge in Scottish trade with the Baltic and easier conditions in the Mediterranean, following the capture of Gibraltar (1705) and Minorca (1708). The grain trade, described in chapter 4, was also well established by the early eighteenth century, with grain rents stored for shipping in a series of girnals (grain stores) along the coast. These included stores at Portmahomack and Cromarty, both built by Lord Tarbat in the 1680s and 1690s, and a store on the Gordon estates, at Ferryton in Resolis. From 1692 the Cromartie estates took a more proactive role in marketing grain by freighting the cargo at its own expense and selling in Edinburgh, rather than selling to an Edinburgh merchant at an agreed price for delivery on the shore in the north. By accepting the risks of shipping and marketing in Edinburgh, a higher profit was achieved. This continued until 1709, when the presence of French privateers increased the risks and thereafter merchants from the south again played a more prominent role by accepting the risks and paying lower prices. A similar pattern is seen in the marketing of grain by Lord Strathnaver from the Sutherland estates.[3]

Imported luxuries

The principal opportunity to increase trade in the early eighteenth century was by the import of consumer goods. Many of these – such as wine and spirits, tea, spices, tobacco and soap – were at first luxuries but became increasingly part of normal household purchases. The growth of this trade was initially fuelled by greater expectations among the land-owning class, particularly so in Easter Ross and the Black Isle where there had been a marked increase in the number of minor land-owning families in the seventeenth century. Although many lairds moved in social circles in Edinburgh and London, and diverted substantial parts of their income to maintaining this lifestyle, they also kept large houses in the north and created a demand for luxury goods. The Cromarty Firth, with Cromarty as its principal port, was well placed to supply approximately twenty-five houses on medieval castle sites in Easter Ross and the Black Isle and to this was added, during the course of the eighteenth century, a similar number of new mansion houses.[4] Because there was only a shallow and narrow navigable channel in the Dornoch Firth, Cromarty was also the principal port for areas further to the north.

Initially the principal imports were wines and spirits, shipped from France, Spain and Portugal – often shipped along with salt as return cargoes for exported salt fish. The Scottish aristocracy, prior to the Union, had claimed the right to import wines and spirits for their own use without the payment of duty. The claim was, however, largely irrelevant since the right to collect customs duties had been sold in 1696 to local 'tax farmers' – usually the principal landowners – who subsequently controlled the customs. This system led to under-collecting of duty to the extent that in 1707 only £30,000 was received from Scotland as a

I N V O I C E of goods fhipped aboard the John and William, John Blyth mafter, for the Murray frith, on account and risk of Mr Gilbert Barkly merchant in Cromarty.

G. B.

2 Casks, No. 1. $120\frac{1}{2}$ tr. $20\frac{1}{2}$
     2. $121\frac{1}{2}$ $21\frac{1}{2}$
       ———
      242 lb. 42
      42
      ——
      200 lb. Annifeed at 19 *fl.*   F. 38 0

1 ditto   3. $124\frac{1}{2}$⎫ 106 lb. Gr. Ginger at *fl.* 42. F. 44 10
     tr. $18\frac{1}{2}$⎭
       Casks   3 6
             ———— F. 85 16

1 ditto   gr. 175⎫ 161 lb. brightMadder at *fl.* 22. F. 35 8
     tr. 14⎭
        Casks   0 12
            ——— 36 0

2 ditto at 50 lb. is 100 Gun Powder at *f.* 29 F. 29 0
         Cask, *&c.*   1 19
             ——— 30 19

135 Iron Pots, different fizes, wt. 4039 lb. at *fl.* $7\frac{3}{4}$ 313 1
            F. 465 16

Duty, pafsport and fhipping,   F. 9 13
Premium of *F.* 500 infured   11 14
            ——— 21 7
           F. 487 3

Commiffion $2\frac{1}{2}$ *per cent.*   12 3
           ———
          F. 499 6

FIGURE 6.1
Account for goods shipped into Cromarty, *c.*1750.

whole – 2 per cent of the English total. The first attempts to reform the system were unsuccessful, mainly because the old officials employed by the tax farmers were appointed to the new posts. However, a purge led to the removal of some of these corrupt officials in 1710.

Supplying the land-owning class with wines, spirits and other luxuries – whether licitly or illicitly – was very much a matter of personal contact and many merchants were themselves sons of minor land-owning families. Urquhart of Greenhill's dealings with Lord Strathnaver at Dunrobin, in the first two decades of the eighteenth century, are illustrative of Cromarty's developing place in this trade. Strathnaver, with Urquhart's assistance, maintained a boat at Cromarty, of five tons burden, which was then used to transport goods to Dunrobin. Urquhart also acted as an agent for Strathnaver by paying customs dues for him and honouring bills drawn on Strathnaver. The range of goods supplied by Urquhart can be illustrated from a range of entries in the Sutherland estate papers. In one typical shipment in 1720 there were foods (flour, sugar and raisins), soap (imported from Danzig), nails, hemp, a variety of alcoholic drinks (brandy, claret, sherry, Canary and Rhenish wine, and Nottingham ale), together with glasses, bottles, corks and hops for brewing.[5]

A number of these were subject to duty but there was also a growing trade in other goods. In 1725 the *Prosperous Margaret*, captained by the Cromarty merchant-captain John Reid and bound for Inverness, was wrecked on the sandbar at Montrose. The cargo, saved and rouped on the shore, shows the increasing demand for a range of imported foodstuffs (not only spices and Mediterranean fruit, but flour and English cheese), tableware (china, glass, earthenware and pewter), leather, cloth, shoes, dyes, metal and ironmongery. The ship, wrecked in January, even had marmalade oranges on board.[6]

In 1751, Reid and his partner, Gilbert Barkly, attempted to imitate the success of the Clyde ports by shipping a cargo of tobacco from Virginia to Inverness. Much of it was for onward distribution to European ports but they also established a snuff-mill at Kirkmichael, in the parish of Resolis, operated by Barkly's brother and in Cromarty a tobacconist set up in business. As a major development of trade the venture failed but it is indicative both of increasing local demand for such goods and of local initiative in responding to the demand.[7]

Smuggling

Smuggling in the Cromarty Firth in the early eighteenth century, as in the rest of Scotland, was based on official connivance in evasion of duties. From 1696 Gordon of Dalpholly had the farm (lease) of the customs for Inverness, which included Cromarty and the Moray ports. His son, Alexander, was appointed collector of customs in 1707 and was only removed in 1714 following complaints from Inverness merchants.[8] These were, in effect, complaints of unfair competition because Gordon and his elder brother, William Gordon of Invergordon, were both evading duty and had established their own tenants as merchants in Cromarty, undercutting the Inverness merchants on whose imports duties were being levied. The Inverness merchants pointed out that Barkly and Elphinstone, the Gordon brothers' frontmen, were 'poor illitrat and wretched tenants ... never known to be worth five pounds of Free Substance in the World ... (and did not) pretend to trade to the value of sixpence before their Master was made Collector'. Subsequently they appeared 'to be very considerable dealers especially in Tobacco, Pepper, Wine, Soap, & Brandy, which, tho' they yield the highest duties, yet these new Traders are able to sell & actually do retail the greater part of their commodities at a less price than the value of the duties'. The complaints led to a 'pretended search' at Inverbreakie by Gordon and his subordinates, which descended into farce when they 'actually found a great quantity of brandy, Fruits, Pepper and other goods in the House of a Widow not far from the said port'. There seems to have been so much contraband in various places that they had been unable to avoid stumbling across some. Barkly and Elphinstone, who were present, 'made a heavy noise, affirming that, if these goods which belonged to them were carried off they would be ruined and undone'. However, they seemed reassured after Gordon spoke privately with them. The Collector then found a way out the problem by deeming it 'necessary not only to go himself but to carry all the officers present along with him to bring horses for carrying off the said goods'. Not surprisingly, by the time they returned everything had been removed. The only possible legal action was against the widow in whose house the goods were seized but this was hardly worth pursuing and the matter 'was soon hushed'.

There were other abuses, including the falsification of fish debentures. One shipment of a 'few haddocks' from Cromarty was entered as a 'parcel of Wet and Dried Codfish' bound for Lisbon, on which a bounty of £196 was claimed. The false document had been signed by a boy, Lawrence Bernard, a servant to one of the merchants involved and when things got hot he was slipped five or six guineas and persuaded to join the cargo on its way to Lisbon. What is striking in these affairs is just how blatant was the evasion.

The firth was also an official quarantine station for ships that had called at ports where cholera had been reported. They were required to wait at anchor for forty days before discharging cargo. Lord Duffus who conducted the investigation into Gordon's conduct only succeeded in making the *Providence* of Fraserburgh – bound for Cromarty with goods from Dunkirk – wait out her quarantine by having her 'remain under my guns the full time'. Several other ships came in from France with only ballast and the merchants 'made no scruple to tell me that they had run their cargos and were not at all afraid of the Collector who was universally known to have been more guilty than any of them'.

Not until the 1750s was smuggling curbed to become the clandestine affair of popular legend. And the aristocracy were slow to change their approach to duty-free drink. In 1757 the respectable Lady Ross of Pitcalnie, Nigg, wrote that 'Starks, the customs officer [at Cromarty], is such a Divle, there is ill bringing anything to this place' and, on another occasion, 'this wine must go in the night time to John Mackenzie's as there is ane Ugly Dog at Cromty who would seize it'. Effective control came not least because customs crews now received a proportion of the value of contraband seized and because, after 1755, fishermen caught smuggling were pressed into the navy. There were also further purges of the staff, suspected of corruption or of Jacobite sympathies, after the Jacobite risings of 1715 and 1745.[9]

Quarrying and building

New mansions for the aristocracy, coastal girnals for grain and more substantial houses for prospering merchants all led to a greater demand for building stone and for skilled masons and squarewrights. Other than over very short distances, stone could only be efficiently transported by water and, as a result, sources of good quality stone close to the coast were exploited. In 1686 George Mackenzie, Viscount Tarbat, began New Tarbat House on the north shore of the Cromarty Firth, as the centre of his enlarged estates, for which he had 660 loads of 'wall stones' boated from the quarry at Newton, outside Cromarty. Sir Thomas Urquhart had earlier referred to a newly discovered source of freestone close to Cromarty and this may have been the same quarry. By 1695 Tarbat had also completed his 'great girnel' at the Ness in Cromarty, beside the harbour, and several merchants in Cromarty built substantial houses in the early years of the eighteenth century. At least five of them survive to the present day. There were also many other buildings as the town expanded into a new area, which came to be known, from the salting of fish carried out there, as Pickletoun.[10]

Ships and boats

The Scottish merchant fleet as a whole had increased as a result of the seizure of ships during the second and third Anglo-Dutch Wars (1664–7 and 1672–4) and the corrupt admiralty court at Cromarty was notorious for its role in declaring ships to be prizes of war – that is, ships trading with the enemy which might legitimately be seized, with the captor receiving both the vessel and its cargo. But trade from Cromarty itself seems to have supported only one or two ships at any one time. In 1675 Alexander Urquhart, master of the *Blessing* of Cromarty, brought slates from Dunrobin for New Tarbat House and in 1685 was engaged to ship Tarbat's grain crop of 400 bolls bere and 72 bolls meal.[11] In 1707 'the Great Barque *Hendret* of Cromarty, John Reid master' shipped Sir Kenneth Mackenzie's meal and oats from the Cromarty Firth to Royston, on the Firth of Forth. These ships may have traded at the same time but in 1710 Cromarty had only the forty-ton *Anne Galley*, compared with twenty-seven vessels in the Inverness precinct as a whole. The *Anne* was jointly owned by a Cromarty merchant, Urquhart of Greenhill, and his brother-in-law Bailie John Steuart of Inverness. In February 1710 she left from Cromarty for 'The Sound' with 258 barrels of Urquhart's 'white herring'. In 1715 she sailed for Barbados, in 1720 for Stockholm, in 1722 for Danzig, and in October 1725, sailing with wine from Bordeaux, she sank off Ushant. The crew were rescued by an Arbroath ship with which she was travelling.[12]

Cromarty's shipping was at much the same level in mid century. The *Betty* and the *Helen and Margaret*, both of Cromarty, appear in the customs books, which are extant from 1742 onwards. However, by 1748 the *Betty* was a Rosemarkie ship and the *Helen and Margaret* was based in Inverness.[13] Two Cromarty merchants, Gilbert Barkly and John Reid, responded to improved trading conditions by having a ninety-ton ship, the *Adventure*, built in the town in 1751. It was probably commissioned with a view to it being used by the British Linen Company to ship flax, since Barkly was initially the BLC's principal contact in the area. However, the BLC became suspicious of Barkly's dealings with them, terminated their contract and bought out Barkly's share in the *Adventure*. This, and other ventures, had overstretched the finances of both men – Reid struggled with debt until his death in 1767 and Barkly, after imprisonment for debt, sought sanctuary at Holyrood and then emigrated to Philadelphia.[14]

The distribution of goods by smaller boats – along with their role in transporting quarry stone – had a significant impact on the local economy. In 1744, of the 178 male heads of households in the town, 14 were fishers, 22 were boatmen, 2 were ferriers and 2 were customs boatmen.[15]

Timber and shipbuilding

Although most woods in the Black Isle and the Easter Ross peninsula had been felled by the seventeenth century, there were remaining forests in the valleys of the rivers that flowed into the Beauly, Cromarty and Dornoch Firths. There was some shipbuilding in Cromarty in the late seventeenth century and the gravestone of a William Swan in St Regulus kirkyard shows a shipwright's tools and a three-masted vessel of *c.*40–50 tons, flying a saltire. A ship of this size may, of course, have been more an aspiration than a reality.

Following the Union of 1707 there was interest from southern merchants, both Scottish and English, in exploiting the timber resources of the Highlands. This was evident by the mid 1720s in the activities of the York Building Company, which had acquired the estates forfeited to the Crown after the 1715 Jacobite rising in order to work timber and minerals.[16] By the same date, the British navy had come to look to the Highlands as an important source of wood, particularly for masts.[17] But the same interest was already there some twenty years earlier. In 1707 Ross of Balnagowan entered into a contract with Francis Plouden, merchant in Edinburgh, William Johnston and Christopher Jackson, both Englishmen resident in Dublin, and Nathaniel Gee, a shipwright in Burntisland and master builder for the Scots African Company. Ross was to sell 12,200 softwood trees from which Gee was to 'build five ships, barks or boats, make tar, split barrel staves and laith wood, saw planks and deals'. The terms of the contract suggest that these were to be made locally and Ross was also proposing to bring a 'Norway man' to the area to make tar – either from pine or, if it could be found, from shale.[18] Cromarty, as the principal port for the Cromarty Firth, was the point to which the merchants' essential stores were delivered. The venture was not successful but both Plouden and Jackson remained active in the north. Plouden's 150-ton *Three Brothers* was in Tain in 1710, engaged to ship timber from the Oykell for Macleod of Cadboll. It was the largest vessel in the north at the time.[19]

Merchants of the royal burgh and in the early eighteenth century

There were three types of merchant active in Scottish burghs in the seventeenth century – packmen or chapmen (who carried goods from place to place), merchants not engaged in foreign trade, and merchant adventurers (who traded overseas).[20] Four documents relating to affairs of the royal burgh of Cromarty in 1669 and 1670 identify thirty-eight individuals as burgesses.[21] Of these only two are given the designation of merchant – one a chapman and the other, John Reid, a skipper. Reid was master of the *Adventure*, which was principally engaged in the grain trade, and there was also the *Blessing*, captained by Alexander Urquhart who, although not a burgess himself, was probably of the family of Urquhart of Newhall who served on the burgh council in 1670. Both Reid and Urquhart can be considered to be merchant adventurers. Another five individuals, from their occupations as glover, tailor, shoemaker, maltman and carpenter, might have claimed the status of merchant along with the principal burgess family, the Clunes. Cromarty's position within the Cromarty Firth also made it a suitable base for masons and squarewrights (later known as house carpenters, who used timber in construction work). The Cromarty master mason, James Dick, was employed on both New Tarbat House and the Inverness Tollbooth, and another master mason, Alexander Mitchell, who worked on Tarbat House in 1729, was sufficiently prosperous to acquire land and become one of the minor heritors in the parish.[22] However, even with these additions, the total remains small.

Other than the laird, the Clunes were the family with the greatest stake in the town's economy in the late seventeenth century. They held land – most of which they had obtained from the burgh – and feued property to others, including many of the fishers, whose houses clustered round the house and barns of Clunes of Dunskaith, in modern-day Gordon's Lane. Indeed, it may be that the fishertown was largely the creation of the Clunes family. Not surprisingly, they were the principal opponents of the laird over the loss of status as a royal burgh.

The Clunes and their allies fought back. Letters to the new laird in 1678 indicate that Alexander Clunes and others had 'designs to make Cromarty a free burgh' – that is, to restore its status as a royal burgh rather than remain as a burgh of barony – and, to this end, they were allegedly in league with the officer commanding troops quartered in Cromarty. The writer referred to this group as the burgh's 'resurrectionists'. Later, in 1704, the laird Sir Kenneth Mackenzie protested that the former Episcopalian minister of the parish, who had married into the Clunes family, was agitating to have the town's status restored.[23] In 1715 this was taken further, perhaps because Mackenzie influence in government had waned with the death of the Earl of Cromartie, and a petition was presented to the Convention of Royal Burghs seeking restoration of the burgh's status. The petition of 1715 continued to have the support of the Clunes family, in this case Thomas Clunes and John Clunes, both designated as merchants. During the course of the legal action they produced evidence of wider support in the form of minutes of a 'debate between the inhabitants of the burgh'.[24] They were, however, unsuccessful.

Although the number of merchants in Cromarty was small there is evidence that they had a keen sense of their status. The burgess families successfully argued that, after the demise of the royal burgh, they held their properties directly from the Crown rather than from the laird. Some, who held only small burgess plots, then incorrectly – but with an obvious sense of pride and importance – described themselves as 'king's barons'. A number of these burgesses were also minor heritors and a division of the parish church in 1702 – that is, an allocation of the floor space among the landowners of the parish – probably arose from their insistence on claiming their rights.[25]

After the Urquharts' affairs fell into disorder in the 1670s, these principal families of the burgh began to use the former private burial ground of the lairds at St Regulus chapel. The stones they erected here were notably elaborate and some are carved with the device of crossed sceptre and spade. Although the sentiment that 'in death no difference is made, betwixt the sceptre and the spade' was commonplace, this was not a usual device on Scottish gravestones. Given what had happened

FIGURE 6.2
Sandilands House (*c*.1700).

to the Urquhart lairds, this symbol of equality in death may have had a
particular local resonance.

Status and wealth were also displayed by building more substantial
houses. These show an increased sense of symmetry in their design and
the most notable to survive is Sandilands, built *c*.1700 for Bernard
Mackenzie. This is a five-bay house with the Mackenzie arms carved
in stone above the door and a large window looking east to the firth.
Houses of similar, elegant proportions were built for the Clunes
family.[26]

Although there were prominent and successful local merchant
families, economic control rested largely with merchants from
Inverness and ambitious local merchants required effective networking,
often established through marriage, with the larger commercial centre.
George Urquhart of Greenhill is a good example. Both his marriages
were into merchant families with Inverness connections, first to
Margaret Steuart, sister of Bailie John Steuart of Inverness and then to
an Elizabeth McLeod. There was always a pull towards Inverness but
Urquhart preferred to be a big fish in the small pool of Cromarty. He
derived his income from his business as a merchant and from factoring
the Cromarty estate and by remaining in the town he retained the social
status of a minor landowner. He styled himself 'of Greenhill', his wife
was known as Lady Greenhill and the family, as Episcopalians, retained

their own chaplain. He also had a place of business at the eastern end of the town whose plaster walls were decorated with a cornice of 'curiously united bunches of grapes with clusters of herring' and its ceiling with a centre piece around which swam 'a shoal of neatly relieved herrings in a sea of plaster'. Urquhart became insolvent in 1724 and his sons all left for England and retained no connection with the town. His daughters, however, remained to be part of 'genteel' society in Cromarty in the mid eighteenth century.[27]

Merchants of the mid eighteenth century

In his study of the merchants of Edinburgh, Tom Devine concluded that there was a considerable turnover in the merchant class. A few of the elite were 'lost' to landownership, many faced bankruptcy in periods of high risk, some families simply died out and many sons went into other careers – a process made easier by the networks on which trade relied, both at home and overseas.[28] A similar pattern can be seen in the much smaller town of Cromarty in the first half of the eighteenth century. The parish registers, which survive from the beginning of the century to 1731, identify eighteen persons designated as merchant (Table 6.1). A survey of householders in 1744 enables identification of those who remained in the town and, when this is combined with a range of other sources, it is possible to form an overview of the fate of the merchants of the period 1700–31 (Tables 6.1 and 6.2). Only five of the eighteen merchant families remained active as merchants in Cromarty in 1744, the loss being due to a combination of geographical mobility, social mobility and misfortune.

Devine found little evidence of upward social mobility among Edinburgh merchants. Cromarty, however, offers two examples from the first half of the eighteenth century. The first is the merchant-captain John Reid, who had been active in shipping grain and other goods for the first earl of Cromartie. Reid's daughter, Elizabeth, married Lord Tarbat's grandson, George Mackenzie of Grandvel, in 1744. By this date Grandvel had sold his small estate of Cromarty – and he died in reduced circumstances in 1748 – but he still moved in the circles of the local aristocracy. His letters reveal him to be a man with a considerable, even obsessive, interest in his personal appearance and in that of his wife – a man conscious of the impression he made in the society in which he moved.[29] The marriage cannot be explained as a convenient arrangement to improve Grandvel's financial situation – two years after his death his widow was still unable to pay the account for his funeral and claimed 'not to have handled above 40 shillings since Sir George died'.[30] Reid had not been especially wealthy and his business had passed to his son, who was a seagoing captain rather than a man

TABLE 6.1   Merchants named in Cromarty OPRs 1700–31.

Merchant	Year	Notes	1744
Alexander Allan	1735	Died 1796. Family of same name ship-builders c.1800 but no connection between them established.	No
Bernard Clunes	1727	1732 tried and convicted for serious assault.	No
Thomas Clunes	1723	Clunes family prominent in burgh in sixteenth century but by 1745 had left Cromarty for lands in Sutherland.	No
Walter Denoon	1714	Later described as boatman and customs officer.	Yes
James Forsyth	1720	Moved to Cromarty from Elgin in 1717. Son, William, trained in London but returned to Cromarty in 1739 and became leading merchant in town. WF died 1800. WF's sons made careers in the East India Company.	Yes
David Geddes	1720	No further record.	No
Robert Gordon of Haughs	1743	Son of the parish minister. Died 1764 after undistinguished career as merchant. Heir, David Gordon, made career in army.	Yes
John Laing	1708	Engaged in trade in salt fish.	No
Mr John Laing	1711	Son of above. Master in Royal High School, Edinburgh and subsequently Inverness Grammar School, but also described as merchant in Cromarty. Emigrated to America (Maryland).	No
Thomas Lindsay	1714	Lands sold to Urquhart of Greenhill c.1720. Family moved to Orkney and flourished as linen merchants. Heir Andrew died in poverty in Cromarty in 1760s.	Yes
William MacCulloch	1727	Left Cromarty for London; in Virginia in 1743; later barrack master at Fort Augustus.	No
George Mackenzie of Muirfield	1714	Son of Revd Bernard Mackenzie, last Episcopalian minister of established church in Cromarty. Family property sold by 1760.	Yes
John Mcleod	1714	Reputedly shot his only son in accident during struggle with customs officers.	No
John Mitchell	1722	Later described as customs officer. It was probably his son who attended university, graduated in 1769 and became minister in Elgin and Ardclach.	Yes
John Reid	1706	No further record.	No
John Reid	1706	Merchant captain; died in 1760s in financial difficulties. Son, John Reid, married daughter of Bailie Steuart of Inverness; emigrated to America.	Yes
John Tulloch	1714	Robert Tulloch, barber, may be related	Yes
George Urquhart of Greenhill	1712	Principal merchant in early eighteenth century. Bankrupt in 1720s. Sons moved to England.	Yes

Source: OPRs; NRAS 0204, Bundle 171

TABLE 6.2   Cromarty merchants in 1744 (other than those recorded above).

Merchant	Year	Notes
Alexander Barkly	1744	Brother, Gilbert Barkly, was the active partner. In financial difficulties by 1751 and emigrated to America, later settling in Bath.
William Galdie	1744	Vintner and innkeeper. Son ran nail works in 1770s.
Mr Alexander Gordon	1744	Proprietor of Ardoch and formerly collector of customs. Son Adam inherited, joined unsuccessfully in business with William Forsyth. Sold estate in 1756 and left area.
Lewis Gordon	1744	Servitor to Sir Kenneth Mackenzie of Cromarty. Resident in London in 1744 and possibly the Ludovic Gordon who later emigrated to Carolina.
Alexander Miller	1744	No information
Alexander Ross	1744	Died 1752. Reputedly the sole Jacobite in Cromarty and left town in 1746.
Alexander Shand	1744	No information

Source: NRAS 0204, Bundle 171.

of business. It seems, rather, that Grandvel judged her to be a suitable companion.

A second example of social mobility is that of the merchants Barkly and Elphinstone, tenants on the Gordon estates of Ardoch or Newhall, who had been set up to trade in goods smuggled by their laird, the collector of customs for the Inverness precinct. Although they were described in 1713 as having been 'poor illitrat and wretched tenants' this was an exaggeration, since Elphinstone was later chamberlain on the Newhall estate, but they undoubtedly rose in social terms. Barkly's son, Gilbert, was for a time the leading merchant in Cromarty but, as a result of bankruptcy and charges of fraud, he emigrated to America in 1752, returning in the 1770s to Bath. While in America he ordered from England 'a table set of blue and white china with the Barkly arms on them' – arms to which he had no obvious entitlement but which presumably enhanced his status in the colonies. Towards the end of his life, however, he wrote that 'from a knowledge of the ungenerous and oppressive disposition of Ross-shire Lairds, I own my prejudice against them to be of long standing' – perhaps indicating that he had not been fully accepted in such circles.[31]

A further change in the social structure was underway in the appearance of minor government posts, principally in the customs and excise services. These posts, which carried secure salaries and pensions, were taken up by some who earlier regarded themselves as merchants. Thus Walter Denoon, described as a merchant in the parish register in 1714, became a customhouse boatman; William MacCulloch, the former chamberlain on the estate, became barrack-master at Fort Augustus; and when Kenneth MacCulloch, a leading tenant, faced financial ruin in the 1750s the factor considered that his only hope was some appointment in the 'public service'.[32]

Religious affiliation was also socially significant. Many, though not all, of the merchant families in the early eighteenth century were united in their allegiance to Episcopalianism and in overt or covert support for the Jacobite cause. The former Episcopalian minister, Bernard Mackenzie, married into the Clunes family and the Reids were linked by marriage to the leading Inverness merchant, Bailie Steuart, also an Episcopalian. An unnamed relation of Urquhart of Greenhill was a sea-captain active in plotting a Jacobite landing at Cromarty in 1719;[33] and Bailie Steuart's Jacobite sympathies are apparent in his letters.[34] This social group mixed easily with the last Mackenzie laird, George Mackenzie – who, although he did not actively support the 1745 rising, nevertheless in 1744 sent a 'picture of King Charles set in gold' to Inverness for repair[35] – and, to a lesser extent, with his Roman Catholic successor, Captain Urquhart, who had been 'out' in the rising of 1715. The importance of this grouping waned in the 1740s with the death of Greenhill, Reid's failure in trade and the growth of anti-catholic sentiments. This was followed in the 1750s by a prolonged patronage dispute with the Roman Catholic laird, and the Episcopalian families were replaced as leading figures in the community by a staunchly Presbyterian faction.

William Forsyth (1719–1800)

Chief among the Presbyterians was William Forsyth, whose father had established himself as a minor merchant in Cromarty in the second decade of the century. Forsyth trained in a London counting house, which was generally thought to provide the best form of commercial education both for learning orderly business methods and making contacts in the business world.[36] Clerks such as Forsyth were often potential partners in the counting house but Forsyth returned to Cromarty on his father's death in 1739. He succeeded as a merchant by applying the same orderly methods he had learned in London, by using his contacts as sources for imports of luxury goods for the aristocracy, and by his acceptability to the British Linen Company, who appointed him their principal agent in the north in 1750. Forsyth's support for the Hanoverian government was an important factor in his success, gaining him the confidence of the BLC.

The goods he shipped to the north included a number of building materials, particularly roof and floor timbers, wainscot boards, lime, slates and nails. He was thus well placed to undertake building projects, with the added advantage that his father had been a mason. Forsyth took the lease of the large quarry at Newton and was responsible for the construction of mills at Rosemarkie, a girnal at New Tarbat, the first phase of the Cromarty harbour, his own house in Cromarty and other buildings in the town.[37]

Forsyth played an important social role in the community for almost fifty years and he was a key figure in the emergence of the 'middling sort' in Cromarty, who were to be central to the flourishing of the town from the mid 1790s. His standing was enhanced from the 1750s when he led opposition to the laird's claim to the right of patronage in the parish church. He was typical of the new middle class beginning to emerge in urban areas. His role as a leader in the community was markedly different from the leadership given by the traditional 'middle men' in rural society – the tacksmen or principal tenants – who resented the increasing role of 'strangers' in their community. This is well illustrated by the language such traditional leaders adopted during the patronage dispute in Nigg, described in chapter 7. Forsyth, in contrast, moved easily in social circles beyond the town. The discrepancy between social and religious groupings created odd alliances. Forsyth, who championed the anti-patronage party in Cromarty, subsequently married the daughter of the minister who had been presented to Nigg in the face of opposition from the congregation.

Notes

1. Daniel Defoe, *A Tour Through the Whole Island of Great Britain* (London, 1985). Lenman in *Living in Atholl* (Edinburgh, 1986), 14 points out that although the tour purported to be in 1720 Defoe had almost certainly not been in Scotland since 1706.
2. Eric J. Graham, *A Maritime History of Scotland 1650 – 1790* (East Linton, 2002).
3. NLS, Dep313, 19 May 1707.
4. David Alston, *A Historical Guide to Ross & Cromarty* (Edinburgh, 1999).
5. NRAS 239, Catalogue of Dunrobin Muniments.
6. NAS, GD23/6/77.
7. A cargo of 70 tons was imported in 1751, on which over £4,000 of duty was payable. Three-quarters was shipped the next spring to Christiansands and Campvere, by the Cromarty merchant John Fraser, acting for Gilbert Barkly (NAS, E504). Fraser's account books (NAS, CS96/1343) show that he was still supplying tobacco in 1756 but he became insolvent shortly afterwards. The tobacconist, David Manson, was supplied by Fraser.
8. PRO, T/168, Report by Lord Duffus Dec 1713 on abuses by Alexander Gordon.
9. NAS, GD199. For the rewarding of customs men and pressing of fishers, see NAS, CE 62/2/1.

10. Monica Clough, 'The Cromartie Estate, 1660–1784: Aspects of Trade and Organization' in J. Baldwin (ed.) *Firthlands of Ross and Sutherland* (Edinburgh, 1986); 95 NAS GD305/153/21.

11. NAS, GD305.

12. See William Mackay (ed.), *The Letter Book of Bailie Steuart of Inverness* (Edinburgh, 1915) and NAS, E502, Fish and corn debentures.

13. Information supplied by Eric Graham (personal communication).

14. NAS, E504, Customs Books; Bank of Scotland Archive, BLC Letter Books.

15. NRAS 0204/Bundle 171.

16. D. Murray, *The York Buildings Company* (Glasgow, 1883).

17. Edmund Burt, *Letters from a Gentleman in the North of Scotland* (London, 1759). New edition (Edinburgh, 1998) ii. 10–11.

18. NAS, GD199, nos 248 and 251.

19. NAS, GD199/250); Eric Graham, *Maritime History of Scotland* (East Linton, 2002).

20. Thomas M. Devine, *Exploring the Scottish Past* (East Linton, 1995), 22.

21. William Mackay Mackenzie, 'The Royal Burgh of Cromarty and the Breaking of the Burgh' in *Transactions of the Gaelic Society of Inverness* (Inverness, 1927), xxxi, 374–91.

22. Highland Council Archive, L/IB/BC 14/114: James Dick, master mason in Cromarty, engaged to build new steeple in Inverness, 1688. Clough, *Two Houses*, notes 'James Dick, Master Mason in this House (Tarbat) 1686'; for Alexander Mitchell see NAS, GD305/147/65 and Valuation Rolls.

23. NRAS 0204/Bundle 191; William Mackay Mackenzie, 'Cromarty: its old chapels and parish church' in *Scottish Ecclesiological Society* (1905).

24. NRAS 0204/Bundles 158 & 171.

25. NRAS 0204/Bundle 159; NAS, CH2/66/4, Minutes of the Presbytery of Chanonry 1747; Betty Wilsher, *Understanding Scottish Graveyards* (Edinburgh, 1985). The erection of new lofts in the church in 1716 may have been a similar assertion of the rights of the former burgesses. Those proposing the changes were the merchants John Laing and John Macleod and, John MacCulloch, one of the principal tenants. See NRAS 0204/Bundle 181.

26. See 1997 survey of Sandilands by Mary Washington College, Virginia and the Robert Gordon University, Aberdeen lodged with Cromarty Courthouse Museum. Clunes properties were Clunes House itself and, probably, Russell House. See survey lodged with Cromarty Courthouse Museum.

27. J. Dallas (ed.), *The Family of Dallas* (Edinburgh, 1921); for Greenhill's marriages see NAS, Register of Sasines and William Mackay (ed.), *The Letter Book of Bailie Steuart of Inverness*, Scottish History Society (Edinburgh, 1915), 183; for his ships Hugh Miller, *Scenes and Legends of the North of Scotland* (Edinburgh, 1994), 246; for the family chaplain NRAS 0204/Bundle 168; for his daughters Hugh Miller, *Memoir of William Forsyth* (London, 1839).

28. Thomas M. Devine, *Exploring the Scottish Past* (East Linton, 1995), 22.

29. NAS, GD23/6/148.

30. NAS, GD23/6/34.

31. PRO, T/168, Report by Lord Duffus Dec 1713 on abuses by Alexander Gordon; NLS, Ac 9907.

32. OPRs and Index to the Register of Sasines for the Sheriffdoms of Inverness, Ross, Cromarty and Sutherland (Edinburgh, 1966); William Mackay (ed.), *Letter Book of Bailie Steuart*, 257; NRAS 0204/Bundle 163.
33. Historical Manuscripts Commission, lvi, Jacobite Papers, 65 & 331.
34. William Mackay (ed.), *Letter Book of Bailie Steuart*, xlvii.
35. NAS, GD23/6/148.
36. David Hancock, *Citizens of the World: London Merchants and the Integration of the British Atlantic Community, 1735–1785* (Cambridge, 1995), 87.
37. NAS, E746/74/51.

Authority and Protest
before the 1760s

Master Gilbert Anderson did so rail against him [Sir Thomas
Urquhart] and his family in the pulpit at several times, both before
his face and in his absence, with such opprobrious termes, more like
a scolding tripe-seller's wife than good minister, squirting the poyson
of detraction and abominable falsehood, unfit for the chair of veritie,
into the ears of his tenandry, who were the only auditors.

Sir Thomas Urquhart, *Ekskybalauron*, 1653

In 1732, William Gordon of Invergordon attempted to enclose the
peat moss at Blackstand, on the commonty at the eastern end of
the Cromarty estate, with trees and 200 yards of feal (turf) dyke,
with the aim of settling smallholders on the land. There was a formal
protest from the factor of the Cromarty estate, William MacCulloch,
on the grounds that this was common land and the moss was used
by Cromarty townsfolk and tenants as a source of fuel – but this was
ignored. The next day '500 persons armed with Durks (and) cudgells'
appeared at Blackstand, 'pulled down ... the dyke ... [and trees] ...
[and] beat and bruised the workmen' – and Gordon abandoned his
attempt at enclosure. The crowd of 500 had been led by the principal
tenants on the Cromarty estate and, in this instance, the interest of these
tenants and of the inhabitants in general coincided with the interest of
their own laird – who wished to pursue his territorial disputes with
Gordon. The laird's support gave the protesters an almost official
mandate but, nevertheless, their action was motivated by the sense
that their traditional right to cut peat was threatened by an 'improving'
landowner.[1]

Occasions like this, when discontent becomes public protest,
are, in any society, indicators of the underlying tensions within the
community – fault lines in the social order which, when they erupt,
reveal the forces that might otherwise have remained hidden both to
outsiders and to future generations. Here it was the tension between
the power of landowners over common land and the traditional

rights of communities. In earlier chapters there have been examples of simmering conflicts in Cromarty between laird and burgesses, and between laird and minister – as illustrated by the quotation at the head of this chapter.

In the early eighteenth century there were frequent protests across Scotland directed at figures of authority, including landowners, customs men, the military and the press gang. Cromarty's prosperity in the first two decades of the century created little general opposition to 'the authorities' as such, but with decline in the early 1720s, protest took a number of forms common in other parts of Scotland. For example, attempts to clamp down on smuggling, which brought much needed trade, led to Col John Cholmley's Regiment being stationed in Cromarty in 1720, following the illegal unloading of ships quarantined in the firth. Popular opinion was, however, for the evaders of duty and against the customs establishment.[2]

The Cromarty grain riot, 1741

Nine years after the Blackstand protest, a similar crowd gathered in the town. The harvest of 1740 had been a failure and the following spring was a time of serious shortages throughout Britain, Ireland and Europe. In Cromarty the community had struggled with the effects of the dearth and were incensed when, in April 1741, a Gourock vessel anchored on the sands at Nigg to ship out grain being sold by Easter Ross lairds, who were taking full advantage of the higher prices offered in the south. At midnight on 6 April a party of thirty men from Cromarty raided the ship and carried off sixty sacks of grain. Their intention was to sell the cargo at a 'fair price' in the town and remit the money to the Gourock merchant, but an attempt by sheriff's officers to recover the grain was met with forceful resistance, which culminated in seizure of the cargo sacks by a large 'meal mob'.

Food riots were not an uncommon feature of eighteenth-century Britain and the historian E. P. Thompson, in *Customs in Common*, has drawn attention to an important feature – what he calls the 'moral economy' of the crowd. He argues that such crowds were often acting within a body of tradition and of expectation that in times of dearth the market in grain would not be allowed free rein and that there would be emergency intervention by those in authority to prevent life-threatening shortages. The actions of the crowd were intended to force or shame the authorities into fulfilling these 'paternalistic' responsibilities, defined by appeal to custom and natural justice.[3]

The raid and subsequent riot in Cromarty were described by Hugh Miller over eighty years later, using oral tradition and documentary sources. Miller's account confirms that the crowd saw themselves as acting in accordance with a set of traditional values. First, there had already been action during the shortage to prevent hoarding and profiteering. The merchants of the town, rather than seeking to benefit, had, with the authority of the sheriff, searched houses for hoarded grain, which was then sold under the supervision of the minister. Second, the people of Cromarty had fulfilled their traditional responsibilities to those less fortunate than themselves – the 'shoals of beggars from the upper part of the country' who had descended on the town. This was despite the fact that some of the Cromarty people had themselves been reduced to gathering shellfish for food. And third, the grain plundered was to be paid for at a reasonable price. To this end it was lodged with a local corn merchant who was 'fully authorised by his neighbours to dole out the contents to the inhabitants and account to Simpson (the merchant whose grain had been seized) for the money'.[4]

The Cromarty riot did not arise from opposition to the market economy as such but was motivated by a belief that in times of crisis the operations of the market should be restrained. Many of those involved were themselves engaged in the market economy. Kenneth MacCulloch, who was prominent in the meal riot, was the leading improver among the tenants on the Cromarty estate in the 1740s and early 1750s. His subsequent failure and bankruptcy were probably the result of legal action against him for his role in the protest.[5] The leader of the raid on the grain ship, which preceded the riot, was a respected artisan – Donald Sandison – a cabinet-maker. According to Hugh Miller, Sandison was one of two Cromarty men who took part in the Porteous riot in Edinburgh in 1736, when a lynch mob hanged the captain of the City Guard who had earlier been responsible for firing on a crowd protesting at the execution of a smuggler.

Those who were vilified in grain riots were not the landowners but the grain dealers, who as middlemen personified the opportunities for profiteering created by an unregulated market. These 'meal mongers' were, in a sense, necessary targets because protest that sought to enforce paternal responsibility could not attack paternal authority as such. For similar reasons, later protests at evictions in Cromarty – and more generally in the Highlands – were directed at the estate factor rather than the laird, who was conveniently assumed to be ignorant of what was done in his name.

Hugh Miller recorded a number of folk tales in which the grain dealer is the villain. One 'meal monger' is portrayed as drowning in quicksand, in an unseemly rush to reach the Tain market, while the ghost of another was said to haunt a remote burial ground, near Navity, constantly tormented by the pains of hunger. The meal mongers were also the target of verses discovered by Miller in the papers to which he had access. Here they were described as 'damned rascals' and 'the worst of all men' – and the verses concluded with the line 'the devil gets villains as soon as they're dead'. Such verses written and circulated after a riot were common in other parts of Britain.[6]

Miller's account is of the community acting very much in unison and in orderly fashion. The crowd comprised 'seven-eighths of the whole inhabitants' of the town and was made up of boys and girls, men and women of all ages – 'from the girl that had not yet left school to the crone that hobbled from her cottage assisted by her crutch'. They were drawn up in a set order of schoolboys, apprentices (wearing their aprons), women and girls, and men (some of whom carried arms, but probably more as symbols than as weapons intended for use).[7] A similar unity of the townspeople, with ordered processions and firing of weapons, had been expressed five months before, not in protest but in celebration at the news that the Cromarty estate had been bought by Captain Urquhart. On both occasions there was an element of formality – a 'theatre of the streets', which rallied support and affirmed a common sense of identity and purpose.[8]

Protest in the pews: disputes in the church 1730s–60s

Tensions within society often erupted in church affairs. The economic relationship between church and people in eighteenth-century Scotland was determined by those landowners who formed the board of heritors in each parish and who were responsible for the church building, manse, glebe, minister's stipend, the school and the schoolmaster's salary. They offset these expenses by charging school fees and pew rents, by making tenants responsible for payment of teinds, and by requiring labour services from tenants for such tasks as roofing the church. Dissent within the church in the eighteenth century was commonly the result of conflict between the largest landowners and independent small landowners, tradesmen and merchants, with disputes often focused on patronage, that is, the hereditary right to appoint the parish minister – a right often vested in the principal landowner. Patronage, having been abolished in 1690, was restored by the British parliament in 1712, although the effects of this were modified by the right of presbyteries to overrule the 'presentation' of a minister. Until 1729 presbyteries, in general, opposed the appointment of ministers presented against the wishes of congregations but from 1730 they began to support patrons in their choices.[9]

From the 1730s, religious life in Easter Ross and the Black Isle was marked by a series of evangelical revivals – such that by 1800 the area was dubbed 'The Holy Land'[10] – and these revivals not only left a mark on the life of individuals but also led to popular opposition to those ministers 'intruded' by patrons on unwilling congregations. Some historians have argued that 'the spread of patronage disputes followed the diffusion of agricultural improvement ... (and) in Perth-shire, Easter Ross and the north-east ... occurred mainly between the 1790s and the 1850s'.[11] However, agrarian change in Easter Ross and the Black Isle was limited in extent until the mid 1790s and consequently the earlier revivals and patronage disputes cannot be linked, in any simple way, to the social disruption caused by the transformation of agriculture. There were patronage disputes, of various forms, before the mid 1790s in Cromarty (1750), Nigg (1752), Kiltearn (1770), Rosskeen (1783), Avoch (1787) and Knockbain (1791) – in every case in parishes in which the revivals had had some influence. In two parishes there were, as a result, secessions from the Established Church. The fact that the revivals preceded substantial agrarian change corresponds with the view of the nineteenth-century historian of the revival, John Kennedy, who claimed in *Days of the Fathers in Ross-shire* that evictions only began in the area after 'the climax of its spiritual prosperity' in the 1780s.[12]

The Nigg revival

The Nigg revival is the earliest instance of a large evangelical revival in the Highlands in the eighteenth century. The revival began in 1739 and was followed, in the 1750s, by the secession of almost the entire congregation in a patronage dispute. It is described in some detail here because it had an important influence on the people of the town and parish of Cromarty – a short ferry crossing away – and, later, on Highland society as a whole, particularly through the role played by lay preachers, known as *Na Daoine* (The Men). *Na Daoine* had their origins a century earlier in the Easter Ross parish of Kiltearn, where they were established by the influential minister, Thomas Hog. As traditional Highland society broke down during the eighteenth century, groups of *Na Daoine* played an important role throughout the north as alternative leaders in times of change and disruption.

The Nigg revival took place under the guidance of the parish minister, John Balfour, who had moved from the neighbouring parish of Logie Easter in 1729. On Balfour's death in 1752, the congregation issued a call to a Mr Bethune. The Crown, however, intervened as patron and presented a candidate, who subsequently withdrew. The Crown then presented a Patrick Grant as minister – a choice rejected by the congregation who made sustained attempts to prevent Grant's induction. They and their supporters within the presbytery and synod were, however, overruled by the General Assembly and the majority of the parish seceded in 1756 to form an independent congregation, which subsequently joined the Secession Church.

In addition to the usual church records, there are three sources for a more detailed account of the Nigg revival and for insight into the motivations of those involved. First, there is a history of the secession congregation written in 1865 by their third minister, John Bennet Munro. Munro's great-grandfather had been one of the leaders of the revival and his father had been the seceding congregation's second minister. Second, there is a pamphlet produced on behalf of the congregation justifying their secession. This is titled *A Pastoral Apology on behalf of a certain flock in Ross-shire* and was printed in 1757. Finally, there are traditions associated with Nigg, and particularly with one of the leading Men of the parish, Donald Roy, collected by his descendant Hugh Miller and published in the 1830s. Miller's account of the role of The Men is usefully supplemented by the novel written by his wife, Lydia, which is set at the time of the Disruption and gives a central place in its plot to The Men.[13]

Munro's history provides valuable information on the religious practices of the congregation after the revival. Central to these were ten praying 'societies'. A monthly prayer meeting had been an established feature of parish life before the revival but the praying societies were, for this parish, an innovation. As a feature of the Scottish church, they had their origin in the Shotts revival of 1630 and, from as early as 1640, had been viewed with suspicion by the General Assembly – and are consequently, for historians, often a hidden feature of church life.[14] In Nigg each society met in a *tigh an leughaidh* (reading-house) and the typical Sunday for a family consisted of private devotions, a meeting at the reading-house, family worship in the home and then the church service, followed by an evening meeting at the reading-house and a final act of family worship. Journeys to and from the church were made in groups, headed by the senior members of the congregation, presumably The Men, who led conversation, which focused on recalling the important points of the sermon. The walk to and from church was itself, as in many dissenting congregations, a public statement of their spiritual independence.[15]

A houſe of heav'n defign'd for good, but turn'd to
    ill,
By craft of heart, ſelf-love, by-ends, and tricks of hell.
Another houſe is reared up, in Preſbyterial ſtate,
A huge one, thatched with patronial ſlate,
Its mines ſo long as *Edinburgh* from *Roſs*, and longer
    too,
The builders ſay, we fear 'tis very true.

FIGURE 7.1
Extract from 'A Pastoral Apology for a Certain Flock in Ross-shire'.

Munro describes the reading-houses as 'at convenient distances from each other' and, since each was attended by 'several families', this suggests that they were located in the dispersed farmtouns of the parish. After the congregation seceded the societies played an important role in the election of elders, in marked contrast to the elders in the Church of Scotland who were often appointed through the influence of the heritors.

There are clear parallels with the evangelical revival in England where John Wesley, at almost exactly the same time, established small groups, called 'classes', whose lay leaders became a central feature of the Methodist movement. Like the praying societies, the classes were a focus for devotion and oversaw the moral life of their members. The position of class leader was something to which ordinary members of the movement might aspire – a further parallel with the position of The Men. This cellular system of organisation within Methodism has been identified as the movement's greatest strength and the key to its rapid expansion. Thus, while the movement's founder, George Whitefield, left 'an overwhelming impression of impassioned eloquence', his more effective disciple, Wesley, left 'a company of men and women closely knit together in a common life'.[16] Accounts of the evangelical revival in the Highlands have tended to emphasise the charismatic role of The Men, who might be compared to Whitefield. The example of Nigg suggests that the place of organisation and structure in the revival has been underestimated.

The praying societies also enabled members of the congregation whose first, and often only, language was Gaelic to familiarise themselves with the text and imagery of the bible. The educational method was well suited to a largely illiterate congregation since it allowed learning to take place in small groups, with a strong emphasis on repetition. Greater access to scripture was almost certainly linked, through the Catechism, to the dogma of the church and the 'closely knit' societies also enforced stricter moral standards on their members. The result was that Balfour declared that he had 'never conversed with more intelligent, savoury, and distinctly exercised Christians'.

Scripture, dogma and an ethical code were augmented by the myths of the Lowland covenanting movement of the seventeenth century, which became an integral part of the congregation's imagery.[17] The revival had its great rituals – not only the annual communion and fast days but also the ceremonial signing of the Covenant, which took place at Nigg on at least two occasions 'in the presence of an immense assemblage of worshippers'. Some signed in their own blood. In addition, The Men adopted the distinctive and quasi-ritualistic dress of a long cloak and a kerchief tied round the head, and wore their hair long. This, together with the attribution of supernatural powers, gave them a status akin, in the minds of believers, to Old Testament

FIGURE 7.2
Donald Roy confronts the Devil in the form of a dog (John McNaught, 2005).

prophets. In these ways the revival offered a richly textured religious
life to its adherents.[18]

Social and economic factors in the Nigg revival

The Men were themselves mostly medium or small tenant farmers,
whose tenure was not immediately threatened by the limited agrarian
reforms of the 1720s and 1730s.[19] However, although there had been
only limited agrarian change by this date, few of the heritors had long-
established links with the parish and the expressed interest of a number of
them in improvement is likely to have altered the traditional relationship
between landlords and tenants. They were regarded as 'strangers',

although one, Ross of Invercassley, was sufficiently sympathetic to the
seceders to allow a site for a new church on the land of his tenant,
William Gair.[20] The heather-thatched church was symbolically built
to exactly the same dimensions as the parish church and remained on
the site until the land passed to Ross of Shandwick, who evicted the
congregation and used the stones in the building of Shandwick House.
The new house was reputedly cursed by one of The Men.

The seceding congregation's own view of the importance of social
cohesion is apparent in the *Pastoral Apology* issued on their behalf.
Their position after the death of Balfour is described as follows: 'Our
shepherd's gone, and left a charge, – that who came next we should
not trust, – before we knew him and loved him.' The presentation of
an unknown, and therefore unloved, minister was seen as the work of
strangers – a key term in their rhetoric.

> Some do know him and love him. – A patron, and some wanton rams,
> not of our fold, ... – he loved the hire, they loved him, – that was the
> rule.
>
> By a strange rule, a stranger to us – His voice and path are unco strange,
> we dare not follow ... A stranger gentleman names a stranger student
> to be our guide to heaven; a few votes of stranger elders force him upon
> us.

The patronage of the parish of Nigg was in the hands of the Crown.
The fact that the Crown had intervened and made a presentation
against the wishes of the people was the result of the influence of
some prominent landowners – and similar influence had led to the
decision of the General Assembly to overturn the decisions of the
presbytery and synod in support of the parishioners. It was such
influence, through channels that extended to Edinburgh and beyond,
which was attacked.

> Another house is reared up, in Presbyterial state,
> A huge one thatched with patronial slate,
> Its mines so long as Edinburgh from Ross, and longer too,
> The builders say, we fear 'tis very true.

The phrase 'longer too' suggests that the network of patronage – the
mines or tunnels of the house thatched with 'patronial slate' – extended
as far as London. In another section, the patron is portrayed as a
chapman, a travelling merchant with a pack of goods. The patron
was a mere 'chapman' because he used the power to appoint ministers
as part of a system of 'trade' in 'honours, posts and pensions'. This
trade was conducted through 'friendly bottles, mutual obligations,
social freedom, display of parts, petty simony, [and] a high taste of
life'. In attacking the 'Chapman-Patron' the Evangelicals of Nigg had

no particular landowner in mind but a system of patronage controlled by commercially motivated 'strangers'. The revival and secession were assertions of a need for community – a community enhanced by the praying societies, led by respected local leaders and opposed to control from without.

Moreover, the traditions associated with both The Men and prominent Evangelical ministers often asserted the supremacy of their spiritual power over the temporal authority of landlords and their factors. One dramatic example of this shows the authority attributed to Men like Donald Roy. The seceders held twice as many fast days as the Established Church – six rather than three – and observing these holidays often brought them into conflict with landowners. On one occasion Donald Roy confronted Duncan Ross of Meikle Kindeace, who had refused to release his servants from work at his mill to observe the fast day. Donald demanded to know 'what right (Ross) had to set his servants to work on a day set aside by the Church of Christ for fasting and humiliation'. His solemn announcement that he would be compelled to complain to 'his Master' was, according to the tradition, sufficient to overawe the landlord.[21]

Divisions in the church in Cromarty

Landownership in the parish of Cromarty was particularly polarised. There was a single major heritor, who owned the Cromarty estate, valued at £1,826 in 1756, while the largest of the other sixteen other heritors held land valued at £219 and the eight smallest each had land valued at less than £10. The small heritors were almost all tradesmen and merchants, and six were also elders. Conflict between the major landowner and the majority of the other heritors was already evident in 1738. The parish schoolmaster had resigned since he was 'going off the country', that is, emigrating, and a young man named David MacCulloch had 'set himself up to teach privately, without being tryed by the presbytery, according to law'. The parish minister proposed the appointment of James Robertson, tutor in Gordon of Ardoch's family, for which he claimed to have the consent of the laird and principal heritor, George Mackenzie of Grandvel. At this point the minor heritors claimed to have already appointed MacCulloch. They met in the church, refused to sit in the same pew as the minister, issued a second call and left, refusing to let the minister see the document. MacCulloch's position as schoolmaster was confirmed and he remained in this position until the 1760s.

Polarisation increased after the Cromarty estate was acquired, in 1741, by Captain John Urquhart. Urquhart was a Roman Catholic and, although initially welcomed, faced growing opposition after 1748 when Gordon of Ardoch attempted to persuade his fellow justices of the peace to implement anti-catholic legislation against Urquhart's household servants – on the basis that one of them was a Roman Catholic teacher, which if true would have contravened the law. Urquhart's factor interpreted this as, in part, linked with Gordon's attempts to encroach on Urquhart's lands. Gordon could not persuade the other justices to act and was also unsuccessful in an attempt to involve the commander of the troops stationed in Cromarty. However, he persuaded the presbytery, and subsequently the synod, to take up the matter and the commissioners to the General Assembly were instructed 'to represent how popery increased ... and ... how priests abounded' in Cromarty. It is interesting to note that Urquhart was supported by some neighbouring Presbyterian landowners, including Sir John Gordon of Invergordon, uncle to Gordon of Ardoch – a fact suggesting a commonality of interest among the larger landowners that transcended religious divisions.

Ardoch had gained the support of the elders, who pursued Urquhart on other matters, principally over Urquhart's claim to the right of patronage in the parish, an issue that came to a head on the death of the minister in 1749. Urquhart sought to exercise his alleged right with, as he saw it, some tact, but without in any way abandoning his claim. His chosen candidate was Thomas Simson and he suggested that the presbytery authorise him to preach for several Sundays so that the congregation could form an opinion of him and he further agreed to find another candidate if any objection could be sustained against Simson's qualifications or character. While Simson was initially accepted by a majority of the heads of families in the parish, the elders opposed Simson on principle, refused to accept any candidate presented by the patron and issued a call to a James Robertson. Robertson, however, withdrew on being offered a university post and the kirk session then called Patrick Henderson. The matter was appealed through the courts of the Church of Scotland and to the Court of Session, with victory going to Gordon and the elders. The decision rested on the patronage of the church being judged to lie with the Crown, not with Urquhart, and Henderson was inducted in 1756 – although only to be deposed for immorality within a few years.[22]

Other disputes had arisen in the meantime. It was a common complaint throughout Scotland that major heritors diverted the parish poor funds to defray their expenditure on the church.[23] The Cromarty kirk session, rightly or wrongly, perceived such a threat from Urquhart and in 1751 allocated funds to 'defend the rights of the poor of the parish to the lands pertaining to them'. Whatever the cause, it led to a clear recording by 1760 of the lands in the parish, which had been bequeathed in 1649 for the benefit of the poor and for the support of the school.[24]

In 1756–7 Urquhart, as the principal heritor, carried out major repairs to the church and following this initiated a 'division' – that is, an allocation of the floor space among the heritors in proportion to their landholdings, which naturally resulted in the allocation to his family of the bulk of the pew space, including the 'eastern gallery' which subsequently became the 'laird's loft'. A number of Urquhart's policies in the management of his estate had aroused resentment and this had led to damage to his property. This included the church building, perhaps in consequence of the division, and in 1759 the estate obtained a sheriff's interdict prohibiting people from 'strolling round the castle, kirk and storehouse and breaking windows'.[25]

Events in Cromarty reveal more complex allegiances than in Nigg, where there was virtually unanimous opposition to an intruded minister. In the Cromarty congregation, voting among heads of families during the patronage dispute was almost equally balanced between the candidates presented by Urquhart and by the kirk session. In July 1750 the laird's presentee was supported by 98 heads of families, the opposing candidate by 111. Urquhart's presentee was, however, opposed by more in the town than in the country, and by almost all of the small heritors.[26] The difference between town and country can be partly explained by the fact that, while in Nigg the congregation were in opposition to the more anonymous operations of Crown presentations, tenants of the Cromarty estate who opposed the laird might risk eviction – as appears to have been the case in one instance recorded by Hugh Miller, who recounts the eviction of Roderick Ross from his tenancy on the Hill. Allowing for the greater influence of the laird, the divisions within the parish of Cromarty nevertheless suggest a less homogeneous society. It is clear, for example, that the elders of the kirk session were not universally respected, as they were in Nigg. There was a proven complaint of 'unsuitable carriage' against one in 1748, two cases in 1755 of elders being 'slandered' by allegations of adultery and theft, and in 1772 the suspension for habitual drunkenness of an elder appointed in 1761. It is reasonable to assume that many of these elders had been appointed because of their social standing, rather than their spiritual qualities – as further evidenced by the fact that in 1756 five elders were also small heritors.[27]

Changing patterns of protest

In Cromarty the late 1740s were a watershed in the social structure of the town, with a new 'middling sort' emerging, who regarded themselves as more genteel than earlier community leaders. They no longer engaged in communal celebrations, as they had on Urquhart's acquisition of the estate, and their protests became more 'polite'. Thus the dispute over the right of patronage in the parish was pursued by legal action and petition, forms increasingly favoured by the 'middling sort' because they were orderly and open procedures, which affirmed the role of the individual in society rather then relying on the anonymous power of the mob.[28]

There was also a significant difference between the 'moral economy' of the meal mob and the principles involved in protest against patronage in the church. Grain riots sought to enforce the responsible exercise of paternalistic authority. The same stance, if applied to patronage, would have led to pressure on patrons to appoint ministers acceptable to the congregation – but when Urquhart sought to do this he was opposed on the principle of patronage itself, not the manner in which he proposed to exercise it. As his factor put it, 'a patron exercising his powers they take to be a creature with 7 heads and 10 horns'.[29] There could, from the point of view of the Evangelical party, be no compromise with such a creature.

An important consequence of patronage disputes becomes apparent here. The 'political space' within which the meal mob operated presupposed paternal power and responsibility – and did not seek to do away with them. There was an expected outcome for the crowd, who believed that the authorities, if subjected to sufficient pressure and reminded of their responsibilities, would intervene in the market. Patronage disputes were, in contrast, often more radical in the demands made. They were not intended to enforce a paternal response from the authorities but rather sought capitulation to the claims of the congregation. In this quite different situation violent action would have been much more dangerous – there was no compromise that could bring it to an end, only victory or defeat. Those areas of the country most influenced by evangelical revivals were not, as is sometimes suggested, necessarily rendered more docile by their religion. However, they did lose the option of engaging in the limited and partly ritualistic challenge to authority that was embodied in the grain riot. Instead they turned of necessity to the more measured forms of protest favoured by the 'middling sort'.

Public protests continued to take place in Cromarty and some involved the use of symbolism and a 'theatre of the streets' – but they were seldom acts that engaged the whole community. Thus, after the French Revolution there was a procession with a 'cap of liberty' and the planting of 'a tree of liberty' on the former site of the town gallows – but this involved only a dozen or so young men.[30] And, while the burning of tar barrels and the parading of effigies continued throughout the nineteenth century, this was to promote particular interests rather than to focus community protest.

Sandy Wood: a personal protest

Sandy Wood is a reminder that protest might take innovative forms. In 1669, after the laird's faction had ousted their opponents from the burgh council, Wood was pursued for debt, apprehended and taken to the house of one of the bailies, where he was kept until a rescue party of women, including the former provost's wife, appeared. The women attacked the two merchants who had pursued Wood, thrust them into a bed where they piled on top of them and 'beat, abuse and scart' them. This was all the more humiliating because it was carried out by women.

Sandy Wood went on to make his own enduring act of protest in another dispute. He was interred, apparently at his own request, beneath a carved tombstone outside the boundary wall of the kirkyard. This was something normally reserved for suicides – but a suicide would not have had a tombstone erected. A tradition was preserved that he had been in dispute over a property boundary and the burial outside the wall was to give him a head start when the dead were raised and called to judgement – so that he could put his side of the argument, at the seat of judgement, before his neighbour.

Notes

1. William Macgill, *Old Ross-shire and Scotland* (Inverness, 1909), no. 786; NRAS 0204/Bundle 18; Highland Council Archive, L/INV/CS 3/22.
2. W. H. Fraser, 'Social Class' in A. Cooke, I. Donnachie, A. MacSween and C. A. Whatley (eds), *Modern Scottish History 1707 to the Present, Volume I: The Transformation of Scotland, 1707 – 1850* (East Linton, 1998) 216; *Calendar of Treasury Papers*, CCXXXIX, no. 35; PRO, T1/123, 168 & 182; T/168.
3. E. P. Thompson, *Customs in Common* (London, 1991), 259–351.
4. Crowds in grain riots throughout Britain frequently paid what was regarded as a just price for what they seized. See A. Randall, A. Charlesworth, R. Sheldon and D. Walsh, 'Markets, Market Culture and Popular Protest in Eighteenth-century Britain and Ireland' in A. Randall and A. Charlesworth (eds), *Markets, Market Culture and Popular Protest in Eighteenth-century Britain and Ireland* (Liverpool, 1996), 19.
5. Hugh Miller, *Scenes and Legends*, 303.
6. For an account of the widespread distrust of middlemen and dealers in the market see Randall et al, 'Markets, Market Culture and Popular Protest in Eighteenth-century Britain and Ireland', 15. Hugh Miller, *Scenes and Legends*, 291–303 and *Tales and Sketches* (Edinburgh, 1863), 265. For similar verses see D. Walsh, A. Randall, R. Sheldon and A. Charlesworth, 'The Cider Tax, Popular Symbolism and Opposition in Mid-Hanoverian England' in A. Randall and A. Charlesworth (eds), *Markets, Market Culture and Popular Protest in Eighteenth-century Britain and Ireland* (Liverpool, 1996), 78.
7. Hugh Miller, *Scenes and Legends*, 299.

AUTHORITY AND PROTEST BEFORE THE 1760s

8. For an account of the importance of public symbolism see J. Brewer, *Party, Ideology and Popular Politics at the Accession of George III* (Cambridge, 1976).

9. Callum G. Brown, *Religion and Society in Scotland since 1707* (Edinburgh, 1997), 18–23, 69.

10. J. N. Hall, *Travels in Scotland* (London, 1807).

11. Callum G. Brown, *Religion and Society*, 78.

12. John Kennedy, *The Days of the Fathers in Ross-shire* (Inverness, 1895), 17.

13. J. B. Munro, 'The First Dissenting Congregation in the Highlands' in *United Presbyterian Magazine* (Glasgow, 1865), New Series, ix. 307–15, 354–360, 401–8. The *Pastoral Apology* is incorrectly attributed to the Revd Patrick Grant in the *Fasti Ecclesiae Scoticanae* and consequently wrongly catalogued in most libraries. The pamphlet is, in fact, an attack on the appointment of Grant. For Donald Roy, see Hugh Miller, *Scenes and Legends*. Lydia Miller's novel *Passages in the Life of an English Heiress* is discussed in Angus Calder, 'The Disruption in Fiction' in S. J. Brown and M. Fry, *Scotland in the Age of the Disruption* (Edinburgh, 1993).

14. A. L. Drummond and J. Bulloch, *The Scottish Church 1688–1843: The Age of the Moderates* (Edinburgh, 1973), 49–51; Callum G. Brown, *Religion and Society*, 15; A. Macrae, *Revivals in the Highlands and Islands in the Nineteenth Century* (Stirling, n.d.), 190. The *Fasti Ecclesiae Scoticanae* suggests that Golspie followed the example of Nigg.

15. Callum G. Brown, *Religion and Society*, 79.

16. G. R. Cragg, *The Church in the Age of Reason* (London, 1970), 145.

17. Allan Macinnes, *Clanship, Commerce and the House of Stuart*, 179; Steven Bruce, 'Social change and collective behaviour: the revival in eighteenth-century Ross-shire', *British Journal of Sociology*, 34 (1983).

18. Callum G. Brown, *Religion and Society*, 80; J. B. Munro, 'The First Dissenting Congregation in the Highlands'; John Kennedy, *Days of the Fathers*, 82.

19. The elders of the secession church who may be presumed to be 'The Men' of the revival were: Donald Roy, formerly an elder in the Church of Scotland, according to Miller 'a farmer with a herd of black cattle'; Nicholas Vass, formerly an elder in the Church of Scotland; John Oag, Shandwick; George Ross, assessor in the Church of Scotland and therefore a man of standing locally whose judgement was respected; similarly, Robert Donaldson, assessor in the Church of Scotland and session clerk of the new session; George Ross, Wester Rarichie, a tenant of *c*.27 acres; Simon Fraser; William Gair: in Balchragan (Ankerville), a tenant of *c*.70 acres, on whose ground the new church was built; John Munro, a tenant of *c*.36 acres at Wester Torran; John Noble, Culnauld; Hugh Hay, Shandwick; and Donald Macandie, at the ferry or in Balnabruach.

20. William Macgill, *Old Ross-shire and Scotland* (Inverness, 1909), no. 105.

21. Callum G. Brown, *Religion and Society*, 80; J. B. Munro, 'The First Dissenting Congregation in the Highlands'.

22. NAS, CH2/672; NRAS 0204/Bundle 97.

23. Callum G. Brown, *Religion and Society*, 77.

24. NAS, CH2/672, 1 July 1751.

25. NRAS 0204/Bundle 36 & 138; Highland Council Archive, HCA/C154/25.

26. NRAS 0204/Bundle 94.

27. NAS, CH2/672; HCA/C154/25.

28. Stena Nenadic, 'Political reform and the Ordering of Middle-class Protest' in Thomas M. Devine (ed.), *Conflict and Stability in Scottish Society, 1700–1850* (Edinburgh, 1990), 68–76.
29. NRAS 0204/Bundle 181.
30. Hugh Miller, *Scenes and Legends* (Edinburgh, 1994), 459.

8

Population and Migration
before the 1760s

None hath a more ancient tenandrie than myself ... Each hamlet
... having its peculiar Clan, as we call it, or name of a kindred,
none whereof will from that position of land bouge with his will
to any other, upon never so great advantages offered unto him, the
interflitting from one parish to another, though conterminal, being
of such a mutual displeasingness, that all and each of them esteem
of it as of an extrusive proscription to the Barbadoes, or depulsory
exile to Malagask.

Sir Thomas Urquhart of Cromarty, *Logopandecteision*, 1653

It would be useful to know much more about the population of
Easter Ross and the Black Isle than we do – but the available data
is incomplete. The conclusions that can be drawn are, therefore,
tentative and are supported more by coherence with the social and
economic changes described in earlier chapters than by hard data on
population levels, age of marriage, mortality rates and emigration.
These tentative conclusions are nonetheless important. For the early
eighteenth century, the evidence suggests two patterns of population movement and growth. First, after the 'ill years' of the late
1690s, there appears to have been a drift of population into the
parishes at the western end of the Black Isle, which bordered the
true Highlands. And, second, there seems to have been a migration
to those centres that had prospered through increased trade in salt
fish, namely Cromarty and Avoch. With the exception of Cromarty,
the established towns in the area did not increase their share of
population. Cromarty, however, increased in size and an informed
guess would estimate growth from *c.*900–50 in 1690 to *c.*1200 in
1760. By the mid century, the increased mobility of the population
became an important factor in estate management – encouraging
both the development of textile manufactures in proto-factories (non-
mechanised factories) and the settling of mailers (cottars or crofters)
on waste ground.

The 'ill years' of the 1690s

In much of Scotland the failure of the harvests of 1695, 1696 and 1698 led to high mortality in 1697 and 1699, and to a significant fall in population. There was, with local variations, a drop in population of 5 to 15 per cent, of which half was the result of death and half the combined result of a fall in births and emigration. While this may not have been 'a lasting disaster but a sharp dislocation quickly repaired', there was nevertheless appalling suffering and the Scottish population may not have been fully restored to earlier levels even by 1755.[1]

In the north there is evidence of harvest failures before 1695 – in Orkney from as early as 1693 – and in Easter Ross grain was distributed to the poor by the Tarbat estate in early 1695, presumably because of a failure the previous year. This corresponds with a tradition, recorded by Hugh Miller in the 1820s, that a fog and east wind in August 1694 destroyed the crop.[2] Flinn's analysis of burials and baptisms from a number of northern parishes, including burials in the parishes of Kirkhill and Kilmorack (Inverness-shire), and baptisms in Kilmorack and Dingwall (Ross-shire), shows that the worst mortality occurred in late 1697 and early 1698 after a good harvest, suggesting that the main cause of death was some disease that spread in the summer and autumn. This is probably a reference to dysentery caused by eating rotten food.[3]

Population distribution: 1690s and 1755

There are two imperfect sources, which allow a comparison to be drawn between population distribution in the early 1690s and in 1755 – the hearth tax returns of 1691 for each parish and a census of Scotland conducted in 1755 by a minister, Alexander Webster, based on information given to him by fellow parish ministers throughout the country. The hearth tax returns, as the name suggests, record the number of hearths, usually one per house unless the family was wealthy. They do *not* give us the size of the population – to estimate which we would need to know the size of the average family who gathered round the hearth. But we can use them to show the distribution of the hearths throughout the area and we can use this as a proxy for the distribution of the population, even without being sure of the actual size of the population. Webster's census can also be used to show the distribution of population in 1755. The value of this comparison is limited because it assumes that both sets of figures are reliable and that family size was similar across the area in 1691. The comparison, with all these health warnings, is shown in Figure 8.1.

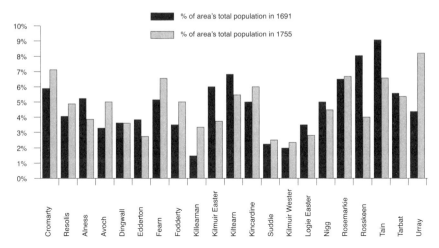

FIGURE 8.1   Population distribution in the Black Isle and Easter Ross, 1691 and 1755.

Two types of parish increased their share of the population. The first is a cluster of rural parishes at the western end of the Black Isle and on the lower reaches of Strath Conon – namely, Fodderty, Killearnan and Urray. The adjoining parish of Urquhart has been omitted from the analysis because part of the parish lay within the shire of Nairn and so no hearth tax data is available in the Ross-shire returns. However, it should be noted that Urquhart in 1755, with 2,590 inhabitants, was the most populous parish in Ross & Cromarty despite having no town or village. There is good evidence that this was a consequence of the Ferintosh estate's privilege of distilling whisky without paying duty. Similarly Fodderty, in 1757, had a 'large stratum of marginal people ... practically all of whom distilled whisky'.[4] This pattern of population distribution and the importance of distilling in Urquhart and Fodderty suggest that small-scale peasant production of whisky may have allowed the area to attract in-migrants and thus rapidly recover population levels after the 1690s. The parishes had access to supplies of bere, water and peat and relatively good overland communications along the drove roads that converged from the north and west at Beauly, the site of large cattle fairs, and then continued south. By the early 1790s these four adjoining parishes were all noted as having particularly high levels of distilling – Killearnan had seven stills of thirty gallons, Urquhart had twenty-nine, Urray was 'abounding with licensed stills' and in Fodderty the people were 'much addicted to the use of spirits'. No other parishes in Ross & Cromarty are similarly described in the Old Statistical Account. In the 1790s Highlanders from Lochaber and Skye were reported as travelling to this area to buy their whisky and the minister of Urray commented that settlers in the parish from the west felt themselves to be within reach of 'their relations and the sepulchres of their fathers'.[5]

The second increase in share of population was in the parishes of Cromarty and Avoch, both places that benefited from the development of fishing in the early eighteenth century. In contrast, other parishes with established towns – Rosemarkie, Dingwall and Tain – show either only a marginal increase, or a fall, in their share of population. Moreover, by 1755 the parish of Cromarty, with 2,096 inhabitants, had a substantially larger population than any of these three parishes.

How big was the town of Cromarty?

Detailed hearth tax returns for Cromarty do not survive, only totals for the shire as a whole. It is possible to make an estimate of the population of the town and parish using a number of assumptions. In 1691 there were 353 hearths in the shire of Cromarty and 84 in that part of the parish of Resolis that lay in the shire of Ross, giving a total of 437 hearths for the two parishes of Cromarty and Resolis. If the relative size of the population of the parishes of Cromarty and Resolis were as in the 1755 census (that is, 2,096:1,371) and if the distribution of hearths reflected the distribution of population, then there were some 260 hearths in the parish of Cromarty. If, further, the balance between town and country within the parish of Cromarty was as in the 1790s (that is, 1,457:727) then there were some 170 hearths in Cromarty itself. These are considerable assumptions but the conclusion is supported by an alternative approach.

A survey of feudal superiorities in the town of Cromarty was drawn up in 1744.[6] After the town lost its status as a royal burgh in the 1680s, those who had held property from the burgh claimed, correctly as it turned out, to hold directly from the Crown rather than through the laird as an intermediary. As a result, properties held in feu from the laird generally post-date the demise of the burgh. Of 230 properties in the town in 1744, over 140 were not held from the laird and so were part of the pre-1680s royal burgh. There is some reason to think that the town grew during the 1680s as a result of trade in grain and salt fish – and so 170 hearths in 1691 is not an unreasonable estimate of the burgh's size.

We can now consider what size of population is indicated by the number of hearths. In 1755 the average family size in the barony of New Tarbat was 4.89. If families were the same size in Cromarty in 1691, the population would have been c.830. This figure should be revised upwards to c.900–50, since a hearth consisted of family and servants, and family size may have been higher in the seventeenth century. On the same assumptions of family size as above, and with the same adjustment for servants in households, the population of the town rose to *c.*1285 in 1744. This is generally consonant with the figure of 2,096 for the parish as a whole in Webster's 1755 census.[7]

There are indications from other sources that Cromarty had grown in size relative to other centres of population between 1691 and the mid eighteenth century. Although it had been expunged from the roll of royal burghs, Cromarty was expected to pay *cess* (tax) in 1697, when it was taxed at five shillings. This compared with two shillings for Dingwall, five shillings for Fortrose and seven shillings for Tain. The relative tax burdens of the towns had changed by the mid eighteenth century. The window tax returns for 1758, the nearest assessment to the 1755 census, show that Cromarty paid the highest tax, being assessed on thirty-one taxable houses, while Tain was assessed on twenty-eight, Fortrose on twenty-six and Dingwall on only four.[8]

In the light of these various strands of evidence we can conclude not only that Cromarty had a higher proportion of the population of Ross & Cromarty in 1755 than in 1691, but also that the population increased between these two dates. Wade's plan of the Cromarty Firth made in 1730 shows the town extending from its old centre below the castle towards the storehouse at the Ness. A third substantial

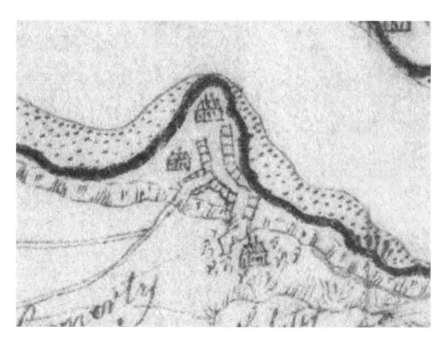

FIGURE 8.2
Cromarty *c.*1730.

building, shown here, may be the house of Sandilands, built by Bernard
Mackenzie c.1700.

Mobility and migration

The old parish registers for Cromarty provide evidence that the growth
of the town was due, in part, to in-migration. There was considerable
under-recording of both births and marriages in the late seventeenth
and early eighteenth centuries. However, the registers show a clear
increase in the number of marriages, and a subsequent increase in the
numbers of births, in the years of prosperity when there were high
exports of salt fish. This is most noticeable between 1714 and 1717.
If the average age of marriage was between twenty and twenty-five,
then few marriages in these years could be of individuals born after the
crisis of the mid 1690s. Instead, we would expect this to be a period
of few marriages, reflecting the high child mortality of 1697–9. Given
the rise in the number of marriages, it seems likely that the increase in
Cromarty's population was partly the result of an in-migration from
other parishes.

The register of marriages provides further evidence to support this.
Persons moving into the parish were more likely to choose marriage
partners from their place of origin and marriages in which one partner
was from another parish were considerably more common before 1721,
when the herring fishing went into decline, than afterwards. In the first
two decades of the century almost 30 per cent of recorded marriages
were to a partner from outwith the parish but this fell to less than 16
per cent in the following decade.

In-migration to the parish is also indicated by the fact that in
the 1740s the Cromarty kirk session was concerned about servants
moving into the parish without a 'certificate' from their own parish.
These certificates gave assurance of their good character and on three
occasions the elders were instructed to inspect certificates in the town
and the country.

Emigration

The Act of Union of 1707 opened up English colonies in North America
to Scots settlers. From then until the outbreak of the American War
of Independence in 1775 most emigrants went to the area that was
to become the United States – the favoured destinations being North
Carolina and Georgia – and between 1735 and 1740 there were
concerted attempts to recruit new settlers, particularly to Georgia,
where warlike Highlanders were seen as a potential barrier to Creek or

Spanish incursions. Emigration then slowed to a trickle between 1741 and 1763.[9]

There are considerable difficulties in quantifying emigration from Cromarty in the early eighteenth century. However, it is clear that individuals, if they considered emigration, were well placed because of Cromarty's position as an embarkation point. In 1735 Captain George Dunbar and Lieutenant Hugh Mackay arrived in Scotland to recruit Highlanders to settle in Georgia. Mackay's instructions were to bring them to Cromarty and in October a group of 177 sailed for Savannah on the *Prince of Wales*. The emigrants were to form a nucleus of Highland settlers in Darien, Georgia. A further group of over forty indentured servants sailed for Georgia in the *Two Brothers* in November 1737. In the same year the *Hope* sailed from Inverness and Cromarty for Carolina with seventy passengers and indentured servants. This vessel was in Cromarty for two weeks before sailing and at least some of the supplies and passengers were taken on there. One man, Alexander Davidson – possibly from Cromarty, since there was someone there of that name – had paid £12 for his passage but was left behind.[10]

It is also clear that the opportunity to emigrate was, in fact, taken up by a number of individuals in Cromarty itself. At least two Cromarty men – Robert Hay and Hugh Anderson – were among the emigrants to Georgia in the 1730s, in 1738 the session clerk emigrated and by the 1740s there were former Cromarty merchants not only in Georgia but also in Carolina, Maryland and Virginia.[11] Later emigrants were able to join a network of established settlers, who retained family connections with the Cromarty area and who assisted the recent arrivals. Britain's role in the Seven Years War (1756–63) also created many overseas trading networks and some of those who served in the armed forces used the opportunity to pursue subsequent commercial ventures throughout the expanded Empire.

There were some unwilling emigrants. Nine individuals from the parish were among those transported as Jacobite rebels after 1746. These were Kenneth Bean, sent to Barbados, three separate Alexander McKenzies sent to Jamaica, and Duncan McKenzie, John McKenzie, Hector McLean, Duncan McLeod and George Hood, the son of Donald Hood and Katherine Hossack, all transported in 1747. There were also some transported criminals, including the wife of John Davidson in Cromarty, convicted of fire-raising in 1750.[12]

Notes

1. A. J. S. Gibson and T. C. Smout, *Prices, Food and Wages in Scotland 1550–1780* (Cambridge, 1995), 166.

2. SRO, GD305/160/38; Hugh Miller, *Scenes and Legends of the North of Scotland* (Edinburgh, 1994), 227.

3. R. E. Tyson, 'Famine in Aberdeenshire, 1696–1699: Anatomy of a Crisis' in D. Stevenson (ed.), *From Lairds to Louns* (Aberdeen, 1986), 45; Michael Flinn, *Scottish Population History* (Cambridge, 1977), 172.

4. Eric Richards and Monica Clough, *Cromartie: Highland Life: 1650–1914* (Aberdeen, 1991), 81.

5. John Sinclair, *Statistical Account of Scotland* (1791–99).

6. NRAS 0204/Bundle 171.

7. This is considerably lower than the 1,400 estimated by Clough as the population of the town in the 1691. See Marinell Ash in *This Noble Harbour* (Edinburgh and Invergordon, 1991), 21 and footnote 5. Clough, however, wrongly takes the 353 hearths to be in the town rather than the shire of Cromarty, while assuming a smaller family size. Richards and Clough, *Cromartie*, 78 give the family size in Tarbat. Family size in Coigach was 5.36 and in Strathpeffer 4.89. Michael Flinn, *Scottish Population History*, 187 notes that 'hearths' included servants.

8. Window tax was levied from 1748. The year 1758 has also been chosen for comparison because at this point Cromarty Castle was uninhabited and its large size does not distort the comparison with other towns. NAS, GD 305/1/164; NAS, E326/1/108.

9. Ian Adams and Meredyth Somerville, *Cargoes of Hope and Despair* (Edinburgh, 1993), 36.

10. Janet Fyfe, 'Cromarty Emigrants and Emigrant Ships' (Cromarty, 1997); Andrew W. Parker, *Scottish Highlanders in Colonial Georgia* (Georgia, 1997), 38–51; William Mackay (ed.), *The Letter Book of Bailie Steuart of Inverness* (Edinburgh, 1915).

11. NAS, CH2/672 13 Nov 1738.

12. Highland Council Archive, INV/HC/1/1; B. G. Seton and J. G. Arnot, *Prisoners of the '45* (Scottish History Society, 1929); A. Livingstone, *The Muster Roll of Prince Charles Edward Stewart's Army 1745–1746* (Aberdeen, 1984).

Part 3
1760s–1843

9

Landownership from *c*.1760

Oh! Is there not some patriot, in whose power
That best, that godly luxury is placed
Of blessing thousands, thousands yet unborn,
Through late prosperity? Some large of soul,
To cheer dejected industry?

James Thomson, *Autumn*

A cottage by the Thames

In 1749 an odd building project was underway in the semi-rural setting of Kew-foot Lane, in Richmond, Surrey, overlooking the Thames. The roof of a simple cottage was removed, the walls heightened, and around this shell a 'capital mansion house' was erected in such a manner that, crossing the threshold and entering the hallway, a visiting gentleman might be told that, although within the refined elegance of a new villa, he stood also inside the original, humble dwelling. An enthusiastic visitor might then be directed to stand on the left of the main door where, in a strange combination of imagination and reality, he would have become a guest in the parlour of the rustic cottage. Perhaps he would also be led to the garden to visit a still simpler structure under the branches of an elm – a wooden bower, furnished with a table and chair, all preserved with equal care and attention. Here, as he paused for a few moments looking towards London, it might have struck him as a time

For those whom wisdom and whom nature charm
To steal themselves from the degenerate crowd,
And soar above this little scene of things;
To tread low-thoughted vice beneath their feet,
To soothe the throbbing passions into peace,
And woo lone quiet in her silent walks.

The construction of this building and the preservation and extension of its grounds was an act of veneration – a tribute, from an ardent admirer, to the memory of the author of these lines, the poet James Thomson, who had died in the previous year. Thomson's wealthy 'fan' – to use a modern term neither would have understood – was George Ross, a rising London merchant, who laid out £9,000 on the project. And although the house would have been appreciated as a pleasing symbol of how commerce, progress, elegance and modernity might remain rooted in nature, it had more particular significances for its owner.

Both Thomson and Ross were migrant Scots – Thomson from the Borders and Ross from Easter Ross. Ross, born in 1708–9, was only nine years younger than the poet. Part of Thomson's appeal was that he presented realistic and detailed descriptions of nature and rural society, particularly the landscape of Scotland seen with some nostalgia from 'exile' in England. But he was also concerned with the need for progress. Thomson did not advocate a return to a primitive, natural life but rather argued for change and development rooted in skilful adaptation to and improvement of nature. Change, as advocated by Thomson, was not to be achieved by sweeping away the old order and imposing a new, but by bringing nature to fruition through skill and endeavour, with science and commerce as essential parts of his vision of progress.

Thomson had been both a close friend of Duncan Forbes of Culloden and an admirer of the Duke of Argyll, and he lauded them in his most popular work *The Seasons* as men who had answered their country's need for 'patriots' to improve agriculture, fisheries, trade and industry. This was a vision which Ross could not only share but, since he had begun his career as confidential clerk to Forbes, he could bask indirectly in the poet's praises. In the *Autumn* section of *The Seasons*, Thomson also provided a potent image of the migration of Scots, like Ross, to London and beyond. Beginning with a description of the gathering of swallows before their flight south, he turns to a panoramic view of storks gathering in the plains at the mouth of the Rhine and then sweeps north in imagination to where the Atlantic surges through the Hebrides and 'boils' around the northern coast of Scotland. From here, where 'nations' of birds come and go, the poet 'sees Caledonia in romantic view', before considering its inhabitants: a 'manly race, of unsubmitting spirit, wise and brave' who, greater than the narrow bounds of their homeland, are 'borne o'er every land' in a migration which brings to new realms their gifts of 'piercing genius' and 'faithful toil'. Thomson turns to the image of a northern sunrise to characterise this migration:

> As from their own clear north in radiant streams
> Bright over Europe bursts the Boreal morn.

This powerful metaphor of the movement of both people and ideas as a Scottish 'enlightenment' must have appealed to Ross, not least because there was an alternative view, commonly held in London. Not everyone admired the Anglo-Scots.

Ross's position is best seen in the light of the careers of similar Scottish merchants based in London in the mid eighteenth century. David Hancock, in his book *Citizens of the World*,[1] studies twenty-three associated London merchants who traded with America between 1735 and 1785, and concludes that this dynamic group shared a number of characteristics. They began their careers in London in mid-life as outsiders, and many, as Scots, were not part of the established merchant and trade structure of the City. Their marginal status encouraged them to look outward and take risks, and they made their fortunes in shipping and trading, in plantations in America and the West Indies, in slaving and, above all, in government contracting. Their wide contacts and logistical skills enabled them to integrate trade on a global basis, something more difficult for established merchants bound by traditional modes of operation. As 'new money' and as 'outsiders' they were a natural focus for envy and resentment.

Their equally natural response was to consolidate their social standing by acquiring villas close to London and larger estates in the English regions or in Scotland. As marks of their status as gentlemen they improved agriculture on these estates, engaged in works of benefit to the community – particularly the encouragement of manufactures, the provision of roads and bridges, and acts of philanthropy – and often ended their careers in public services as MPs. They further manifested their social position by building elegant houses, creating gardens and amassing collections of art. Rosedale House, built around Thomson's cottage, was George Ross's first step on this path.

After Forbes' death in 1747, Ross was patronised by Argyll and by 1754 had gained appointments as the London agent of the Convention of Royal Burghs and the Board of Trustees. He was also a close friend of both General William Amherst, brother of the future Commander-in-Chief of Great Britain, and of the Scottish-born Lord Chief Justice, William Murray, later first Earl of Mansfield. Thus Ross, although a minor figure, was well placed in the web of politics and patronage. His fortunes, like those of other 'citizens of the world', grew with the opportunities presented in the course of the Seven Years War (1756–63), a war fought in Europe, North America, the Caribbean and India.

Ross had worked with Forbes in supplying the Independent Companies in the Highlands in the 1730s and this may have provided him with the skills necessary to set up in London as an 'army agent'. These skills were augmented by his political connections. By contemporary standards, army agents made enormous profits – because the scale on which the war was fought, and its global nature, required skills in procurement, distribution and accounting which only such merchants could provide. By the end of the war Ross was supplying eight regiments. This rose to twenty-one in 1780, comparable with

FIGURE 9.1
Rosedale House, Kewfoot Lane (1749).

the forty-three battalions supplied by Oswald, the richest of the 'associates' studied by Hancock.

It was a common perception that army agents made excess profits and that 'agents, commissaries and contractors ... had fattened ... on the blood of the nation' and some saw government contracting as dominated by a cabal of Scots, Jews and European merchants.[2] Ross continued to act in a manner calculated to establish his status as a gentleman – he bought and improved farms at Kinmylies (Inverness) and near Novar (Ross-shire), acquired the Cromarty estate in 1767 and became MP for Cromarty-shire in 1780. He had come a long way from Kew-foot Lane and set about making Cromarty 'worth an Englishman's while coming all the way from London to see'.[3] His house in Kew-foot Lane remains, as part of the Royal Hospital.

George Ross's development of Cromarty

Ross's title to the estate was not complete until 1772 but he was in effective control from 1767 until his death in 1786. His improvements all exhibited a flair for organisation, bringing together his political contacts, his knowledge of markets in London and the West Indies, his acquaintance with leading architects and engineers, and his insights into improved agriculture in the south of England. Central to his plans was the establishment, in the early 1770s, of a non-mechanised proto-factory, described in chapter 10, which employed 200 to 250 workers in the buildings and over 600 outworkers. The factory used imported Baltic hemp to produce cloth for sacking and bagging, all of which was shipped to London for use in the West Indian trade.

Ross's innovative 'hogyard' was linked with the same overseas trade. Andrew Wight reported in 1781 that it was the only one of its kind he had seen in the course of his extensive survey of husbandry in Scotland.[4] It consisted of a square of buildings and stone walls around a paved central area, 'in a sheltered situation on the shore near the village of Cromarty'. The buildings for breeding sows were on one side, feeding sheds on the opposite side and in the centre spacious buildings for slaughtering, salting and barrelling. The paved area was kept clean by a stream of water.

Pork was cured by salting in barrels and was being shipped from Cromarty from 1777 to both the East and West Indies. There was a crossing of European and Chinese pigs about 1760 by the Leicestershire stockbreeder, Robert Bakewell, which produced the huge pink beasts that were later to be the basis of an expanding trade in pork. Ross's pigs were of an older breed. Wight saw 200 Hampshire hogs, that is, Wessex saddlebacks, in one of Ross's fields, being fattened on potatoes and pease, and also noted that on hot, dry summer days the hogs were driven down to bathe in sea, which was believed to improve the quality of the flesh.

Ross's plan was to encourage the participation of his tenants – the hogyard would breed the pigs, sell them to his tenants for fattening and buy them back at an agreed rate. This was itself an unusual practice. It was more common for a pig breeder to contract out pregnant sows and young feeding pigs to small farmers who supervised farrowing and the rearing of piglets. Ross's system was presumably intended as a means of overcoming the real or perceived lack of local experience and expertise in dealing with breeding sows. Sinclair claimed that Ross's hogyard was unsuccessful because of poor management but the failure in fact resulted from the poor harvest of 1782, with consequent food shortages in 1783.[5]

A third major undertaking was the establishment of a brewery, which was described in 1781 as 'immense' and later as the 'most extensive in the north of Scotland'. There was a sound economic case for this project. Although the quality of ale in Scotland had been improved during the eighteenth century by the use of hops imported from England, in wealthier households a taste had developed for porter – a dark beer

FIGURE 9.2
Cromarty Courthouse (1772). Ross relocated the burgh's mercat cross (1593) to
the front of the new building.

produced from high quality barley. Porter was produced in London and
sold at almost four times the price of Scotch ale. By 1775 the economist
David Loch was urging 'patriotic landowners' throughout Scotland to
establish breweries that would use local grain to produce porter. The
brewery established in Cromarty in the 1770s was set up in accordance
with these views – although it was also, according to the parish minister
and Sir John Sinclair, both writing in the 1790s, intended to discourage
the 'lower ranks' from drinking spirits. However, it relied mainly
on shipping its beers to Inverness – only a negligible quantity was
consumed locally – and operated below its capacity for production.[6]

Ross also secured government funds for the construction of a
harbour (1782–4), designed by the leading civil engineer John Smeaton;
established a nail and spade works; built a courthouse (1772–3) for
the county of Cromarty, partly at his own expense and partly with
government support; built houses for the poor; and, unusually for the
time, erected a church (1783) specifically for Gaelic speakers who had

come from the neighbouring parishes to seek employment in the town. In many of these ventures, Ross worked closely with the leading local merchant, William Forsyth (1719–1800), whose activities have been described in chapter 6.

Ross approached the redesign and improvement of the private grounds of the estate on a grand scale. He demolished the partially ruined Cromarty castle, built an elegant mansion in its place (1772–4) and carried out extensive landscaping of the surrounding policies, replanting Cromarty Hill with hardwoods and reclaiming moorland at a cost of £50,000. He had commissioned plans from the architect John Adam for a new parish church in Cromarty and, while this was not built, it has been suggested that Adam may have had some influence in the building of Cromarty House.

The house has an unusual tunnel below the gardens, a 'tradesman's entrance' through which deliveries might be made to the kitchens. Ross used this device and the topography of his estate to address a 'problem' common to many landowners – how to create landscaped policies for a mansion house in close proximity to a town. Since the town lay between the sea and the bank of the raised beach, with Cromarty House above the bank, the town, although it was within a few hundred metres of the house, was largely hidden from view. The principal public rooms of the house faced north, with a flight of steps leading down from the dining room. From these steps one looked out to the Cromarty Firth, wood and farmland, and to the only other structures above the bank – the Gaelic Chapel and the ruins of the fourteenth-century chapel of St Regulus. The tunnel, running directly below the sight line to St Regulus, created an access to the house while leaving this prospect uninterrupted. From the main entrance to the house, on the south, the view was across a small, artificial lake to the classical façade of a new stable block. Beyond this were the newly built Mains farm and the landscaped woodland of Cromarty Hill, among which was a 'little temple covered with cockle shells ... reared on a solitary corner of the hill'.[7]

Ross also began to remodel the town itself. He acquired all of the properties on the burgh's original high street at the eastern extremity of the burgh – the town having expanded to the west, towards the harbour, leaving its early centre, with the mercat cross and tollbooth, isolated from the main commercial and residential streets. The owners were given new feus in better locations, the buildings of the 'old town' were used for estate employees, and the mercat cross was moved to the front of Ross's imposing new courthouse. Ross's grants of new feus and the injection of money into the local economy led to the building of new houses and the rebuilding of old ones. In the words of Andrew Wight, writing of his visit in 1781, 'houses are every day a-building and neatness and cleanness are studied'.[8]

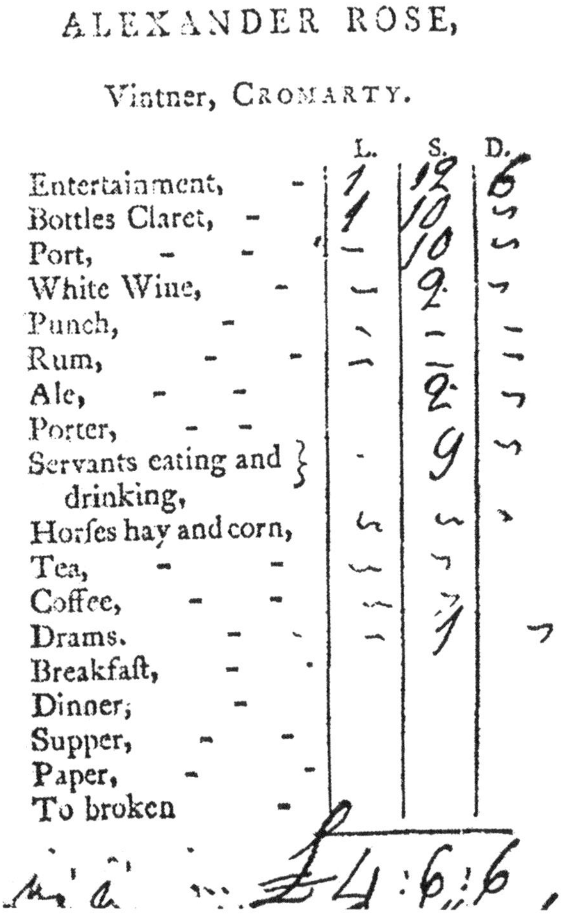
ALEXANDER ROSE,

Vintner, CROMARTY.

	L.	S.	D.
Entertainment,	1	12	6
Bottles Claret,	1	10	–
Port,	–	10	–
White Wine,	–	9	–
Punch,	–	–	–
Rum,	–	–	–
Ale,		2	–
Porter,			
Servants eating and drinking,	-	9	–
Horses hay and corn,	–	–	–
Tea,	–	–	
Coffee,	–	–	
Drams.	–	1	–
Breakfast,			
Dinner;			
Supper,			
Paper,			
To broken			
	£4	6	6

FIGURE 9.3
A bill for accommodation, food and drink in Cromarty, 1780 – a sign of more money circulating in the town.

In the absence of any personal papers it is difficult to form an impression of Ross's character. The management of his estate was generally benevolent, with no eviction of tenants and several acts of generosity, including building houses for the poor and erecting the Gaelic Chapel. On his Inverness estate of Kinmylies he had been similarly sensitive to local opinion and left the popular open ground of Tomnahurich uncultivated for the public to enjoy. Hugh Miller refers to a portrait of Ross and the 'air of dignified benevolence impressed on the features of the handsome old man'. This portrait, perhaps painted by David Martin, hung in Cromarty House with portraits of both Forbes of

Culloden and Lord Mansfield. Ross's dignity appeared to others to be excessive. The *Times* columnist Junius – who was fiercely critical of the Lord Chief Justice, Lord Mansfield's, alleged favouritism towards fellow Scots – wrote of Ross's role in one particular case of backroom dealing, remarking that '... no sale by the candle was ever conducted with greater formality'.

Ross had married in 1738 but his wife, Rachel Kellow, died four years later and his only son, John, pre-deceased Ross *c.*1775 – reputedly by committing suicide, in Cromarty House, following a quarrel with his father over the correct way to carve a joint of meat. Ross had apparently remarked that 'little men cannot afford to neglect little matters', whereon the son left the room and shot himself.[9] When Ross himself died in 1786, a few days after having been elected MP for the northern burghs, the estate passed to his half-nephew, Alexander Gray.

Other estates

Ardoch/Poyntzfield

Adam Gordon inherited Ardoch in 1757 and appears to have substantially rebuilt the mansion house and then sold the estate in 1761 to George Gun Munro (d.1785), the prosperous son of a Caithness minister. The details of Munro's early career are not known but, like George Ross, he was involved in military procurement and, by 1761, he was Commissary of Stores for North Britain and received a knighthood in 1779. He had earlier married a wealthy widow, Mary Poyntz of London, whose fortune was at least in part based on slave plantations in Jamaica. In her honour he renamed the estate Poyntzfield and, according to a parish minister, was 'the first in this part of the country who began improvements in agriculture on a large scale'.[10]

He was succeeded in 1785 by his nephew George Gun Munro II (d.1806), who was then a London insurance broker but subsequently devoted his energies to improvements on the Poyntzfield estate. He provided much of the information for Sir John Sinclair's *Report on the state of agriculture in the northern counties of Scotland* published in 1795. He in turn was succeeded by his brother, Innes Gun Munro (d.1827), who published *A System of Farm Book-keeping based on Actual Practice* in 1821 and established the model estate village of Jemimaville *c.*1820.

Newhall and Braelangwell

Newhall passed to William Gordon in 1772 and was improved by him until his death in 1778. Gordon was educated in Edinburgh and admitted to the Faculty of Advocates in 1768. From an early age he was a friend of the author Henry Mackenzie, who later helped to found the Royal Society of Edinburgh in 1783 and the Highland and Agricultural Society in 1784. Gordon's approach to estate management is indicative of the way in which a practical – and a literally 'hands-on' – involvement in improvement was now considered suitable for a gentleman. In 1778 Mackenzie visited Newhall and reported on Gordon's improvement in the fashionable periodical *The Mirror*. Gordon's letters from Newhall to friends in Edinburgh requested both works of literature and books on agriculture and gardening and he arranged for acknowledged experts to visit him to give advice.[11]

Gordon's improvements were continued by his sister Henrietta, with both her first husband Charles Lockhart (d.1786) and her second husband David Urquhart of Braelangwell (d.1811) who she married in 1787. From this second marriage until her death in 1799 the adjoining estates of Newhall and Braelangwell were managed, and improved, as one. The Newhall estate was then acquired by the trustees of Colin Mackenzie, whose nephew Donald carried out a number of improvements, including the rebuilding of Newhall House. The estate was entailed in 1815 and this was followed by a series of complex legal cases over the liability for payment for the earlier improvements.

David Urquhart of Braelangwell was noted for his 'classical knowledge, philanthropy and engaging manners (which) endeared him to all who knew him'.[12] He died in 1811 and neither of his two sons, by different wives, involved themselves with the estate. Charles was an enthusiast for Greek culture and died fighting in the Greek wars of Independence in 1828; David, a Turko-phile who introduced Turkish baths to Britain, served as an MP for Stafford, interested himself in international affairs and died in Naples in 1877.

Notes

1. David Hancock, *Citizens of the World: London Merchants and the Integration of the British Atlantic Community, 1735–1785* (Cambridge, 1995). For sources for George Ross see my article in the new Dictionary of National Biography.
2. David Hancock, *Citizens of the World*, 221–38. The quotation is from the character Matthew Bramble in Tobias Smollett's *The Expedition of Humphrey Clinker* (1771) referred to by Hancock on page 238.
3. Attributed to George Ross by Hugh Miller in *Scenes and Legends of the North of Scotland* (Edinburgh, 1994), 451.
4. Andrew Wight, *Present State of Husbandry in Scotland* (Edinburgh, 1778–84), iii. 257.
5. NAS, E504; Andrew Wight, *State of Husbandry*, iii. 254 & iv. 730; John Sinclair, *A General view of the agriculture of the northern counties and islands of Scotland* (London, 1795), 63; personal communication from David Soutar, architect, Aberdeen.

6. Andrew Wight, *State of Husbandry*, iii. 253; J. M. Wilson, *Imperial Gazetteer of Scotland* (1853), 321; David Loch, *Essays on the trade, commerce, manufactures and fisheries of Scotland* (Edinburgh, 1775); OSA, *Parish of Cromarty*; John Sinclair, *General view … northern counties*, 65.

7. Hugh Miller, *Scenes and Legends*, 432.

8. Andrew Wight, *State of Husbandry*, iv. 730.

9. Hugh Miller, *Scenes and Legends*, 437.

10. NAS, RH15/44/202, Minute of sale of the estate of Ardoch, 29 June 1761; NAS, GD347/73, Letter from George Gun Munro of Poyntzfield, referring to Lady Munro's next of kin. See also Yseult Hughes, 'What Poyntzfield restoration is revealing' in *Clan Munro Magazine* 19 (1991), 7–12. OSA, *Parish of Kirkmichael and Cullicudden*.

11. NAS, RH15/44/54–55.

12. OSA, *Parish of Kirkmichael and Cullicudden*, 540.

Textiles: 1747–1850s

How by the finest art the native robe
To weave; how, white as hyperborean snow,
To form the lucid lawn.

James Thomson, *Autumn*

Even for those who know Cromarty well, there is a renewed sense of surprise in noting that beside the town's harbour stands an important part of Britain's industrial heritage, unparalleled elsewhere in the country. The three surviving ranges of the Cromarty hemp works, built in the 1770s, were part of a large textile proto-factory – that is, a non-mechanised centre for spinning and weaving. Proto-factories, which brought workers together in a regulated and ordered working environment, were an important stage in the industrial revolution, usually obscured by the subsequent importance of mechanised production. Cromarty's 'manufactory', as it was called, was among the largest in the country and, because it was never mechanised, it is a unique survival making visible this phase of industrial development.

The development of textile production in Cromarty was the achievement of the Cromarty merchant William Forsyth (1719–1800) and of the laird, George Ross (1708/9–86), beginning with the promotion of linen-yarn spinning and leading to the building of the large proto-factory for the production of hemp cloth for sacking and bagging.

Textiles: the 1720s onwards

The growth of the town before 1720 and the absence of any major change in agriculture both helped to retain local population, which would become a potential labour force for textile manufacturing. Moreover, Cromarty's thriving economy in the first two decades of the century, which ran against the trend of the Scottish economy as a whole, had attracted merchants from other parts of the Moray Firth. These included the Forsyth family, from Elgin, who would be central to this development.

In the 1720s steps were taken to promote growth in the Scottish economy, including the establishment in 1727 of the Board of Trustees for Improving Fisheries and Manufactures. The most important subsequent development was the expansion of flax spinning and linen weaving, particularly, after the 1740s, in the production of the coarser fabrics known as 'osnaburgs'. In the 1730s and 1740s female hand-spinners were being recruited beyond the traditional textile-working areas of the central belt and the north east, and there was also a slow increase in the numbers of weavers, sometimes working in small weaving sheds rather than at home. The principal changes in the north came after 1747 when the British Linen Company (BLC), in response to a buoyant market and rising costs in the traditional areas of linen production, turned to the Highlands to satisfy their requirement for a cheap and dependable supply of yarn. The Company judged that they could tap a pool of female labour in the Highlands and that the area's remoteness and the absence of alternative employment would ensure both their requirements of cheapness and dependability. The Company also wanted relatively unskilled spinners, since those around Edinburgh were oriented to spinning a finer yarn than was required to satisfy the demand for coarse linen. The BLC believed that the benefits of employing spinners in peripheral areas would outweigh the additional costs of transport.

There was also a political motivation in promoting the spinning of linen yarn. It was believed that the introduction of manufactures would be a means of integrating the Highlands with the economic, political and social systems of the rest of Britain. The BLC was supported in its pursuit of this objective by both the Board of Trustees and the commissioners administering the annexed estates of the principal Jacobite families who had supported the 1745 rising.[1]

Flax spinning in Cromarty: 1747–c.76

The first move to establish large-scale flax spinning in the north came in 1746 from Lord Morton in Orkney who proposed that spinning be promoted in order to employ the poor on his lands 'in useful manufacture'. Shortly afterwards, on 18 June 1747, Captain Urquhart of Cromarty confirmed that a Duncan Henderson had everything ready for spinning and heckling in Cromarty. The BLC agreed to pay 8d per spindle and 1d commission, and Urquhart sought support from the Board of Trustees for the appointment of a spinning mistress, to teach potential spinners. Since there were problems with the cost of importing flax in small quantities, Urquhart proposed growing flax on his own estate, using imported Riga seed. The BLC confirmed that Urquhart's land was suitable and he sought support from the Board of Trustees for the establishment of a 'lint boor' – an expert in flax growing – who would oversee the raising of flax, and by the end of the year he had made a proposal to erect a lint mill.[2]

Urquhart's enterprise foundered, principally because as a Roman Catholic he was regarded with suspicion by much of the local population. In November 1749 the BLC made a new start by entering into a contract with the Cromarty merchant William Forsyth and supplying him with imported flax. Unlike Urquhart, Forsyth was well regarded in Cromarty, his father having established himself in business there in 1717. Forsyth, moreover, had been trained in accounting and business practice in London before returning to Cromarty on his father's death. The contract offered by the BLC was ideally suited to someone of Forsyth's capabilities and training, for the Company's master spinners, such as Forsyth, were not employees but agents to whom flax was sold, with an agreement to take all the yarn spun, provided it was to sufficient standard. This system both encouraged the agents to control the quality and allowed them some entrepreneurial activity by having some of the yarn woven on their own account. Forsyth, in contrast to Urquhart, made remarkable progress in both spinning and weaving. By November 1749 his spinners had produced 8,000 spindles, 1,208 of which had been whitened and set up for weaving locally, rather than being sent to Edinburgh.[3]

Forsyth was at first simply one merchant among many. In Cromarty, the BLC had also entered into a contract with Robert Gordon and Andrew Lindsay and, in Tain, with a John Reid – but Forsyth quickly rose to become the Company's principal agent in the north mainland and by 1752 he had gained control over the distribution of flax to other agents. Until this point most of the flax that arrived in Cromarty was shipped for delivery to Gilbert Barkly, usually in cargoes of around fifty tons. However, Barkly ran into increasing financial difficulties and fell foul of the BLC over his use of a consignment of Swedish iron, which had arrived in June 1751. By October 1752 he was instructed by the BLC to deliver all the flax and iron in his warehouse to William Forsyth or, alternately, to deliver the key and arrange for the BLC to rent the warehouse. He was also to transfer his one-third share in the ship *Adventure* to the BLC.

In the same year, despite the levels of production already attained, Forsyth petitioned for funding to establish a spinning school in Cromarty. Forsyth's trade continued on much the same basis during the rest of the 1750s and 1760s. He took over Gordon's business on Gordon's retirement in 1765 and entered into a further three-year

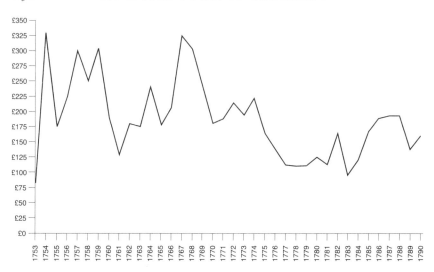

FIGURE 10.1   Value (£ sterling) of linen cloth stamped in Cromarty.

contract with the BLC in 1766. In 1767 he acquired his own ship, the *Elizabeth*, negotiated to import flax and spin yarn on his own account, and by 1772 the value of his imports of flax had risen to £1,300. While the ending of a contractual relationship with the BLC meant that they were no longer obligated to purchase Forsyth's yarns, they continued to do so ad hoc.[4]

Forsyth also continued to have yarn woven locally into cloth but he was unsuccessful in bringing about any significant growth in this sector and the value of the cloth woven in Cromarty rarely amounted to more than £300 (see Figure 10.1). From about 1772 he became involved in the development of the hemp manufactory.

The pool of labour

The promotion of flax spinning in the north had been based on the judgement that there was an available pool of cheap, largely female, labour – generally an important feature of early industrialisation in Scotland. This was particularly so on the fertile lands of Easter Ross and the Black Isle which had retained a high rural population and had the added advantage of being close to the ports through which flax might be imported and finished yarn sent to Edinburgh. The relative economic benefit to the BLC of employing spinners in the north is shown by the fact that in 1749 yarn was spun at Cromarty for 8d a spindle, while in Dundee the cost was 14d.[5]

However, the image of a labour 'pool', to which the manufacturer had only to connect, is misleading. Flax spinning was monotonous and the BLC quickly became aware that in years of good harvest production fell because the spinners were under less economic compulsion to submit to the drudgery of spinning. Moreover, production on the scale required by the BLC required the use of spinning wheels rather than the distaff and this marked a break with a traditional way of life. The distaff was used while going about other tasks; the spinning wheel tied women to the house and made them unavailable for farm work. It was by no means clear to those faced with the 'opportunity' that the change would be economically justified, especially given the low rates of pay – and even if justified it was a sacrifice of a more social lifestyle for one bound to the house. Indeed, the BLC's only similar scheme in the south of Scotland, at Leadhills, foundered because spinners were not willing to work at the rates offered.[6]

There were, not surprisingly, initial difficulties for the BLC in Cromarty and Tain, where only two women came forward.[7] Moreover, the need to train spinners meant that the development of flax spinning was dependent, like many developments in the Scottish economy, on the introduction of at least some skilled labour from elsewhere. In Cromarty this compounded the difficulty of attracting spinners because Urquhart, as a Roman Catholic, was perceived to have brought in 'a considerable number of strangers, craftsmen, servants and other new inhabitants … whose religion was not known or were known to be Papists'.[8] This was coupled with concerns about the moral standards of the incomers. Urquhart's master weaver, Henderson, died in 1748 and one of the weavers, Andrew Spalding, set himself up in his place. Shortly afterwards, Henderson's widow – the spinning mistress, Ann Campbell – became pregnant by Spalding, who lived in the same house. The two refused to appear before the kirk session and left the town.[9] There was a similar adverse reaction to strangers in Inverness in 1765 when a clerk, heckler, weaver and spinning mistress were brought from London to establish the hemp manufactory – one of the men, Thomas Burrel, was dismissed after accusations of 'debauching the women servants' and setting a bad example by his 'turbulent and incorrigible temper and disposition'. And when George Ross introduced lace-makers to Cromarty from Buckinghamshire in the 1770s they were regarded with suspicion because of their habit of drinking gin.[10]

Nevertheless, within weeks the BLC noted that spinners were now 'offering themselves' and by the end of the year the problem in Cromarty had been eased by pressure from the kirk session. Noting 'that now there is a workhouse set up in the town whereby any woman that can work can make her bread', they resolved to revise the poor list and remove all those 'capable of such business'. This action would have had an effect on the poorest members of the population but it

FIGURE 10.2
Linen stamp of William Forsyth, 1750s.

is unlikely, in itself, to have ensured an adequate supply of spinners. In contrast, when Forsyth became involved he not only had 8,000 spindles of yarn produced under his direction in 1749 but these were described to the Board of Trustees as 'fit for Edinburghs' – that is, of a higher quality than required for coarse osnaburgs. He would have required the equivalent of seventy-five full-time spinners to reach his level of production, allowing an average of three spindles of yarn per spinner each week for thirty-five weeks a year.[11] Forsyth's achievement can be attributed to his personal standing in the local community. This was enhanced both by his leading role in championing the rights of the congregation against the laird's claim to the right of patronage and by his moral qualities as perceived by a community under the influence of an evangelical revival.

The labour force grew and six years later, in less than one month between 19 November and 13 December 1755, 3,088 spindles of yarn were produced for Forsyth. The introduction of spinning wheels was reckoned to more than double a spinner's output but even at four times the earlier average of one and a half spindles per week, this level of production would have required over 500 spinners. Forsyth's competitor in Cromarty, Robert Gordon, was operating on a smaller, but still significant, scale – producing 6,000 spindles in one period of 1756, against Forsyth's 8,000 spindles for the same period.[12]

Forsyth was also successful in engaging weavers and encouraging them to produce to a high standard and, despite warnings from the BLC, Forsyth pursued his attempts to produce goods of higher quality. In 1750 he took a seven-year tack of part of the Cromarty links for use as a bleachfield and in February 1754 he sent his first twenty-four pieces of fine linen to the BLC, who complimented him on the quality, finding them good enough for home consumption but advising that they could receive no more. Forsyth stubbornly supplied another twenty pieces in April.[13]

Migrant labour

By the mid-1750s the pool of available – and willing – local labour had been utilised and Forsyth sought, unsuccessfully, to expand by establishing a linen manufactory at New Tarbat, on the north shore of the Cromarty Firth. This location was chosen because the site was on the annexed estates of the Earl of Cromartie and was therefore more clearly eligible for support by the Commissioners of the Annexed Estates. Forsyth proposed to train 'boys and girls from the Highlands' – referring to the true Highlands which adjoined the fertile east coast. In 1743 the Presbytery of Chanonry had already noted that there were many beggars from this area within their bounds and such destitute Highlanders were later to form the core of the labour force for the Inverness proto-factory.[14]

Over a nine-year period Forsyth planned to train, each year, 100 girls in spinning (each taking two weeks to train) and three boys in heckling, one boy in boiling, bleaching and sorting yarn, and twenty boys and girls in weaving. The twenty-four apprentices (in heckling, boiling and weaving) would be bound for three years, accommodated in the building, clothed in uniforms of woollen cloth and linens, and taught English. A master heckler, master weaver, spinning mistress and schoolmaster would be employed and over the nine-year period a total 900 spinners and 192 apprentices would be trained. The plan was first submitted in 1756 and again in 1764, receiving favourable consideration at first but being rejected on both occasions.[15] Although Forsyth's plans for New Tarbat were unrealised, it was the same labour force of displaced Highlanders that justified the subsequent development of proto-factories.

Proto-factories and hemp-working

The proto-factories built in Inverness and Cromarty in the 1760s and 1770s were on a similar scale to the mills appearing in what were to be the key industrialised areas of Britain – and were considerably larger than the weaving-sheds that were already established in many towns. The Cromarty proto-factory can be best understood by comparison with the slightly earlier manufactory in Inverness, established in 1765 by two local merchants, Provost Phineas Mackintosh and Alexander Shaw, in partnership with George Dyer and John Sayce of London. The

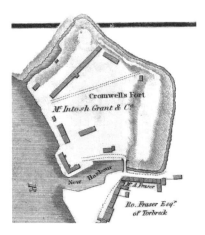

FIGURE 10.3
Inverness Hemp Manufactory (1765) within the embankments of the
Cromwellian Fort at Inverness.

partnership took a ninety-five year lease of a site known as 'Oliver's Fort' – the 'citadel' or fortification built on the banks of the Ness by Cromwell's troops, which by the mid eighteenth century had been pillaged for stone and reduced to 'raised mounds of earth'. Here they set about constructing 'warehouses and workhouses' and proposed to erect a beating mill, heckling house, boiling house and a 'spinning shade [shed]' 400 yards long.[16]

The manufactory used imported Baltic hemp to produce coarse sackcloth for bagging goods traded between London and the West Indies. Since the West Indies remained the principal source of cotton for Britain until 1804–6, demand was high. In 1802 fourteen different kinds of cloth were produced (cotton bagging, wool bagging, biscuit bagging, tarpaulin cloth and ten different kinds of sacking), with demand for each kind varying from year to year.[17]

Sacking required little skill in production and the substantial investment in buildings could thus be economically justified by making effective use of the cheap labour of unskilled 'poor people who had no means of acquiring knowledge in the finer branch of textiles'. A number of visitors noted the consequent composition of the workforce, particularly the employment of destitute young people. For example, in 1768 the factor on the annexed estate of Lovat commented that it would, if continued, 'employ a number of little Creatures, now Begging and Starving'. The employment of the destitute, especially the young, was not only economically advantageous but also socially desirable and Lord Kames commended the manufactory in 1765 as having in this respect 'more utility than any other branch of manufacture in Scotland'.[18]

There was also some technological innovation. The wheels, reels, heckles and looms were 'of different construction from any hitherto used in the country'.[19] This may relate to the function of the long spinning sheds, which were described, in 1768, as being used for 'spinning in the Montrose manner'. Pennant observed this system in Montrose the following year: 'The thread for this cloth is spun here, not by the common wheel, but the hands. Women are employed, who have the flax placed round their wastes [sic], twist a thread with each hand as they receded from a wheel, turned by a boy at the end of a great room.'[20]

The Cromarty manufactory was established by 1772 under the management of William Forsyth, following the acquisition of the Cromarty estate by George Ross in 1767. Ross set up the Cromarty Manufacturing Company, which issued shares at £250 taken up by a number of local landowners. After Ross's death in 1786 the manufactory passed into the control of a London-based company, Dyer and Emmet, who established a third proto-factory on a one-acre

CROMARTY.

FIGURE 10.4
Cromarty from the west, 1799 (Jean-Claude Nattes) showing the hemp
manufactory and harbour.

site at Invergordon before 1811. This operated only until the 1830s. The buildings of the Cromarty manufactory were of stone – more substantial than the wooden spinning sheds in Inverness – and cost over £3,000. There were four ranges, each about eighty yards long, allowing them to be used as spinning walks. In this respect it was similar to the Inverness manufactory and the overall length of the walks, 400 yards, was the same. This was large enough for rope-making to be introduced in Cromarty in 1805.[21]

A substantial number of those employed in the Cromarty manufactory were not residents of the town but Gaelic-speaking Highlanders, who 'on the breaking up of the feudal system ... began to drop into the place in search of employment'.[22] The influx of Gaelic speakers was sufficiently large to warrant the erection of a church for services in Gaelic.

By 1802 the Inverness factory was importing an annual total of 200 tons of hemp and tow and was producing 6,000 pieces of cloth, each 52 yards in length – that is, something in the region of 1,000 yards of cloth per day.[23] Imports of raw material to Cromarty were similar and, like Inverness, the Cromarty factory was capable of producing a daily 1,000 yards. The Inverness labour force, in 1802, consisted of 70 hecklers, 40 yarn dressers, 140 weavers, 50 'pirn boys' and 80 spinners – a total of 380. There were also 1,000 spinners working in their own homes.[24] In the same year the Cromarty manufactory was described as 'nearly equal in all respects' of employment and production to that at Inverness. This suggests some increase in its labour force since 1781 when Wight noted that there were 250 employed 'within the walls' and never less than 600 outworkers.[25]

The economics of the proto-factories

From the 1740s, the BLC had correctly identified the potential of cheap Highland labour for linen spinning. They made use of this for commercial reasons but relied heavily on government subsidies, justified by the state's political objectives of integrating the Highlands with the rest of Britain. The subsequent development of the proto-factories was, in contrast, the initiative of landowners, local entrepreneurs and their London-based partners – and was more clearly justified in commercial terms since it received no state support.

The proto-factories combined technological innovation – the introduction of spinning walks, which were sufficiently important to dictate the design of the buildings – with organisational change. They moved textile manufacture from a system based entirely on 'putting out' to a system more like a production line. The new system had the advantage of being integrated with the old, rather than sweeping it away – and, indeed, in some ways the new system increased the opportunities for 'putting out' in the immediate vicinity of the factory. Home spinners, whose standards had been set in Cromarty by Forsyth during the previous two decades, still numbered some 600 but were now augmented by supervised spinners in the spinning walks. Some processes, such as starching, boiling and dressing of yarn, were centralised in the factory, while others, such as bobbin-winding, were still put out.[26] Home-based weavers were also still active, with perhaps a distinction between established skilled weavers at home and lower skilled and supervised factory weavers.

By centralising some procedures, the proto-factory reduced the time involved in production of cloth and, since production was quicker, less capital was tied up in proportion to output. The achievements of this integrated system can be seen in the following comparison. Between 1750 and 1770, the BLC had imported annually approximately 150 tons of flax for working in the north and they had required several thousand spinners in order to produce yarn, which then had to be woven in Edinburgh.[27] The Cromarty hemp factory imported approximately 100 tons annually and both spun and wove this with a work force of only 850. Unfortunately an accurate series of figures for the output of the Cromarty manufactory survives only for 1819–22, a period when bagging was included in the accounts of linen cloth stamped in Scotland. The value of output in these four years varied between £13,462 and £20,496 and a single reference c.1808 valued the output at £25,000.[28]

The development of proto-factories in the north may be regarded as an early example, albeit a minor one, of the higher speed of industrialisation which is a feature of economically backward economies – as seen in 'late starter' economies in continental Europe and the United States in the nineteenth century. These used imported technology and expertise – and operated on a large scale from the beginning rather than building up from small enterprises.[29] The hemp manufactories, although not mechanised, made use of contemporary expertise to make efficient use of cheap labour, employed on a large scale – and they were, at the time, as much to the fore in revolutionising the organisation of production as those promoting technological change.

Proto-factories, agriculture and population

Although the proto-factories provided men, women and children with work, they did not make use of the productive capacity of families working together as a unit. Dyer and Emmet, who assumed control of the Cromarty factory in the late eighteenth century, also began working hemp in Abingdon, Berkshire where they achieved a higher rate of production. The difference lay in the fact that, in Abingdon, home-based weavers were given out a fixed weight of hemp on which the whole family worked and returned an agreed number of yards of a specified kind of cloth. In contrast, the Cromarty weaver 'received yarn, woof and warp' and wove it in the factory 'without family aid'.[30] Indeed, the proto-factories had been developed precisely in order to make use of the labour of those whose family structure had, in some measure, broken down.

The proto-factories may have created some upward pressure on agricultural wages and Sir John Sinclair noted in 1795 that farm servants were beginning to act in imitation of the 'Cromarty manufacturers and the bold fishermen of Avoch' in purchasing 'more gay attire'. He warned that farm servants might be 'rendered more scarce' and wages might rise. However, Sinclair also noted that the Cromarty and Inverness factories assisted in the settling of mailers on marginal ground, by providing the women and children in the family with a means of enhancing the family income. Thus, while traditional farm servants might expect higher wages, the settling of mailers brought new ground into cultivation and provided a source of more flexible, seasonal farm labour, particularly at harvest. The presence of manufactures was thus aiding in-migration, augmenting rather than decreasing the labour supply in agriculture, and allowing estates to continue with their policies of settling mailers and increasing the area of land under cultivation. This contrasted with the county of Moray where, by 1813, improved agriculture had developed more rapidly and there were fewer manufactures. As a result the area was experiencing a shortage of farm labour and depended on migrant workers from the Highlands of Inverness-shire and from north of the Moray Firth.[31]

Decline and attempts to mechanise

The Cromarty and Inverness manufactories were both at the peak of their production during and immediately after the Napoleonic Wars. Both added rope-making to their output and, at least in Inverness, sailcloth was also produced. In Inverness, employment, including outworkers, had grown to 1,500 by 1804 and by 1818 there was a second manufactory in the town. There was also continued flax-working and, possibly from the 1760s and certainly from the 1770s, a thriving but relatively short-lived manufacture of linen thread centred on Banff and Inverness. In Banff flax was put out to around 4,000 spinners and, from the Inverness enterprise, to 10,000. This, however, declined rapidly from c.1810 – as did employment in the proto-factories over the following two decades.[32]

In 1844 the Commission on the Operation of the Poor Laws reported that there were sixty men and thirty women employed in the

Timothy Pont's map of Tarbat Ness, c.1590
(for detail of Cromarty see p. 22) shows
the old burgh located below the castle
(National Library of Scotland).

1825.

T

W

CROMARTY

TOWN No 1

Opposite. David Aitken's estate plan of 1764 shows the town after its expansion to the west in the early 1700s (Cromarty estate)

Above. John Douglas's estate plan of 1823 shows the town at the height of its growth and the mansion house replacing the castle (Cromarty estate)

Opposite. John Douglas's plan of the town, 1823 (Cromarty estate)

Top. Jean-Claude Nattes visited Cromarty in 1799 and sketched four scenes, two of which were later published – Cromarty from the West (p. 163) and Cromarty Harbour (above). Nattes accurately recorded the landscape but the boats, ships and figures in these prints are all added later. The sentry box on the pier is part of the original sketch.

Above. William Daniell visited Cromarty in 1821 and produced two oil paintings of Cromarty, which differ only in detail. Like Nattes' prints, the boats and ships which throng the firth are works of imagination.

Top. William Daniell also published a print of Cromarty, seen from behind the Courthouse, in *A Voyage Round Great Britain* (Vol. V, 1821)

Above. John Heaviside Clark (1770–1863), known as 'Waterloo Clark' after the sketches he made immediately following the battle, was a prolific engraver and book illustrator. In the 1820s he produced views of a number of Scottish towns, including Cromarty, Dingwall and Tain, in response to the growing opportunities for travel and tourism.

The artist John Muirhead (1863–1927), a friend of Lydia Davidson (granddaughter of Hugh Miller), visited Cromarty in 1884. He produced a number of paintings including views of harvest at Rose Farm, the fishertown, the harbour and, above, 'Hugh Miller's Grammar School'. Miller's school is the cottage in the left foreground, with the new school (1874), with its tower, in the centre of the picture. (Henry and Marian McKenzie Johnston)

Top. In April 1900, Valentines of Dundee visited Cromarty and took photographs. A number were reproduced as postcards and in John Bain's *Cromarty and District* guide. 'In the Fishertown' – a view of Gordon's Lane – was reprinted many times.

Above. Cromarty's *Official Guide*, produced by the Town Council in 1934, used a line drawing of the same view – keeping the creels but removing most of the people

Top left. Sir Kenneth Mackenzie of Cromarty (c.1658–1728) had himself portrayed as a warrior. Fragments of a panel (1702) with the arms of Sir Kenneth and his wife, Anne Campbell, survive in the parish church. John Urquhart, of Craigston and Cromarty (opposite), also appears in military garb.

Top right. Captain John Urquhart of Cromarty (1696–1756)

Above left. George Ross of Pitkerrie and Cromarty (1708/9–1786) was a lawyer and army agent – a sophisticated business man supplying arms, not wielding them

Above right. Catharine Munro Ross of Cromarty, a descendant of George Ross's sister, inherited the Cromarty estate in the late 1840s after a lengthy legal dispute . . .

Top left. . . . and her husband, Hugh Rose, took the name Hugh Rose Ross of Cromarty. He had made his money in the Caribbean, in military contracts, plantations and slavery.

Top right. Walter Charteris Ross (1857–1928) was a professional soldier but his portrait instead reflects the vogue for tartan and the romanticism of the Highlands.

Above left. John Watson, fisherman, painted c.1904 by George Paterson

Above right. Fisherwoman photographed c.1908

Top. John Laing built his house on the burgh's old high street (Causeway) *c*.1700

Above. John Feddes, who had reputedly made money as a buccaneer, built Miller Cottage *c*.1700; and his descendant Hugh Miller (senior), a sea captain, built one of the first new, Georgian-style houses in the town in 1795.

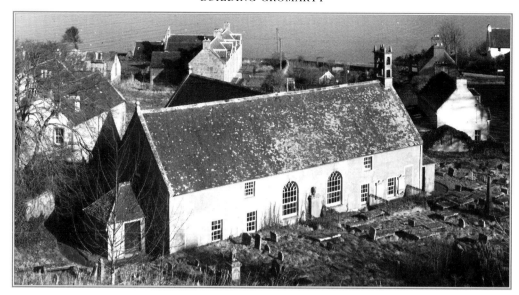

Top. The parish church was enlarged in 1739, with the addition of a new aisle to the north

Above. Initials of pew holders in the front gallery of the north aisle – Thomas Harper and Ann McCulloch, William Elder and Janet McGlashan, Robert Ross and ?

Right. Initials on the old front of the west gallery, obscured when the gallery was extended in the 1750s

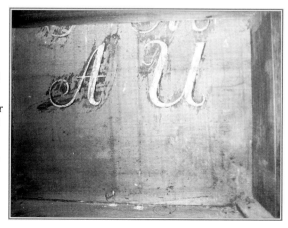

Top. George Ross demolished Cromarty castle and built his mansion house on the site in 1772

Above. In the same year, William Forsyth built his house, set in its own grounds in the town

Top. The houses of Big Vennel (shown here in 1900) were probably built in the 1770s and '80s

Above. George Ross's brewery (1770s) was, in its day, the largest in the north of Scotland

Top. George Ross's hemp manufactory, as it was in the early 1970s. A fifth range (to the left) had already been demolished and the north range (right) was demolished a few years later.

Left. George Ross's town house or courthouse, erected in 1772, seen here in a dilapidated state in 1900

Below. The Courthouse in 1991, restored as a museum

Top. Adam McGlashan, a successful merchant, returned to Cromarty and built McGlashan's Lodge c.1795. It was subsequently owned by Margaret Graham and her husbands – Sir Michael Benignus Clare (Physician General of Jamaicia) and General Sir Hugh Halkett (Commander of the King's Hanoverian army).

Above. Lt Col. David Gordon, a grandson of the parish minister, built his house in 1806 – with an adjoining kitchen block and 'an elegant parterre'

Top. Built in 1828 for Thomas Bain, farmer at Easter Navity, and his wife Helen Watson, this house became the Free Church Manse in the 1850s

Above. The Lodge, on the right, erected by the Wrights and Coopers Society in the 1820s and demolished in 1971

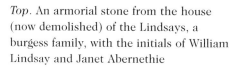

Top. An armorial stone from the house (now demolished) of the Lindsays, a burgess family, with the initials of William Lindsay and Janet Abernethie

Top left. Re-used carving of a winged horse (seventeenth century?)

Above. Kenneth Kemp, tailor, and Isobel Thomson were married c.1711. Their son Thomas married Margaret Williamson. The year 1727 is presumably when their house was built, on the Braehead.

Right. Admiralty boundary markers (First World War)

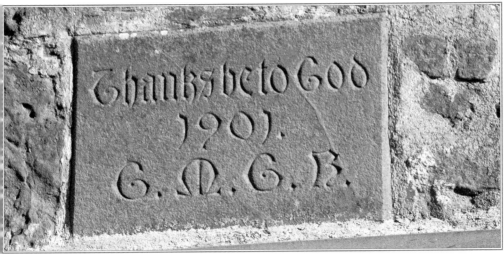

Top. Carved stone from the Masonic Lodge of 1823, subsequently placed in their new lodge built in 1914

Middle. Carved stone on the old brewery with the initials of Gertrude May Gathorne Ross, marking the safe return of her husband, General Walter Ross, from the Boer War

Above. Carved stone on the Gaelic Chapel

Top. Tennis players pose in Edwardian elegance at the courts near the Victoria Hall

Above. A few minutes' walk away, a fisher family pose outside their house

Top. Boy Scouts at camp in fields near Cromarty in August 1912

Above. Fisher boys at the harbour (1910?)

Top. Robertson's Lodge of Freemasons parading behind their lodge

Above. The front of the lodge, built in 1823 and now the Urquhart Snooker Club

Top. The Cromarty Artillery Volunteers, formed in 1860, built the Victoria Hall in 1887, with much assistance in fund raising from 'the ladies of the town'

Above. The Volunteers annual inspection on the Links, with the Cromarty herring boats drawn up on the shore behind and the artillery magazine to the right

THE HARBOUR, CROMARTY

Top. The harbour c.1910 with the schooner *Lily*, the Cromarty Steamship Company's *Croma*, and two other boats, one of which is the *Nimrod*. Beyond is the Fleet, at first both a source of excitement and a tourist attraction.

Above. The dedication of the war memorial, commemorating the death in the First World War of forty-five Cromarty men

Cromarty manufactory, with children 'indirectly employed by assisting fathers and brothers to wind pirns'. In Inverness it was noted that the manufactory: '... employs about 110 men, 150 women, and 20 boys and girls, who work from ten to twelve hours a day, and earn, the men, from 4s to 10s; the women, from 2s to 3s 6d and the children from 1s 6d to 2s a week. Formerly, nearly double the number of persons just stated were employed.' The second Inverness hemp manufactory had closed. It is significant that wages were little changed from the 1s to 10s earned in 1792 and were less than those reported in 1802. The situation for outworkers was similar. The minister of Resolis noted, in 1836, that '... the prices of labour [for the Cromarty factory] are now low and much lower than they have been; but the benefit is notwithstanding very generally felt, and it would be a very great loss to the country, and bear very hard upon the indigent families, should it be withdrawn altogether.'[33] In 1846 a letter from the manager of the Cromarty factory to the Inspector of the Poor at Tain indicated that hemp had been put out to paupers. They presumably worked at the lowest possible rates.[34] Decline was even more marked in the 1840s and early 1850s, and the Cromarty factory closed in 1853. A significant factor in the decline had been the introduction of jute as a fibre for sacking and the working of this material in mechanised factories in Dundee.

Attempts to retain textile production in the north continued to rely on the comparative advantage of lower wages. In Inverness in 1802 there were forty-three cotton weavers, and thirty-six wool weavers and, although the cotton weavers earned 15s per week and the wool weaver 10s to 15s – considerably more than the 8s to 12s earned by hemp weavers – it was recognised that weavers at Inverness worked cheaper 'by 2d in the 1s' than those in the south of Scotland. In Cromarty, Andrew Macrae and Son continued linen spinning from the 1790s until shortly after 1815. Their business relied on the traditional system of putting out to home-based spinners but, even with cheap labour, they became insolvent in 1804 and again in 1817.[35]

There were three attempts to mechanise textile production in the north, all before 1810 – wool carding and spinning, in Inverness and at Braelangwell, in the parish of Resolis, and cotton spinning at Spinningdale in Sutherland. Only the Braelangwell enterprise is considered here. In the 1790s David Urquhart, owner of the Braelangwell estate, erected both a flax mill to scutch locally grown flax and a mill to card and spin wool. In using both jennies and machine carding, Gordon's Mills, as it was known, was typical of many small woollen factories at the end of the eighteenth century. The spinning mill, four storeys high, was in operation from January 1797, under a manager brought in by Urquhart along with others who 'had a knowledge of sorting, scribbling, carding and spinning'. Urquhart, in his application for support from the Board of Manufactures, expressed the hope that the mill would provide employment and 'meliorate the condition of the people, many of whom are yearly emigrating to other countries'. Urquhart also indicated to the Board that he was also taking steps to encourage the weaving of wool.[36]

A number of feus were laid out beside the mills with the intention of creating a small village. There was also a waulk-mill on the estate and by 1810 the enterprise had achieved some success. What Urquhart envisaged was similar to developments in the north of England, where, for example, in the hamlet of Cheadle Hulme in the 1770s a small factory with two carding engines, five spinning jennies and one twisting jenny formed the nucleus of a new village.[37]

Urquhart died in 1811 and, while the spinning mill appears to have been in operation in 1814, there is no evidence of the mills being active in woollen manufacture much after this date and no mention of them in the New Statistical Account of the parish in 1836. Finance and overall management had probably been entirely in the hands of Urquhart himself and, with his death, there was no effective entrepreneur. It would, in any case, have been difficult to compete with the growing industrial centres of the south.

The loss of enterprise

In the 1760s and 1770s textile working was labour intensive and the availability of cheap labour justified investment in proto-factories in the north. Technological change in the production of cotton and woollen goods reduced the relative importance of cheap labour and, at the same time, agrarian change in central Scotland between 1760 and 1790 and migration from the north and west increased the pool of labour in the urbanised central belt. As a result the relative advantage of locating production in the north declined and the additional transport costs of shipping raw materials to the north and of shipping finished goods to markets in the south became prohibitive.

The region's loss of comparative advantage led to a loss of capital and of entrepreneurial skills as the mobile merchant class invested elsewhere. William Forsyth, although he remained in Cromarty until his death, ensured that his sons had careers in the East India Company and left no active business behind him and the sons of Urquhart of Braelangwell both pursued diplomatic careers abroad.[38]

A last remnant

In January 1902 a column in the *Invergordon Times* noted the death of Dannie Allan, a Cromarty weaver who had been thrown out of employment by the closure of the hemp factory but had remained in the town, living in poverty. Until his death in his seventies he dressed as he had done while employed, in a blue bonnet and a blue swallow-tailed coat with brass buttons, an increasingly old-fashioned figure and the last remnant of what had once been a thriving industry.[39]

Notes

1. Alasdair Durie, 'Linen spinning in the north of Scotland, 1746–1773' in *Northern Scotland* (1974–77), ii. 13–36.
2. Bank of Scotland Archive, BLC Letter Book, 18 June 1747 & 27 Aug 1747; NAS, NG1/1, 26 June 1747, 4 Dec 1747, 11 Jan 1748 & 15 July 1748; NAS, CH2/672/2.
3. NAS, NG1/1, 3 Nov 1749.
4. NAS, NG1/1/12, 1 Dec 1752; General Letter Book, 10 July 1772; Scots Letter Book, 22 Jan 1765 and 20 June 1765.
5. Alasdair Durie, 'Linen spinning', 19.
6. Alasdair Durie, 'Linen spinning', 20.
7. BLC Letter Book, 25 June 1747.
8. 'Memorial on the Patronage of the Church of Cromarty, 1754' cited in WM Mackenzie, 'Cromarty: its old chapels and parish church' in Journal of the *Scottish Ecclesiological Society* (Edinburgh, 1905).
9. BLC Minute Book, 29 Aug 1748; NAS, CH2/672/2.
10. NAS, E728/28/1; William Macgill, *Old Ross-shire and Scotland* (Inverness, 1909), no. 855; Hugh Miller, *Scenes and Legends of the North of Scotland* (Edinburgh, 1994), 432.
11. NAS, CH2/672/2, 24 Nov 1747; Durie, 'Linen spinning', 22. Any spinners still using the distaff, as some probably were, would have produced only one and a half spindles per week.
12. NAS, NG1/1/13, 11–12 & 102.
13. BLC Letter Book, 13 Dec 1751, 24 Feb 1754, 28 Feb 1754, 18 April 1754; NRAS 0204/Bundles 39 and 163.
14. NAS, CH2/66/4.
15. NAS, E746/117 aand E746/138/4. It was a rival manufacturer, Sandman of Perth, who developed the site as a linen manufactory.
16. John G. Dunbar (ed.), *Sir William Burrell's Northern Tour, 1758* (East Linton, 1997), 96; NAS, E728/28/1, 2, 3(1) and E787/24; Highland Council Archive, L/IB/BC, 5/19/5, 6/3/15 and 9/7/10.
17. NLS, Ms9646; Andrew Wight, *Present State of Husbandry in Scotland,* (Edinburgh, 1778–1784), iv. 128; James Robertson, *A General View of the Agriculture in the County of Inverness* (London, 1808), 312; OSA, *Parish of Inverness*; NSA, *Parish of Inverness*.
18. NAS, E726/28/1; NAS, E787/24; David Loch, *A tour through most of the trading towns and villages of Scotland* (Edinburgh, 1778), 54–55 (Loch's visit to Cromarty was in 1776); Andrew Wight, *State of Husbandry* (Wight's first visit to Cromarty in 1781 is recorded in Vol. III and his return visit in 1784 in Vol. IV); NAS, E726/28/1.

19. NAS, E726/28/1.

20. Thomas Pennant, *A Tour in Scotland 1769* (London, 1790).

21. For shares, NAS, GD274/40. For the Invergordon factory, William Thom, 'Journal of a tour in the North of Scotland' in *New Agricultural and Commercial Magazine*, i. no. 4 (1811), 285; Tain and District Museum, Cadboll Papers: Cadboll Estate Rent Book 1813, Vol. 2. No mention is made of it in Fraser's survey of 1802 (NLS, Ms9646) and it was noted in 1844 that the enterprise had failed (Commission for Inquiring into Administration of the Poor Laws, *Report*, PP 1844 XXXII–XXVI). The factory buildings – which, as in Cromarty, were of stone – remained in 1843 when they were used as temporary barracks for a regiment of Irish Fusiliers sent north following the Resolis and Rosskeen riots (*Inverness Courier*, 11 Oct 1843). For the cost of the Cromarty factory, see Andrew Wight, *State of Husbandry*, iii. 252. Early insurance records confirm that there were four ranges in 1780, with two more buildings in the centre of the square (Guildhall Library, Sun Insurance Records, Ms 11936/322, entry no. 493826 and Ms 11936/278, entry no. 419830). A fifth range had been added by the 1820s and appears on John Douglas's estate survey of 1823 (Cromarty House archive). The wooden buildings in Inverness were destroyed by fire and stone buildings erected in their place. J. Maclean, *Reminiscences of Clachnacuddin* (Inverness, 1842). In 1815 the Inverness manufactory consisted of two 110 foot-long ranges, each three storeys high, with well-lighted garrets; and a two-storey heckling house, with garrets, between these ranges. A wall formed the fourth side of an area 150ft x 110ft (*Inverness Journal*, 15 Sept 1815). In adjoining buildings were a 'dye-house, dry-house, storehouse, wright's shop, stable etc'. It was offered for sale in 1815 for £2,650 (*Inverness Journal*, 15 Mar 1816). For rope-making in Cromarty, George S. Mackenzie, *A General Survey of the Counties of Ross & Cromarty* (London, 1810), 335.

22. Hugh Miller, *My Schools and Schoolmasters* (Edinburgh, 1993), 455.

23. NLS, Ms9646, p 211. In 1794 its output was reported as being 'upwards of 300,000 yards' – suggesting a consistently high level of production. See James Donaldson, *A General view of the agriculture of the county of Nairn* (London, 1795), 10.

24. NLS, Ms9646, p 211. Hecklers (men) might 'win at piece work' 8s to 12s per week; dressers (men) 8s to 12s per week; weavers (men) 8s to 12s per week; pirn boys 2s to 3s per week; spinners (women) in the factory 4s to 6s per week; and women spinners 'in the country' 4s to 6s per week.

25. NLS, Ms9646, 21. In 1777 there had been 60 looms. David Loch, *Tour*, 54–55.

26. NAS, SC24/21/7.

27. Alasdair Durie, 'Linen spinning'.

28. NAS, NG1/15/1–2; George S. Mackenzie, *General Survey ... Ross & Cromarty*, 335; NLS, Ms9646, 213.

29. A Gershenkron, *Economic Backwardness in Historical Perspective* (Cambridge, 1966).

30. NLS, Ms9646, 210.

31. John Sinclair, *General view of the agriculture of the northern counties and islands of Scotland* (London, 1795), 56–57; William Leslie, *A General View of the Agriculture of the Counties of Moray and Nairn* (London, 1813), 35.

32. For rope working in Cromarty see George S. Mackenzie, *General Survey ... Ross & Cromarty*, 335; for rope-making and sailcloth production in Inverness, see J. Maclean, *Reminiscences of Clachnacuddin*, 45. For Inverness manufactory in 1804, James Robertson, *A General View of the Agriculture in the County of Inverness* (London, 1808), 312. For the second Inverness hemp manufactory, *Inverness Courier*, 9 April 1818. For thread manufacture see, for Banff, Andrew Wight, *State of Husbandry*, iii. 722 and for Inverness, OSA, *Parish of Inverness*. In 1802, between 8,000 and 12,000 spinners were engaged for the Inverness thread manufactory (NLS, Ms9646, 213).

33. PP 1844 XXXII–XXVI, Commission for Inquiring into Administration of the Poor Laws, *Report*; OSA, Parish of Inverness; NSA, *Parish of Kirkmichael and Cullicudden.*

34. Cromarty Courthouse Museum, photocopy of original document.

35. NLS, Ms9646, 216–220; NAS, CS96/1860, 'Andrew Macrae and Son, lint manufacturers, spinning book 1794–1804'.

36. NAS, NG1/2/3, 194 and 244.

37. George S. Mackenzie, *General Survey ... Ross & Cromarty*, 335; Maxine Berg, *The Age of Manufactures, 1700–1820* (London and New York, 1994).

38. Hugh Miller, *Memoir of William Forsyth* (London, 1939); Henrietta Tayler, *The Family of Urquhart* (Aberdeen, 1946).

39. *Invergordon Times*, 15 January 1902.

I I

Economy, Population and Society: 1760s–1790s

... to give
A double harvest to the pining swain,
And teach the labouring hands the sweets of toil?

James Thomson, *Autumn*

Scottish agriculture 1760s–90s

The improvement of agriculture inevitably brought a profound change to life in rural Scotland. The social cost of that change was always considerable but it was less traumatic when improvement was gradual and when it involved local farmers and merchants as tenants of larger, improved holdings. The Highlands suffered more because improvement came late and because the region had largely lost its enterprising tenants – and change was, as a result, rapid and almost entirely imposed from above, by landlords, their factors and a new class of commercial farmers from the south.

The three decades from 1760 to 1790 were the crucial period in the transformation of farming in southern, lowland Scotland – a 'great leap forward' in which a principal driver was the imposition of improving leases, enforced through estate factors and, if necessary, by legal action. These policies, based on the considerable authority exercised by landowners in Scotland, made possible a dramatic increase in the productivity of arable ground with consequent benefits to landowners in the form of higher rents. The most enterprising tenants responded by taking on leases, participating in the growing market economy and sharing in the benefits of improvements. By the early nineteenth century multiple and joint tenancies had almost disappeared, as had the letting of land to subtenants and cottars, and common lands had been either divided or the legal process of division had begun. As a result the rights of private property were extended over a wider area and, with the removal of extensive subletting, a threefold structure of landlord, tenant and landless labourer was established.

Agriculture: the Black Isle and the Northern Lowlands

In the north, however, things were different. There was still a marked contrast in the mid 1790s between Moray, where agriculture had been 'infinitely improved', and the rest of the fertile coastal fringe in the counties of Nairn, Inverness, Ross, Cromarty and Sutherland. John Donaldson, in his 1794 account of agriculture in Moray, judged improvement to have begun in 1768 when the earl of Fife began to grant leases to 'particular substantial and intelligent farmers' of land formerly occupied under multiple tenancies. Other proprietors soon followed his example. A second report on agriculture, written by William Leslie, was published in 1813 and by this date single-tenant farms were the norm. Leases on larger farms were generally for nineteen years and yields were in the region of ten times for bere and eight times for oats. 'Intelligent Moray farmers' were, thereafter, commonly perceived as the driving force for improvement in the north, as farmers from the Lothians had been a generation before.[1]

William Leslie expressed a number of interesting views on the progress of farming. He held an unusually high opinion of improvements in the seventeenth and early eighteenth centuries and disputed some of the conventional wisdom on improvement in the second half of the eighteenth century. He detected no difference between estates managed by a factor and those managed by the landowner, and believed that the improving lease hindered improvement by suppressing ingenuity and preventing adaptation to adverse seasons. It was, he claimed, long leases which led to beneficial change – and by this he meant those which gave tenancy for a lifetime or more, a nineteen-year lease being, in his opinion, a short one. Only when the tenant was placed 'as near as possible to the situation of a landowner on his own land' would improvement be maximised. He supported his case by reference to the practices of English agriculture and specific examples from Moray and Nairn. Leslie's comments suggest that the process of change in Moray before 1800 relied on a local, active farming class who were, given the security of long leases, prepared to engage in improvement. While landlord authority clearly existed – Leslie noted that the baron court still operated – improvement was not entirely landlord led.

The contrasting situation in the Black Isle is revealed in Sir John Sinclair's *General view of the agriculture of the northern counties and islands of Scotland* published in 1795. The survey begins with an extensive description of farming in the Black Isle, based on information supplied by George Munro, proprietor of the estate of Poyntzfield, three miles west of Cromarty. This indicates that the improvements effected in the central lowlands had not been replicated. Sinclair estimated that on the best-conducted farms typical crop yields were six to eight times for barley, five to eight times for oats, seven to ten times for wheat, and six to seven times for pease. However, most tenant farms fell below this with returns of three to four times for barley, two to four times for oats, and three to four times for pease. The minister of Resolis gave similar figures of 3.5 times for barley and only 2.25 times for oats and pease, although he noted that tenants on the shore had higher yields. Low yields also prevailed in much of Sutherland and Caithness, where the average returns across the counties were 4.5–5 times for bere and four to five times for oats, and in Nairn and Inverness, where the return on the poorest fields fell below twofold. These yields contrasted with an English average return on oats of seven to nine times, a return that had already been equalled or exceeded in parts of southern Scotland.[2] There was also a marked contrast with the yields in parts of north-west Sutherland where, under an 'unimproved' system, returns of ten to twelve times were common because there was ample cattle dung and cultivation was by hand tools in lazy beds.[3]

North of Moray there was almost no use of improving leases. Sinclair noted the benefits of long leases but observed that on the Cromarty estate there had not been a formal lease to any of the 'inferior class of tenants ... time out of mind'. The situation in the rest of Ross-shire, Nairn-shire and Inverness-shire was similar and most small tenants had no lease.[4] Since there were few long leases there could be no effective use of improving leases. Sinclair saw other barriers to improvement – the prevalence of small farms, payments of rent in kind, the obligation of tenants to provide personal services to the laird and thirlage to estate mills – but the absence of leases requires particular attention.

Agriculture: the 'native tenantry'

Sinclair attributed much of the lack of progress to the failings of 'the native tenantry'. Grieves on mains farms were normally from the south and landowners were 'forced to look abroad and have recourse to active strangers of skill and ability' in order to find suitably progressive tenants.[5] Proprietors of individual estates echoed Sinclair's views. Gordon of Invergordon was seeking a southern farmer in 1771[6] and Munro of Foulis, in correspondence with his factor in the 1790s, lamented the difficulty in finding a suitable local tenant.[7] Few other farms were of sufficient size to attract southern farmers – although multiple and joint tenancies had been abolished, most holdings were still between fifteen and fifty acres, and farms of even eighty acres were unusual. The tenants of such farms lacked capital and as a result few were enclosed. Moreover, rotations were poor, fallowing was not practised except on the mains farms and there was little variety of manure. Sinclair advocated an increase in the size of farm to between fifty and a hundred acres, but even this was less than the minimum conventionally regarded as desirable.[8]

The unsuitability of local tenants was, in part, the result of their inexperience in dealing with cash rents. Sinclair, however, condescendingly attributed the failure to convert rents to cash to the character of the tenants themselves, claiming that they were likely to squander a cash rent before payment and consequently fall into arrears. Even with payment in kind, he held that the careful oversight of a factor was absolutely indispensable. The perceived need for strict oversight of small tenants through the estate factor, and the large number of small farms, led to the demands made on factors being such as to render their lot one of 'near slavery'. By comparison, factoring in the south of Scotland was, Sinclair says, a sinecure. As a result, there was a shortage of suitable factors in the north and many estates either shared the services of a factor or, in the case of the smaller ones, operated through a ground officer working to the proprietor's instructions.

In Inverness-shire, James Robertson perceived a similar ingrained lack of initiative among tenants such that 'rather than relinquish their slovenly habits ... they adopt the desperate resolution of removing to America'. It is notable than no writer on agriculture on the north saw any difference between the shortcomings of lowland Scots and highland Gaelic tenants – all were damned by the same judgement. Robertson, however, rejected the notion that this was the result of 'constitutional indolence' and attributed it to four factors: a 'prejudice for ancient customs', a 'natural fondness for common pasture' rather than enclosure, a lack of 'permanent interest in their possessions' and the absence of examples from people 'of their own rank'. Robertson attributed the absence of leases more to the attitude of landowners – who were motivated almost solely by commercial interests and believed that their tenants would be 'more submissive in such abject dependence'.[9]

Some of Robertson's other comments provide an explanation for the lack of suitable tenants. He believed that one consequence of the decay of traditional Highland society was a social structure in which there were few 'in the middle ranks of life' and that, as a result, examples of good farming practice were not disseminated. Small tenants could not identify with the few rich farmers who were engaged in improvement and so could not emulate them.[10] There was neither a trickle down of ideas from above nor the possibility of small tenants rising in the world to take on the role of improving farmers.

Robertson's comments confirm what has already been described in earlier chapters – that there was a move away from the area of those with capital and skill, principally local merchants.

Agriculture: landlords and mailers

Although landowners north of Moray found it impossible to bring about substantial improvement through the use of improving leases, they were nevertheless motivated by the same desire as southern landowners – to take greater control of their estates and to increase their income from rents. This is apparent in the notice of sale of the Cromarty estate in 1763, which held out the prospect of the purchaser increasing the rent 'to 10 times its present amount'.[11] Rent rolls, in fact, show that a quite different change in estate management took place.

Holders of small parcels of land were commonly known as mailers, cottagers or cottars. Mailers might hold up to fifteen acres of ground, although according to Sinclair once they held more than ten they were likely to regard themselves as having the superior status of 'tenant'. Most held less. The term 'mailer' indicates that a rent (mail) was paid but the amount, and whether it was in cash or in kind, varied considerably. In the seventeenth and early eighteenth century cottars and subtenants did not appear on estate rent rolls, since they owed their position on the land to the principal tenants or tacksmen and written leases, when they existed, often referred to the tacksmen and 'his subtenants and cottars'.[12] However, from the 1730s some landowners began to exercise greater control over their estates by entering all those on the land in the rent roll. Bringing mailers on to the rent rolls was partly a necessity. Since economic change had reduced the social role of principal tenants as middlemen, standing between lairds and the bulk of the tenantry, estates had little option but to deal directly with all those on their land.

In addition to existing cottars, new mailers could be settled on unimproved ground as a first stage in bringing it into cultivation – and where there were undivided commonties with disputed boundaries, as on the Black Isle, mailers might be used to colonise ground at no risk to the landowner. Although the extensive Mulbuie commonty on the Black Isle was not divided until 1829, this was the culmination of a lengthy legal process and evidence taken in 1814, generally from the oldest tenants, shows that landowners had been actively extending their estates from the 1770s – both by settling mailers on the commonty and by enclosing ground to create plantations of conifers.[13] In Sir John Sinclair's words mailers were 'the aborigines of improvement' bringing ground into cultivation, to be followed by 'the common farmer, the farmer of the higher or last polish, and the land-owner'. Sinclair also regarded mailers as useful because they provided labour at harvest, to both tenants and landlords, and aided work on public highways. Sinclair considered that it might be beneficial to settle mailers in 'small close colonies' with houses laid out each with its own piece of land, making co-operative ploughing possible, and 'The Colony', a farm on the Poyntzfield estate, probably originated in this way. He also recommended a contract between landowners and mailers to encourage good practice, similar to an improving lease.[14]

While the Cromarty rental of 1763 still showed only principal tenants, the 1755 Newhall rental already included all those on the estate. Of ninety-four tenants, forty-four were mailers, that is, 47 per cent of those who worked the land. Almost exactly the same proportion is found on the Easter Ross estate of Pitcalnie in 1734, with sixteen mailers and eighteen other tenants. In 1735, neighbouring Rarichie, a part of the larger Balnagowan estate, had ten mailers and eleven other tenants, and on the Ankerville estate in 1780 there were twenty-two tenants and fourteen mailers.[15]

All this contrasted with southern Scotland. In the south improvements in the three decades after 1760 depended on an estate bureaucracy that was focused on enforcing the conditions of improving leases for larger farms. In the north, with only limited use of improving leases and slow progress in creating larger farms, estates nevertheless did away with the services of tacksmen. The burden of estate management thus increased as landowners or their factors dealt directly with small tenants.

Agriculture: improvement on the Cromarty, Newhall and Poyntzfield estates

Despite the real or perceived problems in finding suitable tenants, the changes effected on both the Cromarty and Newhall estates from the late 1760s exemplify the enthusiasm for improvement and landscaping that characterised the Scottish land-owning class. The proprietors of Cromarty and Newhall engaged with the ideals of improvement in different ways. In the case of Newhall, the young proprietor, William Gordon, ploughed the land himself; in Cromarty, the older and experienced lawyer and businessman, George Ross, sought to develop innovative schemes, drawing inspiration from farming practices in Buckinghamshire.

Agriculture: Cromarty

Ross had earlier purchased and improved both the estate of Kinmylies in Inverness and a farm in Ross-shire and was credited with being the second person to practise improved farming in Inverness-shire. An interesting aspect of Ross's improvements was his attempt to transfer expertise from England through his contacts with Buckinghamshire. He sent his farm manager at Kinmylies to be trained there – an experiment that seems to have been successful since on his return he 'practised the several methods of agricultural improvements, which he had observed in England, with very great success, and paved the way to encourage others to act in a like manner'. The farm manager went on to become factor on the Lovat estates. In Cromarty, Ross brought ploughmen from the same county and used their wives to teach lace-making. However, the ploughmen, naturally, used English ploughs and this led to the problem that they could not be maintained by local plough-wrights. The promotion of lace-making also foundered despite financial support from the Board of Trustees for Manufactures, who granted £40 per annum for three years to promote the production of 'blond mignoned and Trolly laces'.[16]

Ross had sufficient capital to buy up much of the property of small landowners, making possible the creation of larger farms. Rosefarm – probably named after Ross (as Rosedale House in Kew had been) was formed before 1781 from the old lands of Greenhill, and Townlands Farm, tenanted by William Forsyth, probably dates from this period, its eight fields created from rigs previously held by a number of old families in the town. Improvements on Rosefarm, the Mains and Townlands all followed conventional lines. In 1781 Wight reported that hay had been recently introduced as the main food for horses and cows, and noted that grass and clover were sown, and potatoes and turnips cultivated. On Townlands, Forsyth practised an eight-year rotation, which he had taken from the *Gentleman's Magazine*. Rosefarm was enclosed partly with hedge and ditch and partly with stone walls; 'horse hoeing husbandry' was practised; potatoes were grown; but unusually, oxen rather than horses were used for ploughing and carting. A farmhouse and offices had also been built.[17]

In his will Ross instructed his trustees to continue with 'plantations, enclosures and hedges and to create inclosures of 100–150 Scots acres' so as to encourage 'opulent farmers to possess the same'. However, despite having this clear aim, Ross had not introduced long leases and did not pursue the policy of amalgamating smallholdings into larger farms as far as he might have. Newton Farm was said to have remained as four holdings when Alexander Bain, a tenant whom Ross respected, refused the tenancy of the whole and in 1792 the parish minister reported that few amalgamations of small farms had taken place. It would seem that Ross, since he did not use long improving leases, shared Sinclair's view of the general lack of initiative and ability of native tenants and that consequently improvements were restricted to his close associates.[18]

Although no papers relating to his management of the estate have survived, we have some knowledge of his factor, Hugh Rose, who moved to the Sutherland estate c.1784. Sinclair considered him 'one of the most intelligent and sagacious farmers that the North could boast of' and George Dempster of Skibo believed that Rose knew 'the way to set this county [Sutherland] on its legs' and was only prevented from doing so by 'the noble personages themselves', that is the Sutherland family. Like Ross, Hugh Rose favoured improving moors and encouraging fishery and manufactures but, as in Cromarty, there is no suggestion of longer or improving leases being appropriate. His attitude to tenants in Sutherland was paternalistic and he promoted schemes to reward outstanding tenants with 'premiums such as a gown or cloak, or a hat or a coat for excellence ... so that the recipients might stand out at church or market'.[19]

Despite the absence of leases, small tenants were seldom removed from their holdings on the Cromarty estate and Ross also created additional *pendicles* (smallholdings) at Newton and Neilston, perhaps as part of an intention to relocate tenants as the principal farms were consolidated. Summons of removing were raised against a number of tenants in 1784, when Walter Ross became factor.[20] However, this may have been in response to rent arrears resulting from the harvest failure of the previous year and does not, in itself, show that tenants were actually evicted.

Agriculture: Newhall

The small estate of Newhall passed to William Gordon (1745–78) in 1772. Gordon's improvements reflect the intellectual interest in agriculture and estate management that was part of the ethos of the Scottish Enlightenment.[21] As with Ross, Gordon's improvements were a combination of embellishment and commercial ventures. He 'inclosed a considerable piece of ground' and planted 1,000 oaks, including an avenue leading to Newhall House. The Mains farm was also partly enclosed and by 1778 the farmhouse was newly harled and farm offices with slate roofs were under construction. Wheat, turnips and grass were planted, hay was being made, and new ploughs were brought from Edinburgh. As on the Cromarty estate, Gordon encountered problems with local blacksmiths and asked a friend to send '2 horse shoes of Clarke's make, as described in his treatise, as a pattern for the Blockheads of smiths we are blessed with in this country'. Lime was available from shell deposits, which he noted 'answer beyond my most sanguine expectations', and the Mains farm accounts for 1780 suggest returns of more than nine times for oats.

Gordon's active involvement is evident in remarks in his letters, many of which were written in breaks from attending to farm business. On one occasion he remarked that 'having got all my sowing over I am now with servants to take the Hay for a day or two'. At other times he ended brief letters with 'I am in the middle of my hay harvest with the finest weather I ever saw ... time is too precious to add more' and 'I have been these last two days morning to night, accounting with my tenants'. Gordon was not simply overseeing the work of the farm but engaging in farm work himself, thus seeking out and valuing the direct 'experiences of life' as advocated by writers such as his friend, the author Henry Mackenzie. On one occasion he wrote that he thought he 'really would become a Farmer'. This enthusiasm should, however, be set against other experiences, such as 'coursing greyhounds and shooting in the forenoon and drinking good claret in the after'.

Gordon faced two difficulties. He inherited his estate at a time of general failure in credit, which made it difficult to raise capital for improvements, and he experienced problems in marketing his crop and victual rent. In 1773 he attempted, unsuccessfully, to sell his oats locally, from the storehouse, rather than accept an offer from a Portsoy merchant. Whereas in May he was convinced that he could 'dispose of them to very good advantage', in October he was still struggling to sell the last of it. The underdevelopment of the local market would have created similar problems for any improving tenants.

Other than Newhall Mains, the only large single tenancy farm on the estate was Kirkton. Following Gordon's death in 1778 this was set on a nineteen-year lease to Alexander Barkly. The terms of the lease included improving clauses – that the tenant straighten the boundaries, enclose, build stone or mud dykes and erect new farm buildings. These were much less onerous than the detail of many improving leases in the south. However, Barkly failed and gave up the tack. His inadequacies as a tenant are confirmed in correspondence from more successful members of the Barkly family, who had left the area for London and their migration is further confirmation of the general pattern – the loss of the more enterprising members of merchant families.[22]

Agriculture: Poyntzfield

Adam Gordon inherited Ardoch in 1757 and substantially rebuilt the mansion house and then sold the estate in 1761 to Sir George Gun Munro (d.1785). Munro had married Mary Poyntz of London whose money helped him to finance improvements and he renamed the estate Poyntzfield in her honour. According to a parish minister:

> Sir George Munro was the first in this part of the country who began improvements in agriculture on a large scale, by enclosing, planting, draining, liming, fallowing, and sowing green crops on his mains of Poynterfield [sic], which now adds greatly to the beauty and value of that part of the estate.

Munro introduced English ploughs and granted leases in 1782 to two tenants for nineteen and twenty-one years. He was succeeded in 1785 by his nephew George Gun Munro (d.1806) who provided much of the information for Sir John Sinclair's report in 1795. He favoured, among other things, the settling of mailers on moor ground and advocated settling them in 'colonies' where they might share resources.[23]

Fishing: 1760s–90s

George Ross, even before his purchase of the Cromarty estate, actively supported attempts to promote the development of fisheries in the north and in 1759 subscribed £500 to the Inverness Fishing Chamber, set up by the British Fisheries Society under legislation of 1749. The Chamber raised over £11,500 and offered a prize for the first cran of herring caught each season, in order to encourage fishermen to continue an involvement in the fishery.[24] However, it was subsistence fishing that remained of more importance in Cromarty with 'groups of neighbours ... each year forming parties of eight or ten who sailed to Tarbat Ness around mid-summer, where they based themselves for several weeks in encampments, sleeping under the sails of their boats, in order to lay up a store of cured cod and ling for the winter'. There were some short-lived developments in Caithness around 1750 when a fleet of boats is said to have left the Cromarty Firth for Wick, manned by 'mechanics and fishermen'.[25]

The most significant change in the community was a loosening of ties between fishers and the laird. On the Cromarty estate in 1738 there had been eight fishing boats 'of much use some years past' but by 1756 this had fallen to four, with a further three boats having been 'waste' for two or three years. The 1762 Cromarty estate rental is instructive, since it was prepared as the estate changed hands and contains notes on potential increases in income. Although it dealt with salmon netting, oyster and mussel scalps, and ferry rights, it did not suggest replacing those fishing boats that had gone out of use. This unwillingness on the part of the landowner to maintain unproductive fishing boats led, when fishing revived in the late eighteenth century, to greater commercial freedom for fishers themselves and enabled them to enter directly into agreements with southern merchants.[26] The revival of herring fishing, centred on the Caithness fishery, is described in the next chapter.

Trade in salt salmon was also in decline and overseas markets were damaged by the outbreak of the Seven Years War in 1756. By this date the Scottish salmon trade was dominated by John Richardson and Company, the 'Great Fishmonger of Tay'. A new product had been developed from the 1740s with the introduction of 'kitting', that is, the preserving of boiled salmon in ale-based vinegar for the London market, where salt salmon was out of favour. It was also possible to ship fresh salmon from the Tay to London. Richardson dominated the whole trade – fresh, salted and kitted – and by 1771 he was able to report that 'we have a great part of the Scots fishery of salmon in our own hand'.

However, with the decline in the salt salmon trade there was little revival in the north, which was too far from London to ship fresh salmon. Although the Cromarty merchant William Forsyth supplied Richardson with salt salmon from the Rosehall fishings, in Sutherland, in 1771, there is little evidence that the Cromarty Firth yairs were active. In 1758, 400 bolls of salt that had been cellared in Cromarty were sold to a local merchant, John Fraser, and shipped to Norway. In 1763 no rent was received by the Cromarty estate for its salmon fishings and in 1780 the rent of the Newhall stell (stake) net was only £5, half of what was paid for the kelp on the same shore. William Forsyth had exported salmon on his own account to Bilbao, Venice, Rotterdam and Campvere, but this trade ceased by 1766. Low prices limited the viability of commercial fishing and shortened the season, with some fisheries ending in late May when the vats at the fishing station were full, and most yairs were regarded as a means of ensuring a regular supply of fish for consumption rather than as a larger commercial venture.[27]

Mines and quarries

The example of the Brora coal mine in Sutherland had kept before local proprietors the possibility of discovering workable reserves of coal and other minerals on their estates. Captain Urquhart employed a surveyor to search for coal in the 1750s and George Ross also engaged a surveyor in 1768 and had test bores sunk. Further trials were made at Eathie in the mid nineteenth century – but none of these was positive.[28] In 1776 a Mr Jeans of London who had 'a great knowledge in natural History' visited Gordon of Newhall to 'make an essay for Limestone of which there are some appearances on a burnside of mine'. Traces of lead were subsequently found in the lands of Brae within two miles of the sea and, in the belief that this might be a workable vein, Gordon employed twelve miners the following year but the enterprise came to nothing.[29]

Stone quarrying was, however, of greater and enduring importance. The quarry at Newton was leased from 1750 to John Adam and subsequently to William Forsyth, who had the tack from at least 1761 and paid only 10s as against Adam's 16 guineas. Forsyth used its 'excellent stone' for a storehouse across the firth at Milton of New Tarbat in 1764.[30] Aitken's estate map of the previous year shows that the quarry had two sea entrances to allow loading directly onto ships or boats.[31]

The Newton quarry created substantial employment. Ten quarriers appear in the parish registers in the nine years between 1752 and 1760, indicating that quarrying was already a distinct trade differentiated from that of masons, and quarriers appear, at this time, to have been relatively prosperous. A number of new feus in the town in the 1770s were granted to quarriers and one, James Allan, a church elder in Moray, who moved to Newton, joined the Cromarty kirk session and subsequently became its treasurer.

Population and mobility in the late eighteenth century

It might seem that George Ross's development of Cromarty, coupled with estate policies that displaced few tenants, would have led to a significant growth in the population. The evidence, however, does not support this. The population of the town of Cromarty, as reported in the OSA in the early 1790s, was 1,457. Although Webster's census of 1755 must be treated with caution, this suggests an increase of only about 100. Yet it is clear that there was an influx of Gaelic speakers to the town, large enough to warrant the building of the Gaelic Chapel in 1783, with seating for over 450 persons, and, if the census figures are correct, there must have been migration from the town partly offsetting the influx of Gaelic speakers. This suggests increasing mobility rather than growth – a population in a state of flux.

In Resolis, after the failure of the 1782 crop, many farmers dismissed servants and employed their own children from a younger age than previously, thus reducing the opportunities for employment. The population, which was in any case marginally below its 1755 level, fell as a result by a further 11 per cent – from 1,345 in 1780 to 1,199 in 1789. The parish minister in the OSA attributed this to the fact that 'many of the young and stoutest lads have [since 1780] annually gone to Glasgow, and other places in the W and S of Scotland, where the price of labour is high, instead of marrying and settling in the parish, as was the custom formerly'. In the rural part of the parish of Cromarty the population also declined after the dearth of 1782–3 and fell by forty between 1785 and 1790.

In Easter Ross and the Black Isle seasonal migration to the south was also recorded in Rosemarkie, Fodderty, Tarbat and Avoch – especially among 'mailers, villagers and crofters'. In Moray, William Leslie noted in 1813 that the 'manufactories of the south' had carried off 'the avaricious, all the giddy, all captivated by novelty' and David Dale's cotton mills at New Lanark on the Clyde had by 1793 drawn in a considerable labour force from Caithness, Inverness-shire and Argyll. As early as 1778 the Cromarty justices of the peace used the provisions of the Comprehending Act, a piece of legislation which was seldom

FIGURE 11.1
From a satirical print by Richard Newton showing 'A Flight of Scotchmen
descending on London', 1790s.

invoked, to apprehend two factory workers who has 'deserted their
employment' to seek work in the south.[32]

However, the failure of the 1782 harvest also led to migration from
adjoining highland areas into the lowlands of Easter Ross and in the
parishes of Logie Easter and Kilmuir Easter this led to an increase
in population. Later, in the two years after 1793, the population of
Resolis increased as moor was improved and mailers were settled.
These movements – from the north to the industrial areas of the south
and from the true Highlands to the fertile east coast – were coupled
with emigration. Throughout Scotland the importance of each form
of migration varied over time in a complex pattern but these different
streams of population movement had a common source in 'an
increasingly turbulent rural society'.[33]

A further form of temporary migration was for military service. The
press gang was active in the Cromarty Firth, especially from the 1740s,
to the extent that the Cromarty estate found it difficult to find anyone
willing to work near the shore and during the American Wars thirteen
men from Avoch were pressed into the navy. Recruitment into the army
was already common from the late 1740s, when there was a permanent
military detachment in Cromarty, and after the American Revolution
in 1775 there was an increased drive to recruit Highland soldiers. A
recruiting party for MacDonald's Regiment was stationed in the town's
new courthouse in 1776 and two fencible regiments, the Northern
(Duke of Gordon's) Fencibles and the Sutherland Fencibles, also drew
recruits from the town.[34]

The 'circle of gentility'

In the principal Scottish cities, from the middle decades of the eighteenth century, certain styles of life, patterns of consumption and networks of social contacts were beginning to differentiate a middle class from the land-owning class above and the labouring class below. This is most evident in new patterns of housing, which both separated the middle class from the labouring class and displayed their commitment to order and rationality. It is also to be seen in the emergence of new social organisations and patterns of behaviour, which linked the members of the middle class and segregated them from others, and in the growing distinction between private and public life – with the role of middle-class women increasingly restricted to the private sphere.

The process by which a distinct middle class was formed in Cromarty can be traced to beginnings in the mid eighteenth century. Hugh Miller's biography of the merchant William Forsyth, published for the family in 1839, contains valuable analysis of these changes in Cromarty society. He believed that one consequence of the community's prolonged dispute with its Roman Catholic laird in the 1740s and 1750s was that a group of 'persons of somewhat less influence' came to form a 'circle of gentility' in the society of the town, taking on the role that would otherwise have been filled by the laird. This group united minor members of poorer aristocratic families, principally Lady Ardoch (d.1761), Mrs Mackenzie of Scotsburn (d.1812), the daughters of the former merchant Urquhart of Greenhill and the descendants of the parish minister, George Gordon (d.1749). This was augmented by a number of ladies of 'lower pretensions' who were supported by relatives in the south and by 'a few retired half-pay ensigns and lieutenants'. This circle was, according to Miller, held together by the bonds of tea parties, prayer meetings and pride in family descent by some 'silver thread' that connected them to the aristocracy. It was, at least in its tea parties and prayer meetings, markedly different from the group of similar social standing, which in 1741 had celebrated Captain Urquhart's acquisition of the estate with a six-day party involving bonfires, drummers, the firing of volleys and drinking 'ankers of spirits'.[35]

The presence of this genteel group can also be seen in the window tax returns, which, from the 1780s, show that houses were occupied, for a number of years, by both young ladies from minor land-owning families (Miss Sutherland of Clyne, Miss Munro of Foulis and Miss Graham of Drynie) and by army officers of a similar background (Major William Falconer, Captain John Mackenzie and Captain Innes Munro).[36]

In Cromarty, as in the cities, these changes are most evident in the design of new houses. There had already been an expansion and rebuilding of houses in the town in the late seventeenth and early eighteenth centuries. While there is some indication of a greater concern with symmetry at this early date, many of these houses remained large, rambling affairs, often with parts of the building sublet. A clearly different pattern emerges with Forsyth House, c.1772, which is symmetrical and set in its own substantial grounds. Among its innovations was a low tunnel connecting the house to the nearby well on the high street, doing away with the necessity of servants being seen in the front garden.

Notes

1. James Donaldson, *A General View of the Agriculture of Elgin and Moray* (London, 1794), 15; William Leslie, *A General View of the Agriculture of the Counties of Moray and Nairn* (London, 1813), 143 and 350; John Henderson, *A General View of the Agriculture of the County of Sutherland* (London, 1812), 121.
2. John Sinclair, *General view ... northern counties*, 81; OSA, *Parish of Kirkmichael and Cullicudden*; John Henderson, *A General View of the Agriculture of the County of Caithness* (London, 1815) and *General View ... Sutherland*; James Donaldson, *A General view of the agriculture of the county of Nairn* (London, 1794), 14; B. A. Holderness, *Pre-industrial Britain Economy and Society 1500–1700* (London, 1976), 144; Thomas M. Devine, *The Transformation of Rural Scotland* (Edinburgh, 1994), 57.
3. Foulis Castle Archive, volume of printed estate papers. In interpreting Aitken's plan it is assumed that 0.8 of a boll was sown on each acre. This is calculated from Sinclair's account of a typical Black Isle farm (John Sinclair, *General view ... northern counties*, 81) which paid rent of £23 18s. Sinclair estimates rent at 16s per acre, giving a size of 29.88 acres. This required 37 bolls of seed, i.e. 0.8 bolls per acre. This is between the three firlots (0.75 bolls) per acre and 14 pecks (0.875 bolls) per acre reported in the OSA for Brechin (see Thomas M. Devine, *Transformation of Rural Scot*land, 56). John Henderson, *General View ... Sutherland*.
4. John Sinclair, *General view ... northern counties*, 104; James Robertson, *General View ... Inverness*, 94; James Donaldson, *General view ... Nairn*, 12.
5. John Sinclair, *General view ... northern counties*, 53.
6. NAS, RH15/44/41.
7. Foulis Castle Archive, Evidence in the case of Miss Mary Seymour v George Munro of Culrain.
8. John Sinclair, *General view ... northern counties*, 55.
9. James Robertson, *General View ... Inverness*, 94.
10. John Sinclair, *General view ... northern counties*, 303.
11. NRAS 0204/ printed notice of sale.
12. See, for example, NRAS 0204/Bundle 86, Lease of the Loaning of Davidston, 1743.
13. See Highland Council Archive, *Mackenzie of Scatwell v Magistrates of Fortrose*, printed volume in Fraser Macintosh collection.
14. John Sinclair, *General view ... northern counties*, 56–7 & 70.

15. Pitcalnie NAS, GD199/300 ; Rarichie NAS, SC34/29; Ankerville NAS, RH15/44/242.
16. Andrew Wight, *Present State of Husbandry in Scotland* (Edinburgh, 1778–84) ii. 247; James Robertson, *General View ... Inverness*, 396. Lace-making: NAS, NG1/1/19, Petition from George Ross of Pitkerry, Esq. 22 Jan 1772. The failure of the enterprise is recorded by Hugh Miller, *Scenes and Legends* (Edinburgh, 1994), 432. Ploughmen: John Sinclair, *General view ... northern counties*, 22.
17. Andrew Wight, *State of Husbandry*, iii. 258–9.
18. Ross's will: FN Reid, *The Earls of Ross* (London, 1894), 124. Cromarty Courthouse Museum, Bain MS. OSA, *Parish of Cromarty*.
19. J. Ferguson (ed.), *The Letters of George Dempster* (n.p., 1934), 167; John Sinclair, *General view ... northern counties*, 129.
20. NAS, SC24/4/1.
21. Gordon's improvements are detailed in a series of letters from him in NAS, RH15/44/54–55.
22. NLS, 9907/2. Alexander Barkly's brother, who supported many members of the family, was Aeneas Barkly, a successful sugar merchant in London. Aeneas's son, Henry, became colonial governor of the Cape, South Africa. See Mona Macmillan, *Sir Henry Barkly: Mediator and Moderator* (Cape Town, 1970). Alexander's uncle, Gilbert, had already emigrated to Philadelphia.
23. NAS, RH15/44/202, Minute of sale of the estate of Ardoch, 29 Jan 1761; NAS, GD347/73, Letter from George Gun Munro of Poyntzfield, referring to Lady Munro's next of kin. OSA, *Parish of Kirkmichael and Cullicudden*. Sinclair, *General view ... northern counties*, 41.
24. NAS, GD146/7 'List of subscribers in the Fishing Chamber of Inverness 1759'.
25. Hugh Miller, *Scenes and Legends*, 267; Hugh Miller, *Tales and Sketches*, 156–8.
26. NAS, GD159/10; NRAS 0204/Bundles 86 and 157.
27. Ian A. Robertson, *The Tay Salmon Fisheries* (Glasgow, 1998), 57–94; NAS, E504; NAS, RH15/44 (Newhall rentals); M. Mackenzie, *A View of the Salmon Fishery of Scotland* (London, 1834), 6.
28. St Andrews University Archive, ms. TA140:B8E43, 'Diary of Alexander Oswald Brodie 1843', 164 notes that a well in Cromarty 'occupies the place of a shaft driven by a shrewd Earl of Cromarty through the older sandstone in search of coal'. However, Thomas Telford noted in 1802 that the shaft was sunk by George Ross of Cromarty in the mid eighteenth century. Thomas Telford, *Survey and Report of the Coasts and Central Highlands of Scotland*, 1802, 10. For Urquhart's survey, see NRAS 0204/John Urquhart's Account Book 1752. The surveyor was a Mr Wetherby. For Ross's survey, North of England Institute of Mining and Mechanical Engineers, Watson Collection, Colliery View Book, NRO 3410/Wat/2/10/47, 1 Aug 1768 and Miscellaneous Collections, Borings and Sinkings, NRO 3410/ZA/12/57, 1 Aug 1768.
29. NAS, RH15/44/54–55.
30. This storehouse was on the opposite shore of the Cromarty Firth where there was 'no tolerable stone'.
31. NRAS 0204/Bundle 39 and 157; Highland Council Archive, Minutes of the Commissioners of Supply for the County of Cromarty; NAS, E746/74/46 and 51; David Aitken's survey of the Cromarty Estate (Cromarty House archive).

32. Iain Donnachie and G. Hewitt, *Historic New Lanark* (Edinburgh, 1993), 39. For the use of the Comprehending Act, see Highland Council Archive, Minutes of the Commissioners of Supply for the County of Cromarty. For the provisions of the Comprehending Act, and the fact that it was unusual for it to be invoked, see A. E. Whetstone, *Scottish County Government in the Eighteenth and Nineteenth Centuries* (Edinburgh, 1981).

33. Malcolm Gray, 'The Course of Scottish Emigration, 1750–1914: Enduring influences and Changing Circumstances' in Thomas M. Devine (ed.), *Scottish Emigration and Scottish Society* (Edinburgh, 1992), 16.

34. NRAS 0204/Bundle 11, John Gorry to Lady Urquhart, 15 Mar 1757; OSA; NRAS 0204/Bundles 86 & 97 refer to the 'officer commanding at Cromarty' in 1748 and to the 'military in Cromarty' being in want of meal when the mill was out of order after storms in the winter of 1756/57; NAS, SC24/7.

35. Hugh Miller, *Memoir of William Forsyth* (London, 1839); reprinted in *Tales and Sketches* (Edinburgh, 1863); NRAS 0204/Bundle 168.

36. NAS, E326.

Landownership and the Local Economy: 1790s–1840s

Inverness will have a serious rival in Cromarty ... which is obviously the best adapted to become the grand depot, the great granary and storehouse of merchandise and trade, in the northern end of the Island of Great Britain; and when the day shall arise (and come it will) that Government will assuredly see the utility and vast importance of a naval establishment at this port, Cromarty will be seen to rise rapidly and become the general mart of the North.

Sir John Sinclair, 1795

The sixty years from 1790 to 1850 saw Cromarty's dramatic growth as a commercial centre and its equally dramatic decline as Invergordon rose to become the principal port in the firth. Many of the buildings of twenty-first-century Cromarty are from this period of prosperity, reflecting the wealth created by the rising middle class. Landowners played a surprisingly limited role in the growth of the economy, and for almost the whole of this period there was no proactive management of the Cromarty estate.

Succession, entail and the 'Cromarty bastardy case'

George Ross of Cromarty died in 1786 with no direct heir. After his father's death, Ross's mother, Catherine Fraser – of the family of Fraser of Achnagairn – had married for a second time, to John Gray of Overskibo. A grandson of this second marriage, Alexander Gray (c.1741–1820), became Ross's business partner in the London army agency, Ross and Ogilvie. George Ross became an MP in 1780 and, since the holding of an army agency was a disqualification from sitting in the House of Commons, he retired from the business in favour of Alexander. On Ross's death, Alexander succeeded him, changing his name to Alexander Gray Ross of Cromarty.

George Ross's estate had, however, been substantially diminished because, towards the end of his life, he had sustained a substantial financial loss through the failure of John Fraser, a London merchant and a relation through his mother. Fraser's debts of over £90,000 included some £43,000 owed to Ross. This in turn prevented Ross from repaying money he had borrowed to improve the Cromarty estate and Alexander Gray Ross inherited the problem. Outstanding debts remained a significant burden on the estate, such that in the early 1800s payments of interest amounted to almost £2,000 on an income of just over £2,700.[1]

However, the army agency grew with the advent of the war with France in 1793. When George Ross had handed over the agency to Alexander in 1780, they were contracted to twenty-one regiments. By 1796 the annual turnover was in excess of £1 million. Yet the commercial fortunes of war were unpredictable and the partners in the agency became bankrupt in 1804. At this point, it seemed that the Cromarty estate might be sold. There was, however, legal argument as to whether or not George Ross had entailed the Cromarty estate – had he done so it would have been protected from creditors. Ultimately this claim was unsuccessful and in 1815 the estate was placed in the hands of trustees in bankruptcy. Alexander Gray Ross died in London in 1820, having leased Cromarty House to a series of tenants from the 1790s and, apparently, having taken little personal interest in the Cromarty property. His death was followed by a further lengthy dispute – 'the Cromarty bastardy case'. Gray Ross had an illegitimate son and subsequently married the mother, which would have legitimated the child in Scots law but not in English law. The couple married in Scotland but they were domiciled in England. English law was eventually held to apply, the illegitimate son did not inherit and the estate passed to Catharine Munro, a direct descendant of George Ross's sister.

Catharine Munro's husband, Hugh Rose, had made a fortune at a young age supplying the British army in the West Indies during the Napoleonic Wars. By the 1820s he was already recognised as a noted improver in the area and in 1830, when it seemed that the Cromarty succession case had been resolved, the *Inverness Courier* observed that:

> A wide field of improvement is thus opened up. The town of Cromarty with its various beauties and advantages – its great natural capabilities, excellent harbour, and central situation for commerce – will afford full scope for that zeal, public spirit, and judgement which Mr Rose has already displayed in his extensive improvements in Ross-shire.[2]

The legal process further delayed this until 1847 – from which date there was a radical change in estate management.

Newhall and Braelangwell

After the death of Henrietta Urquhart in 1799, the Newhall estate was acquired by the trustees of a Colin Mackenzie, whose nephew Donald carried out a number of improvements, including the rebuilding of Newhall House. The estate was entailed in 1815 and this was followed by a series of complex legal cases over liability for payment for the earlier improvements.

The Braelangwell estate remained in Urquhart hands and was further improved in the first two decades of the nineteenth century. By the 1820s a further factor was coming into play in landownership – the Highlands were becoming romanticised. This received a considerable boost in George IV's visit to Edinburgh in 1822, during which he wore the kilt and leading members of Scottish society were instructed by Sir Walter Scott, as master of ceremonies, to appear in their 'traditional' clan tartans – an instruction that led to a flurry of creative invention. The king's own costume was supplied by George Hunter, an Edinburgh merchant whose daughter had married Urquhart of Braelangwell.

The couple's son, David Urquhart, was clearly caught up in the romance of the Highlands and for decades pursued the case that the Urquharts of Braelangwell were the hereditary chiefs of the Clan Urquhart. This was false both as a matter of genealogy and in the notion that the Urquharts had ever been a Highland clan – but it was indicative of the manner in which families in the eastern lowlands were influenced by the redefinition of Highland identity.[3] The small Braelangwell estate and its tenants were however largely irrelevant to David Urquhart. He played a role on the world stage as a linguist and diplomat – remembered at his death in 1877 for having presented the pope with a plan for world peace and for introducing Turkish baths to Britain. The claim to be a Highland chief may have been part of the persona he wished to present on his European travels but by 1839 he had sold Braelangwell to Lt General Hastings Fraser.

The management of most estates now owed nothing to a traditional relationship between landlord and tenant – after the late 1840s the farms were run on a commercial basis and the moors were used for sport. The duties and responsibilities taken on by the laird – for example, to entertain tenants on the wedding of his son or to relieve poverty – were those of any Victorian landowner.[4]

Agriculture 1790s–1815

The new breed of commercial farmers

The Napoleonic Wars of 1793–1815 led to consistently high, though fluctuating, grain prices as a result of restrictions on imports from abroad and increased demand from a larger army and navy. The price of barley, for example, rose from 16s per boll in 1790 to as high as 50s in 1800. Similarly high prices obtained in the last years of war. These trends produced increased returns for tenants of productive farms throughout Scotland and, as market prices rose, wheat cultivation in the north expanded – 10,000 bolls of wheat were grown in Easter Ross in 1812, compared to only 2,000 in 1802 – and the importance of exports of wheat can be seen in the details of shipping recorded in local newspapers. Local marketing also became easier with the opening of a corn market in Dingwall in 1806.[5]

In addition to the increasing importance of wheat, there was a sustained local market for barley for distilling at Ferintosh. Production had originally been in numerous small stills but in 1780 a group of merchants formed a company, which built a larger distillery, and in 1780 the customs authority appointed a 'tidesman' to supervise shipping of spirits.[6] Although the 'Ferintosh privilege' of duty-free distilling was rescinded in 1786, and the large distillery failed, the parish almost immediately became a centre for small-scale licit distilling under the new regulations, with twenty-nine stills in 1798 and a rapidly expanding population. There was also, until the 1820s, a thriving trade in illicitly distilled spirits in the north and both the licit and the illicit trade kept demand for barley high.

Higher prices enabled landowners to raise rents but, since rents were still lower than in the Lothians, the area became attractive to tenants from the south. There was also, by this date, recognised expertise among Moray farmers and some moved into the area. Thus, for the first time, there was a substantial body of experienced, improving tenants and in 1793 the Ross-shire Farming Society was formed, with both a Black Isle and an Easter Ross committee.[7]

Improvement was taken up more quickly on some estates than on others. The Cromarty estate initiated changes as early as 1794–5, while Braelangwell and Newhall continued earlier policies of estate management until 1814. The opportunity for larger scale improvements opened a debate on the value of settling 'mailers', that is, smallholders given uncultivated ground, who initially paid either no rent or minimal rent. Sir John Sinclair's view on the advantages of settling mailers – the 'aborigines of improvement', as he described them – has been outlined in chapter 11. George Mackenzie of Coul, in his *Survey of the Counties of Ross & Cromarty*, written for the Board of Agriculture in 1808, argued that the policy was unsustainable. The holdings created could not support a family and attempts to introduce manufactures as supplementary employment had failed. If the land brought into cultivation by mailers was subsequently consolidated into a larger farm then the mailers were simply moved on and condemned to constant poverty. Moreover mailers, according to Mackenzie, interfered with

other improvements because they impoverished the land by digging pits
for earth to add to their middens and allowed their cattle to wander,
breaking down fences and enclosures.[8] The policy of settling mailers
was gradually abandoned but different estates moved towards this
change at a different pace.

The Cromarty estate

In the mid 1790s a family named Middleton arrived in Cromarty from
Berwickshire. They originated from near Darlington but had farmed at
Norham-on-Tweed since the 1770s. There were three brothers – William
Middleton, who took the lease of Kirkton farm on the Newhall estate;
George Middleton, who before 1795 revived the trade in salt pork from
Cromarty and from 1801, or before, took a long lease of Davidston
farm; and a Thomas Middleton, who in 1807 supplied carts, men and
horses for the rebuilding of Newhall House. William was drowned near
Kirkton in 1794, along with his grieve, who had come to the area with
them, and nothing more is known of Thomas. George had taken on
the lease of Kirkton by 1803 and also had the lease of Newhall Mains
before 1807.[9]

George Middleton's recognised expertise allowed him to raise
capital for his improvements. By 1803 he had borrowed £400 from the
Cromarty estate and, in 1804, a further £500 from Charles Lockhart
of Kindeace, using his property near Cromarty harbour as security. He
was also allowed to run up arrears of rent amounting, at his death in
1810, to almost £400. Writing in 1836, Hugh Miller saw Middleton as
the key improver of the period, whose innovations included building the
first steam thrashing-mill. He grew wheat, although he considered that
it was not prudent to risk sowing too much of this crop, and by sowing
Polish oats, rather than older varieties, he was achieving a sixteenfold
return. Middleton also engaged in other business – trade in salt cod
and pork, the tenancy of the meal and flour mill at Braelangwell, and
a short-lived attempt to ship flagstone from a quarry at Davidston.[10]
The improvements to Davidston can be seen on the estate maps of
1823 in the form of larger, consolidated fields forming a 300-acre farm.
The farm had been created by the removal of eleven tenants – among
forty-five on the estate who were served with summons of removal in
1794 and 1795. There was, understandably, resentment and in 1815
Middleton's house was damaged by a mob who suspected him of
hoarding grain.[11]

The 1823 map shows other changes on the estate. There were now
thirty-five holdings rather than the minimum of forty-five which appear
in the summons of removal in 1795. Of these, eleven were farms of over
seventy acres, a size considered viable by at least some improvers, and
this accounted for 71 per cent of arable ground on the estate. There
were now only fifteen holdings of fifteen acres and under, of which

nine were the recently formed 'Neilston pendicles'. The effect of these changes is evident in the fall of almost 10 per cent in the population of the rural part of the parish of Cromarty between 1791 and 1821, and in increased emigration, particularly after 1808.

The Newhall and Braelangwell estates

David Urquhart of Braelangwell (1748–1811) married Henrietta Gordon of Newhall, who had succeeded to the Newhall estate on the death of her brother William in 1778. From the time of their marriage in 1786 the estates were jointly managed. Urquhart died in 1811, Henrietta having predeceased him in 1799, and the Braelangwell estate was sold in 1812 – some of it to the Newhall estate.[12] Both Urquhart and Gordon were enthusiastic improvers, coupling agricultural change with the promotion of textile production, but their improvements were largely restricted to the Mains farm and the grounds of what was, by 1810, a 'very comfortable modern house' at Braelangwell. These included enclosures, a plantation of young oaks and an orchard of thirteen acres, the largest in the north of Scotland. Shell-marl, found in a shallow loch

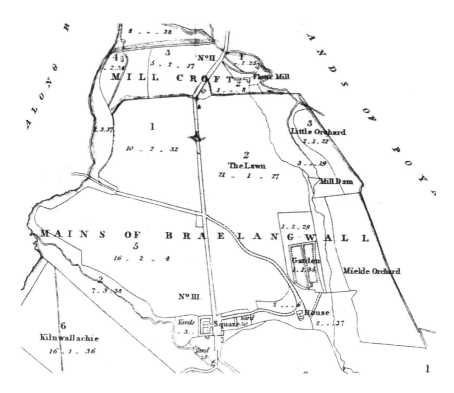

FIGURE 12.1
Braelangwell in 1812 – its orchard was the largest in the north of Scotland.

nearby, was used extensively as manure. Newhall was sold in 1799 and substantial improvements, including the rebuilding of Newhall House and erection of new farm buildings, commenced in 1806.[13]

On the Braelangwell estate, in 1801, there were no substantial single-tenancy farms and a map of the estate made in 1812, prior to its sale, shows no significant change from this position.[14] An analysis of the Newhall rental of 1816, shows that there were seventy-four mailers and fifty-five other tenants, only two of which – Resolis and Kirkton – were in substantial single tenancies. The raising of summons of removal against seventy-six tenants on the Newhall estate in 1814 probably indicates an intention to reorganise tenancies to create larger holdings and by 1819 a number of nineteen-year improving leases were being granted.[15]

Estate villages

Many estates pursuing policies of improvement also attempted to establish estate villages. These were created throughout the Highlands from c.1750 as centres for tradesmen, who hitherto had been based on the farmtouns. It was the intention that the new settlements would also become the focus for development of manufactures – but this was seldom achieved.[16] The Newhall estate laid out Gordon's Mills in lots in the 1790s and Poyntzfield created Jemimaville before 1820. Gordon's Mills came to little after the failure of the wool-carding and spinning mill around which it was based, but Jemimaville grew despite being established only shortly before the collapse of grain prices at the end of the Napoleonic Wars. By the early 1820s its inn had become a social centre for the unmarried male labourers employed on those neighbouring farms which had introduced the bothy system of farm labour[17] and by the 1840s there was additional employment in small-scale shipbuilding, established by an Aberdeen merchant.[18]

Agriculture: improvement after 1815

At the end of the Napoleonic Wars in 1815 foreign grain flooded the British market and prices tumbled to their lowest level for twenty years. Tenants in the north attempted to compensate for the fall by supplying barley to illicit distillers – and even leading figures in the farming community came to rely on this market for their produce. However, new legislation in 1823 was spectacularly successful in encouraging licit distilling and clamping down on the illicit trade. It was, consequently, the partial recovery of wheat prices after 1825 that had a more enduring effect. Over the next decade both large and small farmers turned to wheat growing. However, concentration on one crop tended to be counter-productive over time and in 1836 Miller noted that 'during the past ten years every farmer in the parish has reared and exported wheat; but the inevitable effects of over-production have already become apparent; the value of this grain is sinking fast'.[19]

Fluctuations in the grain price made returns uncertain and militated against large-scale improvement, particularly on estates that were entailed or controlled by judicial factors, and by the mid 1830s the spread of improvement was limited. The eastern part of parish of Cromarty was generally improved but not the western, and in Resolis there were only three large farms, of which one was 'largely waste although capable of improvement'. On some farms the limited improvements of the eighteenth century had either not been extended, as at Poyntzfield, or, as at Braelangwell, had been neglected.[20]

The progress of improvement in Easter Ross and the Black Isle as a whole can be judged from the 1831 census. In the parish of Cromarty, consolidation of farms into larger tenancies had continued and by 1831 there were only eighteen farms in the parish, of which twelve employed farm labour – the remaining six being worked solely by their tenants. This was the lowest number of smallholdings in any parish in the east of Ross & Cromarty. The parish of Resolis, in contrast, has sixty-eight smallholdings and the average size of farms that employed labourers was much smaller.

Where farms had been improved, yields had increased. On Millcroft of Braelangwell in 1844 both manure and bonemeal were being bought in and the return on barley was 7.6 times and on oats 5.4 times.[21] In the same year there were the first imports of South American guano, for use as manure,[22] and from the mid 1850s part of the disused Cromarty factory became a guano store. Although change was underway, the area contrasted with the north-east of Scotland where the agricultural revolution could be said to be complete by 1840.[23] Hugh Miller was employed as accountant in the Commercial Bank in Cromarty from 1834 to 1839, a position which enabled him to observe the financial affairs of both merchants and farmers. He noted that small farms were proving uneconomic in the face of competition and that tenants of such farms – who had been 'a comparatively comfortable class some sixty or eighty years before, used to give dowries to their daughters, and leave well stocked farms to their sons' – were now 'falling into straightened circumstances'.[24]

The 'provision trade'

The production of barrelled salt pork, established by George Ross in the 1770s, initially failed following the poor harvest of 1782–3 but was reviving by 1788 and grew significantly with the arrival of George Middleton, whose trade in salt pork and bacon amounted to 112 tons by 1808. Ten years later the annual value of the pork trade from Cromarty was £30,000.[25]

Pigs were common in the town – too common for those who sought to promote the town as a 'place of summer resort' – and the lane which ran past Middleton's slaughter houses and curing yard is still known as the 'Slooch moochd', a rendering of the Gaelic *slochd na muic* (the pigs' pass). One of the leading provision merchants, Robert Ross, rose to be, as his gravestone recorded, 'The Friend of Hugh Miller, Provost of Cromarty for 20 years and Agent for the Commercial Bank for 43 years'.

Fishing: 1790s–1840s

The Caithness herring fishery

In the later eighteenth and early nineteenth centuries fishing in the Moray Firth was focused on expanded trade in salmon shipped to London, a newly developed lobster fishery and, most importantly, a revival of the Caithness fisheries. As in the seventeenth century, this seems to have begun with an expansion of the cod fishery, which may have helped fishermen to accumulate capital to equip boats, but it quickly became a boom in herring fishing.[26]

The involvement of some northern fishing communities with merchants from the south of Scotland was also important. Falls of Dunbar began buying both cod and herring in Caithness in the 1780s and also dealt with fishermen in Avoch. After Falls' bankruptcy in 1788, the Northumberland Fishing Company dealt with Avoch, while in Caithness the cod fishery seems to have been largely taken over by London-based smacks, who were said in 1811 to have overfished and destroyed the fishery. The subsequent development of the Caithness herring fishery was encouraged both by southern firms and by local merchants and by 1811 the herring catch had risen to 60,000 barrels.[27] A crucial factor had been the introduction in 1785 of a government bounty on herring caught and cured. Earlier bounties had encouraged the building of large vessels, which could operate as herring busses. The new system, which operated with various changes until 1829, increased the income of herring fishers themselves and thus financed improvements to their fishing boats and gear. This led in turn to increased catches and allowed fishers to reinvest in yet larger boats and more nets – something which was possible because fishers now owned their boats rather than holding them from local landowners.[28]

The Caithness herring fishery was initially prosecuted mainly by local fishermen who worked seasonally and also held small plots of land. In the late 1780s around 100 boats fished from Wick and nearby Staxigoe. By the mid 1790s the reputation of Caithness cured herring had grown and there were around 200 boats. The success of the Caithness fishery drew in fishers from communities along the north and west coasts and from the Moray Firth. By 1806 there were between twenty and thirty boats on the east coast of Sutherland. Cromarty boats were gradually absorbed into this process, and they were fishing from Caithness for a twenty-year period from around 1790 to 1810. The fishery that the Cromarty boats had joined was operated on the 'engagement' system, by which curers undertook to pay boats at a fixed rate for all herring caught – together with a daily bottle of whisky.[29]

There was further progress after 1808 when government fisheries officers were appointed and a series of controls, implemented through them, began to establish a reputation for quality Scottish herring. These controls included larger net meshes; shaking fish out of nets at sea rather than on shore; a maximum of 1,250 herring per barrel, with a standard thirty-two-gallon barrel and a specified thickness of wood; gutting and curing within twenty-four hours of catching, with the use of gutting knives rather than hand; sorting and grading of fish; and the introduction of the crown brand.[30] The bounty on the catch was doubled in 1809 and the number of boats engaged in the Caithness fishery increased dramatically.

The Cromarty fishery district

With this growth, Wick harbour became congested and, despite the construction of a new harbour by the British Fisheries Society, both boats and curers began to look for additional bases to the south, often in small and difficult harbours. In the first decade of the century, according to Hugh Miller, Cromarty fishermen returning from Caithness in September had been aware of shoals of herring in the Moray Firth, sometimes more than off Caithness. In Cromarty itself fishing had been boosted by a revival of cod fishery, and in 1808 the Cromarty merchant, George Middleton, exported 110 tons of salt cod, but there were no merchants willing to cure herring until 1815, when George and Hugh Ross employed coopers in Cromarty and fishermen were persuaded not to go to Caithness.[31] This venture was unsuccessful but a run of good herring seasons followed and an Aberdeen-based company, formed in 1819, established curing stations around the Moray Firth employing almost all the boats. In 1821 herring fishing was reported to be 'going on with great spirit' with twenty Irish fishing boats employed by the curers and the 'beach and green [had] the appearance of a continual fair'.[32] The curers were probably 'A. Gordon and Co' who, in 1826, employed thirteen coopers in Cromarty, including six apprentices.[33] By

FIGURE 12.2
Seal of the French consul at Cromarty, 1830s, perhaps established to support
French fishing boats.

September of this year there were 'no fewer than 200 women engaged
in cleaning and salting the fish ... while 29 masted vessels lay in the firth
waiting to convey the barrels, on being made up, to various ports'.[34]
The Cromarty fishery district had become the eighth largest herring
station in Britain, curing 20,000 barrels annually.[35]

The policy that government should be involved in the control
and development of fishing was replaced during the late 1820s by
an emphasis on free trade and laissez-faire economics, resulting in
the withdrawal of bounties and the abolishing of salt duty by 1829.
Herring fishing survived these changes but there was a general decline
with the loss of the West Indian market after the abolition of slavery
in 1833 and the decline of the Irish market with the famine of the
1840s. Recovery came with the development of the Eastern European
and Baltic markets, in which quality was of greater importance and
in which the full benefits of the improvements in quality achieved
after 1809 were realised. Crown branding continued, at a fee of 4d a
barrel from 1858, but by then large curers could market on their own

reputation. The Caithness fishery grew further until it reached a peak in the 1850s, with 1100 boats in Wick alone.

The prosperity of the Cromarty fishery district did not, however, survive the decline of the 1830s and 1840s. This was something of a puzzle at the time. In 1849 one observer was of the opinion that 'in curing convenience, in fishing ground and in means of navigation, Cromarty has few, or no equal on the Scottish coast; and yet, strange to say, the herring fishing lies nearly dormant and in a state of neglect, which better times alone can re-animate'.[36] French vessels that cured herring on board were, however, in the port.[37]

The failure of Cromarty to revive can be accounted for in three ways. First, there had been the growth further south of significant new ports at Fraserburgh (1820s) and Peterhead (1830s), with larger harbours able to operate on a larger scale and benefit from the expanding Baltic trade. These ports could by this time draw on an increasingly mobile labour force of gutters, packers and fishers. Second, the accelerated pace of innovation in fishing gear after 1830 meant that, once the Cromarty fishing had declined, it was almost impossible for local fishermen to re-enter the trade in competition with the better equipped fishers from other areas. Even in the 1820s many Cromarty boats were manned by only four men, although larger boats had been common elsewhere for some time.[38] Finally, there appears to have been an important element of choice in the strategies pursued by different fishing communities. By the 1790s a contrast was already being drawn between the 'bold fishermen' of Avoch and the fishers of the Cromarty Firth, who did not venture far from their home ports.[39] This was, however, not simply a matter of character. Cromarty offered alternative sources of employment and, at the time, a growing local market for white fish. In this context, line fishing provided secure, if limited, returns while herring catches fluctuated and might well prove a 'fause lippenin' – a false trust.

In contrast, the Avoch fishermen, engaged by Falls of Dunbar and the Northumberland Fishing Company, had a secure market for their catch, justifying investment in larger boats and longer journeys in search of fish. The longer established tradition in Avoch of involvement with southern merchants and the continual upgrading of equipment appears to have helped this community to revive its herring fishery after the decline of the 1830s, while the Cromarty community concentrated on line fishing.

Salmon and lobster fisheries

Two years after the introduction of the new herring bounty in 1785, salmon fishing was transformed by a key advance made by George Dempster (of Dunnichen and later Skibo) who 'discovered the

exporting of fish in ice to London'.[40] Dempster was a Member of
Parliament and in London, in 1786, met with an Alexander Dalrymple
of the East India Company. Dalrymple had spent time in China and
told Dempster that Chinese 'coolies' used crushed ice to preserve
perishable goods in transit. In 1787 Dempster persuaded the Tay fish
merchant Richardson to experiment with this method. Until this point
the export of fresh salmon to London, wrapped in straw, had stopped
with warmer weather in April or May. The use of ice extended the
season considerably and this was coupled with a continued trade
in kitted salmon, preserved in vinegar, during the summer months.
The marketing of fresh salmon to London was contemporary with
a further development – the shipping of live lobsters, a trade which
expanded from around 1785, with hundreds of thousands of lobsters
being supplied each year in 'well smacks': 30,000 were caught off the
Sutherland coast in 1807, 40,000 off Caithness in 1811, and 70,000
off Portmahomack in 1792.[41] Salmon netting was entirely in the
hands of estate owners but the lobster fishery was a useful addition to
the income of fishing families.

Increased demand, once fresh salmon could be provided, led to
improved design and increased use of stake nets. A stake net consisted
of a row of poles driven into the seabed, carrying a leader net that
directed fish into a pound at the seaward end. These appeared first on

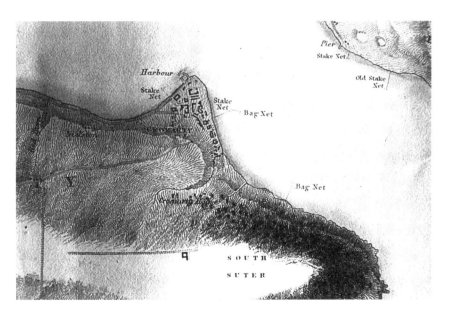

FIGURE 12.3
Stake and bag nets for salmon in the Cromarty Firth, 1830s.

the Tay shortly after 1800, around Montrose in 1807 and were also in use on the Solway from an early date.[42] Stake nets required more active management than yairs: it was, in a sense, the tide which did the fishing in a yair, leaving fish trapped on the sand at low water. The cost of the additional labour required by stake nets could only be borne with higher market prices.

At some fishing stations salmon were only kitted, not shipped fresh. James Grubb, who leased the Newhall and Ardoch salmon fishing, boiled and pickled 1,130 salmon and 1,299 grilse between January and August 1816. These were shipped to London and Berwick.[43] In the same year vinegar was supplied from a storehouse in Cromarty to a John Stevenson who had the lease of the Chanonry salmon fishing.[44] It was, however, the trade in iced fresh fish that came to dominate and the Aberdeen-based Hogarth & Company controlled most of the fishings from the 1830s. Salmon fishing provided only limited local employment, with two or three fishers and a manager in Cromarty in 1841 and 1851.

The expansion of stake netting had an immediate impact on river fisheries. The concern was not now the destruction of salmon fry in yairs but the number of fish caught, especially breeding fish. The Conon, which recorded a catch of 7,656 fish before stake netting, had only 633 afterwards, while the stake nets in the lower waters of the Cromarty Firth trapped 6,500. By 1816 the river fishery on the Ness had become 'a losing concern'.[45] Protests and legal action by proprietors of river fishings led to the Tay stake nets being declared illegal in 1819, a judgement based on an early Scots statute that banned 'fixed engines' in rivers. The difficulty in interpretation lay in determining what constituted a river and what a part of the sea.

Further actions were brought and decided case by case. A stake net at Redcastle on the Beauly Firth was declared illegal, stake nets near Fort George were deemed to be in tidal waters, and the legality of nets between the two was contested. In 1834 stake nets in the Cromarty Firth were still 'in their full glory' and 'the rivers nearly useless'.[46] These 'fixed engines' became illegal in the Cromarty Firth in the 1850s, following a Court of Session decision. Hugh Miller, writing in the *Witness*, responded to the decision that the Cromarty Firth was not a part of the sea by satirically describing their lordships as great geographers who had discovered a previously unknown river wider than the Mississippi.

Cromarty harbour

Cromarty's role as an entrepôt had been secured by the construction of the harbour piers, between 1781 and 1784, which allowed ships of up to

EDINBURGH, ABERDEEN, INVERNESS,
AND CROMARTY

STEAM PACKET.

 THE BRILLIANT of 90 Horse Power, continues to SAIL from Leith every Monday Morning for Inverness, Cromarty, and Invergordon— calling at Aberdeen, and all the intermediate Ports, and leaves Inverness, Cromarty, and Invergordon for Aberdeen and Leith—every Wednesday Morning at the following hours, viz :—

On WEDNESDAY 30th July, from Inverness at 3 o'clock, and from CROMARTY and INVERGORDON at 6 o'clock in the Morning.

The BRILLIANT has excellent Bed accommodation and a female Steward in the Lad. .' Cabins. Passengers from Inverness, may either embark at the hour of Sailing or on the preceding evening.

Carriages, Goods, and Sheep carried at moderate freight.

Farther information will be obtained of the Shoremasters, at Inverness, Cromarty, and Invergordon.

Aberdeen, 15th July, 1828.

FIGURE 12.4
Steam ships and the new harbour at Invergordon reduced Cromarty's trade.

350 tons burden to load and unload safely and led to a marked increase in trade over the following quarter century.[47] The term 'emporium' was commonly used for a centre that acted as a general market for goods of all kinds. Inverness was so described by Pennant in the 1760s but, in 1794, Sir John Sinclair judged that Cromarty might overtake Inverness as the 'general emporium' of the north. However, Cromarty's trade was threatened by the north side of the firth, which was becoming better connected into the expanding network of improved roads. The establishment in 1803 of the Commission for Highland Roads and Bridges, in response to Thomas Telford's report of the previous year, led to the construction of bridges over the Conon in 1809 and the Beauly in 1811, thus expanding the road network from Inverness into Easter Ross. The roads themselves were improved from 1807 when additional funds were raised by making some roads on the east coast into toll roads. Initially there was some limited benefit to Cromarty in improved roads and from 1821 the Geddes Hotel in Inverness ran a conveyance every ten days from Inverness to Cromarty to take passengers to the London smacks – a journey which took five hours.[48]

A harbour pier built on the north shore of the firth, at Balintraid, in 1821 posed the first serious threat to Cromarty's trade. In 1822 Robertson of Kindeace wrote to the *Inverness Journal* to encourage use of Balintraid, remarking that 'a few interested people in Cromarty will

ANNO QUARTO

GULIELMI IV. REGIS.

****

Cap. xlviii.

An Act for preserving and maintaining the Piers and Harbour of *Cromarty*.   [16th *June* 1834.]

WHEREAS an Act was passed in the Twenty-fifth Year of the Reign of His late Majesty King *George* the Third, intituled *An Act for the better preserving and maintaining* 25 G. 3. c. 39. *the Piers and Harbour of* Cromarty, *in* North Britain, which Act has expired: And whereas by virtue of the Powers granted by the said recited Act, Piers, Quays, Jetties, and other Buildings and Works, were erected and completed for the Improvement of the Harbour of *Cromarty* in the County of *Cromarty*, and the Accommodation of Vessels resorting thereto, and have proved of great public Utility; but the same cannot be preserved and maintained unless some of the Provisions of the said recited Act be continued in this Act, and further Powers and Authorities be granted to the Trustees hereby appointed: May it therefore please Your Majesty that it may be enacted; and be it enacted by the King's most Excellent Majesty, by and with the Advice and Consent of the Lords Spiritual and Temporal, and Commons, in this present Parliament assembled, and by the Authority of the same, That it shall Trustees. and may be lawful to and for the Member of Parliament for the Burgh of *Cromarty*, the Sheriff Depute of the United Counties of *Ross* and *Cromarty*, the Provost of the said Burgh of *Cromarty*, the Proprietor of the Estate and Barony of *Cromarty*, and the Baron Baillie of the said Barony of *Cromarty*, for the Time being, and the Judicial Factor of the Estate of *Cromarty* appointed or to be appointed by the Court of Session in *Scotland* during the Sequestration of the said Estate, or any Three or more of them assembled together (who are hereby appointed Trustees for putting this Act into execution),

[*Local.*]   14 *O*   cution),

FIGURE 12.5
The Cromarty Harbour Act, 1834 – part of the attempt to revive trade in the face of competition from Invergordon.

do all they can to oppose any change in the present system'.[49] This was followed by the harbour pier built at Invergordon in 1828, augmenting the landing piers for the Invergordon–Balblair ferry already constructed at the expense of the Commissioners of Highland Roads and Bridges.

From this point Cromarty's trade began a rapid decline. It was already 'very trifling' in 1835 and by 1843 two-thirds of Ross & Cromarty's imports and exports were passing through Invergordon's more central harbour. Robert Carruthers, the editor of the *Inverness Courier*, observed that Invergordon 'bids fair to eclipse Cromarty as an emporium for trade'. In Cromarty there were already 'many ruinous and tottering buildings'.[50] An Act of Parliament in 1834 reconstituted Cromarty Harbour Trust and in 1836 there was expenditure of £800 to improve its facilities, but to no avail.[51] At the 1841 census there were only four men employed as boatmen in the town and only one carter and three porters – a far cry from a few decades before. Cromarty remained a convenient port of call for emigrant ships sailing to Canada but this too declined after 1850 with the introduction of steam ships, sailing from west-coast ports.

From the completion of the harbour in 1784 there had been hopes that the Cromarty Firth would become a base for the Navy and in 1803, following a report by Thomas Telford in the previous year, the Committee on the Survey of the Coasts and Central Highlands of Scotland confirmed that 'for the perfect accommodation of a squadron, or even a fleet, there seems to be nothing wanting but storehouses upon the shore'.[52] Twenty years earlier George Ross had 'entertained sanguine hopes that government one day will establish a dry dock near the harbour for repairing ships of war in their northern expeditions' and in 1802 Edward Fraser of Reelig drew attention to the potential, which he believed Telford had missed, of using the quarry below Newton as a dock.[53] None of these schemes were realised, although naval vessels appeared from time to time.

Timber and shipbuilding

A few estates, such as Newhall, created plantations in the early and mid eighteenth century and when the Newhall timber matured in the 1770s, the laird explored the possibilities of shipping it for use as rails on wagon roads at the Carron iron works. However, most plantations on the Black Isle were established in the second half of the century, some such as those at Redcastle (1801–2) and Tarradale (c.1770) created by enclosing parts of the Mulbuie commonty. The hardwoods on Cromarty Hill were planted in the 1770s, using earlier softwoods for shelter, and although there was considerable damage to all standing timber from gales in 1818, the woods on the Cromarty estate remained an important asset, with an estimated value in 1843 of £20,000. There were two timber yards in the town in 1834, both of which were still in operation in 1850. Most timber was shipped south from the firth, much of it for pit props, and when ownership of the Cromarty estate was clarified in the late 1840s, systematic felling led to a temporary increase in activity at Cromarty harbour.[54]

Locally grown wood had, however, limited uses and there was also a trade in imported wood. Lucille Campey has recently demonstrated the interconnection between import of timber from Canada and emigration. The same vessels that shipped timber from Canada, carried emigrants on their outward voyage – the combined trade both making the enterprise viable and reducing the cost of emigration. Some imported timber was landed in the Cromarty Firth but the benefits of this went again to Invergordon, where a 'woodyard for foreign timber' was opened in 1849.[55]

Despite the limitations in the size of local timber, shipbuilding was established at Cromarty shortly before 1810, when a ship of 123 tons was under construction, and over the next twenty years at least twelve vessels were launched, the largest of 160 tons.[56] There is no record of shipbuilding between 1830 and 1850, when Cromarty's trade was in decline, and the last ship was built in 1855. The main shipbuilder was Hugh Allan, who had transferred his business to Cromarty from Beauly in the first decade of the nineteenth century, at a time when Cromarty's trade was flourishing and there was a ready supply of timber in the firth.[57] In 1844 a ship was under construction on the shore at Jemimaville, in this case the initiative of an Aberdeen merchant.[58]

Brewing

High grain prices during the Napoleonic Wars led to the bankruptcy of the tenant of the Cromarty brewery in 1803. There was a partial revival in its trade after the collapse of grain prices in 1815 and the only surviving set of accounts, for the year 1818–19, show that sales rose to over £2,000. Nevertheless, the enterprise remained vulnerable. Its sales were achieved by the tenant travelling to Fortrose, Nairn, Inverness, Dingwall and Tain to take orders and it faced increasing competition from the trade in both licit and illicit whisky. Another tenant became bankrupt in the 1830s and the brewery was defunct by the 1850s.[59]

Not only did brewing fail but Cromarty and the surrounding area did not initially benefit significantly from the burgeoning trade in whisky. The demand for Scotch whisky, which had been growing from the mid eighteenth century, increased towards 1800 as a result of greater urbanisation and the interruption of imports of French wines and spirits during the Napoleonic Wars. Increased taxation on malt, stills and spirits encouraged illicit production, which flourished until 1822 when considerably harsher punishments were imposed on those found guilty of illicit distilling. Illicit production was at its highest in those parts of the Highlands which bordered the fertile 'corn lands' of the eastern coastal fringe and where there were good supplies of water and peat. A degree of remoteness was an advantage in avoiding detection – although, given the connivance of the land-owning magistracy, who relied on the illicit trade to market their grain, this was of lesser importance until 1822. Tom Devine and others have highlighted the importance of illicit distilling in the local economy and stressed its significance as evidence of enterprise in Highland peasant society, contrary to the image of indolence and inertia often given by Victorian commentators.[60]

The eastern Black Isle was at a disadvantage in the illicit trade because it had poor supplies of peat and, to a lesser extent, because it was at a distance from the overland routes by which whisky was smuggled south. As a consequence the area failed to benefit – precisely at the time when mailers were being encouraged to settle on unimproved ground. These households had, as a result, to rely more on increasingly poorly paid work in flax and hemp spinning.

As pressure increased to suppress the illicit trade, licit whisky stills were established at Ardoch and Braelangwell – and, very briefly, at Cromarty. The Ardoch distillery was established in 1816 and failed in 1824, but that at Braelangwell was still 'famed for its excellent whisky' in 1836 and employed three brewers, a maltman and a resident exciseman, although its manager had been accused of fraud.[61] In the century before 1850, the overall effect of legislation and of the increasing popularity of spirits was to remove brewing and distilling from its position as an integral part of the local economy and turn it into a larger scale industry – located in those areas best suited to production.

The spiral of decline

It is difficult to know just why Cromarty, with its wealth and the experience of its merchant community, failed to recover from the decline of the 1830s and 1840s. The answer probably lies in the loss of confidence brought about by the failure of so many sectors of the economy at much the same time – and by the lack of local leadership. The succession to ownership of the Cromarty estate was still unresolved, other landowners were absentees, the leaders of the merchant class were elderly and conservative in their outlook, and the town council formed in 1834 was ineffective.

Notes

1. Cromarty Courthouse Museum, Cromarty Estate Factors Accounts, 1803–11.
2. *Inverness Courier*, 23 June 1830.

3. Henrietta Tayler, *The Family of Urquhart* (Aberdeen, 1946), 258–60; William Ferguson, 'The Urquharts of Cromarty' in *Scottish Genealogist*, vi. Part 2 (1959), 16–18.

4. *Inverness Courier*, 26 April 1849 (wedding of laird's son) and *Northern Ensign*, 15 July 1850 (formation of female industrial school by Mrs Ross).

5. Ian R. M. Mowat, *Easter Ross 1750–1850: The Double Frontier* (Edinburgh, 1981), 36–42.

6. NAS, CE62/2/1.

7. John Sinclair, *A General view of the agriculture of the northern counties and islands of Scotland* (London, 1795), 67.

8. George S. Mackenzie, *A General Survey of the Counties of Ross & Cromarty* (London, 1808).

9. John Sinclair, *General view ... northern counties*; Middleton family papers; Highland Council Archive, DI32; NAS, SC24/4/1.

10. Cromarty Courthouse Museum, Cromarty Estate Factors accounts, 1803–13; NSA, *Parish of Cromarty*; John Henderson, *A General View of the Agriculture of the County of Caithness* (London, 1815), 331; NAS, SC24/4/1; NAS, E504/17 Twenty-four tons of flagstone shipped for George Middleton on 1 Dec 1795.

11. John Douglas, 'Cromarty estate plans, 1823' (Cromarty House archive); NAS, SC24/4/1, Cromarty estate, summons of removing, 1795; Highland Council Archive, Minute Book of Commissioners of Supply for the County of Cromarty, attack on Middleton's property.

12. Henrietta Tayler, *Family of Urquhart*.

13. George S. Mackenzie, *General Survey ... Ross & Cromarty*, 335; OSA, *Parish of Kirkmichael and Cullicudden*; Highland Council Archive, D32.

14. Highland Council Archive, D32.

15. NAS SC24/4/1, summons of removal; Highland Council Archive, D32, Newhall estate rental.

16. N. Allen, 'Highland Planned Villages' in *Highland Vernacular Building* (Edinburgh, 1989).

17. Hugh Miller, *My Schools and Schoolmasters* (Edinburgh 1993), 226.

18. Cromarty Courthouse Museum, Procurator Fiscal v Catherine Sinclair or Macdonald, 1841.

19. NSA, *Parish of Cromarty*.

20. NSA, *Parish of Cromarty*; NSA, *Parish of Kirkmichael and Cullicudden*.

21. NAS, SC24/16/3, Braelangwell Papers, Produce of the farm of Millcroft of Braelangwell, 1844.

22. Transactions of the Highland Agricultural Society of Scotland (1877).

23. Ian Carter, *Farm Life in Northeast Scotland 1840–1914* (Edinburgh, 1979), 22.

24. Hugh Miller, *My Schools and Schoolmasters*, 492.

25. George S. Mackenzie, *General Survey ... Ross & Cromarty*, 335.

26. Malcolm Gray, *The Fishing Industries of Scotland 1790–1914* (Aberdeen, 1978), 29.

27. Malcolm Gray, *Fishing Industries*, 29; John Henderson, *A General View of the Agriculture of the County of Caithness* (London, 1815); OSA, *Parish of Avoch*.

28. James Coull, *The Sea Fisheries of Scotland* (Edinburgh, 1996), 71.

29. J. Malcolm Gray, *Fishing Industries*, 29–30; John Henderson, *General View of the Agriculture of the County of Sutherland* (London, 1811); Hugh Miller, *Tales and Sketches* (Edinburgh, 1863), 160; James Coull, *Sea Fisheries*, 63.

30. James Coull, *Sea Fisheries*, 107.

31. George S. Mackenzie, *A General Survey of the Counties of Ross & Cromarty* (London, 1810); Hugh Miller, *Tales and Sketches*, 163; Cromarty Courthouse Museum, 'State of Herring Fishing Conjunctly twixt George and Hugh Ross, Cromarty, 1815'.

32. *Inverness Courier*, 23 Aug 1821.

33. NAS, SC24, 1826 Militia List. The register of sasines refers to Alexander Gordon, fishcurer, a brother of James Gordon, merchant in Copenhagen.

34. Robert Chalmers, *The Picture of Scotland* (Edinburgh, 1827), 320.

35. Ian R. M. Mowat, *Easter Ross 1750–1850: The Double Frontier* (Edinburgh, 1981), 50.

36. J. Thomson, *The Value and Importance of the Scottish Fisheries* (London, 1849), 33.

37. St Andrews University Archive, ms. TA140:B8E43, 'Diary of Alexander Oswald Brodie', 163.

38. Hugh Miller, *Tales and Sketches*, 171.

39. John Sinclair, *General view ... northern counties*; OSA; Ian Mowat, *Easter Ross*, 47.

40. M. Mackenzie, *A View of the Salmon Fishery of Scotland* (London, 1834), 7; Elizabeth David, *The Harvest of the Cold Months* (London, 1994).

41. John Henderson, *General View ... Caithness* and *General View ... Sutherland*.

42. Bruce Walker, 'Salmon Fishing' in G. Jackson and SGE Lythe, *The Port of Montrose* (New York, 1993), 188; M. Mackenzie, *Salmon Fishery*, 7.

43. NAS, CS96/843.

44. CRMCH/SC/11/112.

45. M. Mackenzie, *Salmon Fishery*, 55.

46. M. Mackenzie, *Salmon Fishery*, 90.

47. OSA, *Parish of Cromarty*; George S. Mackenzie, *A General Survey of the Counties of Ross & Cromarty* (London, 1810), 334.

48. *Inverness Courier*, 17 May 1821.

49. *Inverness Journal*, 6 Sept 1822.

50. Commissioners Appointed to Inquire into the State of Municipal Corporations in Scotland, *Report* (1835); Robert Carruthers, *The Highland Notebook; or, Sketches and Anecdotes* (Edinburgh, 1843), 287; St Andrews University Archive, ms. TA140:B8E43, 'Diary of Alexander Oswald Brodie'.

51. Cromarty Courthouse Museum, Cromarty Harbour Trust Minutes.

52. Thomas Telford, *Survey and Report of the Coasts and Central Highlands of Scotland*, 4th Report (1803).

53. Andrew Wight, *Present State of Husbandry in Scotland* (Edinburgh, 1778–84), iii. 253; NLS, Ms9646, 202.

54. Mackenzie of Scatwell v Magistrates of Fortrose, Division of the Mulbuie Commonty (Highland Council Archive, Fraser Macintosh Collection), 85–8; *Inverness Courier*, 5 Feb 1818; St Andrews University Archive, ms. TA140: B8E43, 'Diary of Alexander Oswald Brodie 1843'; P. and G. Anderson, *Guide*, 1834 and 1850 editions; *Inverness Courier*, 7 Sept 1847.

55. Lucille H. Campey, 'The Regional Characteristics of Scottish Emigration to British North America, 1784–1854' (unpublished PhD thesis, University of Aberdeen, 1997); *Inverness Courier*, 19 July 1849.
56. George S. Mackenzie, *General Survey ... Ross & Cromarty*, 335; Iain Hustwick, *Moray Firth Ships and Trade* (Aberdeen, 1994), 158.
57. *Inverness Courier*, 6 Jan 1830. Article by Hugh Miller, who argues that there was also shipbuilding in Cromarty *c*.1700.
58. Cromarty Courthouse Museum, Papers in Procurator Fiscal v Margaret Macdonald or Sinclair, 1845.
59. Cromarty Courthouse Museum, Cromarty Estate Factors Accounts, 1803–19 (bankrupt tenant of brewery); *Inverness Courier*, 2 April 1818 (tenant of brewery travelling to take orders); Cromarty Courthouse Museum, papers in sequestration of D. Bain & Sons; J. M. Wilson, *Imperial Gazetteer of Scotland* (1853), 321. Tenants included Mr Davidson of Findhorn in 1795 (John Sinclair, *General view of the agriculture of the northern counties and islands of Scotland* (London, 1795), 63); Archibald Rhind, a manager of the 'brewerie' died 1798 (gravestone); and Alexander Peter, brewer, died 1829, aged 85 (gravestone).
60. Thomas M. Devine, *From Clanship to Crofters' War* (Manchester, 1994), 119–34.
61. *Inverness Journal*, 12 Dec 1816 (opening of Ardoch distillery); SRO, CS96/4117, Inventory of effects of Duncan Montgomery, distiller, Ardoch, 1824; NAS, SC24, Cromarty militia list, 1826 (distiller); NSA, Parish *of Kirkmichael and Cullicudden* (Braelangwell distillery); NAS, SC24, Resolis militia list, 1831; *Inverness Journal*, 5 Mar 1830 (charge of fraud against George Andrews, distiller, Braelangwell).

13

Population and Emigration:
1790s–1851

The *Cleopatra* as she swept past the town of Cromarty was greeted
with three cheers by crowds of the inhabitants and the emigrants
returned the salute but mingled with the dash of the waves and
the murmurs of the breeze their faint huzzas seemed rather sounds
of wailing and lamentation than of a congratulatory farewell.

Hugh Miller, 1831

Cromarty's population 1790s–1851

Figure 13.1 shows the population of the parishes of Cromarty and
Resolis between 1790 and 1851. The town of Cromarty grew
from 1801 until 1831, while the population of the rural part
of the parish was relatively constant, unlike Resolis where it increased
as a result of the policy of settling and retaining mailers on the
estates.

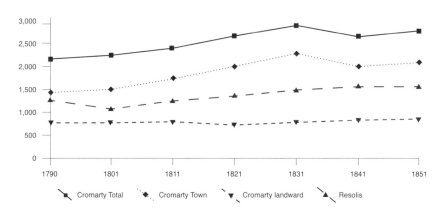

FIGURE 13.1   Population: parishes of Cromarty and Resolis 1790–1851.

Population mobility 1790s–1840s

The Scottish census of 1841 recorded whether or not individuals were born 'within the county' in which the census was taken. The relevant county, in the case of the parish of Cromarty, was taken by the returning officer to be Cromarty-shire and, since this consisted of little more than the parish, the census returns give a unique indication of local migration. Almost 29 per cent of the population of the town of Cromarty and 31 per cent of the inhabitants of the rural part of the parish had been born outside the county. A more detailed examination of the returns shows that the hemp factory accounted for much of this in-migration. Sixty-nine per cent of the forty-eight hemp spinners, all female, had moved into the town, while 42 per cent of the fifty-two male workers – hecklers, weavers, flax dressers and sacking workers – had done so. In contrast, only three individuals in the fishing community were not natives of the parish.

The 13 per cent fall in the town's population in the decade before 1841 was followed by a 2 per cent increase by 1851 – but this was well below the national average. Charles Withers has shown the importance of migration from the Highlands in the growth of Scottish cities in the mid nineteenth century and the particular importance of Cromarty and Dingwall in migration to Edinburgh, Leith, Perth, Dundee, Aberdeen and Stirling.[1] From other sources it is known that hemp workers migrated to Dundee as the Cromarty manufactory declined.[2] Cromarty appears to have been, for many individuals, a stage in a series of movements from rural parishes to the urban centres of the south.

Military service

During the Napoleonic Wars 75,000 fighting men were recruited from a Highland population of 300,000.[3] The Cromarty and Resolis militia lists of 1814 and 1825 show the effect that this had. The militia lists comprise all adult males between the ages of 17 and 45, and on the basis of population increase we would expect the 1825 list to have some 10 per cent more men than in 1814. Instead it has over 40 per cent more. The additional 30 per cent, amounting to 100 men, were those in military service in 1814.[4] This is confirmed by a similarly high figure of men in military service in 1804.[5]

Emigration after the mid eighteenth century

Emigrants who left the north after the mid eighteenth century were often able to join a network of established settlers, who retained family connections with the Cromarty area and who assisted the recent arrivals. For example, in 1763 Aeneas Urquhart from the parish of Resolis sailed from London to Philadelphia along with his cousin, James Forbes. Urquhart stayed with Gilbert Barkly, who had emigrated from Cromarty in the 1750s and was in partnership with Mr Hay, possibly related to the Robert Hay who had left Cromarty in 1737. Barkly also had dealings in America with Alexander Reid, the son of Captain John Reid – Barkly's erstwhile partner in Cromarty. Forbes was to assist a Mr Ross, whose name suggests that he had a connection with the north.[6]

Lady Ross of Pitcalnie, in Nigg, was sufficiently concerned at the numbers emigrating after 1763 to write to the Cromarty merchant, Forsyth, 'anent the peoples going to America'.[7] The emigrants included John Rose, the son of the factor on the Cromarty estate, who settled in Pennsylvania[8] – further evidence that the opportunity to emigrate was being taken up by merchants and professionals. Miller recorded a story in the 1820s of two brothers from Cromarty who went to America during the Revolution hoping to join their father, Donald Munro, who was already there. Father and sons found themselves on opposite sides in the conflict and the father accidentally killed the sons.[9] It would be easy to dismiss this tale were it not for the facts that Miller names the father and there were two women in Cromarty in Miller's day who were daughters of Lt General James Munro of the loyalist North Carolina Highlanders.[10]

Marjory Harper suggests that there were patterns of emigration distinctive of highland and lowland areas. In the former, emigration was generally of whole families, sometimes as part of wider community groups, who were seeking to transport their old way of life to a new geographical setting. In the latter, most emigrants were individuals seeking to improve their own circumstances.[11] Emigrants from Cromarty in the eighteenth century, as far as can be judged from the individuals identified, were of the second kind – and they were more pulled away by the attraction of new opportunities than pushed out by reduced economic circumstances. Although they made use of family connections, they were often single when they emigrated and were prepared to move on if circumstances changed. Since these emigrants were not part of a communal emigration, in which the preservation of a way of life was central, they were freer to adapt new lifestyles. Alexander Ross from the farmtoun of Peddieston enlisted with his two brothers in Fraser's Highlanders in 1757, settled in Canada, married a French-Canadian and the couple's children were brought up as Roman Catholic, French-speakers. It is almost impossible that Ross himself would have been a Roman Catholic in the parish of Cromarty.[12]

Members of merchant families, or those who aspired to improve their situation, were also attracted to service in the East India Company.

James Barkly, a Cromarty merchant (*fl.*1720) had two sons who became captains of EIC ships in the 1770s.[13] Charles Grant, an apprentice to the prominent Cromarty merchant, William Forsyth, became one of the EIC directors and Forsyth's sons both made their careers in India – the elder son, John, was a senior merchant in the Company's Bengal establishment at his death *c.*1825. James Forbes (1755–1810), a grandson of Barkly who was financially supported by Forsyth after the death of his (Forbes) father, subsequently made a successful career in Calcutta.[14]

For those from merchant families, particularly those who left as young men, there was sometimes the option to return – to Britain, if not to Cromarty itself – since their social identity was not tied wholly to a community overseas. Thus the former estate factor, MacCulloch, returned to be barrack-master at Fort Augustus in the 1740s and Gilbert Barkly, having emigrated in 1751, settled in Bath after the American Revolution. James Forbes returned from Calcutta in 1810, after thirty years in India, only to die within a few days of reaching Cromarty. Some of those who returned brought considerable wealth with them – one of the largest houses in the town was built *c.*1795 by Adam McGlashan who had prospered as a merchant overseas, probably in the Newfoundland fur trade.[15]

Towards the end of the eighteenth century the connection of local landowning families with the West Indies provided increasing opportunities for aspiring young men. George Gun Munro of Poyntzfield, for example, acquired land in an established British colony, Jamaica, through his marriage in 1760 to Mrs Poyntz, sister of the island's Chief Justice, and the family later had important holdings in Grenada. And Hugh Rose, who later acquired the Cromarty estate through his second marriage, made a substantial fortune as part of a company that supplied the British forces in the West Indies during the 1790s. The wars of 1793–1815 brought further territory – Trinidad, St Lucia and the three territories (Demerara, Berbice and Essequibo) that were to become British Guiana. Rose was subsequently in partnership with the son of another Ross-shire laird, Macleod of Geanies, in cotton, sugar and coffee plantations there.[16]

The extent of emigration to the West Indies by those lower in the social scale can only be gleaned through individual examples. Hugh Miller's school friend, Alexander Finlay, went to Jamaica in 1816 and became proprietor of the Twickenham Park Estate at Spanish Town, and Gustavus Forbes, a former neighbour of Finlay, was also somewhere in Jamaica. Alexander Munro 'of Grenada' died in 1819, leaving property in the town and Charles Mackenzie, a sailor and subsequently a carpenter in Jamaica, died there in the 1820s. There were also individuals from the Caribbean in Cromarty – Mrs John Ross of 'Demeraray' was among the subscribers in Cromarty to the Meikle

Ferry Disaster Fund in 1809, John Hossack 'of Demerara' subscribed his name to an address to the king in 1820, Daniel Ross 'from Berbice' appeared in the Cromarty militia list of 1826, John Munro 'late of Demerara' died in Cromarty in 1835 and a West Indian 'mulatto' boy was a member of the same class as Miller in the Cromarty school c.1815.[17] There was also a story told of the Cromarty laird, Hugh Rose Ross. His first wife, Arabella Phipps, who he had married c.1800, died in 1806 in Bayfield House, Nigg. She was said to have been murdered by her husband's 'quadroon' mistress, who had been brought back from the Caribbean as a servant.

Cromarty as an emigration port

The general level of emigration from the Black Isle and Easter Ross slowly increased after 1815 as a result of the economic depression, which was the result of the collapse of grain prices, and the reversal of government policy, which now favoured emigration to British colonies. However, an equally important factor was the development of the Canadian timber trade, which had become important when the

NOTICE TO INTENDING EMIGRANTS
TO THE
British Settlements of North America

FOR PICTOU AND QUEBEC
THE STRONG OAK BUILT BARQUE
SUPERIOR
Register, 308 tons,   500 Tons Burthen
DONALD MANSON, Commander,

Will be on the Berth at CROMARTY on the 10th April, and will be departed from thence on the 18th April, for SCRABSTER ROADS, where she will remain for two days for the embarkation of Passengers.

FIGURE 13.2
Notice to intending emigrants to North America, April 1842. The captain of the *Superior*, Donald Manson, was a native of the town.

FIGURE 13.3
Working drawing for Cromarty's Emigration Stone (Richard Kindersley)
erected in 2002 as part of the celebrations to mark the bi-centenary of the
birth of Hugh Miller.

Napoleonic Wars closed off supply from the Baltic. Ships sailing for Canadian timber from Aberdeen and Leith began to carry an outward 'cargo' of emigrants – and despite the restrictions of the Passenger Act this was still at relatively low cost. In this context, both Cromarty and Thurso, where ships could call with only a minor deviation from their route, became 'Highland gateways to British America'.[18]

Ship owners employed local agents to attract emigrants from throughout the north and east Highlands and organise their collection from the embarkation port. Between 1814 and 1822 most emigrant ships calling at Cromarty were from Aberdeen, using a variety of agents, but thereafter William Allan, a Leith shipping broker, established himself as the principal agent, achieving dominance by 1831. His leading position was challenged from the following year by Duncan MacLennan, an Inverness lawyer. MacLennan often accompanied passengers on the voyage and also acquired plots of land in Upper Canada where they could settle. In 1839 he entered into a partnership with a Caithness agent, John Sutherland, and from the 1840s they controlled much of the business in the Highlands and Thurso came into its own as an embarkation port from this date.[19]

Emigration was important business for the town because emigrants were expected to supply both their own food and the goods necessary for their new life in Canada. Much of this might be purchased in the embarkation port and they would also arrive in advance of the sailing, taking accommodation in the town. The principal agents employed local subagents, who were likely to have a stake in supplying both the ships and their passengers. These included William Watson, a local ironmonger, who acted for William Allan; and MacLennan's subagents William Munro, a clothier and grocer, Alexander Macpherson, merchant, and John Mowat.[20]

The vast majority of those who sailed on emigrant ships from Cromarty were from the true Highlands – many displaced by clearances, particularly in Sutherland. While there was also emigration from the lowlands of Easter Ross and the Black Isle, it is impossible to give an accurate estimate of emigrants from Cromarty itself. The Commission on the Poor Laws reported in 1844 that there had been emigration from the parish to America 'in recent years'. In this respect Cromarty was, within the Black Isle, similar to Fortrose, where thirty of 'the labouring class' had left for Canada in the previous three years, and Resolis, where there had been 'much emigration in last 20 years, all to Canada'. However, this was not the common pattern. Eight parishes reported that there was little emigration and two mentioned only seasonal migration to the south of Scotland.[21]

One factor in these variations may be the role of earlier emigrants in encouraging others to follow. For example, James Mustard moved from Cromarty in the late 1790s, probably as a result of the removal of tenants on Davidston farm. He went first to Edinburgh, then to Pennsylvania and, in 1801, to York County, Ontario. In this he was typical of the enterprising and mobile individual emigrants mentioned above. He was followed to Canada by five brothers and two cousins – and, more than twenty years later, by several related Bains, Hoods and Mustards who emigrated from the parish of Cromarty, some to Ontario and some to Prince Edward Island. Although this was not the emigration of a community group seeking to maintain a way of life – as in some emigrations from the west Highlands – family links were clearly important.[22]

A few emigrant ships also sailed from Cromarty to Australia, a voyage of about 100 days. In 1838 three ships, the *Vestal, Asia* and *Lady McNaughton*, took emigrants to this destination but it was afterwards more common for them to join larger ships sailing from Glasgow or Liverpool.[23]

Notes

1. Charles W. J. Withers, *Urban Highlanders* (East Linton, 1998), 96.
2. Ian R. M. Mowat, *Easter Ross 1750–1850: The Double Frontier* (Edinburgh, 1981), 57.
3. Thomas M. Devine, *From Clanship to Crofters' War* (Manchester, 1994), 135.
4. Some men from Cromarty were prisoners of war held in Valenciennes. *Inverness Journal*, 14 July 1809.
5. In 1804, 209 men in the County of Cromarty were in service in 1804. L. Colley, *Britons: Forging the Nation 1707–1832* (London, 1994), Appendix 2.
6. NLS, Ac 9907.
7. NAS, GD199. Marinell Ash, *This Noble Harbour* (Edinburgh and Invergordon, 1991), 76 argues that Cromarty was probably a major port of emigration from the 1760s. This may be too strong a claim – but certainly Cromarty was, and remained, a convenient point of departure for emigrants from the eastern Highlands.
8. Cromarty Estate papers, Barony of Cromarty Cartulary, Vol. I, New Series, XXV, Trust disposition of lands of Torran, Nigg, 1795.
9. Hugh Miller, *Scenes and Legends of the North of Scotland* (Edinburgh, 1994).
10. Highland Council Archive, Index to Register of Sasines, 10 Feb 1827. The North Carolina Highlanders were a 1,400-strong force loyal to the British Crown. They were defeated at the attack on Moore's Creek Bridge (NC) in 1776 and reformed after the successful invasion of the south in 1780.
11. Marjory Harper, *Emigration from North-East Scotland, Volume 1: Willing Exiles* (Aberdeen, 1988).
12. Information from the family history of Geneva Bazin (personal communication). 'Papists' were identified in Webster's census of 1755 and those in Cromarty were all associated with the household of Captain Urquhart.

13. Andrew Barkly (1741–90) and Charles Barkly (d.1776 by drowning in River Hooghly).

14. Forbes served for thirty-six years in Calcutta, returned to Cromarty in 1810 and died on the day of his arrival (gravestone in East Church, Cromarty). His mother's relation (uncle?), Alexander Barkly, married Christian Urquhart and it is possible that this is the same James Forbes who went to Philadelphia with his 'cousin' Aeneas Urquhart in 1763 (NLS, Ac 9907/1–8). If he left America for India at the outbreak of the American War of Independence he would have been in India for almost thirty-six years in 1810. He would have been only eight in 1763 – Aeneas Urquhart noted that he hoped to attend 'college'.

15. The house was originally called McGlashan's Lodge, subsequently Clare Lodge and now Bellevue.

16. R. W. and J. Munro, *Tain Through the Centuries* (Tain, 1966), 109.

17. Hugh Miller in Michael Shortland (ed.), *From Stone Mason to Geologist: Hugh Miller's Memoir* (Edinburgh, 1995), 107 (mulatto pupil in Cromarty), 235–9 (school fellows in Caribbean); NAS, SC24/15/1 (Alexander Munro of Grenada); NAS, SC24/16/4 (Charles Mackenzie, carpenter, Jamaica); *Inverness Journal*, 3 Nov 1811 (Mrs John Ross, Demeraray); *Inverness Journal*, 21 April 1820 (John Hossack of Demerara); Gravestone of 'John Munro, late of Demerara' in Gaelic Chapel, Cromarty; NAS, SC24/4/1, Cromarty militia list, 1826 (Daniel Ross, Berbice). Ross died in 1827 aged thirty-six (gravestone, Gaelic Chapel, Cromarty).

18. Lucille H. Campey, *Fast Sailing and Copper-bottomed: Aberdeen Sailing Ships and the Emigrant Scots They carried to Canada, 1774–1855* (Toronto, 2002), 59.

19. Lucille H. Campey, *Fast Sailing and Copper-bottomed*, 59–63.

20. Janet Fyfe, *Cromarty Emigrants and Emigrant Ships* (Cromarty, 1998).

21. PP 1844 XXXII–XXVI, Commission for Inquiring into Administration of the Poor Laws, *Report*.

22. Janet Fyfe, *Cromarty Emigrants*; and correspondence from Nancy Gloger, Ontario (descendant of James Mustard).

23. Janet Fyfe, *Cromarty Emigrants*.

14

Town, Society and Identity:
1790s–1840s

The town of Cromarty is pleasantly situated in the eastern part of the parish, on a low alluvial promontory, washed on two of its sides by the sea. It is irregularly built, exhibiting on its more ancient streets and lanes, that homely Flemish style of architecture characteristic of all our older towns of the north ; and displaying throughout that total disregard of general plan, which is said to obtain in the cities and villages of a free country.

Hugh Miller, 1836

From the mid 1790s until the early 1830s, Cromarty enjoyed a period of growth and prosperity, greater and more sustained than any earlier boom. This was also a time of profound social change, both in movements of people into and from the town and in the emergence of new social groupings. Hugh Miller was born into this bustling community on 10 October 1802 and he grew through an often troubled childhood and adolescence to become an influential journalist, scientist, folklorist, churchman and social commentator. His perceptive observations on his own community are an especially valuable resource.

The rise of the middle class

Commenting on the changing social structure of the town, Miller noted that towards the end of the century an 'independent middle class' was, in Cromarty as throughout Scotland, in the process of emerging as commerce flourished. This was first exemplified in the prominence of the local merchant William Forsyth and his family. However, it was not until the mid 1790s that this grouping was increased by a growing number of prosperous farmers, merchants and professional men. The professions expanded in the early nineteenth century – the office of procurator fiscal was created in 1807; fisheries districts, including one

The Cottage in which Hugh Miller was born.

FIGURE 14.1
The cottage where Hugh Miller was born, the larger house built by his father and
the Gaelic Chapel on the hill behind.

based on Cromarty, were established in 1808, each controlled by a
fisheries officer; newly established banks employed their own agents;
the customs and excise service expanded; and, as more attention was
given to education, the number of privately employed schoolmasters
increased. The national census of 1831 recognised this trend and
specifically recorded the number of 'educated men' in each town. There
were thirty in Cromarty – but more in Tain (fifty-one), Dingwall (forty-
eight) and Invergordon (thirty-five).

Many of the better-off merchants and professional men were drawn
into the circle of 'genteel' society, which was apparent as a group in
1807 when a visitor to Cromarty, Norton Hall, described 'a number
of genteel people ... many as well and as fashionably dressed as any
in the city of London'. Another, Robert Forsyth, described 'a small
genteel society, consisting of several respectable families'. The emerging
middle class in Cromarty can by 1820 be identified in the signatories
of a loyal address to the king. The thirty named individuals included
two 'in the Customs', the excise officer, the fishery officer, the sheriff
clerk, the factory manager, the two ministers, the schoolmaster and nine
merchants.[1]

The middle class and the growth of the town

Although the merchant William Forsyth had built an elegant house in Cromarty in 1772, the first houses to rival this did not appear until the mid 1790s. From then, and especially between 1810 and 1830, there was both an expansion of the town into new, regularly laid out streets and, in all parts of the burgh, the building of a new style of house for merchants, prosperous farmers and professional men. This was in contrast to the 'total disregard of general plan' characteristic of the older town, as noted by Hugh Miller in the quotation at the head of this chapter. In 1797 Miller's own sea-captain father built 'a respectable dwelling, which cost him about four hundred pounds'[2]; in the same year, Adam McGlashan, who had prospered in Newfoundland, returned to the town and built McGlashan's Lodge (later Clare Lodge,

FIGURE 14.2
The house and business premises (1808) of Andrew Macrae, merchant. This was later the Commercial Bank and, from 1889, John Bain's shop.

now Bellevue); and at about the same time George Middleton built 'a dwelling house with garden behind, storehouses, a slaughter house and outhouses for curing pork and fish' conveniently situated by the harbour (now part of the Royal Hotel).[3]

By 1804 'an increased rage for building' was reported and the view, remarkable to modern ears, was expressed that 'Cromarty bids fair to rival the great Royal Burgh of Inverness'.[4] A merchant named Macrae, who had been bankrupt in 1803 owing £10,000, was in 1808 able to build a substantial house with business premises at the corner of Church Street and the High Street, overlooking – and indeed looking down on – Forsyth House. On the opposite corner was another fine house, built c.1803 by the merchant James Thomson. Lt Col David Gordon, the son of a local merchant and grandson of a minister of the parish, erected a three-storey house (now St Ann's) in 1807–8 on the family's ground in Church Street, with parlour and dining room on the ground floor, drawing room and bedroom on the first floor, two bedrooms on the second floor, and a kitchen in an adjoining wing, with a garden behind and a 'handsome parterre' between the front door and the street.[5]

A large plot adjoining what is now Bank Street was feued c.1805 to a Murdoch Ross, who had flourished as a butcher with the revival of Cromarty's trade in pork. His second son, who began his career as a pork curer, rose to professional status as agent for the Commercial Bank and built the largest house on the site in the 1820s. This also served as his place of business. Perhaps because of the need to separate business and family space, it was one of the first buildings in the town to be constructed two rooms deep.

From c.1810 new feus were laid out in a grid of streets between the town and the harbour, soon named Rose Street, Barkly Street, George Street (later Duke Street) and Credit Place (subsequently George Street, after briefly, and ambitiously, becoming George Square). At least six of the houses in this area were built speculatively by Hugh Ross, a local merchant and shoremaster, and rented to the excise officer, surgeon, fishery officer and one of the town's sea captains. One of the houses subsequently became a ladies' boarding school and another a 'tavern and hotel' with a coffee room that provided its customers with London, Edinburgh and Inverness newspapers. With the success of commercial agriculture during the Napoleonic Wars, there were also new houses for prosperous farmers, as, for example, Dr George Macdonald, who farmed Newton and built his house (Maryness, George Street) overlooking the harbour c.1815, and Alexander Simpson of Navity, whose house in the High Street (No. 18) dates from 1817.[6]

New houses, wherever they were located in the town, were symmetrical and fronted the road, in contrast to older 'gable end on' houses. Where possible, they were set in their own grounds and they had more ornamentation – in pediments for the main door, more carefully worked details on *rybats* (surrounds) and cornices, and carved *skewputts* (the bottom stone of the gable skew). Where the grounds were large enough, they had stables or gig sheds and a carriage entrance with gateposts. Well laid-out gardens were also important and McGlashan's Lodge, the largest house, was surrounded by 'pleasure grounds'. Advertisements for the sale or rent of houses sometimes named the house carpenter responsible for the building and drew attention to such features as 'stone and woodwork finished in superior style'. The outlook could be important – from upper windows of one house there was 'a most beautiful and comely view of the harbour and Frith [*sic*.] of Cromarty' – and the location might be promoted as 'spacious and airy' or in 'a clean, well-aired and healthy situation'.[7] In all, a group of thirteen houses, either set in their own ground or with ornamented entrances or windows, can be dated to the period between the mid 1790s and the mid 1830s but the members of the new middle class were not significantly segregated from others in the town. Two of the largest houses, McGlashan's Lodge and Col Gordon's, faced or overlooked the cottages of the fishers.

Many of these, and other more modest houses of the same period, have well-lit, first-floor dining rooms with ornamented fireplaces – reflecting the importance of social eating in the bonding of the emerging 'middling sort'.[8] The bank agent, Robert Ross, built his house (now Old Bank House, Bank Street) in the 1820s, with windows enlarged by sidelights to provide better illumination. An inventory of 1822 for the house of the recently deceased chief customs officer (now Roseville, High Street) shows that one of the four principal rooms in the house was a dining room – the others being a kitchen and two bedrooms. The

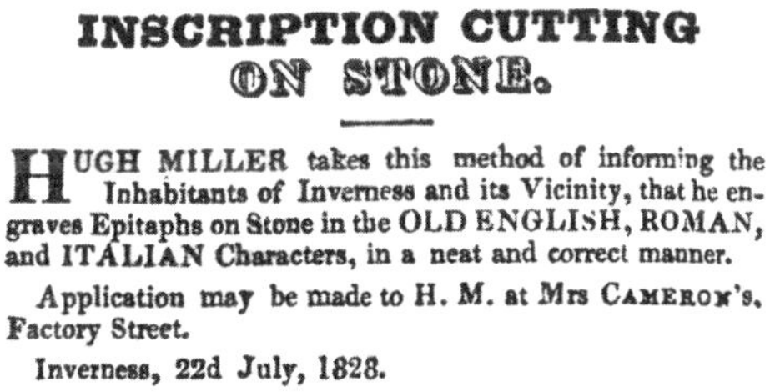

INSCRIPTION CUTTING
ON STONE.

HUGH MILLER takes this method of informing the Inhabitants of Inverness and its Vicinity, that he engraves Epitaphs on Stone in the OLD ENGLISH, ROMAN, and ITALIAN Characters, in a neat and correct manner.

Application may be made to H. M. at Mrs CAMERON's, Factory Street.

Inverness, 22d July, 1828.

FIGURE 14.3
Hugh Miller worked as a stone carver, appealing to those who wanted better quality gravestones.

dining room, on the better-lit first floor, had mahogany furniture, the cutlery was silver and the wall was hung with prints.[9]

A concern with appearance extended beyond death in the developing taste for well-carved gravestones, whose elegance and symmetry was similar to the new style of houses in the town. Epitaphs became more elaborate and, in addition to the details of birth, death and occupation, they stressed virtues of integrity, benevolence and piety. Long and faithful service to employers – such as the East India Company, banks and the customs service – was praised; and on one stone it was noted that two brothers had been 'partners in a successful business [pork curing] for a period of over 60 years'.[10]

Civic society

The emerging middle class initiated a number of improvements to the town and, despite Cromarty having no burgh council, its merchants and professional men began to exercise greater authority by using the office of justice of the peace to influence local affairs. The justices' meetings were held jointly with the commissioners of supply for the county of Cromarty, who had responsibility for the county's roads and bridges. The number of justices increased in 1788 with the appointment of local merchants and the joint body subsequently turned their attention to the improvement of the town. In 1797 the streets were 'causeyed' – that is, cobbled – at the considerable cost of £141 and there was lobbying for the establishment of a daily postal service.[11]

A growing sense of civic pride is evident in the provision of a uniform for the town constable in 1797 and in 1804 the justices applauded the fact that the drill sergeant of the Loyal Cromarty Volunteers was establishing a fife and drum band.[12] Cromarty presented itself to the outside world as a busy, thriving and fashionable small town. This is seen in an oil painting by the artist Daniell, produced by him in 1820 in two versions that differ only in detail.[13] The firth teems with shipping and Cromarty itself glows in a golden light. In James Clark's series of prints of towns in the area produced in the mid 1820s, Cromarty is equally busy and notable for the fashionable golf players in the foreground.

The Reform Act of 1832 gave Cromarty a town council for the first time since the 'breaking of the burgh' in 1670 and in November 1833 nine men of the 'middling sort' were elected – the prosperous farmer and doctor, George Macdonald, became provost, with the other councillors being three merchants, two 'provision merchants' dealing in salt pork, a baker, a cabinet-maker and Hugh Ross, who was house builder, merchant and shoremaster. Hugh Miller described this group as 'consisting of elderly or middle-aged men ... sound Evangelicals, but decidedly Conservative in their leanings'. Opposing them was a body of younger men who were 'staunch Liberals, but great Moderates' in church affairs. However, Cromarty was already in decline and the lack of council funds inhibited effective action by the council.[14]

Education, entertainment and the arts

The 'middling sort' took a keen interest in education as a means of bettering themselves. Hugh Miller describes how, in about 1815, 'some of the wealthier tradesmen of the town', dissatisfied with the parish schoolmaster, established their own private school. There were a number of other ventures at the same time and, in addition to the larger 'adventure schools' run by men, the increasing demand for education created the opportunity for widows and unmarried women in reduced circumstances to open their own 'dame schools'. In 1809 there was a girls' boarding school, in 1830 a Miss Bruce began a private day school and in 1835 a similar establishment was begun by Elizabeth Smith.[15]

The provision of education as a charitable activity was also a concern of the middle class. Charles Grant, who had been apprenticed to William Forsyth and rose to be a director of the East India Company, provided funds for a Sunday school for forty children, which was probably active from at least as early as 1800. However, the principal charitable schools appeared in the late 1820s. The Cromarty Friendly Society, also known as the Ladies Society, established a school in 1829 which was taught by a Mrs Macdonald and in 1832 the 'Links Day and Sunday School' was formed, taught by a Mr Denoon on 'Sheriff Wood's monitorial system', that is, with older pupils taking responsibility for the teaching of younger pupils. Fees were charged at the Links school, but it was described a 'society school' rather than a private venture. It received a glowing report in 1831, with one boy able to perform feats of mental arithmetic, giving the result of multiplying two six-figure numbers in under eight minutes, and another reading his own verses on 'Hearing a Lark Sing on the Evening of a Tempestuous Day', and much of this seems to have been due to the qualities of the teacher, Mr Denoon. In 1833 the two schools had eighty-six pupils, more than the fifty-six attending the parish school. The rural population had long been served by a school at Davidston, run by the Society for the Propagation of Christian Knowledge. Adult self-improvement was also valued. A reading room was opened in 1821 to take London, Edinburgh and Inverness papers and by 1831 there was also a reading club with a circulating library.[16]

The middle class were drawn together socially in a number of other activities, many of which began as pursuits of the minor aristocracy and gradually came to involve a wider range of merchants and professionals.

A golf society – in effect for both golf and dining – was formed in the 1750s and a local merchant began to supply golf clubs.[17] This society involved principally members of landed families but its activities focused on the dining room of the merchant William Forsyth, whose house overlooked the Cromarty links where the game was played.

Public, as well as private, dinners were increasingly important. These were held in the various lodges, in the Crown Inn, and later in Mann's Hotel, to mark occasions such as the election of the local MP in 1837, Hugh Miller's appointment as editor of the *Witness* in 1839 and the marriage of the laird in 1849. The earlier New Inn had printed bills of fare from 1780, listing the drinks and other services available to its customers. Once again, the practice of lavish dining at inns appears to have begun with landed families, especially those who were commissioners of supply for the county and attended courts in Cromarty.[18]

There were formal balls in the town from at least 1772, when one was held to mark the completion of the courthouse. On this occasion two clerks and the foreman of the nail works, who had not been invited, vented their feelings by breaking the town cross into pieces – both their exclusion and their resentment being indications of a changing class structure. By the early nineteenth century, balls had become a recognised feature of local social life. For example, a ball was organised 'for the behoof of the poor' by the estate factor, Walter Ross, in 1818 and another was held in the factory buildings in 1836 to celebrate the marriage of the manager. Three separate balls were held in 1849 to celebrate the laird's marriage and by 1851 there were two dancing masters, recorded in the census returns.[19]

The Loyal Cromarty Volunteers

Social bonding and a sense of common purpose were not restricted to the middle class and experience of communal action was increased by the formation of local volunteer forces after 1794. Volunteers in wealthy Lowland towns were an elite and Lowland county volunteers were composed of small proprietors, 'opulent' tenants, 'industrious manufacturers' and 'ingenious mechanics'. However, those in Highland burghs were more broadly based and often 'less carefully chosen'. Indeed, a food riot in Dingwall in 1796 appears to have been led by the volunteer force.[20]

The sheer numbers joining the volunteers in the north suggests participation by a wider cross-section of society. The Nigg Militia, formed in 1795, had ninety members and a company of similar size was formed in Cromarty. The Cromarty company was disbanded in 1802 but reformed the following year with two companies and an establishment of 160 men. In 1806 it had four companies and an establishment of 328. When the Local Militia Act of 1808 ended all pay for volunteers, most units disbanded and 'only a few, very elite corps survived' – yet we find the Cromarty volunteers finally being stood down only in 1818. The volunteers remained a potent symbol and their colours were displayed at a subscription ball held in the town in 1850.[21]

'Britishness'

An important aspect of common identity to develop during the course of the eighteenth century was the sense of a shared 'Britishness'. Linda Colley's study of the forging of British identity argues that it was built on common strands of Protestantism, shared economic objectives, the monarchy, and fear of catholic, continental Europe as an external enemy. These can all be seen in Cromarty. The community's staunch Protestantism had been strengthened by disputes with their Roman Catholic laird in the mid eighteenth century and later, in 1779, when a collection was organised by the kirk session for 'the Protestant Interest at Edinburgh' in order to support their opposition to 'the late Popish Bill', over £12 was raised, more than twice the amount that the 'Protestant Interest' thought sufficient. Of this total, £2 10s was contributed from the factory, the poorest section of the community. Almost fifty years later, Hugh Miller was the only adult male in the town unwilling to sign a petition opposing Roman Catholic emancipation. The area had benefited from the state's economic policies, especially from government funding for the harbour, and the town was firmly Hanoverian. The popularity of the volunteer militia, formed as defence against French invasion, has been described above.[22]

Cromarty was reaping clear benefits from the expanding British Empire and associated overseas trade. The markets for its principal outputs – hemp bagging, salt pork and salt herring – were wholly or partly in the Caribbean and the wealth of individuals who had made money abroad was displayed in the new houses of the town. There were opportunities for young men in the colonies and the poorest section of the community benefited by charitable donations from overseas, for example from William Fraser who owned a sugar plantation in Guyana.[23]

Some critics of Colley's work suggest that it was the social elite who accepted and promoted British identity and doubt the extent to which popular British patriotism involved the bulk of the population.[24] The evidence from Cromarty suggests that, by the 1790s, British identity was espoused by the townspeople in general. Hugh Miller had direct evidence from the 1790s of a Cromarty salmon fisher – hardly one of the social elite – who insisted on drinking a toast to the king (George III) with two unwilling English drovers after concluding a bargain and of a local ship's captain who participated in a 'Liberty and Equality' demonstration but insisted that his vessel fly the Union flag. Miller also reported how the 'threatened invasion knots the people still more firmly together, and they began to hate the French, not merely as national, but as personal enemies'.[25]

Friendly societies

The sense of common identity was also expressed in the emergence of a number of friendly societies in the 1820s. In 1830, 201 members of the Free Gardeners paraded through the town and at the laying of the foundation stone of their Lodge (now the Cromarty Arms) in the following year there were deputations of thirty men each from three other societies – the Freemasons, The Society of Wrights and Coopers (also known as the Hammermen), and the Cromarty Friendly Society. The Wrights and Hammermen, with 120 members, built a substantial lodge at about the same time.[26]

In 1831 Hugh Miller, writing in the *Inverness Courier*, captured the pageant of the friendly societies' public ceremonies and, at a point when the town's economy was already beginning to decline, suggested that they were an embodiment of sound moral values and inner strength.

> All the members were adorned with bouquets; a profusion of rods and arches, enwreathed with a countless variety of flowering shrubs, and with branches of trees rustled over their heads; pendants and sashes of blue silk intermingled their shining folds; swords, and the different symbols of the lodge glittered to the sun from amid this heraldic forest of natural and artificial beauty ... But there was a deeper pleasure to be derived by the spectacle of this pageant ... In that class of men which includes the operative mechanic and common tradesman, there is a close connexion between morals and outward appearance; and when our late monarch complimented the Scotch on that care which the common people bestowed upon their dress, he, in fact, paid a compliment to their prudence and worth. All the members of the Society were attired in a neat and tasteful manner – no slight proof that that distressing depression of trade which for a considerable time past has borne so heavy on the northern districts, has not yet subdued the spirit of the people.[27]

The four friendly societies were all strong supporters of the reform candidate in the election of 1832, with the Gardeners' lodge hung with banners proclaiming 'The cause of the People' and 'Liberty and Reform'.[28]

The societies provided benefits to their members by the support of sick members and widows but they were also a locus for ceremony, symbolism and pageantry. These ceremonies, such as the pouring of chalices of corn, wine, and oil over the foundation stone, were carried out in public with the blessing of the church and the Moderate minister of the Gaelic Chapel offered up the concluding prayer. This prayer focused on the 'principle of Union' – that is, the sense of fellowship and solidarity which united the members of the lodge.[29] There may have been some underlying tension between the two churches in Cromarty in this matter, since the Evangelical congregation in Nigg had been earlier strongly opposed to its members taking the Masonic oath.[30] But if there was such a tension it did not stop widespread participation in the activities of the societies.

In 1815 there were 312 adult males in the parish of Cromarty between the ages of seventeen and forty-five and, in 1808, 328 members of the Loyal Cromarty Volunteers. This suggests that membership of the volunteers was the norm. The number of males of militia age had increased to 444 in 1825, remaining at a similar level until 1831, and in 1829 there were over 320 members of one or other of the friendly societies. Joint membership of a number of societies was possible and this might reduce the proportion of the population participating – but other evidence suggests a high rate. In 1843 the average reported membership of Free Gardeners lodges in Scotland was 103 and trades societies, such as the Wrights and Coopers, had an average of eighty-nine members.[31] Cromarty in the same year had three societies with memberships of 180, 140 and 130, the largest being probably the Gardeners.[32] Once again, participation in such an organisation appears to have been the norm for an able bodied male in steady employment.

Just over 5 per cent of the population of Scotland were members of friendly societies. In Cromarty, with a population in the parish of 2,662 in 1841, the level of participation was almost 17 per cent. Levitt and Smout in *The State of the Scottish Working Class in 1843* suggest that, since working-class males were equal to about four-fifths of all adult males and adult males (that is, males over eighteen years) were about a quarter of the population, then 'as many as one working man in four or five belonged to a friendly society'.[33] In Cromarty the same assumptions would lead to the conclusion that three out of every four working men were members.

The friendly societies, being contributory organisations, did not include the poorest members of society and excluded, as new members, those suffering from chronic illness, who might become a drain on their resources. The Freemasons, however, whose members were generally better off, appear to have taken on the charitable role of providing for some of the poorest in the community. They incorporated meal and coal stores in their new Lodge (1823), and these were used to store goods

for distribution to the poor. It was only the Freemasons who survived
Cromarty's economic decline – the Friendly Society's building (1819)
became the Free Church school, the Gardeners Lodge was acquired
by Munro of Poyntzfield by the 1850s and later became the Cromarty
Arms Hotel, and the Wrights and Coopers Lodge, although used by
other organisations for some time, was a net store by the 1880s and
was demolished in 1973.

Segregation: rank and gender

As the classes formed bonds that united them, they also tended to
emphasise their distinction from other classes. A developed sense not
only of civic pride but also of ordered social rank is evident in the
procession at the laying of the foundation stone of the Free Gardeners
Lodge in 1830. This was preceded by a band of musicians and headed
by 'the Magistrates, and other respectable Gentlemen of the Town'.
The Cromarty Friendly Society followed and then the Freemasons,
Hammermen and Gardeners.[34] The Cromarty Friendly Society had
been formed in 1802 and it was probably the same society that later
ran the Cromarty Charity School. Its membership comprised 'nearly all
the ladies and gentlemen of the place' – justifying its prominent place
in the procession, ahead of the older Freemasons lodge.[35] But there was
a further degree of social segregation in membership of, on one hand,
the Masonic Lodge and, on the other, of the larger societies of the Free
Gardeners and the Wrights and Hammermen. Thus, to celebrate the
marriage of the laird in 1849, the 'gentlemen of the town' dined at
the Masonic Lodge, while the 'trades' ate in the Wrights and Coopers
Lodge.[36]

Hugh Miller observed that a consequence of the emergence of
distinct social classes was that, in the fifty years between the 1780s and
the 1830s, amusements 'instead of interesting the entire community
... (were) confined to insulated parties and single individuals'. Thus
communal games, public practical jokes and common activities on
holidays had all disappeared. There was also a decline in open mockery
of what was ludicrous and laughter at eccentricities was now 'smuggled
... as secretly as if it were the subject of a tax'. Miller implies that the
pressure to conform to public moral standards became a matter of
conforming to the expectations of a particular group rather than the
local community as a whole.[37]

The role of middle-class women became more clearly distinguished
from that of middle-class men. This resulted in greater leisure time for
the women of better-off families, allowing them to cultivate interests
in literature, music and art. Thus Miller noted that, in the 1820s, there
was 'a small but very choice circle of intellectual ladies' and in Miller's

own boyhood there had been a school for young ladies, teaching drawing and composition, run by a Miss Bond.[38] As amusement and leisure became more private it became desirable to create enclosed gardens with high perimeter walls. It is difficult to date the numerous examples of these that survive, but Miller noted the building of one in the 1840s.[39]

The Church: revivals, division and disruption

The religious revivals and protests against patronage of the mid eighteenth century showed local communities largely united among themselves in opposition to the power of landowners within the church. By the late eighteenth century, society had changed and so did the nature of religious revivals and protest in the church.

The increasingly mobile work force of the east Highlands was also more mobile in participation in religion. Revivals became commonly associated with large gatherings and now characteristically centred on the conversion of young men and women, whose experience of 'awakening' was often accompanied by 'violent bodily excitement'. This was very different from the well-ordered and disciplined conduct of, for example, the Nigg revival of the mid eighteenth century -- and some disapproved.[40] The first surviving references to awakenings in Cromarty are among the members of the Gaelic Chapel congregation after the appointment of Alexander MacAdam as their first minister in 1782. The marginalised nature of the Gaelic speakers is seen in the two Men (lay leaders) of this congregation identified by Revd John Kennedy in his *Days of the Fathers in Ross-shire* – Roderick Mackenzie (Rory Phadrig) who was 'awakened' in the 1780s, and John Clark, who appears to have been a contemporary. Neither remained settled in Cromarty – Mackenzie later moved to Contin and Clark emigrated to America. Clark was remembered for having declared at a prayer meeting that 'not a builder or tailor in Cromarty could be saved'. This was interpreted by Kennedy as having a 'spiritual' meaning – referring to the 'builders who rejected the corner-stone' and those who 'patched with rags a righteousness for themselves' – but it was heard at the time as an attack on the better-off section of the community and betrays a tension in the town between established artisans and tradesmen on one hand and the recently settled, and poorer, Gaelic speakers on the other.[41]

Annual communion services too, especially in revived congregations, attracted large crowds, with gatherings of up to 10,000 people reported on some occasions.[42] There seem to have been large communions in Cromarty from the early 1790s, following the revival, and, while the large congregations were welcomed, there is evidence of some unease.

In 1794, for example, two constables were employed at a cost of 5s each to 'watch the kirk doors during divine service at the time of communion'.[43]

The Church of Scotland as a whole was divided into two parties. The Evangelicals stressed the personal nature of religious experience, accepted or encouraged revivals, and opposed patronage in the church; the Moderates espoused the rationalist values of the Scottish enlightenment, rejected what they saw as the unreasoned 'enthusiasm' of revivals, and were prepared to compromise with the established secular powers in the appointment of ministers. Tensions mounted after the Evangelicals gained a majority in the General Assembly in 1834 but the government refused to introduce reforming legislation which would give congregations the right to choose their ministers and this led to the Disruption – the secession of a third of the ministers in 1843 to form the Free Church. It was one of the most significant events in nineteenth-century Scotland.

Easter Ross and the Black Isle were notably strong in their support for the Free Church. This was, in part, the legacy of evangelical revivals and patronage disputes in the eighteenth century and, in part, the result of revivals in the early nineteenth century. However, there was a different pattern of support in town and country. In the rural Highlands adherence to the Free Church was particularly strong among small tenant farmers, farm workers and unskilled labourers and Hugh Miller wrote of the county of Sutherland that 'all who are not creatures of the proprietor ... are devotedly attached to the disestablished ministers'. The schism in the church has consequently been portrayed as, in effect, a class conflict between 'small tenantry on the one hand, sheep farmers, factors and proprietors on the other'.[44] But in the rural lowlands of the south and north-east of Scotland the influence of the Evangelical party varied from parish to parish and in urban areas the poorest classes often remained in the Established Church, while it was merchants and skilled artisans who joined the secession. The contrast can be seen within the Black Isle. Resolis followed the rural Highland pattern – almost the whole congregation seceded, with the exception of a few of the larger farmers and the principal landowners, and it was reported that one landowner had dismissed his servants who joined the Free Church. In Cromarty the majority of the congregation of the Gaelic Chapel, the poorest section of the community, did not join the secession and this pattern of religious adherence was closer to that of urban parishes.[45]

In Cromarty, this reflected earlier tensions between English and Gaelic speakers in the town. A growing sense of solidarity among the labourers and weavers who formed the congregation of the Gaelic Chapel had led to an attempt in the 1820s to have its status enhanced. It was proposed to achieve this either by giving the two ministers joint responsibility for the whole parish or by erecting a new parish for the minister of the Gaelic Chapel. The 'English' congregation successfully resisted the proposal, partly because the minister of the Gaelic Chapel was a Moderate rather than an Evangelical.[46] At the Disruption the Gaelic Chapel minister and a large part of the congregation remained, as a result of this antagonism, within the Established Church. This created some strange situations. Many of the Gaelic speakers who adhered to the Established Church worked in the hemp factory – while the factory manager joined the Free Church and allowed the factory buildings to be used for Free Church services until a new church could be built.

Those Gaelic speakers who did join the Free Church soon found themselves in conflict with the rest of the congregation and this led to an unparalleled, although short-lived, secession with the Free Church congregation itself following the appointment of the Revd David Wilkie as minister in 1848. The precise reasons for the split cannot now be determined but a wooden building erected by the breakaway group was described in a newspaper report as a 'station house for Gaelic speakers' and its erection as an 'act of justice'. These seceders may have associated themselves with the Nigg seceders (now part of the United Presbyterian Church) but were drawn back to the Free Church four years later when the minister, with whom they had been dissatisfied, resigned. He had earlier signed his name in a Bible, still held in the local church, as ' the much oppressed David Wilkie'. This embarrassing division in the parish which was had been home to both Hugh Miller, the leading lay figure in the Free Church, and Alexander Stewart, one of its most eminent ministers, went unreported in its newspaper, the *Witness*.[47]

The Resolis Riot

In Resolis an attempt to induct a new minister to the Established Church in September 1843 led to a riot in Resolis and a jail breaking at Cromarty to release one of the rioters, Margaret Cameron, who had been taken prisoner. Revd Thomas Brown, in his semi-authorised history of the Disruption published in 1884, described the rioters as 'gentle hearted men forced into collision with the law'. Although there were some 'gentle hearted men' present, Brown was far from the truth.[48]

The riot at Resolis was in response to the planned induction of Revd John Mackenzie of Rogart, as a replacement for the widely respected Donald Sage, who had joined the Free Church. It was part of a series of inductions around the Cromarty Firth. The first edition of the *News of the World* reported the induction of another John Mackenzie, minister of Cromarty's Gaelic Chapel, to the church of Rosskeen (Invergordon) on Tuesday 19 September. The three ministers who attended and Sir

Hugh and Lady Fraser of Braelangwell were assaulted with sticks and stones by a crowd, some of whom were also carrying reaping hooks. They retreated to Lower Kincraig where the induction was held in private. One family in the parish who had not joined the Free Church had the turf roof of their house torn off and on the following Sunday a party of gentlemen – including Hugh Rose Ross of Cromarty and his son, the sheriff substitute and the procurator fiscal – were driven away from the church by a crowd and Lady Ross of Balnagowan, who arrived by coach, was pelted with stones. Hugh Rose Ross attempted to return to his house at Calrossie but, finding it surrounded by a crowd, spent the night wandering in the plantations of trees, before making his way to Tain.

However, on Wednesday 27 September an induction at Kiltearn went off peaceably. This was attributed to the restraining influence of the Revd Dr MacDonald of Kiltearn whose powerful preaching in Gaelic the previous Sunday had dissuaded the people from interfering. The induction at Resolis was the following day and, as a precaution, the armed Cromarty coastguard had been instructed to patrol the inner firth to prevent sympathisers crossing from the north shore. Resistance at Resolis had been well organised and when the church bell was rung as a signal a crowd of 'men, women and lads' gathered in front of the church. The men were armed with sticks and the women gathered piles of stones. They prevented a group of justices of the peace, the procurator fiscal, sheriff's officer and assistant sheriff-substitute from entering, stoned the carriage of the sheriff when he arrived and drove them all back to the nearby manse. A Free Church minister who was present, James Macdonald of Urray, was unable to influence them.

> Some of them called out my name. I addressed them on their highly improper and lawless conduct and frequently and earnestly begged of them to desist and go home, but they would not be advised by me. I endeavoured to explain to them the consequences of their actions but they would not listen – they assaulted and threatened me and said they would never sit to hear me preach. I told them I could not help that and ... that they (the Mob) were doing the cause of the free church the greatest infamy, and bringing the cause of Christ into dishonour by their lawless and sinful conduct that day.

Mr Macdonald also repeated the justifications given by the rioters, which included their desire not to be 'behind other parishes' such as Rosskeen which has resisted an induction and their wish to secure the whole of the crop from the glebe lands for Mr Sage.

The authorities, led by the Lord Lieutenant, Colonel Baillie, decided to proceed with the induction in the church rather than in private and this led to a number of confrontations during the afternoon. The crowd had grown to somewhere between 100 and 200 people and, in a series of skirmishes, the Lord Lieutenant was struck with a stick by a stableman or groom, Andrew Holm, and, soon after, Mr Sage's dairymaid Margaret Cameron was arrested. Margaret Cameron's arrest came after a decision had been made to send for the armed coastguard. While they waited, William Watson, a Cromarty merchant and JP, had been noting down names of those he recognised. Watson and Mr Shaw Mackenzie, the patron who had chosen Mr Mackenzie as minister, then went forward to talk to the people. Alexander Fraser, a twenty-year-old labourer, pressed a stick to Watson's chest saying, 'Be off as you have no business here.'

> On seeing this several of the women threw stones at me and I thought it prudent to retire, which I did backwards. I was closely followed by Margaret Cameron, holding stones in her hands and threatening me with injury. She followed me so far and so closely that Provost Cameron of Dingwall came up and seized hold of her when in the act of throwing a stone.

The two Camerons – provost and dairymaid – rolled together into the ditch and when Mr Watson gave assistance Margaret was, she claimed, roughly handled, dragged across the ground and held by the throat until she nearly suffocated. She cried out 'Murder' as she lay on the ground and someone put a hand over her mouth to silence her. She was handed over to the sheriff officer and taken off to Cromarty. Shortly afterwards the coastguard arrived, the Riot Act was read – a formal procedure which authorised firing on the crowd – and a volley of pistol shots were discharged over the heads of the rioters. This only provoked a renewed attack by the crowd, described by Lt Thomson of the coastguard.

> The rioters assailed us with such violence at this time that my crew were forced back along with the authorities and other gentlemen present. At this time I was struck on the side with a stone which knocked me over. Another stone struck me on the crown of the head which cut me severely. By these blows I was rendered nearly insensible and when endeavouring to raise myself from the ground I received two severe blows on the loins from stones.

A private induction was held that evening at Fortrose, while at Jemimaville the sheriff officer's gig was removed from the stable of the Inn and broken up on the shore. The following afternoon, Friday 29 September, 100 men and women began to march to Cromarty. They approached a mason James Holm, a Free Church elder, who was working on the new church for the congregation and asked him to join them. He refused but after they had left thought that, in his words 'there might be a *barry* [row] between them and the people of Cromarty and he might be of some use for peace.' He caught up with the crowd at Shoremill and as he walked with them urged them to be peaceful.

The pattern of events was similar to the previous day. At Cromarty, Holm and the highly respected Cromarty Free Church minister Alexander Stewart – the 'gentle hearted men' of Brown's account – were unable to influence the crowd. They unsuccessfully attempted to have bail granted and then Mr Stewart spoke at some length from the steps of the jail.

> I can only state generally that it was to the effect – That I claimed to be heard as a friend – that mobbing and stoning and most especially forcing prisons and liberating prisoners was an outrage on all law and order – that the people of Cromarty had been quite peaceable at the recent settlement in this place – that such conduct injured our cause and very likely we might get the blame of it – that they ought rather to show their sentiments of the Moderates by indignantly disowning them and having nothing to do with them.

Although admired as a preacher Mr Stewart was not noted for the power of his voice and James Holm had not been able to hear him because of the noise from the crowd. Holm himself shouted, 'For God's sake, keep peace.' The jailbreak that followed was, in fact, initiated mainly by three brothers from Cullicudden, all quarriers – John, Donald and Thomas Urquhart – and a group of drunken fishermen celebrating a wedding. One of these, Robert Hogg, known as Property, shouted to the Resolis men that they should free Margaret Cameron, and James Watson, the bridegroom, supported him with the cry, 'Come away and break open the prison door and get out the woman and I will give you a dance at my wedding.' The jailbreak went ahead, although Hogg and Watson had drunk too much to help in any practical way. The crowd, with Margaret Cameron, marched out of Cromarty 'brandishing their sticks with great glee'. The Urquhart brothers stopped for about twenty minutes at Duncan Ellison's spirit shop to refresh themselves but soon caught up with the crowd and an hour later many gathered for a glass of whisky at the Jemimaville Inn.

The following Wednesday, 4 October, the *Inverness Courier* claimed that 'the law was in complete abeyance'. A myth was already beginning to take shape, with the claims that some of the women had in fact been men in disguise and that the rioters now kept nightly watches on the houses of the heritors and the authorities, knew all their movements and were sending threatening letters. On the same day 200 men of the 87th Royal Irish Fusiliers arrived at Invergordon on the steamer *Duke of Richmond* and were quartered in the old factory building. A coastguard cutter with fifteen men also arrived and before the end of the day seven Rosskeen rioters were arrested.

Their treatment was to cause controversy. The soldiers had set up a guardhouse in a building formerly used by the Commercial Bank and the prisoners were handed over by the superintendent of police for Ross-shire to the Fusiliers who locked them up overnight in the disused bank safe. An action for damages raised by one of the prisoners was finally settled in 1847 and although the award was only £200 the total cost to the authorities, including legal fees, was £1,700. It was also claimed that the Fusiliers had threatened that anyone who opposed them would be 'cut down like standing corn'.

The next evening, Friday 5 October, the soldiers, coastguard and special constables crossed to Resolis, where three people were arrested. During the next few days more were apprehended and imprisoned in Dingwall and Cromarty. Within a week it was felt that order had been restored and the Fusiliers were marched through the Black Isle to Fort George, where they were to be quartered for the winter, still within a day's march of any possible disturbance.

The Resolis rioters and the jailbreakers were tried at the High Court in Edinburgh on 10 and 11 January 1844. Twelve people were indicted on charges of riot or jail breaking, four of whom did not appear and were declared outlaw – Thomas Urquhart (quarrier, Cullicudden), Eppy Aird (wife of Donald Watson, shoemaker, Balblair), William Fraser (shoemaker and fisherman, Ferryton) and David Mackenzie (crofter, Bleaching Green, Bog of Cullicudden). They must presumably have left the district for good. John Urquhart (quarrier, Cullicudden) was sentenced to nine months' imprisonment, on a recommendation of leniency from the jury; the charges against his brother Donald Urquhart (quarrier, Cullicudden) were found not proven. Andrew Holm (groom) and Alexander Fraser (shoemaker, Ferryton) changed their plea during the trial to guilty and were sentenced to six months' imprisonment. The case against Robert Hogg (fisherman, Cromarty) was found not proven. Charges of jailbreaking against Donald Murray (mason, Jemimaville), John Finlayson (weaver, Cromarty) and Colin Davidson (shoemaker, Jemimaville) were dropped. No charge had been brought against Margaret Cameron.

The Resolis Riot was markedly different from the grain riot in Cromarty a century before, when an armed crowd gathered but acted with the support of, rather than in opposition to, the local leaders of the community. The crowd at Resolis and Cromarty were less biddable and some of those assaulted by the crowd, such as John Grigor, the procurator fiscal, and James Hill, assistant sheriff-substitute and manager of the factory, were themselves leading members of the Free Church in Cromarty. A significant role in the riot was played by younger men and woman, many of whom were casual farm labourers or workers in relatively unskilled trades such as quarrying. Just as the revivals of the early nineteenth century were more volatile in form than in the eighteenth century, and the participants more mobile, so there was a more volatile and mobile element within the protesting crowd. While there was some attempt by Free Church elders and ministers to influence them, much of what happened was beyond their control. The crowd was more clearly proletarian and merchants, leading tenants and prominent tradesmen, who had led community resistance a century before, were now more commonly aligned with the forces of law and order.

There is a view of this period of Highland history which holds that the clearances and the Disruption are parallel and linked events – the landowning class removed their tenants for economic gain, and the tenants in turn supported the Free Church in order to appoint their own ministers, rather than have this power in the hands of the lairds. This is a caricature, which has some basis in reality, but it is an oversimplification because it ignores the true effects of the breakdown of traditional society. The events at Resolis and Cromarty reveal the competing interests of the relatively secure merchants, tradesmen and artisans of Cromarty on the one hand and the growing numbers of displaced individuals with little secure employment, willing to resort to mob violence.

Three smaller riots between 1815 and 1847 provide further evidence of a tension between the poorer sections of society and the leaders of the Evangelical party. Two of these were grain riots in which action was directed against families whose heads were, or would become, elders of the Free Church. In 1815 there was an attack on the house of the Middleton family, who were suspected of hoarding grain. The Middletons had initiated improvements at Davidston in the mid 1790s with the displacement of a number of small tenants. Later there was similar resentment towards Dr Macdonald of Newton farm, whose single tenancy had been made possible by the eviction of four families in the early 1840s. Extensive grain riots took place around the Moray Firth in 1847 and those in Cromarty were triggered by MacDonald's purchase of a substantial quantity of oatmeal from a local merchant. The third case of riot was in 1841, when there was popular opposition in Resolis to the roup of the tools of the Jemimaville blacksmith, as the result of action taken to recover debts by John Forsyth, a Cromarty merchant. Forsyth was to become, like Middleton and Macdonald, an elder of the Free Church.[49]

Notes

1. J. N. Hall, *Travels in Scotland* (1807), 488–90; Robert Forsyth, *The Beauties of Scotland* (Edinburgh, 1806), 531; *Inverness Journal*, 21 April 1820.
2. Hugh Miller, *My Schools and Schoolmasters* (Edinburgh, 1993), 11.

3. *Inverness Journal*, 29 June 1810. Middleton's feu was granted in 1796 (Register of Sasines). The buildings are now the Royal Hotel.

4. Cromarty Courthouse Museum, copy of letter from Robert McKid, 17 April 1804, on the possible sale of the Cromarty estate.

5. *Inverness Journal*, 10 Jan 1812.

6. Cromarty House archive, John Douglas, Plan of the estate of Cromarty, 1823 (George Square); NAS SC25/44/3, Dingwall Sheriff Court, Will of Hugh Ross, 1839; *Inverness Journal*, 28 Feb 1812 (tavern and hotel, with coffee room); *Inverness Journal*, 17 April 1812 (ladies' boarding school in 'corner house near the pier'). Other information from the Register of Sasines.

7. NAS, SC24/21/3, Roll of Electors 1841 (Clare Lodge); *Inverness Journal*, 29 June 1810; *Inverness Journal*, 6 Dec 1816.

8. Stena Nenadic, 'Middle-Rank Consumers and Domestic Culture in Edinburgh and Glasgow 1720–1840' in *Past and Present* 145 (1994), 122–56.

9. CRMCH/SC/11/138/2.

10. Cromarty, Cromarty Courthouse Museum, survey of gravestones in Cromarty East Church kirkyard.

11. NAS, SC24/16/3 (causeying of streets).

12. NAS, SC24/21/4 and Inverness Archive, Minutes of the Commissioners of Supply for the County of Cromarty. On the respective roles of the justices of the peace and commissioners of supply see A. E. Whetstone, *Scottish County Government in the Eighteenth and Nineteenth Centuries* (Edinburgh, 1981).

13. The originals of Daniell's oil paintings of Cromarty are held by Lord Cromartie and Lord Gough.

14. *Inverness Journal*, 8 Nov 1833 (election of Cromarty Town Council); Hugh Miller, *My Schools and Schoolmasters*, 471.

15. Hugh Miller, *My Schools and Schoolmasters*, 122; *Inverness Journal*, 3 Nov 1811 (girls' boarding school); Cromarty Kirk Session papers, *Answers made by Schoolmasters to Queries circulated in 1838*.

16. *Inverness Courier*, 22 June 1831 (inspection of Cromarty Charity School); *Inverness Courier*, 15 Jan 1821 (opening of reading room in Cromarty).

17. The golf club is described by Miller in *Memoir of William Forsyth* (London, 1839) as formed 'in the early and more active days of Mr Forsyth' and can be more accurately dated from the sale of golf clubs by a Cromarty merchant in 1755 – see NAS, CS96/1343.

18. *Inverness Courier*, 23 Aug 1837 (election of MP); *Inverness Courier*, 26 Apr 1849 (marriage of Duncan Ross of Cromarty); NAS, SC24/21/7 (printed bills from New Inn, Cromarty). In 1779 two of the commissioners of supply found the bill from the New Inn 'extravagant' and suggested that it was settled by the merchant William Forsyth and the Cromarty factor, Hugh Rose.

19. Hugh Miller, *Scenes and Legends*, 433; *Inverness Courier*, 16 Apr 1818 (ball in aid of poor); *Inverness Courier*, 24 Feb 1836 (marriage of Walter Hill).

20. A. E. Whetstone, *Scottish County Government in the Eighteenth and Nineteenth Centuries* (Edinburgh, 1981), 102 and note 56.

21. Information on Cromarty Volunteers from Scottish Services Museum. *Inverness Journal*, 2 Apr 1818 (Cromarty Volunteers disbanded); *Invergordon Times*, 17 Jan 1850 (subscription ball).

22. Linda Colley, *Britons: Forging the Nation 1707–1837* (London, 1992); NAS CH2/672/2 (collection by Cromarty Kirk Session for 'the Protestant Interest' in Edinburgh); Hugh Miller, *My Schools and Schoolmasters*, 453.
23. PRO PROB11/1780, will of William Fraser of Berbice, 1831.
24. See, for example, E. P. Thompson's 'Which Britons?' in *Dissent* (Summer, 1993).
25. Hugh Miller, *Scenes and Legends*, 458–65.
26. *Inverness Courier*, 29 July 1829; 9 Dec 1829; 21 April 1830; 25 May 1831.
27. *Inverness Courier*, 27 July 1831.
28. *Inverness Courier*, 25 May 1831.
29. *Inverness Courier*, 21 April 1830.
30. John Martin, *Church Chronicles of Nigg* (1991), 29.
31. Ian Levitt and T. C. Smout, *The State of the Scottish Working Class in 1843* (Edinburgh, 1979), table 6B.
32. PP 1844 XXXII–XXVI, Commission for Inquiring into Administration of the Poor Laws, *Report*.
33. Levitt and Smout, *The State of the Scottish Working Class*, 132.
34. *Inverness Courier*, 30 April 1830. Report written by Hugh Miller.
35. *Inverness Courier*, 22 June 1831. Report on the inspection of the Cromarty Charity School.
36. *Inverness Courier*, 26 Apr 1849.
37. Hugh Miller, *William Forsyth* (London, 1839), 79–86.
38. Hugh Miller, *My Schools and Schoolmaster* (Edinburgh, 1993), 82.
39. Peter Bayne, *The Life and Letters of Hugh Miller* (Edinburgh, 1871). Another walled garden, at the banker Robert Ross's house, was feued from the Cromarty estate in 1861.
40. John Kennedy, *The Days of the Fathers in Ross-shire* (Inverness, 1895), 234.
41. John Kennedy, *Days of the Fathers*, 105–7.
42. John Kennedy, *Days of the Fathers*, 220.
43. NAS CH2/672/2, 299.
44. P. L. M. Hillis, 'The Sociology of the Disruption' in S. J. Brown and M. Fry (eds), *Scotland in the Age of the Disruption* (Edinburgh, 1993), 46; James Hunter, *The Making of the Crofting Community* (Edinburgh, 1976), 104.
45. P. L. M. Hillis, 'The Sociology of the Disruption', 46.
46. Hugh Miller, *My Schools and Schoolmasters*, 456.
47. *Inverness Courier*, 28 Mar 1850 reported the opening of the wooden church, with a Mr Macgrigor as missionary. The *Northern Ensign* 20 June 1850 refers to the two congregations and the impending move of the Revd David Wilkie to Forfar, implying that this was likely to remove the cause of the division. *Inverness Courier*, 27 Dec 1849 (connection with Nigg seceders).
48. Thomas Brown, *Annals of the Disruption* (Edinburgh, 1884).
49. Highland Council Archive, Minutes of the Commissioners of Supply for the County of Cromarty, 1815; Cromarty Courthouse Museum, MS 'History of the Bains of Newton'; Marinell Ash, *This Noble Harbour*, 125; Cromarty Courthouse Museum, Procurator Fiscal v Margaret Sinclair, 1841.

Part 4
After 1843

15

Living with Decline: 1843–1900

That little burgh [Cromarty] is a [whited sepulchre]; for we defy thee, whoever thou art, to produce a town, not even Naples and Stamboul excepted, which combines in equal degree the quality of external loveliness with abomination and filth within ... We have visited very strange places in our day; we have climbed the garrets of the West port, and plunged into the dens of the Cowgate; we have explored the thieves district of old Pye street, and dived among the troglodytes of the Minories; but we solemnly swear that never our eyes and our noses have been assaulted with such a concentration of intensely abominable filth as that which almost knocked us down, twelve years ago, each time we ventured to pass the doors, or enter the dwellings, of the fishers of Cromarty.

Alexander Oswald Brodie, 1855

The town of Cromarty took considerable pride in the appointment of Hugh Miller as editor of the national church newspaper the *Witness* in 1839 and in his subsequent role in the public life of Scotland. His fame was confirmed by the part he played in the Disruption of 1843 – and, indeed, it may have been Miller who coined the name 'Free Church' for those members of the Church of Scotland who broke away to gain the freedom to appoint their own ministers. Cromarty's role in what was a defining moment of Scottish history ought to have been a high point – but their pride was tempered by a harsh economic reality. Almost everything that had made the town successful was being lost and Cromarty was in disastrous decline. Its trade in salt herring had gone, the hand-loom hemp factory was running down as mechanised jute production grew in Dundee, smaller enterprises such as shipbuilding, the pork trade and brewing had failed, and, most importantly, its seaborne trade had been lost to the new harbour at Invergordon.

Miller's success brought a further irony. He had already made the folklore and traditional history of his home town known through his

Scenes and Legends of the North of Scotland published in 1834 and now, through his biographical *My Schools and Schoolmasters*, first published in as a serious of articles in the *Witness*, he would make the detail of life in early nineteenth-century Cromarty available to readers throughout Scotland. Its people for a time lived with a public profile probably greater than any other small town in the country. But by 1855, when *My Schools and Schoolmasters* appeared in book form, it was a public image of Cromarty's prosperous, but vanished, past. On his visits home, Miller found the town becoming a 'second deserted village' and he had, in any case, almost ceased to comment on contemporary Highland affairs by this time.[1] Miller's suicide in late 1856 came at a time when the town had fallen on some of its hardest times.

In the year of the Disruption itself, 1843, one visitor to the town, Alexander Oswald Brodie, employed by the Stevensons who were building Cromarty's lighthouse, wrote in his diary that it was 'a miserable place in the last stages of decay'.[2] It was almost certainly Brodie who later responded to the publication of *My Schools and Schoolmaster* in 1855 with a review containing a scathing account of the town. In a style reminiscent of the extravagance of Sir Thomas Urquhart, he wrote the words quoted at the head of this chapter.[3]

From the 1840s to the late 1880s descriptions of Cromarty's economy and condition remained generally negative. A short-lived revival in 1856, during the Crimean War, was in marked contrast to the town's usual 'gloomy and sombre look'; in 1875 it was 'a town to let', with 'streets deserted and silent, houses roofless and windowless'; in 1880 it was 'simply a fishing village … singular among northern town in showing no signs of progress or prosperity … with empty houses and shops'; and in 1885 'trade was at a low ebb … there was no money circulating' and it was 'a town buried alive'.[4]

These impressions were borne out by official statistical information. By the time of the report of the Commission on the Poor Laws in Scotland in 1844, Cromarty had more paupers – 161 individuals – than any other parish in east Ross & Cromarty except Tain, and many in Cromarty, who had formerly been partly or fully employed, had been forced to go south.[5] The local Dorcas Society, established in 1846 to educate destitute children, provide clothing for the poor and give employment to older women as knitters, recognised in 1850 that it was Cromarty's isolation which 'rendered employment to the poor and aged females impossible' and in 1857 it was supporting ninety-six widows, sixty-one spinsters and thirty-four old men. The Society's prospectus in 1846 had graphically outlined the extent of child poverty: 'A greater part of these children are almost naked, particularly the boys – they having in many instances no undergarments, neither shoes nor stockings, and their upper garments unwashed rags'.[6]

PARISH OF CROMARTY.

Abstract of Accounts

From Whitsunday, 1896, to Whitsunday, 1897,

WITH

LIST OF POOR

Chargeable to the Parish during the Year,

SHOWING

INDIVIDUAL COSTS;

ALSO,

KLEIN BEQUEST, WITH LIST OF RECIPIENTS,

AND ALSO

Statement of the Income and Expenditure of the
School Board of the Parish, with
H.M.I. Reports.

DINGWALL:
PRINTED AT THE ROSS-SHIRE PRINTING WORKS.

FIGURE 15.1
Annual Accounts of the Parish Council listing every individual who received poor
relief.

There was also a series of sequestrations of local merchants and farmers as the economy declined during the remaining years of the century – Alexander Simpson, farmer at Navity (1846), Peter Fraser, baker (1840), John Duncan, farmer at Cromarty Mains (1841), William Watson, merchant (1842), John Yule, innkeeper (1849), John Fraser, saddler (1859), Jeremiah Joyner, grocer (1860), John Mackay, merchant (1870), Charles Michie, chemist and bookseller (1870), Kenneth Mackenzie, tailor (1887), and James Hogg, fishcurer (1886).

Population and migration

The population of the town continued to fall from its peak of 2,215 recorded at the 1831 census, with a 25 per cent drop in the single decade between 1851 and 1861 (see Figure 15.2). In these ten years almost 500 people left the town. The decline in male employment in this decade amounted to 110 jobs, with the principal losses being in textile working (44), building trades (24), and shoemaking and tailoring (26). At the same time the number of fishermen increased from 82 to 103, to constitute almost 30 per cent of the working male population in 1861. Many of the workers in the hemp factory, displaced when the factory finally closed in 1853, appear to have moved on to Dundee, where individuals originating from Cromarty made up a significant proportion of the 160 Highland-born paupers recorded in Dundee's East Poorhouse between 1856 and 1878.[7]

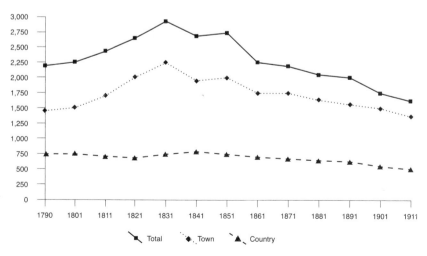

FIGURE 15.2   Population: parish of Cromarty 1790–1911.

Decline in the town's population continued, although at a slower rate, for the rest of the century with the loss of a further 270 people by 1901. Emigration became an increasingly attractive option, not only to North America but to Australia and New Zealand, and reports abounded in the local newspapers of the departure of the more prominent emigrants, including the popular Free Church minister, Mr McEachern, who accepted a call to a parish in Australia in 1868.[8] Some became important figures in their adopted countries and among the most notable was James Ross (1848–1913), the son of a Cromarty ships captain, who went on to be one of the principal engineers on the Canadian Pacific Railway and, through his later business ventures, came to be known as the 'Coal King of Canada'.[9]

Links with at least some emigrants were maintained and in the autumn of 1889 the town used these contacts to organise a shooting match with a team in New Zealand – with the teams competing on the same day in the two countries and the scores, sent by mail, arriving in March of the following year.[10] But the loss of those who were the most dynamic in the community left its mark and an article in 1897 accurately commented that 'the old days are gone when Cromarty could keep its own' and described it as 'a town of old men and women and young children'.[11]

Agriculture

Cromarty's economy returned to reliance on its earliest source of wealth – the farmlands of the Black Isle. In the Scottish lowlands as a whole the period from the 1840s to the 1870s has been described as the era of 'high farming' during which most of the advances were made that would sustain agriculture until the 1940s. There were new and larger farm buildings, massive expenditure on field drainage, which did away with uneven ridged fields and made possible the use of new machinery, including reapers, binders and seed drills, and links to markets by the ever-growing network of railway lines.[12] The northern lowlands, such as the Black Isle, lagged behind in these improvements and, as in the late eighteenth century, when change did come it was all the more rapid – and all the more disruptive of traditional rural society.

Renewed impetus for improvement of agriculture on the Cromarty estate came in 1847, with the settlement of the court case over the disputed succession. The estate finally passed into the control of Hugh Rose of Glastullich, who had inherited through his wife, Catharine Munro, and had taken the name Hugh Rose Ross. In 1849 Ross's eldest son, George William Holmes Ross (1825–83) married Adelaide Lucy Davidson, a descendant of Henry Davidson, who had been clerk to the first George Ross of Cromarty and whose family, having made a fortune in sugar, had bought and restored Tulloch Castle in Dingwall. Their wedding was the occasion for a major refurbishment and redecoration of Cromarty House, where the ornate wallpaper still hangs in the drawing room.

Hugh Rose Ross was described as 'the greatest rural improver of Ross-shire ... who has drained, planted, built and embellished his estate around Calrossie for the long period of 48 years'. His forty miles of hedges were the best kept in Ross-shire and in 1840 he had established a works near Tain producing agricultural drainage tiles for field drains, with a water-driven mill to prepare the clay and two kilns, each with a capacity for 25,000 tiles.[13] In 1846, the year before Ross secured his title to the Cromarty estate, the Corn Laws had been repealed. Since 1815 this legislation had protected British landowners and farmers by keeping the price of grain and bread artificially high and, by way of compensation for the repeal, Parliament passed the Drainage Act, which offered landowners low interest loans for drainage schemes. This all seemed to augur well. In 1849 the Cromarty estate took a loan of £10,000 under the Drainage Act[14] and the management was placed in the hands of a dynamic factor, Strachan, who began enlarging and draining a number of farms.

An unsympathetic contemporary account of the changes that followed Strachan's appointment, and of his 'tyrannical oppression', is preserved in a manuscript history of the Bain family of Newton, who were removed as part of these improvements.[15] This personal perspective on the improvements is a valuable reminder of the bitterness attached to lowland, as well as highland, clearance. According to its author the changes reduced the number of tenant farmers on the estate from thirty to ten, only half of whom were former tenants. The factor Strachan is portrayed as 'full of vainglory and void of all principle' – not only evicting tenants but also refusing compensation for improvements and refusing to allow widows to retain tenancies. He is also accused of insensitivity towards the environment, defacing the beauty of the estate by tearing up hedges, cutting wood and leaving areas uncultivated for game. Hugh Miller, writing in the 1850s, also lamented the destruction of these hedgerows.[16] Strachan's 'new farmers' were, it was claimed, out of touch with the land and 'better at calculating the returns on paper than superintending the work'. It is interesting that in the Bain history no blame is attached to the 'old laird', nor to his son (George William Holmes Ross) who was in the army and so, it was argued, unaware of Strachan's actions – nor to the son's wife, who 'knew nothing of estate management'. The fracture in the structure of society was between those who traditionally worked, and cherished, the land and the new class of factors and commercial farmers.

The detail of the social changes brought about by improvement can be seen in the differences between the census returns of 1841 and 1851.

On the farmtoun of Peddieston, for example, the population fell from thirty-nine, in thirteen households, to twenty-three, in eight households, and the number of adults of working age (thirteen and over) fell from twenty-one to eleven. Not only was there a smaller population but many of those on the farm had moved there from elsewhere and most of those born locally were the children of incoming agricultural labourers. Only three adults, two of them elderly women paupers, remained of the working population of 1841.

Some small farms simply disappeared, such as a smallholding at Navity described in detail, some fifty years later in 1892. It had been worked by two brothers, Robert and Daniel Williamson (known as Robie-Danie and Danie-Robie), who were, even in the late 1840s, old-fashioned and preserved an older form of life.[17]

> The brothers lived in a small, mud-built, thatch-roofed hut of three apartments, occupying the centre of an 'acre of land' ... The piece of land, surrounded on all sides by a dry-stone dyke, the brothers managed, without help, to cultivate. The situation of the hut was northward and southward, the entrance being to the east, one window looking to that direction, and two to the west. At the north end of the ground was a moat of primitive construction; the water in which, green and slimy and moving with frogs and their young, moistened the land under cultivation. A small bridge of rustic make spanned the moat. Crossing the bridge you came to what was known as the fruit garden ... This part of the ground was separated from the rest of the land by a stone dyke coped with turf to the depth of from six to eight inches. Passing the door of the hut to your right, and turning the corner to the south, you came upon a plot at the rear of their dwelling. This was the flower garden tastefully laid out, and where grew 'London pride,' 'dusty millers,' and sorrel wood, mint, thyme and such like old fashioned flowers. It was well kept and free of weeds. The remainder of the 'acre' was always under crop of the same description – potatoes, barley, and oats. The brothers tilled the field with a primitive looking worn-out spade, the barrow being a wooden one with iron 'tynds', drawn by one or other of them. The manure was seaweed gathered on the shore, and brought from thence in a creel of their own make on the back up the steep bracken braes in a zig-zag path, never deviated from; along with which they invariably carried in one of those short-necked black jars a supply of water from St Bennet's Well, specially for quenching their thirst. For boiling the potatoes and greens sea water got from a hole scooped in a rock about three hundred yards to the south-west of the well (still to be seen) was used, in order, it is supposed, to save their supply of salt. For other domestic purposes water from the pools around the hut was got ... At the north end of the hut stood a large heap of brushwood, tree roots, and turf, the accumulated gatherings of years, seldom broken on, the firewood for daily use being gathered nightly from the neighbouring wood and moor.

The hut had three apartments, the southmost being at one time a weaving shop, but had become a sort of store or lumber-room for old chests, ancient dram-drinking glasses of crystal, empty bottles &c. The middle apartment was both sitting room and kitchen. Here the food was prepared and the table spread daily. The fireplace stood against a stone wall which supported the roof, the smoke finding its way towards the clouds through an opening immediately over the hearth … The furniture of both sitting room and kitchen was a table and several chairs, with sundry hardware and other utensils. The apartment to the north was their only bed-room, and contained a four poster bed, a chest or two, and a couple of chairs.

… On week days as well as Sundays Robie-Danie donned a blue cloth jacket with brass buttons, a vest of the same texture, and linen trousers, all manufactured and made by themselves. His head covering had originally been a 'Glengarry', but long wear had considerably changed its appearance. Danie-Robie's work-a-day suit was entirely linen, also their own make. Being the one who attended church … on that day he dressed in a coat of blue cloth of the swallow-tail make, with brass buttons; vest and trousers of the same cloth; his head topped with a silk 'beaver' much weathered and brown, worn sailor-like fashion.

… In their declining years the brothers took a fancy and kept a dog of the terrier species that it might worry or, at least, scare away the rats and other 'uncanny vermin' which invested [sic] the hut as well as the turf stack … They at the same time made pets of a bantam cock and mate, the former to crow and, as the brothers said, tell them of whenever friend or stranger from a distance was to pay them a visit, a belief still to be met with in some out-of-the-way country places. The loom end of the hut was occupied by the fowls.

… All implements of husbandry required for the 'acre', such as wheel-barrows, harrows, pick and axe handles, were made by the brothers, their tools consisting of a large clasp-knife, a saw, and an axe – the latter used only to do the rougher kind of work. The wheels of the barrows were very primitive-looking affairs, made of several pieces of undressed wood clamped together, a hole being left in the centre for the wooden axle to work in.

… They knitted their own stockings, performed their washing and beetling, and made their shoes. These resembled somewhat the shoe of today, only they were made on the straight principle, not 'rights and lefts'. They thrashed and dressed their barley and oats, the neighbouring farmers taking it in turn to carting the grain to the mill, three miles distant, to be made into meal.

… Of books they had a goodly collection, such works as Boston's *Fourfold State*, Baxter's *Call to the Unconverted*, Howie's *Scotch Worthies*, Newton's *Works*, Traill's *Select Writings*, Flavel's *Works*, and Bunyan's *Pilgrim's Progress* being well to the front. Latterly they came to patronise the book canvasser on his stated visits to Cromarty, and to take from him in parts, to be afterwards bound for them by a friend in Cromarty, such books, chiefly of a religious nature, as took their fancy.

... Not long after the brothers' death, the hut was used as a barracks, or bothy, by masons employed at the new steading for Navity farm, and afterwards the 'auld clay biggin' was thrown down, and now the ploughshare passes over where it stood.

Whatever the social cost, the improvements of the late 1840s and 1850s carried out under Hugh Rose Ross increased yields and were continued by his son, George, whose initials 'GWHR' are displayed on the row of model farm labourers' cottages built at Cromarty Mains. However, the end of the American Civil War in 1865 led quickly to the import of cheap grain from the United States and to a consequent fall in prices. Thomas Middleton, the great-grandson of the improving farmer George Middleton, had the tenancy of three large farms near Cromarty, with in total over 1,100 arable acres, and kept accounting records over a thirty-year period from 1871. By the 1890s average profits at 18s 7d per arable acre were almost half the level they had been in the 1870s, when they peaked at just over £2.[18] Not surprisingly, in the 1890s the population of the rural part of the parish fell, with a loss of one hundred people between 1891 and 1901 (see Figure 15.3).

Throughout Scotland farmers close to centres of urban population diversified into production of milk, fruit and vegetables but this was more difficult where there were only small towns and Cromarty did not have a daily supply of milk until 1893 when Mr Lumsden, who farmed Navity, began deliveries.[19] One area of growth had been the production of disease free seed potatoes, which had increased in importance since the middle of the century. Shipments of potatoes from Cromarty harbour were reported each year from the 1880s and shortly after 1900 those promoting the Cromarty & Dingwall Light Railway, which was to run along the north shore of the Black Isle, provided estimates of the freight which the line might carry. The crops grown annually for export

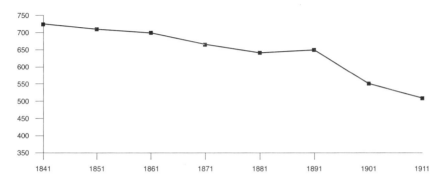

FIGURE 15.3   Population: parish of Cromarty (landward) 1841–1911.

averaged 15,000 quarters (c.1,500 tons) of oats and barley, 5,000 tons
of hay and 5,000 tons of potatoes.[20]

Resolis: agitation for smallholdings

Unlike the parish of Cromarty, Resolis had retained a large number of
smallholdings and, from the 1880s, there was agitation to create more.
At a meeting of 150 crofters and small farmers in April 1883 they
articulated their need for more small farms, through their chairman,
John Maclennan, the tenant of Resolis Mains.[21] There were also
concerns about the lack of security for small tenants. In 1889 Munro
of Poyntzfield evicted a number of smallholders, including a Hugh
Munro whose family had farmed for 100 years at the Colony, an early
settlement of mailers on moor ground. Another had been turned off
the Cromarty estate in 1866, when two farms were consolidated, and
granted moorland by Poyntzfield at 4s 6d per acre for the first seven
years, 9s for the next seven years and 11s 6d for the remaining seven
years. However, as they did not fall under the protection of the Crofting
Acts, they could be – and were – removed.[22]

Fishing

In 1836 Hugh Miller wrote in the *New Statistical Account* of Cromarty
that herring seemed to have left the firth and 'many of the fishermen, in
consequence of a series of expensive and ill remunerated exertions, have
sunk into abject poverty'. They continued to fish for herring but had
to make longer journeys, leaving Cromarty for the fishing season, often
on the west coast. The involvement of the Cromarty fishers in herring
fishing was driven by the changing market price, the pattern of which
was as follows:

1835–42:	rising prices
1842–51:	a drop and then steady lower prices
1852–56:	rising prices
1857–74:	fluctuating prices with no clear trend
1875–83:	a sudden rise followed by fluctuations at a higher level than before
1884–mid 90s:	collapse of prices and crisis
mid 90s–1914:	boom years but with fish landed at fewer centres

In some years the Cromarty fishermen did not pursue herring fishing.
In 1868, in a time of fluctuating prices, only three of eighteen boats
were engaged because the men would not accept the low wages on

offer and in 1871 there was criticism that the men were slow to accept new practices – both the Cromarty and Portmahomack fishermen were being described as lazy for following the 'old system' of not shooting their nets until they saw herring playing in the water.[23] As catches in the Moray Firth fell it became common for the fishermen to sail to the west coast in late April for the herring fishing, leading to a request from the fishermen in 1894 for a change in the date of the communion service in both the Free and Established churches. In 1932 one old man recalled the Sunday evening prayer service held 'before our fifteen great sailing boats departed for the West Coast fishing'.[24]

In 1891 there were fifty-five Cromarty boats, but of these only seventeen were '1st class', that is, over thirty feet. In contrast Avoch had thirty-eight '1st class' vessels.[25] In 1895, after the crisis in the industry, it was reported that the Cromarty herring boats – the large boats – had been lying in mud off Alness for two years.[26] With the revival of the mid 1890s, herring were again caught within the Cromarty fishery district, which ran from Portmahomack to Avoch, but all those for curing were landed at Portmahomack, where nine boats were engaged to curers by the turn of the century. However, this fishery soon declined and after 1903 no boats were engaged and landings of herring were minimal.[27] There was also a decline in the number of boats sailing to pursue the west coast herring fishery – whereas in 1891 'the town sent a fine fleet to the Castlebay fishing', in 1910 it sent only one boat.[28] An early photograph of the Cromarty Artillery Volunteers parading for inspection on the links, probably in the 1890s, shows the herring boats drawn up and stored for the winter.

Line fishing was a more reliable, but less lucrative, source of income and in 1848 the Aberdeen-based Hogarth & Company built a curing shed for haddock on the links and engaged all the Cromarty fishers.[29] From the 1860s there was, however, a significant threat to line fishing from inshore trawlers working in the firth, a threat that increased in the 1880s with the advent of steam trawlers. In January 1885 twelve Cromarty boats, loaded with stones as weapons, attacked a stream trawler operating opposite the town and later in the month a group of fishermen, returning from training with the Naval Reserve, assaulted the crew of a steam trawler at Invergordon. A Cromarty fish merchant named Hogg, who had bought fish from the trawlermen, had his barrels thrown into the water.[30] A number of public protest meetings were held in the town over the next five years, and one local fisherman, Alexander Reid, emerged as a leader. Some protection was gained by 1888, when trawlers were excluded from the firths, with extensions to this limit in 1890 and 1892, but there was still a problem with illegal trawling.

The line fishery also required a source of bait. Lugworm was dug on the shore but more important were the mussel beds of the Cromarty Firth. The Earl of Cromartie claimed the right to these under a charter of 1698 but this was contested by the Cromarty fishermen who believed that they had a traditional right to take mussels from the beds in Nigg bay. In 1837 they pursued the matter as far as the Court of Session – where the case was decided in their favour – but it was a hollow victory for no one thereafter took responsibility for restocking or managing the beds and within forty years they were almost wholly depleted. The Cromartie estate's title to the oyster beds was, however, unambiguous and a short-lived attempt was made in 1872 to exploit these, with an English oyster farmer, Mr Musset, being brought to the firth and eight smacks engaged to dredge for the shellfish.[31]

Salmon fishery

From the 1850s fixed salmon nets and traps became illegal within the waters of the Cromarty Firth, a position confirmed by statute with the Salmon Fisheries Act of 1862. From this date coastal salmon-fishing stations were created along the east coast, those close to Cromarty – to the south at Navity and MacFarquhar's Bed and to the north at Castlecraig – being operated from a base on the links. The catch in the Cromarty nets alone was reported as averaging one hundred a day in August 1881.[32]

The decline of catches in the line fishery in turn led to increased poaching of salmon and sea trout. In 1896 there was said to be 'wholesale poaching of salmon by Cromarty fishermen, who pretend to be fishing for flounders' and two years before, in April 1894, there was what almost amounted to a sea fight between two boats of Cromarty fishermen and thirteen bailiffs over a catch of sea trout. A month later seventeen bailiffs armed with cudgels confiscated a further basket of fish in the town.[33]

The Cromarty fishing community

In the early part of the nineteenth century the Cromarty fishing community was surprisingly small. The militia list of 1814, which names all men in the parish between the ages of 17 and 45, has only twenty-five fishermen: seven aged between 17 and 29, and eighteen in the age range 30 to 45. This was no doubt the effect of the Napoleonic Wars which had led many fishers into the navy and, with peace, their numbers probably increased as young men returned from service. In 1841 the census returns show that there were eighty-two fishermen and numbers thereafter rose steeply, as children born in the 1820s and 1830s grew to working age. Ten years later, in 1851, numbers had increased to 103. This increase was, however, at the very time when opportunities had become limited because of the failure of the Cromarty fishery district to recover from the slump of the 1830s. Thus, in 1843 a visitor described Cromarty's fishertown as characterised by 'dilapidated houses ... pigs ... children ... dead mussels, (and) rotten fish'. In the harbour there were 'a number of fishing boats ... the poor fellows ... scarcely getting a single herring'.[34] The number of fishermen fell slightly, to ninety-three in 1871, but by the census of 1891 the fisher community – men, women and children – made up almost half the population of the burgh, 620 of the 1308 inhabitants.

There is also evidence that the fishing community was becoming increasingly marginalised. The tradition in the north of Scotland was for more churchgoers to be 'adherents' of the church rather than communicant members. Nevertheless, it is notable that no fishermen or women were communicant members of the Free Church after the Disruption and although there was no tradition of anything other than infant baptism, in 1857 the Free Church minister, Mr McEachern, christened eleven children described as 'young fishermen and fisherwomen ... some of whom were talking to their fathers during the ceremony'.[35] The omission of infant baptism suggests that their families had had no active connection with either the Established or Free churches. This appears to have been remedied by the Free Church during Mr McEachern's ministry and a number of men and women from the fishertown became communicant members after 1860. When the new church was built in 1867 with a seating capacity of 900, its large size was regarded as in part due to the growing numbers of fisher folk.[36] The Established Church responded in the 1880s with the erection of a mission hall in the fishertown itself, a corrugated iron hut mounted on wooden stilts. Its physical proximity to the parish church, a matter of few hundred yards, emphasised the great social distance between the two sections of the community.

The fishers began to appear more and more as a distinct and different class. Donald A. Mackenzie (1873–1936), son of the Cromarty sheriff clerk, wrote that 'in my boyhood they sat in their own corner of the church; the boys sat on their own forms (the "second forms") in each class in the school, and were not allowed to leave their corner of the playground'. It was only the introduction of football in the 1880s which led to fisher boys and town boys playing together.[37]

By the mid-1870s the state of the fishertown – especially its middens and pigs – was being seen as a barrier to the development of Cromarty as a tourist destination. This, and the continuing division in the community, became particularly apparent in 1897–8 when Mackenzie published a series of ten articles entitled 'Cromarty Idylls' in the Dingwall newspaper, the North Star. The first four of these were about the fisher community. Mackenzie praised the hardiness of the fishers but caused great offence by some of his remarks. He described the houses of the fisher folk as 'often miserable hovels, grimy with smoke, and redolent with the nauseous odour of fish entrails and the bark of lines', the dialect as 'rough and uncouth, abounding in gutturals, like a thing they despised and which they willingly spat out' and the people as 'a strange mixture of blood, with traces of Highland, and Gypsy and English mingling'. The first recorded reference to the fisher dialect had been an article in the *Invergordon Times* in August 1867 in which an anonymous contributor described it as a hybrid of Caithness and Buchan and stated that it had been the general dialect of the town but was gradually becoming peculiar to the fishing community. This was disputed in a letter published the following week, whose author claimed that the fisher dialect was quite distinct from the 'pure English' spoken in the town.

In response to the 'Cromarty Idylls' a crowd of around 200 fishermen assembled in Cromarty, paraded an effigy of Mackenzie's father (Alexander H. Mackenzie) through the streets and burned it outside the family house in Barkly Street. D. A. Mackenzie's brother, William Mackay Mackenzie (later an eminent historian and secretary to the Royal Commission for the Ancient and Historical Monuments of Scotland) wrote an open letter from Glasgow remonstrating with the fishermen, claiming that the 'Cromarty Idylls' had been accurate in showing both the fishers' strong and weak points. He alleged two failings of the community – their improper practice of allowing the women, showing bare legs and thighs, to carry men out to their boats and their neglect of their children, who were often left hungry. He added that the mob had insulted and assaulted young women, and regretted that they had attacked a number of those in the town who had striven to help them, including those promoting the building of new houses for the fishers.

Hopes of revival

The Crimean War 1854–6

At a number of points it seemed that economic revival of the town might be achieved. The hope that the Navy might make greater use of the sheltered anchorage of the Cromarty Firth seemed about to be realised when a number of ships of the Baltic Fleet, commanded by Vice-Admiral Charles Napier, over-wintered there in 1854–5, and the principal Cromarty hotel was renamed the 'Admiral Napier' in his honour.[38] The vessels were *Dragon, Basilisk, Vulture, Rosmund, Cossack* (20 guns), *Magician* (16 guns), *Arrogant* (46 guns) and *Odin* (36 guns)[39] and their presence was keenly anticipated.

> Should the crews of these vessels be half so fond of fun and frolic as those of the smaller craft now in the bay, the ancient village will undoubtedly be kept in a state of boisterous jollity ... The sailors appear in a very gay style, bedecked with artificial flowers and long streamers of gaudy ribbons

... They go into the country in large parties with colours displayed and accompanied by music.[40]

However, the town came closest to significant material benefit from the war with the conversion of the disused hemp factory buildings to barracks for the Ross-shire Militia.[41] This was officially sanctioned in November 1855 and the converted buildings, almost complete in April 1856, were to be capable of accommodating 1,000 men, although only 320 beds had been put up for the time being. There was also a military hospital in part of one wing. In the town, quarters were being found for twenty to thirty officers, a site had been fixed for a shore battery on the links, and the Reeds Park, to the east, was being made ready as a rifle range. The town council had played its part by paving one side of Church Street to a sufficient width that officers might promenade arm in arm with their ladies and 'show off their military gait'. As all this was made ready, workmen were seen in the streets and the town seemed 'lively and cheerful'.

However, the Peace of Paris had already ended the war in March 1856 and in July the order was given that the whole station was to be dismantled and equipment shipped to Edinburgh for sale. There was an attempt in the following year to have the militia stores moved from Dingwall to Cromarty, but this was staunchly and successfully resisted by Dingwall Town Council.[42]

A fleet anchorage?

Thereafter, Cromarty's greatest hope lay in the use of the Cromarty Firth as a fleet anchorage, with benefits similar to those realised with the over-wintering of the Baltic Fleet in 1854–5. The first visit of the Channel Fleet took place in August 1863 and, until the moment of its arrival, it was not known where the ships would anchor within the firth. The Artillery Volunteers were drawn up on the links at Cromarty but, when the fleet sailed past and headed for Invergordon, they refused to fire a salute. The decision had been determined by the railway connection to Invergordon, completed earlier in the year.[43]

Attempts to have it anchor at Cromarty were made without success at the Channel Fleet's second visit in 1874 and this remained a source of resentment for decades. In 1883 the local MP, Mr Pender, was challenged at a public meeting as to 'why the Channel Squadron anchored in a guttery puddle [Invergordon] when there was a good anchorage at Cromarty'.[44] But no amount of colourful rhetoric could hide Cromarty's comparative disadvantage.

Transport

Cromarty's growing isolation in relation to the improved transport network of the eastern Highlands not only took the fleet to Invergordon

FOR LONDON,
THE
SMACK CALEDONIA,
GEO. MACDONALD, MASTER,

WILL Sail from CROMARTY, on Thursday the 21st current, and call at the Ferry of Kessock same day, and off Findhorn, Burghead, and other ports in the Frith next day, wind and weather permitting.

Inverness, 23d July, 1828.

FOR LEITH,
THE SMACK LIZARD,
JOHN FRASER, MASTER,

WILL Sail from CROMARTY on Saturday the 2d August, wind and weather permitting.

Inverness, 23d July, 1828.

FIGURE 15.4
Advertisements for smacks sailing from Cromarty all this had disappeared by
the 1870s.

but affected all aspects of the town's trade. The improvements brought about by the Commission for Highland Roads and Bridges in the first half of the nineteenth century had linked Dingwall and Easter Ross to Inverness and the south by bridging the rivers Conon (in 1809) and Beauly (in 1811). The advance of the railway network reinforced this. The railway had come to Inverness in 1854 and the line north reached Dingwall in 1862, Invergordon in 1863, Bonar Bridge in 1864, Golspie in 1868, Helmsdale in 1870 and, finally, Wick and Thurso in 1874, with the connection from Dingwall to Skye completed in 1870. A report in a Dumfries newspaper of a journey north in 1865 tellingly mentioned Cromarty but only as 'seen in the distance' from a railway carriage.[45]

In 1875 a correspondent in the *Inverness Advertiser* declared that Cromarty had been 'flourishing until the railway brought death and stagnation'. This might have been an exaggeration but what was clearly significant was the resultant loss of seaborne trade. Before the coming of the 'iron horse ... trade was carried to the town by 5 London smacks, 5 Leith Smacks, 2 Aberdeen smacks and 1 Dundee smack'. These had all been lost and both Invergordon and Dingwall – 'a swamp built town' – had 'gained life by Cromarty's death'.[46]

In 1865 a scheme for a Black Isle railway was proposed and a public meeting was called in the town urging the extension of the proposed line to Cromarty. Although a 'large and influential committee' was appointed and the project taken up 'with great spirit', the Black Isle railway was not only thirty years away but would never reach Cromarty. Nevertheless the prospect of a railway connection was a powerful idea and in his election address in Cromarty in 1872, the sitting MP, Pender, mooted a narrow gauge railway for the Black Isle as a solution.⁴⁷

After the Highland Railway completed the line to Fortrose in late 1893 there was continued pressure from Cromarty for a connection. The Light Railway Act, which came into force in 1896, relaxed the regulations on rail weight, signalling and staffing for railways with a maximum speed of 25 mph and, with construction made easier, surveys were completed in the same year for both a Fortrose–Cromarty link by the Highland Railway and a Dingwall–Cromarty line by the West Highland Railway Company. It was the latter that was to be pursued, though not to completion, through the formation of a new body – the Cromarty & Dingwall Light Railway Company. This was despite an initial set back in the departure of its principal backer, Colonel Ross, for military service in India in 1897. By 1902, after Ross returned, a Parliamentary Provisional Order was in place, but construction did not begin until 1914 – and the line was never completed.⁴⁸

It was therefore improvements in road and sea links that proved to be the more important for Cromarty. In the 1860s the Cromarty–Nigg ferry ran irregularly, with complaints from travellers of waiting for hours on the far side, and the road to the Balblair–Invergordon ferry was in poor repair. The link to Nigg was, in reality, of little importance and the attraction of operating the ferry was threatened when, in September 1899, the boat was swamped and a ferryman drowned. More significantly, complaints were still being made in 1890 about the lack of connection between Cromarty and Invergordon, which was 'a life and death matter' for the town. When the Black Isle railway opened in 1893 the Post Office still favoured sending mail via Invergordon, but this was opposed by the town council who wanted mail delivered via Fortrose using the new line. A compromise was reached with the morning mail coming from Fortrose and the afternoon delivery from Invergordon and it was this link, and the contract for delivery of mail, which would sustain the Cromarty–Invergordon ferry until well into the next century.⁴⁹

In 1893 Captain Black of the steamer *Earnholm*, which had been trading since the 1880s, bought a paddle steamer, the *New Undaunted*, to provide a regular service between Inverness, Nairn, Cromarty, Invergordon and Dingwall.⁵⁰ In the same year a group of local merchants and tradesmen formed the Cromarty Steamship Company and bought two small steamers, the *Speedwell* and the *Venture*, to provide a regular service to Invergordon. These were later replaced by the *Saga* in 1903 and, in 1913, by their first new built ship, the *Sutors*, constructed by the Rose Street Foundry, Inverness. The company traded at a loss from its foundation until after 1903 but the commitment of the local directors and the substantial number of local investors allowed the operation to survive for the benefit of the town.⁵¹

Tourism

'A place of summer resort'

By the 1820s general improvements in transport in Scotland, especially the advent of steam-powered vessels, had made possible the beginnings of mass tourism in the north. These visitors were less prepared to accept the conditions tolerated by earlier travellers. One commentator noted in 1828 that steamers were already passing through the Caledonian canal 'in the great rout of the tender legged, tender skinned, tender stomached tourists, who require well-aired flealess sheets – chicken broth – and no trouble'. Conditions in Cromarty – the 'abominable filth' described by Brodie in 1843 – were unlikely to attract this clientele.[52]

In October 1848 a public meeting in Cromarty resolved that the town council should use the powers of the Police Act to have the streets lighted and cleaned and in the following year the council elected as provost Sir George Gun Munro of Poyntzfield, on the strength of his commitment to establish gas and water supplies and 'macadamise' the streets. Munro's aim was to promote Cromarty as 'a place of summer resort' and thus improve its trade. Seaside tourism was by this date well established in Scotland. Cromarty had had a bathing house from as early as 1777 but it was probably more recent examples, such as cottages let for bathing on the coast east of Inverness, which the town sought to emulate. There was also a growing perception that the health of middle-class urban families might be preserved or restored by taking a house in the country, or by the coast, for the summer season.[53]

The water supply was complete by the end of the following year but it soon became apparent that it was a failure, because the springs provided insufficient pressure to carry the water to the town. There was also discontent that no action had been taken on a gas supply and the streets remained dirty. Neither were bathing machines a success. Nevertheless, there was still optimism in 1856 when a new hotel opened, which it was hoped would lead to 'a large influx of strangers, tourists and sea bathers'.[54]

With improvements in transport, day trippers were also becoming a potential source of income. Cromarty's annual games in May 1857 attracted a steamer chartered by Inverness Royal Academy. More came to see naval vessels in the firth, particularly after the Crimean War had raised public awareness of, and pride in, the Navy. HMS *Pembroke* drew 'hundreds of people' to see the drilling of coastguard volunteers in 1857 and in 1862 the attraction of the 'magnificent war frigate' HMS *St George* was such that crowds travelled on a Sunday from Alness and Dingwall to view her, leading to public criticism in the local press. However, once the railway reached Invergordon in the following year it was easier for visitors to travel there, a disadvantage that became most

FIGURE 15.5
HMS *Pembroke* trained members of the Coast Guard Volunteers at Cromarty,
1857.

apparent with the second visit of the Channel Fleet to the firth in 1874.
Cromarty gained little benefit.[55]

Hugh Miller's birthplace

The town's greatest asset was its image as the birthplace of Hugh Miller.
By 1859, three years after Miller's death at his own hand, the skyline
was dominated by a monument topped with a three-ton statue of Miller
by the sculptor Handyside Ritchie. In the same year a Mr Dickson
published *Cromarty: Being a Tourist's Visit to the Birthplace of Hugh
Miller*, based on his visit in the previous year. Miller's mother lived in
the cottage where Hugh had been born until her death in 1863 and, in
the following year, the family arranged for its repair and improvement,
with railings erected around it. The *Invergordon Times* reported that it
would then be 'pleasing to visit the humble cottage in which was born
one of Scotland's most gifted and genial sons'.[56]

In 1867 a series of articles by 'DRM' appeared in the local press
describing a visit to Cromarty, originally planned for six days but

extended to ten as a result of the 'variety of diversions' available. The problem apparently was 'not what to do, but when to do it'. The town's people, especially its 'upper classes', were hospitable, there was sea fishing and many 'endeared spots' to visit. But central to the attraction was that 'wherever one turns the spirit of Hugh Miller is to be found, fresh and fragrant as ever'. Moreover, one might encounter the real-life characters described by him, such as the simple-minded 'Captain' Mackay who, as a boy, had been devoted to Miller, and who welcomed DRM and his party at the harbour.[57]

Only four years later a different picture was painted by 'JK' who had made a special trip to Cromarty. Surprisingly, having asked at the hotel about the location of Miller's birthplace, he could get no information. Then 'weary and wet I paced the town and made frequent inquiries … eventually found the street and was directed by a rather genteel person but to the wrong house … (and) finally found the birthplace unoccupied and in a most lamentable state of decay, the roof fallen in and a small garden plot in barbarous condition'. In JK's opinion 'the life-like statue of this intellectual hero' overlooked a 'wreck' and suggested a 'sad reflection on the loyalty of the inhabitants'.[58]

A group from Inverness, calling on the steamer *Eilean Dubh* in 1880, following the extension of the harbour pier to accommodate such vessels, had a similar experience. Miller's cottage was 'rapidly falling into decay' and at the monument they were surrounded by a group of 'tattered children' who begged for money in exchange for dancing a hornpipe. The author of the piece admitted that Cromarty 'would be a charming resort in summer but for one thing, it is cut off from the line of the railway – the artery of life – and is, as it were, far out into the sea'.[59]

An English traveller in the same year, inspired by Miller's *My Schools and Schoolmasters* and *Scenes and Legends*, had similar views, although he found more positive features. The thatched cottage where Miller was born was pointed out with pride by the inhabitants, who were kind, hospitable and 'with a lot more intelligence than we expected'. In a match between visitors and locals the cricket team played to a high standard. And, although Cromarty appeared so deserted that it would be 'safe to discharge a cannon in the streets', on which grass grew, such a place where 'steam was never seen and there was no noise' might be regarded as a pleasing contrast to the bustle of the city. But improvements were needed and a 'better means of bringing such places of interest into easier access'. The writer had only reached his destination by being given passage from Invergordon by some fishermen 'gayan doon to Cromarty'.[60]

From 1882 a new steamer, the *Earnholm*, was carrying visitors between ports in the Moray Firth and this may have been one spur to improvement. By 1887 visitors from Buckie on the *Earnholm* were

The Sutors of Cromarty from "Uncle Sandy's" Garden.

FIGURE 15.6
Hugh Miller as a visitor attraction – a view of Uncle Sandy's garden.

able to see Hugh Miller's cottage in a good state of preservation, with Miller's collection of fossils and other artefacts put into good order by his son, who had created a museum in the cottage. A report of a visit by steamer from Aberdeen in 1889 makes it clear that Hugh Miller remained the principal attraction of the town. Visitors were not only shown his birthplace but also his uncles' house and the grammar school he had attended by the shore.[61] The old school was painted in 1884 by the Scottish artist John Muirhead, on a visit to Cromarty, during which he also produced paintings of Gordon's Lane, harvest at Rosefarm and fishing boats on the shore.

From 1893 the paddle steamer *New Undaunted* went, on Tuesdays and Fridays, from Inverness to Nairn, connecting with a train, and from there on to Cromarty and Invergordon, before returning by the same route. Its timetable specifically allowed for an hour in Cromarty to visit Hugh Miller's cottage.[62] Before the end of the century the cottage had been handed over to the town council, who maintained it until 1938, making it an integral part of the effort to promote Cromarty.

The promotion of Cromarty

An anonymous correspondent in the *Inverness Advertiser* in 1875, drew attention, as others had done, to the dereliction and poverty in the town, but proposed a solution in the form of a plan to develop Cromarty's potential. First, it was necessary to establish suitable bathing accommodation – Cromarty, with its sheltered position, had, he argued, the capacity to exceed Nairn and become 'the Brighton of the North'. Second, the town should promote itself as a 'hydropathic establishment' where 'sick people might wander with Hugh Miller's work in hand over the classic ground', which might be considered 'the Italy of Scotland' lying as it did between two expanses of water, with 'Cromarty like Brindisi in the heel of the boot'. And, finally, there was a need to remedy the state of the fishertown by removing pigs and dunghills. Hydropathy was a sufficiently amorphous body of thought to accommodate Cromarty's combination of sea air, bathing, pleasant walks and amusements.[63]

From 1889 Cromarty had an indefatigable advocate in the person of John Bain, a local draper, who believed that Cromarty's future lay with tourism and not in 'Utopian notions of a railway terminus and an English fleet anchorage'. Bain placed two new bathing machines on the

CROMARTY FROM THE HILL.

VISITORS' GUIDE.

HOTELS.
CROMARTY ARMS.   COMMERCIAL.

WALKS.
1. To the Monument.
2. Along the Shore Road westward.
3. Along the Cliffs (ascending beyond the Bathing Vans).
4. Through Morial's Den, from Gate on Shore Road, as far as Newton Farm. Return by High Road.
5. Eathie Burn (see Miller's "Scenes and Legends," Chap. XXXI.). Leaving Newton Smithy on the right, pass by Navity Farmhouse to the Beach. Proceed westward a short distance.

6. To the Dropping Cave. Take the path along the Shore to the east for some distance past the Shooting Range.
7. Round the Hill. Take the road leading to Cromarty House, and enter the Wood after passing St Regulus Burying-Ground (well worth a visit). Follow the path along the Cliffs as far as Gate opening on to level ground. Either turn sharp to the right or take the path leading straight on (the latter leads to the Look-Out). This walk, which is allowed to be one of the finest in Scotland, may be varied by taking the lower path.
8. To Macfarquhar's Bed. Passing by Cromarty House Stables, proceed past the Mains Farm, and cross straight over Hill to the Sea.

The Library is open to Visitors. Terms, 1s per annum. Attendance, Mondays, at eight P.M.

Cromarty Bowling and Tennis Green, off High Street.

Hugh Miller's Birthplace and Museum, &c Church Street.

BOATING.
The numerous Caves on both sides of the Firth may be visited ; also the Golf Course at Nigg.

Post Delivery, 3.45 P.M. ; Dispatch, 10 P.M.

Keys for the Bathing Vans are kept at the Cromarty Shop, where views of the district may also be had.

FIGURE 15.7
Visitors' Guide from the *Cromarty News*, 1891.

beach and he promoted his views through a regular column 'Cromarty Observations' – from 1893 'Cromarty Notes' – in the *Invergordon Times*, by frequent articles in the *Ross-shire Journal* and, for eighteen months in 1891–2, through his own weekly paper, the *Cromarty News*. He argued for better accommodation, with a reliable piped water supply; bathing facilities; a recreation ground with tennis and bowls; boats for hire; tree planting and public seating; a public urinal; the covering of open drains and removal of ruinous houses and sheds; a daily ferry link to Invergordon; repairs to roads and pavements; cleaning of the beach; and improvement to walks around the town. In 1890 he financed and published 'Cromarty and Neighbourhood' as a guide to the town, with sketches of local scenery, and sent a hundred copies, at his own expense, to hotels in the south, and followed this in August 1900 with an album of sixteen photographs of the town and district.[64]

An editorial in the *North Star* in October 1897 summarised the niche market at which the town was aiming: 'Cromarty people observe that they who once visit them, come again. This is because Cromarty is unique among watering-places. It has a special clientele – those who appreciate old-worldliness, its unconventionalities, its remoteness from the ordinary haunts of the holiday maker.'[65]

The social structures of the town

As Cromarty plunged into economic decline in the 1840s, its social networks became the more important as means of combating poverty, giving a sense of purpose and maintaining community spirit. The principal organisations in early nineteenth-century Cromarty have been described in chapter 14 – the church, the Loyal Cromarty Volunteers and the various friendly societies, namely the Freemasons, the Free Gardeners, the Wrights and Coopers (the Hammermen), and the Cromarty Friendly Society. The Volunteers were disbanded in 1817; by the 1840s the Gardeners and Hammermen had dissolved, while the Freemasons continued into the 1850s but then became moribund; and the community was not only split between the Established and Free churches after 1843, but experienced a short-lived schism within the Cromarty Free Church itself in the late 1840s. The sense of community was also diminished by emigration, by increasing consciousness of social class and by the 'churn' of population, as displaced people moved from rural areas into the town before moving on to the larger urban centres. Social division was exacerbated by the growing proportion of the town's population who were living in poverty, especially the still expanding fishing community.

However, some new organisations were being formed. A Dorcas Society was established in 1846 by a Mrs Paterson, wife of the officer commanding the coastguard, and a debating society was established in 1840, meeting in the Wrights and Coopers Lodge, but it is not clear for how many years it met.[66] There were also successors to the uniformed Loyal Cromarty Volunteers. In the autumn of 1853, with war with Russia imminent, the government resolved to recruit a volunteer coast guard, thus allowing members of the regular Coast Guard Service to be called up by the Navy. Recruiting began in early 1854 with the intention of recruiting 6,000 men in England, 1,500 in Scotland and 1,000 in Ireland. By August the Scottish contingent had been enrolled, all able-bodied fishermen, and in Avoch they paraded proudly 'distinguished by knots of red ribbons on their breasts'. [67]

In was not, however, until after the Crimean War that training of the Volunteers took place. HMS *Pembroke* arrived at Cromarty in 1857 and the steamer *Commodore* brought 261 volunteers from the coast of the Moray Firth for instruction in gunnery and small arms. The drilling attracted hundreds of spectators and this continued into the autumn, when it was promised that the ship would 'astonish the natives with their great guns'.[68] The formation of the Coastguard Volunteers may have laid the ground for the strong tradition of fishermen serving in the Royal Naval Volunteer Reserve. One outcome of the extended visit of HMS *Pembroke* was the marriage of a sailor, John Shepherd, to a young Cromarty woman, Catherine Fidler or Finlayson – and the fecundity of their son, James, led to Shepherd becoming one of the most common names in the twentieth-century town.

In June 1859 the town council began again to campaign for the creation of a shore battery at Cromarty, no action having been taken since 1856.[69] Late in the same year artillery and rifle volunteer companies began to be formed throughout the UK. A corps of artillery was formed in Cromarty but made little progress, although individual volunteers wrote to the newspapers arguing for the importance of fortifying either Cromarty or nearby Navity, where '400 men could be landed in five minutes' and 'in twenty minutes more the Black Isle would be in possession of the enemy'. The lack of enthusiasm in Cromarty was deemed by some 'not a credit to Hugh Miller's native town' and with the encouragement of Colonel Ross, the laird, as commandant, they were practising firing shot and shell fortnightly during the summer of 1861.[70] The Volunteer Artillery did not bring any significant employment but it was an important focus of activity and a source of pride for the men of the community. They competed in rifle and carbine shooting competitions, which became part of the celebrations at New Year, established a fife and drum band in 1868, their annual inspection and dinner was an important social occasion, and their drill hall, completed in 1887 and named the Victoria Hall, became the main indoor social space in the town.[71]

The 'war excitement' of 1854–6 had also led to a demand for news and to the opening of reading rooms in Dingwall, Avoch, Fortrose, Rosemarkie and Tain.[72] In Cromarty it was not until 1859 that the Mechanics Institute was formed which purchased newspapers. It had sixty-six members, who were also provided with six large maps and a few standard works of reference. Throughout Britain mechanics institutes were usually founded and governed by the paternalistic middle class and this was the case in Cromarty, where the venture was supported by the laird, provost, bank agent and commanding officer of the coastguard. The same year saw the formation of a temperance society and the Band of Hope was created in 1860. An active minister in the Free Church, Mr McEachern, helped to establish the Mutual Improvement Association, which met in the Masonic Lodge from 1866. This was an interesting development since these organisations, increasingly common in mid nineteenth-century Scotland, were run by their own members and, unlike the mechanics institutes, did not shun political or religious controversy. There was also a revival of the Masonic Lodge, which culminated in 1870 with a 'dinner, tea and ball' involving sixty of the brethren, their wives and friends, which ran from 6 p.m. to 1 a.m., with songs, speeches, string and wind instruments, and 'more splendid decoration of the hall, with flags and evergreens, than ever seen even by oldest brethren' – and all of this with 'no intoxicating drinks'.[73]

The Free Church, having recovered from its local schism of the late 1840s, was a major force in the town, with its new church building completed in 1867, and in 1871, when the burgh's population was 1,481, the congregation had 1,300 adherents, 900 above and 400 below the age of fourteen. The church also ran the largest school in the town and there was an active Young Men's Christian Association (YMCA) formed in 1871, a lodge of the temperance organisation the International Order of Good Templars, formed in 1872, and many concerts and lectures, including one organised in 1875 by the YMCA at which Edward Tew of Nairn used a 'magic lantern' to show 130 dissolving views, recreating a voyage from Aberdeen to the Arctic. This was presented to an audience of 600 in the factory buildings.[74]

There appear to have been reasonably cordial relations with the Established Church. The committee that ran the Dorcas Society was interdenominational and in 1871 a lecture to support the Society and the YMCA was held in the Free Church school, with the laird, Colonel Ross – who was a member of the Established Church – in the chair. In 1872 the ministers agreed to a joint Sunday School Christmas entertainment in the factory buildings, arranged by 'the Misses Ross, the Misses Graham and other young ladies of the town'. Three Christmas trees were placed at intervals with over 600 'useful and ornamental gifts' and, after an opening hymn and prayer, the gifts were distributed and there was a magic lantern show provided by the lighthouse keeper, Mr Ritson, before the children dispersed with parcels of fruit and cake. In 1881, at a meeting of the YMCA, the chair was taken by the Church of Scotland minister, Mr Scott, because the Free Church minister, Mr Elder, was ill, and when a new minister, Mr Mackay, was inducted in 1883 Mr Scott was present and spoke of his hope for unity with the new incumbent.[75]

There were perhaps greater tensions within the Established Church itself. In the 'Gaelic Chapel case' of 1831 the minister of the Gaelic Chapel had unsuccessfully attempted to have either a parish created for him within the bounds of the parish of Cromarty or to have a collegiate charge created, with the two ministers having equal status. This was now a thing of the past but there remained a lack of cooperation between the congregations, both of which remained in the established Church of Scotland after the Disruption of 1843. The well-respected John Maclennan was appointed as minister of the Gaelic Chapel in 1849 but remained only until 1851. He was followed, in 1852, by Walter Ross Munro under whom the Chapel's congregation suffered a considerable decline, no doubt in part due to migration from the town, but perhaps also caused by Munro himself, who was eventually deposed for drunkenness in 1874. Over the next fifteen years three ministers served the congregation, one of whom, Donald Macleod, remained for little more than two weeks. In 1858 the chapel was described as 'an old, sorry dilapidated building ... The roof is broken, the windows freely admit not only the light but the elements as well; the doors are choked up with nettles, and should you approach to look inside, the damp, mouldy walls, and the decaying ghostly pews, are the sights that reward your curiosity.' During the 1880s, however, the roof was re-slated with funds raised by public subscription.[76]

When a vacancy occurred in 1888 it proved impossible to find a Gaelic-speaking minister. After nine months, the presbytery considered appointing a probationer from Resolis who could read some Gaelic but could not preach in the language. However, the proposal to appoint him was opposed by Mr Scott, the minister of the parish church, whose appeal was upheld by the synod. The congregation was now less than 150 and it was claimed that only 50 or so preferred to worship in Gaelic. Following an investigation by commissioners appointed by the General Assembly, and despite the views of those who thought it should be closed, the Chapel's last minister, Alexander Macpherson, was appointed in 1893 and remained until his death in 1918. The unusual origins of the chapel meant that it was the last congregation in the Established Church in Scotland in which the right of patronage remained, in this case exercised by the Crown.

The congregation had, however, shrunk even further to eighteen communicants and fifty-three adherents, even before Macpherson was appointed. During the long vacancy of 1888–93 the church was described by John Bain, writing in the *Invergordon Times*, as 'a Cave of Adullam for a few discontents' and Macpherson's incumbency was marked by constant bickering with the congregation of the parish church. Repairs to the building were carried out following Macpherson's appointment in 1893 but there was a tragic accident in the course of this work when the church officer, William Taylor, fell to his death through the rotten floor of the tower, where he had climbed in order to attach a rope to the bell.[77]

Although the activities of the Masonic Lodge, the Volunteers and the Free Church, with its associated organisations, led to a revival of community spirit in the late 1860s and 1870s, this seems to have run its course by the 1880s. There had been no corresponding revival of Cromarty's economy and this may have taken its toll on voluntary effort. The town was divided by a number of disputes, many of them involving Duncan Ross (1851–87), who succeeded to the Cromarty estate on the death of his father in November 1883. Early in the following year the Inspector of Poor, Robert Ferguson, died and two rival candidates emerged – Ferguson's son, who had carried out the work during his father's last illness, and the laird's candidate, Alexander Mackay, son of the harbour master. Support among the townspeople was strongly in favour of Ferguson and against Mackay who was 'a stranger' – but the case was appealed through the sheriff court to the Court of Session, where it was decided in favour of Mackay.[78] During the course of these court actions Ross carried out repairs to the road on the Chapel Brae, leading up to Cromarty Hill, which included replacing a stone dyke with a wire fence, placed in such a way that it left the road a few feet narrower. The fence became the principal issue at the next town council elections and it was subsequently torn down during the night.[79] In the course of an earlier dispute Ross had a bucket of 'noxious substances' emptied over him by a group of fishermen. Ross died young in 1887 and was succeeded by his brother Walter (1857–1928), a more effective laird who was instrumental in coordinating local efforts to have a drill hall erected. The Victoria Hall, completed in 1887, was the first of a number of new public buildings in the town. However, Ross left for military service in India in 1889, appointing Geoffrey St Quentin as factor, a post he retained until 1901.

There were further disputes as a result of the strength of the local temperance and Sunday observance campaigns. The influential Free Church minister, Mr McEachern, left for Australia in 1868 and later in the year it was observed that his voice was missed in connection with the refusal of a licence to Mr Couper, who wanted to establish an inn at the shore. Fifty fishermen subsequently petitioned regarding the lack of 'a public house convenient for them when leaving early in the morning' and pointing out that Mr Couper had offered to supply them with coffee 'for a small remuneration'.[80] Abuse of alcohol was certainly a problem within the community, but it appears that McEachern would have been a voice of pragmatism rather than for strict abstinence. The decision to refuse was, in fact, reversed by the justices of peace.

McEachern's successor, Mr Elder, remained until 1882 but latterly suffered from poor health and in 1883 a new Free Church minister, Mr Mackay, was appointed. Mackay also supported the temperance movement and at a licensing meeting in April 1884 he proposed a motion seeking to restrict the number of licensed premises, there being then one licence for every 200 inhabitants, and also opposed 'grocers' licences' (what would later be called 'off licences'). There were more extreme views. A Thomas Skinner declared, 'Sweep all away – if half the dockan is cut away it remains still.'[81]

In 1889, following a campaign for Sabbath observance, the Sunday postal service from Invergordon was discontinued, with the result that no mail was delivered on either Sunday or Monday, and in the same year Margaret Macrae, who had spent £70 on improvement to the Victoria Inn, in Church Street, was refused a licence. Subsequent letters to the press complained of the influence of the Good Templars, who acted like a 'secret society'.[82] These campaigns, and the greater social responsibility of the Free Church, may have driven a wedge between them and the Established Church. Walter Scott was appointed to the parish church in 1876 and remained until his death in 1925, but after Mr Mackay, of the Free Church, left in 1895 and was succeeded by Mr Macnicol, Mr Scott had no effective working relationship with his fellow minister.[83]

Education

The fortunes of private schools – generally known as 'adventure schools' when run by men and 'dame schools' when run by women – declined with Cromarty's economic downturn of the 1840s. The parish school continued as before but the Free Church school, formed after the Disruption in 1843, became the more important institution, operating from the schoolroom on the Braehead build in 1819 by the Cromarty Friendly Society. Its teachers included Miss Bruce, who had been running her own private school since 1830, and who was herself the daughter of a teacher. In 1868 the school had 150 boys and an unspecified number of girls on the roll.

There had been two 'society schools' in the 1830s but by 1846 there was only a single charitable school, run by the Dorcas Society, taught by Miss Macdonald and providing for some twenty-five 'bereaved and destitute' children. The school run by the Society for the Propagation of Christian Knowledge continued at Davidston, supported by the Middleton family.

The Education (Scotland) Act of 1872 created a Board of Education for Scotland and local, elected school boards – thus taking education out of the hands of the churches – and established the legal responsibility of parents to see that all children between the ages of five and thirteen received education in reading, writing and arithmetic. There was an exemption for children aged over ten who could show that they had achieved an adequate standard. The Act provided for the partial funding of education from the local property tax but fees could also be charged for attendance, with poor parents able to apply to the parochial board for support. Free primary education was introduced in 1890 and the age for compulsory education was extended to fourteen in 1901.

New schools were built in Cromarty and at Peddieston, west of Davidston, both under the control of the Cromarty School Board; and, in Resolis, at Newhall and Cullicudden. The buildings at Cromarty and Peddieston were completed in 1876, both designed by the Tain architect Alexander Maitland, the Cromarty school being described variously as 'Oxford style' and 'French Gothic'. At its opening the children marched through the town, preceded by the Artillery Volunteers' band, and the school was decorated with flags supplied by the coastguard.

In 1877 there were 235 pupils at Cromarty, but an average attendance of only 151 – 64 per cent. At Peddieston, the attendance was similar – thirty-five from a roll of fifty-three. By the early 1880s Cromarty had over 300 pupils and just over 350 pupils by 1893, in which year there were ninety at Peddieston. In Cromarty this now included a small secondary department, with around twenty pupils, created in 1891. Attendance had increased and generally averaged between 85 and 90 per cent, although it might be lower depending on the demands of farm work. The actions pursued in court for non-attendance of children were usually against parents in the fisher community, making Alexander H. Mackenzie, the attendance officer or 'whipper in', something of a hate figure for some families. This was an aggravating factor in the dispute, described earlier in this chapter, which led to the burning in effigy of Mackenzie in 1897.

The Cromarty school building was enlarged in 1890 to allow for secondary education. There were also evening 'continuation classes', which in Cromarty attracted about twenty adults. To encourage pupils to remain for secondary education, there were three small bursaries of £3, and a more substantial one of £20. Thereafter there were two university bursaries of £13 and £42 10s – the latter established in 1889 by the Denoon family, whose relation had excelled as a local teacher sixty years before. The first Cromarty pupil to receive his schooling wholly under the state system and then graduate from university was Walter Johnstone, the son of the Cromarty druggist (chemist), who graduated with an MA from Edinburgh in 1890 and then went on to take a medical degree. The first woman graduate would not be until 1912, when John Bain's daughter, Lilly, was awarded her MA by Glasgow University.

The perceived success of the school, and to some extent the salaries of its teachers, depended on the reports of inspectors, who seldom enthused but might occasionally, and with apparent reluctance, praise. In 1893, for example, the 'general behaviour of the children was commendable ... [although] some of the finer points of discipline were wanting' and reading was 'fluent and not altogether devoid of expression'.[84]

Sport[85]

By the mid nineteenth century organised team sport began to play a significant part in community life throughout Scotland. There were a number of reasons. Sport had gained social approval and was seen as a manly and improving activity, established rules were emerging from the chaos of folk football and shinty, there was increased leisure time (with a half-day Saturday holiday for skilled workers from the 1850s and for unskilled workers from the 1890s) and improved transport meant that opposing teams could travel to play each other. The need for free time and money, for equipment and travel, meant that such sporting activity only gradually trickled down from the better off to the working class.

Cricket became very popular in Scotland between about 1860 and 1914. The first recorded cricket match in Cromarty was decidedly upper class when, in 1862, HMS *St George*, a frigate with 86 guns and 880 men, including midshipman HRH Prince Alfred, visited the town. The officers, including the prince, were invited by Colonel Ross to play cricket in the 'fine demesnes of Cromarty House' and Mr Smith of Tain was engaged to produce stereoscopic views of the ship and the match. A Cromarty team, perhaps with a less exclusive membership, is recorded in 1868, playing against Invergordon, whose first match had been played the previous year. By 1878 there were clubs in Tain, Dingwall, Beauly, Inverness, Invergordon, Fortrose and Cromarty, with almost all the local schools, including Cromarty, also running teams. Local cricket was formalised in 1893 when the North of Scotland Cricket Association was established but instead of encouraging the spread of the game, this formalisation may have led to a decline in those communities unable to provide pitches of the standard required for league and cup matches. By 1896 it was reported that cricket in Cromarty was 'a lost art'.[86]

The more plebeian sport of football was often connected with New Year celebrations, which were gradually moving from Old New Year's Day (12 January) to 1 January. Cromarty, or at least its younger inhabitants, seems to have made the transition about 1880 and in 1882 there was a New Year match, over-twenties against under-twenties, played under the still novel Association rules – but with a disputed goal because it was too dark to see if it had gone in or not. Four years earlier, in 1878, there is a reference to both the 'Hugh Miller Football Club' and to a match played against Invergordon, but this may have been to older rules. Football remained popular but, both in cricket and football, Cromarty's isolation made it difficult and expensive to play matches against other towns and villages. The town's teams did not become part of North of Scotland Cricket Association or the Highland Football League, both formed in 1893. Matches could, however, be played against teams from naval ships once the fleet began to make regular appearances in the firth.

A Cromarty curling club was formed in 1889 – very much a game for the better off – but it came into conflict with the commercial interest of salmon fishing, since the curlers used the same pond from which ice was taken to stock the ice house on the links. Also in 1889 a Recreation Grounds Committee was formed to establish a bowling green and tennis court and, across the ferry in Nigg, a golf club was set up. The recreation ground made slow progress and a separate tennis club was formed which rented part of the factory grounds. Like curling, these activities – bowling, tennis and golf – were for the middle class, but the vogue for forming recreational associations was more widespread, as attested by the Cromarty shop assistants, who formed their own rambling club.

Local politics

From the mid 1880s, as the economy declined and social action faltered, there was understandable criticism of the town council as ineffective – its members were elected unopposed and seldom met. The man who changed this was John Bain (1860–1938), already mentioned in connection with the promotion of tourism to Cromarty, whose life provides a lesson in community leadership.

Bain was born in 1860, the third child of a farm servant, James Bain (1825–63), who was employed at Allerton farm but died at the age of thirty-nine. John was engaged as a pageboy by Captain Graham, agent for the Caledonian Bank, but soon left, possibly after some dispute, and by the age of twenty-one was a draper's assistant in Caernarfon. He married Tabitha Gayer in Festiniog in 1887 and in 1889 returned to Cromarty to establish his own draper's business in the Caledonian Bank's former premises at the junction of Church Street, High Street and Forsyth Place, with the promise that it would be 'the largest and cheapest in the Black Isle for clothing, boots and shoes'. Almost immediately he became involved in the establishment of the Cromarty

Literary Society and also undertook to write a regular column for the *Invergordon Times*, which appeared from June 1889 as 'Cromarty Observations'. His first piece promoted a vision of Cromarty as a holiday resort, praised a fellow townsman (also named John Bain, but not related) for planting trees on the links some twenty years before, criticised those seeking to keep the Gaelic Chapel open and poked fun at the singing in the Free Church, of which he was an active and devoted member.

Bain continued, in his own words 'creating not so much a chronicle of Cromarty news as a perpetual series of criticisms aimed at making the crooked straight and dealing out suggestions for reform in all directions'. He attacked the 'foolishness of no mail on Sundays or Mondays', argued for greater cleanliness in the town and criticised the inaction of the town council. In November 1890 he was himself nominated to the council – this was done without his consent but he came third in the poll and accepted the place. In early 1891 he planted trees on the Braehead, above the links, at his own expense, an action that was criticised by a number of his fellow councillors, who formally censured him for doing so without their permission. Bain resigned in protest and on 30 April responded in style with the first edition of the *Cromarty News*, which would run as a local weekly newspaper until September 1892. It was mostly written by Bain himself, under a variety of pseudonyms, and was often devoted to attacks on, or mockery of, the town council.

The council was presided over by an elderly provost, the banker James Taylor, who had 'ruled a stolid Town Council with stern decorum' since 1880 and had been an office bearer in the Free Church since 1843. Bain was sympathetic to Taylor and his principal adversaries were other councillors – Donald Junor, whose shop was on the opposite corner to Bain's at the junction of High Street and Church Street, John Junner, a tailor (Miller Lane) whose power base was in the Gaelic Chapel congregation, and James Ross, agent for the Commercial Bank. Ross's antagonism was such that the *Invergordon Times* report of the meeting at which Bain had resigned had been met by Ross with an action for defamation against its publisher. There was also the druggist Walter Johnstone, 'so domineering that people were often afraid to ask for things', and, although a Liberal like Bain, frequently an opponent.[87]

The council's antipathy continued unabated and when, in July, Bain pulled out weeds along the Paye (the old entrance road to the town), he was censured for this act, described by Walter Johnstone, as one of 'uncalled for impudence'. Bain replied with an edition of the *Cromarty News* in which he implied that the councillors were themselves weeds – and urged that they be 'torn up by the roots'. In later editions 'Stinging Nettle' became one of Bain's pseudonyms and verses appeared declaring that:

You dare not plant a tree or shrub, or pull a dock or thistle,
You dare not run or ride, or pray or preach, or sing or whistle,
You dare not venture an opinion, commend good or denounce ill,
Until you get permission from the Cromarty Town Council.

Bain also set about forming an amenities society, with the provost as honorary president, which pursued the objectives of planting trees (as Bain had done on the Braehead), improving footpaths (as, one might argue, he had done at the Paye) and placing seats around the town.

Bain, Junor and Junner had all been elected members of the School Board, but here Bain, with Thomas Middleton (farmer, Davidson) and Mr Mackay (Free Church minister), formed a majority. Their heated meetings were fully reported in the *News*, to the fury of Junor, and in August 1891 Bain was also elected to the Parochial Board, defeating both Junor and Junner. Bain then stood unsuccessfully at the town council election in November, with no fewer than ten candidates contesting the four vacancies. If nothing else he had engendered unprecedented interest in the affairs of the council. Those elected were James Taylor (the provost), James F. Thomson (Taylor's accountant at the Caledonian Bank), and two candidates put forward as supporters of the ruling faction – Mr Copland (the schoolmaster), and Hugh Mackenzie (draper, 9 High Street). Provost Taylor died in early 1893 and was replaced by Walter Johnstone.

The *Cromarty News* ran until September 1892, at which point Bain resumed his column in the *Invergordon Times*. Over the next eight years he campaigned for an improved water supply (completed in 1896), better communications (achieved through the Cromarty Steamship Company, which he founded in 1893) and environmental improvements (through the Amenities Society). This was not without difficulties. For example, the town council was not enthusiastic about proposals for a new water supply, fearing that it would be too expensive, and it was Bain and other gentlemen, rather than the council, who met for discussions with the laird, Colonel Ross, on his return from India in 1893. At this point the proposal was known as 'the Free Church water scheme' and a series of lectures were being held in the Victoria Hall in aid of the project. Eventually the council was won over. Bain also became president of the Ploughman's Union, which campaigned for better working conditions for farm workers – a cause to which he must have felt drawn because his own father had been a ploughman.

There were other social developments – and other disputes – during the 1890s. A successful fund-raising campaign begun in 1891 led to the building of a cottage hospital in 1893, at a cost of £1,010. Some argued that there would be much greater benefit arising from the provision of better housing and, to promote this, the Cromarty Building Company was formed, which acquired ground at the east end of the town and

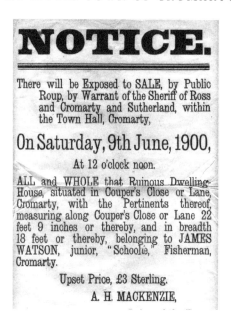

NOTICE.

There will be Exposed to SALE, by Public Roup, by Warrant of the Sheriff of Ross and Cromarty and Sutherland, within the Town Hall, Cromarty,

On Saturday, 9th June, 1900,

At 12 o'clock noon.

ALL and WHOLE that Ruinous Dwelling-House, situated in Couper's Close or Lane, Cromarty, with the Pertinents thereof, measuring along Couper's Close or Lane 22 feet 9 inches or thereby, and in breadth 18 feet or thereby, belonging to JAMES WATSON, junior, "Schoolie," Fisherman, Cromarty.

Upset Price, £3 Sterling.

A. H. MACKENZIE,

FIGURE 15.8
A derelict house for sale, 1900.

began erecting a terrace of model houses for 'the working and fishing classes'. The first house, of what would become Nicol Terrace, was completed in 1897. Both the churches built new halls to enable them to expand their activities, the Free Church in 1898 and the parish church in 1900.

In 1900 Bain again stood for election to the town council, this time defeating his old rival John Junner. He stood on a manifesto of promoting Cromarty as a health resort, improving the Cromarty–Nigg ferry and encouraging cooperation in the town. He also argued for 'so managing the liquor trade as to bring the town a revenue which could be spent for the public good'. Bain was elected but his election leaflet had not carried the name of the printer and, on this basis, the defeated candidate (Junner) petitioned the sheriff to have the election declared void. The sheriff ruled that, although technically wrong, it had not made a difference to the result and that to use such a trifling matter to try to unseat Bain was unjustified. Since both parties were at fault he ordered both to make a two-guinea donation to the Cottage Hospital. When John Bain returned to Cromarty that evening, by ferry from Invergordon, he was carried shoulder high up the pier by his supporters and pulled in a pony trap through the town in a torchlight procession.

Notes

1. Krisztina Fenyö, *Contempt, Sympathy and Romance: Lowland Perceptions of the Highlands and the Clearances during the Famine Years, 1845–1855* (East Linton, 2000).
2. St Andrews University Archive, ms. TA140:B8E43, 'Diary of Alexander Oswald Brodie 1843'.
3. From the Scottish Review quoted in *Inverness Advertiser*, 23 Oct 1855.
4. *Invergordon Times*, 30 Apr 1856; *Inverness Advertiser*, 20 Apr 1875; *Inverness Advertiser*, 3 June 1880; *Invergordon Times*, 21 Jan 1885.
5. Commission for inquiring into the administration and practical operation of the poor laws in Scotland, Report (London, 1844).
6. *Inverness Advertiser*, 2 Jan 1850 (Dorcas Society Annual Report); *Inverness Advertiser*, 13 Jan 1857 (Dorcas Society Annual Report); Cromarty Courthouse Museum, Dorcas Society Papers.
7. Charles W. J. Withers, *Urban Highlanders* (East Linton, 1998), 114.
8. *Invergordon Times*, 22 July 1868.
9. Eric H. Malcolm, *Heroes and Others* (Cromarty, 2003).
10. *Invergordon Times*, 12 Mar 1890.
11. *North Star*, 30 Dec 1897.
12. Gavin Sprott, 'Lowland Agriculture and Society' in Cooke, Donnachie, MacSween and Whatley (eds), *Modern Scottish History 1707 to the Present, Volume 2: The Modernisation of Scotland, 1850 to the Present* (East Linton, 1998).
13. *Inverness Courier*, 28 Feb 1843.
14. Security on such loans was recorded in the Register of Sasines.
15. Cromarty Courthouse Museum, Bain MS.
16. Peter Bayne, *Life and Letters of Hugh Miller* (Edinburgh, 1871), ii. 442.
17. *Cromarty News* 1891–2.
18. Middleton family papers.
19. *Invergordon Times*, 19 Apr 1893.
20. Eric H. Malcolm, *The Cromarty & Dingwall Light Railway* (Cromarty, 1993).
21. *Invergordon Times*, 25 April 1883.
22. *Invergordon Times*, 16 Jan 1889.
23. *Invergordon Times*, 8 July 1868 & 16 Aug 1871.
24. Cromarty Courthouse Museum, John Bain's Scrapbook, original in the possession of Prof. W. Bain, Glasgow.
25. NAS AF38/155/25.
26. *Invergordon Times*, 18 Sep 1895.
27. NAS AF15/15/3.
28. 'How I Ran a Newspaper', address by John Bain to the Cromarty Literary Society, 1910.
29. *Inverness Courier*, 3 Oct 1848.
30. *Inverness Advertiser*, 16 Jan & 30 Jan 1885.
31. *Invergordon Times*, 31 Jan 1872.
32. *Invergordon Times*, 3 Aug 1881.
33. *Invergordon Times*, 5 Aug 1896.
34. St Andrews University Archive, ms. TA140:B8E43, 'Diary of Alexander Oswald Brodie 1843', 161–3.

35. *Inverness Advertiser*, 17 Feb 1857.
36. *Invergordon Times*, 20 Mar 1867.
37. Donald A. Mackenzie, 'Cromarty Dialects and Folk-lore' in *Transactions of the Rymour Club* (Edinburgh, 1928).
38. *Inverness Advertiser*, 19 June 1855.
39. *Inverness Advertiser*, 19 Dec 1854, 2, 23 & 30 Jan 1855.
40. *Inverness Advertiser*, 23 Jan 1855.
41. *Inverness Advertiser*, 1 May, 23 Oct, 27 Nov & 18 Dec 1855; 22 & 30 April, 1856.
42. *Inverness Advertiser*, 10 Mar 1857.
43. *Invergordon Times*, 5 Aug & 12 Aug 1863.
44. *Invergordon Times*, 26 Aug, 2 Sep & 9 Sep 1874; 22 Aug 1883.
45. *Invergordon Times*, 11 Jan 1865.
46. *Inverness Advertiser*, 20 Apr 1875.
47. *Inverness Advertiser*, 18 Aug 1865; *Invergordon Times*, 24 Jan 1872.
48. For a full account see Eric H. Malcolm, *The Cromarty & Dingwall Light Railway* (Cromarty, 1993). *Invergordon Times*, 21 Oct 1896 & 22 Sep 1897.
49. *Invergordon Times*, 18 Sep 1861 & 5 Feb 1862; 2 Apr 1890; 26 July 1893; 27 Sept 1899.
50. *Invergordon Times*, 12 July 1893.
51. *Ross-shire Journal*, 8 Mar 1895 and Cromarty Courthouse Museum, John Bain's Scrapbook, original in the possession of Prof. W. Bain, Glasgow.
52. Alastair J. Durie, *Scotland for the Holidays: Tourism in Scotland c1780 – 1939* (East Linton, 2003), 49–50; Anon, *The Jew Exile: A Pedestrian Tour and Residence in the Most Remote and Untravelled Districts of the Highlands and Islands of Scotland, Under Persecution* (London, 1928); St Andrews University Archive, ms. TA140:B8E43, 'Diary of Alexander Oswald Brodie, 1843'.
53. *Inverness Courier*, 26 Oct 1848 & 22 Nov 1849. For bathing machines in Cromarty see NAS CH2/672/2, 267. In 1821 the *Inverness Journal* (8 June) carried an advertisement for bathing machines at Sea Bank, Inverness, with fruits in season and refreshments served at the beach.
54. *Northern Ensign*, 20 June 1850, 23 Nov 1850 & 18 Dec 1851; *Invergordon Times*, 7 August 1867; *Inverness Advertiser*, 24 June 1856.
55. *Inverness Advertiser*, 25 May & 16 June 1857; *Invergordon Times*, 21 May 1862; *Invergordon Times*, 26 Aug 1874.
56. N. Dickson, *Cromarty: Being a Tourist's Visit to the Birthplace of Hugh Miller* (Glasgow, 1859); *Invergordon Times*, 6 June 1859, 10 June 1863 & 22 June 1864 quoting the *Dundee Advertiser*.
57. *Invergordon Times*, 7 Aug, 21 Aug, 28 Aug, 4 Sep & 18 Sep 1867.
58. *Inverness Advertiser*, 3 March 1871.
59. *Inverness Advertiser*, 3 June 1880.
60. *Invergordon Times*, 25 Jan 1882.
61. *Invergordon Times*, 8 Feb 1882; 20 July 1887; 15 Aug 1888 & 29 May 1889.
62. *Invergordon Times*, 12 July 1893.
63. *Inverness Advertiser*, 11 May 1875; Alasdair Durie, *Scotland for the Holidays*, 101.
64. *Invergordon Times*, 9 & 12 Jun 1889; 23 July 1890; 29 Aug 1900.
65. *North Star*, 21 Oct 1897.

66. *Inverness Courier*, 10 Apr 1844.

67. *The Times*, 3 Mar 1854; *Inverness Advertiser*, 10 Jan & 1 Aug 1854.

68. *Inverness Advertiser*, 16 June & 26 Oct 1857.

69. *Invergordon Times*, 1 June 1859.

70. *Invergordon Times*, 9 Mar & 1 June 1860; 31 July 1861.

71. *Inverness Advertiser*, 20 Jan 1865; *Invergordon Times*, 10 Oct 1866, 5 Aug 1868 & 23 Oct 1872.

72. *Inverness Advertiser*, 29 Aug & 21 Nov 1854, 20 Mar 1855.

73. Jonathan Rose, *The Intellectual Life of the British Working Classes* (London, 2002), 65; *Inverness Advertiser*, 29 Mar & 13 Sep 1859, 24 Feb 1860; *Invergordon Times*, 19 Jan 1870.

74. *Inverness Advertiser*, 12 May 1871, 5 Feb 1875.

75. *Invergordon Times*, 29 Jan 1873, 19 Jan 1881, 23 May 1883.

76. N. Dickson, *Cromarty: Being a Tourist's Visit to the Birthplace of Hugh Miller* (Glasgow, 1859); Report of General Assembly Commissioners, 1889.

77. *Invergordon Times*, 12 June 1889 & 11 Oct 1893.

78. *Invergordon Times*, numerous editions during 1884 and 1885.

79. *Inverness Advertiser*, 23 Jan 1885.

80. *Invergordon Times*, 28 Oct 1868.

81. *Invergordon Times*, 2 April 1884.

82. *Invergordon Times*, 29 May 1889.

83. Isabella MacLean, *Your Father and I* (East Linton, 1998), 92.

84. Cromarty Courthouse Museum, school board papers.

85. This section is largely based on a talk given by Sandy Thomson to the Cromarty History Society.

86. *Invergordon Times*, 21 May 1862, 17 June 1868, 1 Jan 1896.

87. Comments on the individuals are from Isabella MacLean, *Your Father and I* (East Linton, 1998).

16

The Twentieth Century

Are we so many, and are our resources so great, that we can afford
to war with each other and not with the social stagnation, decay,
and misery that meets us on every hand? Let us give up applying
the microscope to every little fault and failing, and weighing every
thoughtless word and expression in the balance. Let us sink all minor
and personal interests in the desire for the achievement of our one
great aim, the improvement of the town and her advancement to that
position which we believe she is fitted and destined to occupy.

John Bain, *Cromarty News*

In August 1902 a crowd of about 1,500 people, including a number
of distinguished guests, gathered at the base of the Hugh Miller
monument to begin a day of celebrations to mark the centenary of
Miller's birth. In his opening remarks the master of ceremonies, Arthur
Bignold MP, asked, with little apparent confidence, if it was 'too much
to hope that this year of the Centenary of Hugh Miller will also be
marked as the dawn of a happy future for his birth-place?' For much
of the following century Cromarty would have to find an appropriate
balance between hope and realism in the face of continued decline.

The poor state of the town's affairs was evident in the local response
to an appeal, launched earlier in the year, for funds to create a reading
room, library and museum to be known as the Hugh Miller Institute.
Although £350 had been raised, a quarter of this had come from the
United States and the colonies, and it was only the support of Andrew
Carnegie that brought the project to a successful conclusion, two
years later, at a cost of £1,250. Carnegie also funded the publication
of an account of the centenary celebrations, whose concluding pages
reminded readers that Cromarty, because of its isolation, had 'not
shared to any extent in the prosperity of recent times' and suggested
that, when there was a revival, it would be 'largely on account of its
picturesque surroundings' which, along with Miller's reputation, had
given the town a growing reputation as a summer resort.[1]

The sustained campaign to attract visitors to Cromarty, which was then underway, had little immediate success. In 1913 a townsman, George Mackenzie, commented that 'during the past ten or fifteen years a good deal was done to boom the town as a holiday resort, but it made not the least headway, the accommodation for visitors being limited and the visitor traffic quite insufficient to warrant speculation in building'. A large proportion of those who did visit were 'natives home on holiday'. Only 'the periodic visits of H.M. Fleets' had, Mackenzie claimed, saved the town's trade from 'utter stagnation', introducing a welcome 'tonic into its extremely anaemic economic system'.[2]

It is in these early years of the century that the people and buildings of Cromarty come into clearer focus in the growing number of photographs taken in and around the town. Valentines of Dundee visited in April 1900 to take a number of views, which were produced as postcards and in an album of sixteen photographs published by John Bain, the local draper. These showed Cromarty's picturesque surroundings – in panoramas from the east and west, and views of the Eathie burn and waterfall, the natural arch at MacFarquhar's Bed and the shoreline of the North Sutor. Miller's birthplace and monument were included, along with the Town Hall (courthouse) and Gaelic Chapel, and there was a photograph of the High Street, with the Jubilee Fountain erected in 1897. There were also two views of the fishertown – one looking down the Big Vennel and the other along Gordon's Lane – and a carefully posed group of three young fisherwomen by a boat on the shore, two of them with creels on their backs and a third sitting knitting.

These were followed c.1907 by a series taken by A.T. Wood, an Invergordon photographer, and published as hand-tinted views by Jessie Macleod and Alexander Hossack for sale from their shop in Church Street. These featured Church Street ('The House of the late Captain Graham'), the Jubilee Fountain and Forsyth House (by then used as the Established Church manse), Cromarty House, its gardens with the Sutors in the background, the harbour, the town seen from the Denny, and a carefully posed view of a tidier Big Vennel with fishermen and women taking centre stage. Even more so than in Valentine's photographs, the people of the fishertown were displayed as objects of curiosity for the visitor.

Bain produced a second album shortly afterwards, entitled *Cromarty Firth*, with the notable difference that by this time visits of naval ships were an integral part of the attraction of the area, and five of the fifteen views in this publication showed the fleet in the firth. But the novelty soon wore off and in 1908 the *Invergordon Times* noted that the fleet no longer attracted crowds as it had once done.[3]

By c.1908 both Bain and another Cromarty man, Willie John Smith, had become enthusiastic amateur photographers. Smith was born in a house in Church Street overlooking the fishertown, and although the family moved to Duke Street it may have been his personal knowledge of his former neighbours which allowed him, in the years around 1910, to take over fifty portraits of the fisher folk at work or in relaxed poses by their houses. The scenes are packed with the gear of a line fishing-community – leather thigh-length sea boots, creels, baskets, lines, barrels, lug spades for digging bait, tubs, basins filled with mussels, and fish, drying on the walls by the door or for sale at the market by the shore. By the shore are the open-decked, single-masted yawls used for line fishing. Bain, a staunch champion of the fishers in their battles against the depredations of the steam trawlers, generally showed a different face of Cromarty in his own photographs. In his lens Edwardian families picnic, play tennis or bowls, and walk in the woods on the Sutor. He also recorded the pageantry of naval funerals, troops marching through the town and busy scenes outside shops in High Street, Church Street and Bank Street. When contrasted with Smith's photographs of the fishers, it was as if there were two towns, coexisting – sometimes uneasily – alongside each other.

Isabella MacLean, wife of the minister of the United Free Church, lived in Cromarty between 1912 and 1919, and later described similar contrasts between the social classes.[4] The MacLeans were on unusually good terms with the Established Church minister, Mr Scott, and his wife, who were 'both people of ample private means and lived in old-fashioned style, dined late and dressed for dinner and had a sufficient staff of servants indoors and out ... They were people of the most impeccable personal behaviour but they were conservative and Auld Kirk to a degree. They took no cognizance of or interest in such things as evangelical preaching, temperance reform or schemes for the education and betterment of the masses. They would have been kind to the poor of their congregation but very definitely "the poor".' She added that Mrs Scott was 'a terrific snob'.

There were also the three elderly Graham sisters, unmarried daughters of Captain Graham whose house (Clare Lodge, later Bellevue) in Church Street, overlooking the fishertown, was one of the largest in Cromarty. They 'lived in great style' on the proceeds of their family's antiques, jewellery and paintings, and were 'charming ladies, full of kindness and good works but so helpless that I doubt any one of them ever washed a dish in her life'. The second of the sisters, Miss Nancy, helped Mrs MacLean with the annual distribution to seventy poor people of money from a trust fund and 'knew every single person in the fisher town whereas I [Isabella MacLean] could never distinguish between Mrs Watson Leezie, Mrs Watson Ovens and Mrs Watson Bodders. The Big Vennel and the Little Vennel [the two principal streets in the fishertown] were places of mystery to me.'

Isabella MacLean also reveals the tragedy lurking in some of Willie John Smith's images of the fishers. The fiddler Blind Benjie, who

MacLean describes as 'probably defective in a harmless, well-meaning kind of way', appears in a number of these. He lived with his sister and brought in a good deal of money from his playing for sailors when the fleet was in. He might appear to have been a quaint 'character' but Mr MacLean suspected that his sister did not treat him well and, after the war, she had him put into the Black Isle poorhouse, in Fortrose, where he died after a few months, having waited in vain each day for her to visit him. The greater desperation of some in this divided society can also be judged by the fact that the bodies of two newly born children were found within the course of twelve months – one at the 'targets' to the east of Cromarty, the other near Shoremill to the west.

In 1901 the laird, Colonel (later General) Walter Charteris Ross, returned from South Africa, seriously wounded with half of his jaw shot away. His arrival was a cause for celebration in expectation of what he might achieve for the town and his estate, and he was pulled in his carriage through the streets by a crowd of local people. There was, in their minds, no doubt that Cromarty would benefit from his return.[5] His second wife, Gertrude, as an act of thanksgiving for his safe return converted part of the former brewery into accommodation for retired and impoverished estate workers. At the end of 1903 an heir was born and the town band paraded, bonfires were lit, and a 'cake and wine banquet' was provided.[6]

Ross, with his wife, was actively involved in Cromarty society. As principal heritor he approved and funded a major internal renovation of the parish church, which succeeded in retaining much of the building's character and fittings, but allowed for modern pews to be introduced in part of the ground floor. The family were also involved in the building of a Scottish Episcopal church, designed by the Inverness architect Alexander Ross. This was begun in 1908 and completed in 1912, although its planned steeple was never added. He supported the establishment of a Working Men's Club in 1902, for which he provided daily newspapers, chaired the committee to establish a branch of the Boys Brigade in 1908 and, when Boy Scouts were formed in 1912, he obliged with a lecture on tiger hunting in India.[7] Mrs Ross, the daughter of a wealthy brewer, was seen by some of the more old-fashioned in Cromarty as being not quite of the right class. She regularly gave Christmas gifts of money – and rabbits! – to the poor in the town but she 'gave herself airs' and, when she first arrived, tried without success to have people curtsey to her.[8]

On his return to Cromarty, Ross was almost immediately elected to a vacancy on the parish council and also became chairman of the Harbour Trust, which soon drew up plans for much needed repairs – but he failed in an attempt to be elected to the school board in 1903. He lent support to an abortive plan to have an 'isolation

All Saints' Church, Cromarty

FIGURE 16.1
The Church of St Regulus and All Saints (1912). The proposed tower was
never built.

hospital' created in the factory buildings, a scheme which foundered
because the cost of the ambitious project would have been borne by
other local authorities in the county.[9] More importantly he involved
himself once more in the plan to create a railway link to Cromarty
and became the main driving force behind the Cromarty & Dingwall
Light Railway Company, formed in 1902. The Company overcame
the problems posed by uncooperative landowners, put together the
funding package with public and private sector support and in 1913
entered into a contract with Nott, Brodie & Co. of Bristol to build
the eighteen-mile line for the fixed price of £96,000. The first sod was

ceremonially cut at Cromarty on 13 February 1914 by Lady Bignold, wife of the local MP and company chairman Sir Arthur Bignold, and the aim was to complete the line by 1916.

Earlier, John Bain had helped connect Cromarty to Invergordon through the Cromarty Steamship Company, by means of which visitors could reach the town. The Cromarty–Nigg ferry was improved in 1906 with the gift of a steam launch by Andrew Carnegie. It made half a dozen runs each day, timed so as to connect with the *Saga* from Invergordon and thus allow Dingwall and Invergordon golfers to play the eighteen-hole course at Dunskaith, on the Nigg side. John Watson took over the service in 1909, with a new boat, and was rumoured to be prepared to offer reduced weekly fares to golfers.[10] Watson's vessel, the *Enterprise*, carried many troops across the firth during the Great War, allowing him to build up his business in later years.

The fleet

Since the turn of the century the town had felt the increasing presence of the Royal Navy. There had been no visits of the fleet to the Cromarty Firth since 1888 but, as the perceived threat from German naval power in northern waters increased, the navy returned and from 1900 the fleet appeared every year. A number of houses in the town were let out to officers and their families, including the parish manse since the minister, Mr Scott, preferred to use his wife's house, Rosenberg.

The creation of a naval base in the Cromarty Firth became a tantalizing prize. Initial hopes were partially dashed in 1903 with the decision to create a base at Rosyth, with the Cromarty Firth as only a subsidiary 'shelter anchorage'. However, Admiral Sir John Fisher, who had become First Sea Lord in October 1902, was a strong advocate for the Cromarty Firth as a safer and more strategically placed base. Fisher promoted the new Dreadnought class battleship, which first appeared in the firth in 1907, and of submarines, which arrived the following year. The area benefited increasingly from naval visits – in July 1907, for example, there were 14,500 navy men in the firth – although Cromarty still felt that too much of the gain went to Invergordon. In 1909 a proposal was made at a meeting of ratepayers that the town council should provide two free pints of beer for every sailor on shore leave in Cromarty on a Sunday afternoon, with the cost being met from the burgh's Common Good. The novel idea was not accepted. A number of naval funerals from this period were recorded in photographs by John Bain – funerals for men such Arthur Netherwood, interred with full naval honours in March 1908 after he was killed by the breaking of a steel hawser on board HMS *Cochrane*.

Admiral Sir John Fisher's enthusiasm for the Cromarty Firth was continued by Winston Churchill, who became First Lord of the Admiralty in October 1911, and in March 1912 Churchill announced to the House of Commons plans for the creation of 'a floating second-class naval base and war anchorage … fortified on a sufficient scale to deter armoured attack'. The endemic rivalry between the army and navy, who were jointly responsible for the defence of naval ports, immediately came to the fore. Plans were drawn up by the War Office for defences consisting of three 9.2-inch guns, six 4-inch guns and eight searchlights, with barracks and other support, all at an estimated cost of £121,500, together with an annual manning cost of £15,000. After studying the proposals the Admiralty concluded that armament could be supplied from naval stocks at a cost of £69,906 and the annual costs could be reduced to £11,600. Following a visit in September 1912 by Churchill and Commander Donald John Munro, then King's Harbourmaster at Rosyth, the Admiralty were instructed to take responsibility and a little more than a year later Munro was appointed King's Harbourmaster at Cromarty.

Three 9.2-inch Mk VIII guns from the redundant battleships *Powerful* and *Terrible* were utilised, two mounted on the North Sutor and one on the South Sutor. These batteries were augmented by six 4-inch Quick Firing Mk III guns from the cruisers *Pandora* and *Prometheus*. The batteries were manned by the Royal Marine Artillery, commanded by Col Lewis Conway Gordon, with the troops accommodated in the obsolete battleship *Renown*, until accommodation on shore could be provided. Workmen were accommodated in a specially built barrack at Nigg and in the old hemp factory at Cromarty. The guns were landed in April 1914 on the north shore and at Cromarty harbour and pulled into position by specially built traction engines. It was also decided to station a torpedo boat flotilla in the firth, with moorings laid at Alness and Invergordon, and to site a temporary seaplane base on the links at Cromarty – the first such base in Britain. Munro also placed a boom defence across the entrance to the firth to prevent its waters being penetrated by enemy submarines.

The impact of this activity on the town was spectacular. Within the space of a single month in early 1914 the contractor's work at the forts was completed, a new Masonic Lodge was opened, work began on the Cromarty–Dingwall railway, an extension to the harbour commenced and the town council, playing its own part in the defence of the coastline, accepted a 64-pound gun from the War Office, which was mounted on the Braehead by the lighthouse and coastguard station. One lasting impact of the military presence was a definitive change in the name of the headlands at the entrance to the firth in 1913, from the East and West Sutor to the North and South Sutor – the Admiralty being unable to cope with the local sense of direction.

Land and housing on the eve of war

Legislation by Lloyd George's government in 1910 provides historians with a detailed insight into land-ownership and housing conditions in the years leading up to war. His budget of 1909, and the related Finance Act of April 1910, advanced the campaign for radical land reform by empowering the Inland Revenue to value every separately occupied land holding in the United Kingdom. The survey was to distinguish the value of the site from the total value, which included buildings, and a base line of 1909 values was to be used to tax (at 20 per cent) any subsequent increase in site value – which campaigners argued was an 'unearned increment'. The survey, carried out between 1910 and 1914, was unprecedented in Scotland and, in England, was the most comprehensive survey of land holding since the Domesday Book.[11] The Inland Revenue Field Books, used to gather information, provide a detailed guide to who owned property, its value and the condition of houses and other buildings.

The survey shows the continued dominance of the major landowners in rural areas. In the parish of Resolis there were 230 occupied properties, of which 133 were owned by the principal landowner, Shaw Mackenzie of Newhall. The two other old estates, Poyntzfield and Braelangwell, owned fourteen and thirteen properties. Much of the housing stock was in poor condition. There were, in all, 215 houses, of which 90 were thatched and 4 partially thatched. Forty-six of the houses, almost all of them thatched, were deemed to be in poor, very poor or ruinous condition. In the town of Cromarty there were 334 properties, of which 237 were residential – but, as a number of these were 'half houses' (houses which had been structurally divided into two units), the number of individual residences was 260. Fifty houses were thatched.

The Inland Revenue survey was supplemented in 1913 with comments from George Mackenzie (1881–1950), youngest son of Alexander H. Mackenzie (assessor for the burgh).[12] Mackenzie identified seventy-three houses that had been demolished since the Ordnance Survey of 1871, of which twenty-seven had been replaced by public buildings, and he detailed the overall decline in housing stock between 1841 and 1911 – from 342 houses to 279. The only new houses in the previous twenty years had been the four erected at Nichol Terrace by the Cromarty Building Company in 1897–8 and the substantial block of houses on George Street, taken on by the Admiralty for the Coastguard in 1904–5. This last project was the cause of a local tragedy. The site had been acquired at a high price by one of the local bank agents, James F. Thomson, on the basis that the houses he built would be let to the Admiralty for twenty-five years at £147 10s. Thomson had, however, run into financial difficulties, ownership passed to the Admiralty in

1905–6 and the following year the rateable value was reassessed, reducing it by £36 10s. Thomson had grossly overestimated the value of the buildings and committed suicide by shooting himself in the factory buildings.

According to Mackenzie, it was only the Admiralty works on the Sutor and at the harbour, with the prospect of service men being based in the town, which began to reverse the economic decline. A 'Glasgow syndicate' expressed an interest in land near the Free Church, with a view to building a hotel, and on Bank Street a notice appeared announcing that the 'Cromarty Picture Playhouse will shortly be erected on this site'. Eight commercial premises in the town also enlarged or improved their establishments. Cromarty, it seemed, had 'risen from its ashes, Phoenix-like; ... humming with industry' and all this was 'thanks to the Admiralty and the Admiralty alone'.

The 'Great War'

War with Germany was declared on 3 August 1914. The part-time Territorial Force was immediately called up and, within two days, troops arrived in Cromarty from the 4th (Ross Highland) and 6th (Moray) Battalions of the Seaforth Highlanders and from the 4th Queens Own Cameron Highlanders, who together formed the Seaforth and Cameron Brigade of the Highland Division. After a few weeks spent improving coastal defences at Cromarty and Nigg, the Brigade moved with the rest of the division to Bedford and by November they were in France.

The 3rd (Reserve) Battalion of the Seaforth Highlanders remained stationed at camps at Newton and Cromarty Mains. In October a further Battalion, the 10th (Reserve), was formed in Cromarty and during the war years there were also men of the 3rd (Reserve) Battalions of the Cameronians (Scottish Rifles) and the Black Watch (Royal Highlanders) garrisoned in the camps. All these reserve battalions, each of 1,000 men, were training units, supplying drafts to the regular battalions in France.

Over ninety years later Jean Campbell (Mrs Newell) can still recall the excitement of wartime Cromarty for a six-year-old girl – a sentry stationed near the end of her street, searchlights on the links, fields full of huts, an invitation with her mother to a concert in the camps (where she saw a xylophone for the first time), parades at the parish church, where her father was beadle, with a band leading the soldiers back to camp and, at church services, organists and singers of the highest calibre. From these Sundays, the sound of Handel's 'Comfort ye, comfort ye', sung at a Christmas service, stayed with her – and the memory of a young, talented organist soon to embark for France who

G v R 1

HE whom this scroll commemorates
was numbered among those who,
at the call of King and Country, left all
that was dear to them, endured hardness,
faced danger, and finally passed out of
the sight of men by the path of duty
and self-sacrifice, giving up their own
lives that others might live in freedom.
Let those who come after see to it
that his name be not forgotten.

*Gunner Alexander Hossack
Royal Garrison Artillery*

FIGURE 16.2
Alexander Hossack, of 39 Gordons Lane, died of pneumonia at Cromarty
Military Hospital on 24 February 1919

sat and stared at his hands, fearing that they would be injured on the
battlefield.

Isabella MacLean, the UF minister's wife, experienced similar
excitement but also anxiety. She returned to Cromarty from holiday in
Aberdeen on 4 August to find the town in a state of intense activity. 'We
had first-aid classes, got our spare rooms ready to receive casualties,

drew up lists of blankets and bedding we could spare and were altogether as excited and unhappy as possible.'[13] A military hospital was, however, soon established with 226 beds and it should be remembered that with so many living in close quarters there were hazards simply from infectious disease. For example, Private Alex Neil of the Cameronians died at Cromarty on 12 October 1918, a victim of the spreading influenza pandemic, which would kill more people worldwide than the war itself. The scale of the military presence is shown by the seventy-four graves from the 1914–18 war in the Cromarty cemetery. Fourteen of these are crew of HMS *Natal*, seven unidentified, who were among the 338 lost when the ship blew up an anchor in the firth on 30 December 1915. The parish of Cromarty would lose forty-five men before the end of the Great War – a disproportionately high loss, resulting from the combination of army and navy service common to seagoing communities.

Training for the Seaforths took place in trenches dug on Cromarty Hill, east of the Mains farm, where conditions, to some extent, prepared men for what was to come. In December 1914, Private James Livesey of the 3rd Seaforths – the 'Dirty Third' – wrote the comic verses of 'The Cromarty Mudlarks'.[14]

They call us the Cromarty Mudlarks, the 9th in the blooming Fort
    [Fort George]
Wouldn't let us in beside 'em, for they're of a different sort.
So we stayed outside on the common, in a hut and an iron shed,
Glad of a good roof o'er us, glad of a good dry bed.

Yes, we're the Cromarty Mudlarks, we are the 'Dirty Third',
Why should we get this nickname? Mebbe you've never heard –,
The 9th, they stay in the barracks, and drill in the barracks
    Square,
They've fires, and brushes, and polish, and such like luxuries there.

But what of the Cromarty Mudlarks? What shall we say for these?
Covered with mud to the boot-tops, mud almost up to the knees;
Living for months under canvas, while the rain comes again and
    again,
And the whole of the camp is a quagmire, and never a ditch nor a
    drain.

Each night every soldier wonders if the tent pegs will hold it fast
Or whether the tent will go sailing, torn by the stormy blast.
Each night every one of us wonders, as the rain comes trickling
    through
What if the tent went off and left us, what we would then have to
    do?

But with morn comes a lull in the weather, and we hear the 'Fall In'
    for parade,

And we're out once again in the quagmire the rain and the
      tramping have made.
Then off we go for a route march. Sing as we march along
For what is the use of grousing? Better a cheer and song.

What if we're caught in a rain storm, with still three miles to go?
We only change the chorus 'While the Stormy Winds Do Blow'.
No fire to dry OUR things by, they have to dry on our backs,
No polish for OUR boots, boys, they'll never more be black.

And that's our side of the story. Mebbe you've never heard
Why we're the CROMARTY MUDLARKS, why we're the DIRTY
      THIRD.

They called us the Cromarty Mudlarks, the 9th in the blooming
      Fort
Wouldn't let us in beside 'em, for they're of a different sort,
      But when we get to the Front, boys, mebbe we'll lead the way,
      And show that the Cromarty Mudlarks are just as good as they.

For all those who completed training in the Cromarty mud, the
journey to the battlefront in France began with embarkation at the
harbour, usually to join a troop ship at Invergordon. One soldier
later remembered this emotional moment, leaving in darkness from
Cromarty as the sound of the pipes played them out and then faded
over the water.

Although the war economy benefited the town, construction of
the Cromarty–Dingwall railway stalled and then went into reverse.
The initial problem was a shortage of labour, both because of the
numbers volunteering to fight in France and the higher wages offered
on government construction contracts, such as the creation of the naval
base in Scapa Flow. Then in early 1917 the permanent way material
– both the four miles of track between Cromarty and Jemimaville which
had been laid and all that in stock, which was practically everything
needed to finish the job – was commandeered and removed by the
Ministry of Munitions for use in France.

With the outbreak of war, the railway's staunchest supporter,
General Ross of Cromarty, had returned to the army as Brigadier-
General, commanding the 152nd Brigade of the Highland Division. Lt
Alan Mackintosh, who came to be known as 'the poet of the Highland
Division', described him in one of his three 'studies in war psychology'
published in his posthumous War, The Liberator in 1918. Mackintosh
led a raid on a German trench on 16 May 1916. Before leaving the
party were addressed by Ross:

'You're going to help make the name of the regiment, and the fame of
the North, tonight, men. I've heard that in Flanders yesterday the Bosche
came up against Scotsmen again and got the worst of it. Now you'll show

'em today that Scotland can give them the worst of it here, too. Scotland for ever. Lead on, Mr Mackintosh, and good luck,' and the raiding party file up the long communication trench to the front line.[15]

Mackintosh, an English-born, Oxford-educated Scot with family connections to Alness, was able to achieve popularity with the soldiers of the Highland Division, partly through his comic verse, and, at the same time, to write poetic verse of lasting value, which captured his own feelings and those of his fellow officers and men. He served with the 5th Seaforths, won a military cross, was wounded in 1916 and spent the next year serving in England. But he chose to return to active service and was killed in November 1917 while attached to the 4th Seaforths at Metz. Having experienced trench warfare, lost many friends and shared in the comradeship of those who 'jest and curse together on the razor-edge of death', he was one of those who felt there was almost no option but death in battle. He was left less able to deal with the prospect of peace than with the continuation of war:

> For nations have heard the tidings, they have sworn that wars shall
> cease,
> And it's all one damned long Sunday walk down the straight, flat
> road of peace ...
> Treading a road that is paved with family dinner and teas,
> A sensible dull suburban road planted with decorous trees ...
> And a God like a super-bishop in an apron and nice top-hat –
> O, God, you are God of battles. Forbid that we come to that.

Mackintosh's verse revealed the fracture in society between those who had experienced the horror of trench warfare, which was, literally, unspeakable – and would never be adequately communicated either during or after the war to the civilian population at home.[16]

Cromarty's economy between the wars

In February 1919 John Bain wrote a piece for the *Ross-shire Journal* entitled 'The Reconstruction of Cromarty', which began with a statement that encapsulated the contradiction of the war – that in the years since the creation of a naval base in the firth in 1913 and during the subsequent war, with all the horror which that involved, the town of Cromarty had experienced the five most prosperous years of its entire history. It had been eighty years since the town had experienced its great decline – when the factory, shipbuilding yard, brewery, shipping trade and pork trade came to an end in rapid succession – and the boost provided by the wartime economy had been badly needed. But fortunately, as Bain said, wars come to an end and Cromarty had to seek a new direction for the future. He argued for improvements to the town's streets and pavements, the return to public use of buildings taken over for the war effort – the library in the Hugh Miller Institute, the Victoria Hall and the church hall – all of which would help Cromarty to develop as a tourist destination, and for the development of fishing.[17] War had brought the bonus of the telephone and an electricity supply to the town, although the latter was an intermittent supply run from a generator at the army camp at Newton.

Although the war was over, the navy would remain a mainstay of the town's economy for some time to come. The Atlantic Fleet, known as the Home Fleet from the mid 1930s, came twice a year on spring and autumn cruises, each time staying for between three and six weeks. The ships anchored in a line three or four miles long between Invergordon and the Sutors, with the largest ships, the battle cruisers such as *Tiger*, *Renown*, *Repulse*, *Hood*, *Courageous* and *Furious*, anchored off Cromarty. Each of these large ships carried 1,000 to 1,400 men and the visits of the fleet were both important social occasions and a significant boost to the economy of the town. Cromarty's shops included naval outfitters, the hotels, shops and other establishments benefited, and Cromarty House was, in effect, run as 'a very discrete boarding house for the wives of Admirals and the like'.[18]

The end of the war had brought renewed hopes for the completion of the Cromarty & Dingwall Light Railway but these were not to be realised. With an increase in costs, mainly because of higher wages, the company did not have sufficient funds and, despite considering alternatives – including narrow-gauge and overhead railways – the sums could not be made to add up. Despite persistent lobbying by General Ross and others, the necessary support from government could not be secured and on 15 December 1925, at a special meeting of the directors held in the Royal Hotel, it was decided to wind up the company. When all was said and done, there had been such significant improvements in roads and road transport since the pre-war period that the business case for investment in the railway had been seriously weakened.[19]

However, the pre-war bi-weekly sailings between Leith, Aberdeen, Inverness and Cromarty had ended, leaving the town, as one commentator put it, 'marooned'.[20] The Cromarty–Invergordon ferry continued, with the contract for delivering mail to Cromarty, run by the Cromarty Steamship Company until 1927, when the route was taken over by John Watson, using the *Ailsa*. This vessel, built in 1906, was steel hulled and a superior vessel to the wooden-hulled ships which had operated on the route.

The harbour had been left in a poor state after its use by the Admiralty and required a new bridge between the west pier and the outer mole. Initially only £1,000, half the cost, was offered by the Treasury. There was lobbying by farmers, traders and merchants who all required access to the outer pier and in 1933 the Coast Line, which shipped goods to and from Cromarty, threatened to withdraw their service because of the problem. It was 1936 before funds were secured and the new bridge was completed the following year, followed by dredging of the harbour basin in 1938.

Salvage work on the wreck of the *Natal* was begun in 1928, with non-ferrous metal removed first. The demolition of the hull began in

FIGURE 16.3
Cromarty Guidebook, 1934.

1930, bringing some badly needed trade to the harbour, but the collapse of the market for scrap metal brought this to an end the following year. Work recommenced in 1937, using the *Disperser* as the salvage vessel. This continued until 1939 and a second vessel, the *Osterhav*, was also broken up on the shore.

The town succeeded for a time in attracting more visitors. The Royal Hotel was significantly improved in 1930 and in 1934 the town council published 'Cromarty – The Official Guide', an attractive pamphlet written by George Mackenzie, who had been editor of the Inverness newspaper the *Northern Chronicle* since 1920, having previously worked as a journalist in Dingwall, British Guiana and Dundee. The Guide put a positive spin on the failure to complete the Cromarty–Dingwall railway by pointing out that 'luckily no ugly railway line scars [Cromarty's] fair face'. Its front cover was a colour sketch of Gordon's Lane in the fishertown, with creels and a fisher woman baiting a line. The poorest part of the town, whose smell and dirt had been such an embarrassment, was becoming a selling point, as the fishing community, which had been at its heart, declined. John Bain, in a lecture to the Cromarty Literary Society in 1929, commented, 'If you were to ask me what I consider to be the chief difference between the Cromarty of sixty years ago and the Cromarty of today, I should answer – the long way greater cleanliness of today's town'.

The guide promoted Cromarty as 'one of the most bracing and health-giving holiday resorts in Scotland ... an ideal spot for the jaded city dweller in which to restore his vital energies' and offered 'the young and virile abundant scope for recreation', with boating, fishing, swimming in the harbour basin, tennis, bowling, football, quoits, walking and, across the ferry at Nigg, an eighteen-hole golf course. The town was credited with 'quite a romantic history', with associations with Robert the Bruce, James IV, the Earl of Bothwell, Sir Thomas Urquhart, Prince Charlie's Jacobite army and, of course, Hugh Miller. It was 'an old-world burgh ... a strange mixture of the old and the new' but, apart from its seventeenth-century houses on Church Street, it had 'few buildings of particular note'. The following year there was not enough holiday accommodation in Cromarty for all who wanted to come and there were many good seasons in the years before 1939, with the annual regatta becoming a particularly successful event attracting hundreds of people.

These successes, however, could not mask the underlying dire state of Cromarty's economy. In 1937 there were sixty-two people unemployed – fifty-three men and nine women. Although there were some new opportunities in the development of forestry, described later in this chapter, these did not compensate for the decay of the town's traditional staples of agriculture and fishing.

Agriculture between the wars

The Great War had seen government intervention to increase production of cereals and potatoes, and Thomas Middleton (1863–1943), of Rosefarm, became Secretary to the Ministry of Agriculture, advising on wartime production, and was later knighted for his services to agriculture. High wartime market prices allowed farms to operate at a profit during the years of conflict but a prolonged depression in agriculture set in between 1921 and the outbreak of war in 1939. There was a downward trend in prices in both arable and livestock sectors, and farmers consequently sought to reduce costs by cutting farm workers' wages, which, unlike in England, were not regulated.

Government policy between the wars was primarily designed to safeguard English arable farming, with subsidies for beet (1925) and wheat (1932). At the same time excise duty on whisky was increased, sales dropped, distilling was cut back and, consequently, barley production fell. Subsidies for barley and oats were only introduced in 1937 and in the same year regulated minimum wages were introduced for farm workers. The price of beef had also dropped during the 1920s and, although a cattle subsidy was introduced in 1934, many Scots farmers and farm workers had left the land, gone south or emigrated.

In 1923 General Ross sold off many of the Cromarty estate farms to the sitting tenants and various members of the Middleton family became owners. Sir Thomas Middleton and his brother, Walter, acquired Rosefarm; and two other brothers, Frank and Kenneth, bought Newton. Dr G.G. Middleton, who bought Davidston, was later president of the National Farmers' Union of Scotland and in 1933 was appointed to a committee set up by the Secretary of State to address the 'barley crisis'.

The end of the fishing community

By 1913 Cromarty had no herring boats, although fishermen still went to the herring fishery as hired men and young women followed the herring fleets as gutters and packers. Line fishing, however, continued. There were considerable difficulties during the war years but the fish caught secured higher prices. In the Cromarty Fishery District, which extended along the coast from the small fishing village of Inver, east of Tain, to Avoch, the average value of each landing by boats fishing with lines fell in the first year of war, from £1.59 in 1913 to £1.45 in 1914, but then rose steeply to £5.97 in 1918.

The first yawls with motors appeared in the district in July 1918 and their comparative advantage soon began to show. The value of each of their landings was soon between two and three times that of a sailing yawl, and by 1928 the average catch of a sailing yawl was only £1.43.[21] Cromarty at this time had only three boats fitted with motors – the first to appear had been dubbed 'the clever yawlie' (from the Scots meaning of 'clever' as 'fast'). Two motor yawls continued in the 1930s, the *Alice* and the *Ella*, but in 1934 the Finlayson family who owned the *Alice* left for Ullapool, sailing from the harbour with the boat piled high with their furniture.

The fishers could no longer afford to modernise their gear and the community was in dire straits. Peter Anson, who described all the fishing communities along the east coast of Scotland in the late 1920s, wrote that 'the few fishermen left here eke out an existence by line fishing in small open boats'.[22] The cost of living as reflected in the price index in 1928 was almost twice as high as in 1914, but the income of these line fishers was the same.[23] Although, in 1934, the *Ross-shire Journal* proclaimed 'Cromarty Wakes Up' when a group of public-spirited men put up money to acquire a motorboat seine netter, the *Prevail*,[24] such efforts did little to save the community. The venture failed and the *Prevail* was sold in 1938.

In a recording made for Cromarty Museum in 1993, Annie Hogg and her brother Bobby recalled the day in 1928 when their father told them he was 'daen wi the sea'. Bobby remembered his father telling him that the four crew of the yawl had fished with twelve lines, each with 600 hooks – 7,200 hooks in all, each hand baited by their wives – and had caught nineteen haddock. On an earlier occasion there had been no fish at all. His decision was a welcome end to a long struggle and Annie recalled her mother saying 'I gaen down on my knees and thanked God'.

Population and emigration between the wars

Cromarty's population was sustained between 1911 and 1921, but then tumbled from 1126 to 837 in the next decade, a fall of 26 per cent, much of this due to the decline in fishing and to migration of men, women and children from the fisher community to elsewhere in Scotland and overseas (see Figure 16.4).[25] This human outflow was aided by a smaller number of earlier emigrants, who had established themselves abroad and subsequently assisted the emigration of their relatives. A number of interrelated Finlayson families, for example, established themselves in New York, Cleveland, Philadelphia and Milwaukee from the early years of the century and were the anchor points for subsequent emigrants. Often the husband would be first, followed by his wife, and then children, nephews, nieces – and sometimes parents.

One trade which had given many from the fishing community mobility was that of shipwright or ships carpenter. There was work

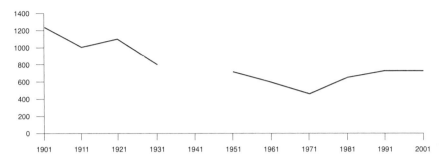

FIGURE 16.4 Population: town of Cromarty 1901–2001.

both on the Clyde and in the USA and a number of men moved between these locations. Gilbert Hogg, for example, went alone to Philadelphia in 1893 at the age of thirty-seven, and to New York in 1905, this time accompanied by John MacLennan (thirty-eight). They both stayed for nine months, returned to Govan and Glasgow, and went again to New York in 1907.

The outflow of fisher families was augmented by farm workers seeking better conditions in the south or overseas, some taking advantage of the Empire Settlement Act of 1922, which offered larger holdings and better conditions in the Dominions. There was also the continual drain from the town of those who did well in education and entered the professions.

Local government

The Housing Act of 1924 provided local authorities with an annual subsidy of £9 per house for council houses, which if passed on to the tenants reduced rent by between a third and a quarter. The theory behind the Housing Act was that such new houses would accommodate the better-off tenants, who would then free up other housing for the less well off. Cromarty's first council housing, three blocks of semi-detached houses, were planned in 1920 and built in the late 1920s, and in 1935 a further three blocks, one block being bungalows, were completed, bringing the stock to twelve dwellings. The first tenants included one of the schoolteachers and a bank clerk. In 1939 properties at 47–51 High Street were purchased by the town council so that the houses and the entrance to town could be improved.

A comprehensive reform of local government was implemented by the Local Government (Scotland) Act of 1929, which abolished parish councils and local school boards, and reduced the powers of small burghs. Most powers were transferred to the county councils. Nevertheless, the Cromarty Town Council had some achievements in the 1930s. A permanent mains supply for electric light was turned on in January 1935, largely as the result of the efforts of a local shopkeeper and town councillor, D. R. Mackenzie, who was subsequently elected provost in 1936. Under his leadership the town council approached their MP, Malcolm MacDonald, during his visit to Cromarty in 1936 and asked for his support in moves to find a national body willing to take over responsibility for Hugh Miller's birthplace. Their campaign was aided by a visit in the following year by Ramsay MacDonald who spoke to the Literary Society on Miller's life and work, and the Commercial Bank marked the occasion by donating the desk that Miller had used as an accountant in the bank. The following year the National Trust for Scotland, formed in 1931, agreed to take over the cottage if £500 could be raised by a national appeal, with the Trust donating the first £100. Renovation and the formal handing over of the property took place in 1938.

Cromarty society between the wars

The term 'social capital' has been commonly used since the late 1980s to describe the extent to which individuals within a community form and join organisations, create networks of contacts and participate in civic and community affairs. In both Britain and the United States the late nineteenth century is seen as a time when much social capital was first created, evident in the flourishing of organisations to promote, for example, sport, education, self-help and charity. This tide of participation continued to flow through the first half of the twentieth century and the connections forged between individuals were important both in seeing them through periods of difficulty, including war and economic depression, and in allowing them to make most effective use of opportunities for personal or community advancement.[26]

Cromarty's high social capital is evident in the descriptions, in the previous chapter, of late nineteenth-century society in the town. From this base, the war years brought much new activity to the community and 1920 saw the revival of many organisations that had temporarily fallen into abeyance. Cricket and tennis clubs were re-formed and when the Admiralty, to the disappointment of the townspeople, disposed of the recreation park they had created, rather than handing it over to the town council, the Reeds Park at the east of the town was made available by the laird for sport. A new minister in the United Free Church began to organise adult education classes, on the model of the Workers Educational Association, and local politics came alive with the debate over temperance, with the possibility of the town becoming a 'dry burgh'.[27]

The existence of local clubs and the ability to organise social events allowed the community to make the most of the spring and autumn visits of the Home Fleet and of the continued presence of the Royal Marines, who manned the Sutor forts during the early 1920s. Cromarty consequently sustained a level of social life well above the economic standing of the town. Eric Malcolm, in *The Cromarty We Knew*, describes these events in the 1930s with affection.[28]

> [HMS *Tiger*'s] football team played Cromarty nearly every week ... they took on our Territorials and ex-Servicemen at rifle shooting ... and ran weekly dances in the Victoria Hall with their own ship's band. The local young ladies had the time of their lives; *Hood*'s dance on a Thursday, *Renown*'s dance on a Friday and *Tiger*'s on a Saturday. The Marines ... played Cromarty at football regularly and there were frequent billiard matches ... There were even bowling matches, four rinks a side. Towards the end of the Fleet's stay, the town would run a series of farewell dances in a gesture of friendship – one for each ship ... And occasionally some sixty local ladies would be entertained to a dance aboard the *Renown*, when the quarterdeck would be enclosed with awnings and decorated with flags and coloured lights ... There were ships' concerts too.

For the community as a whole 'to have hundreds of [young sailors] ashore ... at any one time produced an explosion of energy'.

The relative prosperity brought by the fleet helped sustain a body of middle-class families in the town – shopkeepers, bankers, professional men and farmers – who 'populated' its key organisations, including the town council. General Ross, who had been knighted in 1919, died in 1928 and was succeeded by his son, George (1903–76), better known as Geordie, who joined the Seaforths in 1923 but 'retired' in 1926 – reputedly 'cashiered for going out with a horse without leave, and breaking its knees'.[29] Although he remained in Cromarty, he was a less effective laird than his father and did not act as a leader of the community in any significant way. As a result, more was left to the local middle class.

In the churches, some old divisions were being healed. In 1900 two Scottish denominations, the Free Church (formed at the Disruption of 1843) and the United Presbyterian Church (an amalgamation of earlier seceding churches), joined to form the United Free Church. In many parts of the Highlands a section of the Free Church refused to enter this union and continued under the banner of the Free Church – commonly known as the 'Wee Frees'. The United Free Church, over the next thirty years, negotiated a union with the Established Church, which was accomplished in 1929.

In Cromarty there was, unusually for the Highlands, no 'Wee Free' remnant in 1900 – and, unlike some fishing communities, no evangelical sects – with the result that all Presbyterians in the community were members of one body from 1929. This was not to say that there were no tensions and the congregations continued to meet separately. On 25 January 1932, a disastrous fire gutted the United Free Church building but the opportunity to merge the congregations was not taken up and the decision was made to rebuild. The church was reopened in May 1933. However, by November of that year there was a double vacancy – the 'old kirk' minister Mr Moore had left for Wick in 1932 and the UF minister, Mr Burnett, retired after a long illness. James Fyfe was appointed minister of the united congregation in 1934. Two years later there was a proposal to close the old parish church and although a majority voted in favour – sixty-two for, fifty-two against – it was not the 75 per cent majority required by church law. The debate continued in 1937 but a protest against closure of the old parish church, signed by over 200 people, brought the matter to an end. Over the next sixty years the declining congregation was left with the burden of two buildings to maintain and it was not until the mid 1990s that the historic old parish church was declared redundant.

The active middle class in the town continued to run many social services, including the Cottage Hospital, and the GP, Dr Daniel Johnstone, who was Parish Medical Officer until the parish council was abolished in 1929, gave generously of his services. But there was another side to the town. The long decline of the fishing community from the prosperity of the early nineteenth century and the descent of many families into poverty had, in many ways, divided the fisher folk and the town folk. This was evident in the incident in 1897, described in the previous chapter, when a crowd of 200 fisher folk burned the town clerk, A. H. Mackenzie, in effigy. His son, D. A. Mackenzie, whose articles in the *North Star* had ignited the affair, later wrote that 'in an ethnical or social sense' the parish of Cromarty was, like Caesar's Gaul, divided into three parts – the fishers, the townsfolk and, in the landward part, the 'Gaelickers'.[30] One resident of the fishertown, in an oral history interview in the 1990s, talked of the division within the town as being 'like Beirut'.

The divide was also apparent to outsiders. In 1959 Elizabeth Jane Cameron, writing as Jane Duncan, published *My Friends the Miss Boyds*, the first of nineteen titles featuring Janet Sandison, a character loosely based on Cameron herself. As a child she had spent holidays on her grandparents' croft at the Colony, above Jemimaville and the Colony became the fictional Reachfar of her stories. The nearby Achcraggan of her books was a combination of Jemimaville and Cromarty. She was in no doubt as to the division in the community.

I have never, later in my life, been so aware of the gulf fixed between two races of people as I was of the gulf between the land and sea people of Achcraggan. They had nothing in common except the church, and even there, there was a deep-rooted difference. The land people tended to be tall and fair of skin, the sea people short and sallow; the land people were soft and slow of speech, the sea people shrill-voiced and rapid; to the land people fish were repellently dirty and stinking, to the sea people dirt and stink were the main characteristics of farm animals. The two races had nothing in common except their belief in God, and yet here came the deepest difference of all. The sea people claimed they were God's chosen because His only son had made his friends among the fisher folk of Galilee. The land people claimed that they were the Lord's chosen because he had put His first created man on earth to live in Eden, a garden. There was nothing to be done about it. The grown men fought over the issue at the [inn]; the grown women fought over it in the village shops, and the children fought over it in the school playground. Grown ups and children could be controlled only by the greater powers vested in the persons of ... the minister and ... the schoolmaster. Civil war simmered always just below the surface of Achcraggan life.[31]

Paradoxically, the more the fishing community declined the more it became emblematic of Cromarty's distinct identity, and the fisher dialect and fishermen featured in the first wireless broadcasts from the town on the BBC Scottish Home Service in 1938. This was the year of the 'Urquhart Celebrations', which were a high point of civic pride for the burgh. The recently formed Saltire Society had been persuaded to erect a memorial to Sir Thomas Urquhart in the old parish church, Hugh Miller's Cottage was handed over to the National Trust for Scotland, and the town council obtained both a new grant of arms from Lord Lyon and a provost's chain. It was also in 1938 that the decision was taken that the naval base and anchorage of Invergordon should again be protected, in response to the growing threat from Nazi Germany.

The Second World War

The Sutor forts were re-armed during 1939, this time manned by the Royal Artillery rather than the marines. There were two six-inch Mk VII BL guns on the South Sutor, for close defence and to support the 'examination service', which was to inspect incoming vessels, and two similar guns on the North Sutor, on forty-five degree mountings, to be used for counter-bombardment. In 1940 a third battery was added at Nigg, responsible for the inner defences of the firth. Together these formed Cromarty Fire Command, controlled from the Fire Command Post on the South Sutor, whose role was to prevent entry of hostile or suspicious vessels and to engage any ships attempting to bombard the port or anchorage. The defences of the firth also included a mine laying base, under naval control, which mined the outer Moray Firth; a Chain Home Low Radar Station above the South Sutor fort; a Royal Observer Corps post on Cromarty Hill; and a barrage balloon base on Cromarty links.

Troops arrived in Cromarty a few days after war was declared and a number of houses in the town were commandeered as billets. There were also more than 1,000 Newfoundland lumberjacks on the Black Isle, many in camps near Glenurquhart farm, and, from 1944 men of the Polish pioneer corps, camped in huts on Cromarty links. The Polish troops, who stayed until 1945, used the redundant Gaelic Chapel for Sunday mass and were the last people to worship in the building, before its roof collapsed in 1952. It was an unexpected end for a Presbyterian church. The pioneers left their mark on Cromarty, in an inscription, in Polish and English, on the concrete supports of a bridge they replaced on the drive to Cromarty House – 'Erected by the Polish Pioneer Platoon of the 24th Silesian Inf Br – November 1945'. Also in 1944, a Norwegian coastal artillery training unit was established at Nigg and soon afterwards relocated to naval barracks in Cromarty.

As in the First World War, even if not on the same scale, the presence of troops brought trade to businesses and enlivened the town. There were concerts in the Victoria Hall and recreational facilities in the West Church Hall, much of it supported by local voluntary effort. But unlike the First Word War, fighting ships rarely entered the firth during the years of conflict and one of the most common and striking memories of local residents would be the departure of the fleet, which had meant so much to the town, in September 1939. Eric Malcolm captures the emotional bond between the town and what its people thought of as, in more than the usual sense, 'our ships'.

> The Fleet left quietly one Sunday afternoon, watched by thousands of folk on both shores of the firth, who well knew that they were witnessing a unique and never-to-be repeated spectacle ... Most of the big ships survived the war, but many did not. *Courageous*, *Royal Oak*, *Hood*, *Repulse* and *Barnham* all went to the bottom ... Apart from the Hood ... just names to most, but to us here, well-loved and familiar friends. And, even worse, destroyed with them were the lives of thousands of fine young men. Among the smaller ships – the cruisers, the destroyers, the escort ships – and especially the submarines – the mortality rate was even higher.[32]

Eight months later the town was directly struck by bitter tragedy. In April 1940 the *Disperser*, a salvage vessel which had been working on the wreck of the *Natal* before being requisitioned by the Admiralty, was sent north to Scapa Flow. The clumsy vessel foundered at her moorings in Kirkwall Bay during a storm and went down with the loss of all hands. Of the twelve crew lost, six were from Cromarty. As a result of the efforts of the town clerk, Mr Gaskell, and the MP, Malcolm MacDonald, the bodies were, unusually for wartime, brought home for burial. These deaths, with the thirty-three war dead commemorated on the town's memorial, marked the true impact of the war on Cromarty.

Cromarty's economy after 1945

With the end of the war Cromarty again faced an economic downturn. Plans under the 1946 New Towns Act to create a new town between Evanton and Invergordon, with a smaller new town on the Black Isle at Balblair – all based on proposals to ship Canadian wheat from Halifax, Nova Scotia, for trans-shipment to Europe – came to nothing. Resolis had not, in any case, been sympathetic. One correspondent to the *Ross-shire Journal* argued that the parish's future should be based on local agriculture and consideration given to reclaiming Udale Bay as a dairy farm, on the Dutch model of polders.[33]

Yet, despite the economic problems, Cromarty was not included with those scheduled for attention under the Board of Trade's Highland Development Scheme of 1948.[34] The county council, who were the planning authority, were sufficiently concerned about the state of the town to commission an economic survey, which was carried out the following year. The analysis of employment in this report can be compared with that of 1962, undertaken by students from Edinburgh College of Art (Table 16.1). In 1950 a number of new council houses had been completed and this had supported employment in the building

TABLE 16.1 Employment in 1950 and 1962.

Employment	1950				1962			
	Male	Female	Total		Male	Female	Total	
Agriculture	33	4	37	14%	36	4	40	19%
Salmon fishing	13	0	13	5%	3	0	3	1%
Forestry	23	3	26	9%	19	1	20	10%
Building trades	29	0	29	11%	16	0	16	8%
Distribution/retail	46	24	70	26%	23	26	49	24%
Personal services	3	42	45	16%	5	26	31	15%
National & local government	24	4	28	10%	14	1	15	7%
Transport	8	1	9	3%	4	0	4	2%
Professional	15	0	15	5%	7	12	19	9%
Hydro electricity	0	0	0	0%	2	0	2	1%
Miscellaneous	2	0	2	1%	9	0	9	4%
Total	196	78	274	100%	138	70	208	100%

trades; local government, including the squad working on the roads, was a significant employer; and the numbers employed in distribution and retail reflected the number of shops which the war had sustained and which were still in business. Fishing was now restricted to the salmon fishery, and agriculture and forestry were mainstays of the economy – but all, in their time, suffered major decline.

Salmon fishing[35]

The six coastal salmon netting stations operated from Cromarty – Castlecraig, Cromarty, Gallow Hill, St Bennet's, Eathie and Learnie – each employed four men, of which thirteen lived in Cromarty in 1950. They used 25-foot cobles designed with shallow draft and wide beam, to give the necessary stability for hauling nets, and there was also a motor boat, used to move the cobles to and from the stations and to bring the catch back to the harbour. Smaller sixteen-foot cobles were used at St Bennet's and Eathie where the crew lived in bothies and the boats were hauled up by winch onto the shore. The daily catch might vary from nothing to several hundred fish, and a typical yearly catch for a station would be 1,000 salmon.

Salmon netting ended in 1984 when the rights were bought up by the Atlantic Salmon Trust, whose aim was to allow the fish to run up to the rivers to sustain commercial angling with rod-and-line. The main driving force was, however, the fall in the catch and increasing costs, with employment available in oil related industries – sale of the fishing rights to the Trust offered a means by which something could be recovered by the fishing companies. Thereafter, fish farming of salmon and sea trout was developed by the Cromarty Salmon Company, a local venture. Their cages, some of them wooden, were destroyed by a north-westerly gale in February 1989 and the trout stranded in their thousands on the shore – from where they found their way into many household freezers and kitchens. Nevertheless, the farm restocked and expanded to twenty-four cages in 1996 before declining, as it became apparent that the waters of the firth were less suitable than the faster moving waters of the west coast sea lochs. By the turn of the century there were no fish farms and attempts, from time to time, to farm mussels had also failed.

Agriculture

The Agriculture Act of 1947 and the Agriculture (Scotland) Act of 1948 provided a framework for government support of farming, which allowed farmers to plan and thus encouraged private investment. This investment led to grater mechanisation which, coupled with advances in agricultural science, gave significantly greater yields in all sectors. Subsidies on production brought new land into cultivation in the 1960s and 1970s, to the east of Cromarty Mains, finally removing the network of First World War training trenches, and on the moor between Newton and Davidston, where three iron-age enclosures were ploughed under. The specialist production of seed potatoes continued to develop, especially at Rosefarm.

The expansion of cultivation was achieved with a diminishing workforce, although the numbers in the town of Cromarty employed in agriculture remained stable until the 1960s. Thereafter, in common with the rest of Scotland, the numbers fell to the point where employment in agriculture became of less importance to the local economy than at any time in the area's history. While the farm labour force shrank, UK, and later European, subsidies supported farm owners and tenants, especially those on larger farms, who formed a prosperous, relatively secure rural class, active in local affairs. This was similar to their social position in the days of Cromarty's prosperity in the early nineteenth century, and they were, in the later twentieth century, one of the few groups, besides the lairds, with the time to serve in local government, to the point where the form of government in the county council could well be described as a combination of aristocracy and 'agritocracy'. Farmers were also often local entrepreneurs and, with their understanding of the economy, were key figures in bringing new industries to the area in the 1970s and in arguing for improvements to the region's infrastructure. This influence diminished considerably, although at the end of the century around 20 per cent of elected Highland councillors still had a direct interest in some form of agriculture, while the sector employed less than 2 per cent of the population.

Ongoing restructuring of support for agriculture from the 1990s, the diminishing economic importance of farming for the local economy and the fact that farms are no longer small rural centres of population, all point to the question: what do farmers now provide for the wider community? The answer was once clear – food and employment – but now that this is no longer so, there is a need to redefine the centuries-old relationship between those who work the rich 'cornlands' of the Black Isle, the rest of the area's residents and those who, through their taxes, supply the continuing subsidies.

Forestry

Forestry was one sector of employment that was growing in the Black Isle in the post-war years. Prior to 1914, Britain, as a maritime power, had easy access to overseas sources of timber, especially from Canada, but the First World War closed the sea lanes and brought extensive felling of the limited stocks of native woods. This was a significant change to the landscape of the north. The crisis was recognised by the Government who appointed the Acland Committee, which reported in 1917 and recommended the setting up of a state forest service to create a strategic reserve. As a result the Forestry Commission was established in 1919, with the power to acquire and plant suitable land.

The first acquisitions on the Black Isle were in 1926 and thereafter separate forest units were established, first at Findon and Kessock, and then, in the 1930s, on the Mulbuie ridge and at Kilcoy. These were joined to form a single Black Isle forest unit in 1963. The expansion onto the Mulbuie heathland required preparation of the ground by deep ploughing using tractor-drawn ploughs, and the Newhall blacksmith, Leslie Smith, helped design and produce many of the implements which made this possible.

The Forestry Commission provided much-needed employment, including work for a number of St Kildans resettled after the evacuation of the island in 1930. The Commission also provided housing and created small new communities, such as Mounthigh. By the 1950s there were nine or ten foresters on the Black Isle and a workforce of 200 to 250, including seasonal workers. A significant number of women were employed both in full-time and seasonal jobs. In Cromarty itself, there were twenty-six forestry workers in 1950 and twenty in 1962 – in both years about 10 per cent of the employed people in the town.

By the 1950s a network of nine nurseries totalling sixty hectares made the Black Isle the largest forest nursery in Britain, with up to 20 million transplants each year and, at Blackstand, an annual production of one tonne of seed. First mechanisation, then the run down of the nurseries, which closed in 1983, and finally the contracting out of work, led to a rapid and marked reduction in the numbers employed from the 1970s. By the 1990s there was no one employed in this sector in the town.[36]

Low ebb[37]

Between 1950 and 1962 the number of employed people in Cromarty fell by 24 per cent and the fall in male employment was an even higher 30 per cent. Cromarty reached its lowest recorded population at the 1971 census, with only 484 inhabitants – less than 22 per cent of its peak population of 2,215 in 1831. The fall had been continuous since the end of the war in 1945, with a loss of about 120 inhabitants in both the 1950s and the 1960s. There was a disproportionately high reduction in the numbers of working-age men. At a meeting with their MP in 1965 town councillors outlined some of the problems – salmon fishing employed only five men, where it had earlier employed fifteen, several businesses including a bank and a garage had closed down, farming was more mechanised and the school faced down-grading from a junior secondary to a primary. The only new jobs were two full-time and twelve part-time in a battery chicken farm at the site of a former army camp on the South Sutor. In 1968 the relocation of the lifeboat from Cromarty, where it had been established in 1911, to Invergordon was a further blow to the pride of a community so closely linked to the sea.

There had, however, been some development within the firth with the opening of the Invergordon grain distillery in 1961, soon to become the largest in Europe employing about 400 people for a time in the early 1960s, and from Cromarty's perspective the Balblair–Invergordon ferry became vitally important as a link to the opportunity of employment there.

Two members of the town council, 'Daldon' Ross and Donald Matheson, showed considerable initiative in seeking ideas for the regeneration of Cromarty. A Cromarty Development Committee was formed, which importantly forged alliances with bodies outside the town and in 1961 commissioned a report on development potential from a firm of chartered architects. The report accepted the view put forward to the consultants by Michael Dower of the Civic Trust that 'the new economic lifeblood of Cromarty must come from tourists, holiday makers and people coming to live in the town'. It went on to list priorities for action to preserve the built heritage, describing Cromarty as 'a town of unique architectural interest and charm'.[38]

FIGURE 16.5
Plans for Cromarty in 1962 – Forsyth House as a hotel with walls demolished to create a 'town square' in front.

FIGURE 16.6
Cromarty Guidebook, 1967.

This was followed in 1962 by an extensive study by students from Edinburgh College of Art's Town and Country Planning Department, who spent a number of weeks in the town, surveyed buildings, and made proposals for development.[39] They thought revitalisation would come principally from tourism, but saw too the possibility of promoting crafts as a new source of employment. They also recognised that housing developments could attract people to retire to Cromarty, with the result that these newcomers would be active in preserving the character of the town.

A public appeal had been launched to restore the eighteenth-century courthouse, with a target of £6,000 of which £1,500 had been raised by 1963. Some of this had been contributed by the National Trust for Scotland, who later undertook the renovation of Miller House and a small cottage, renamed Lydia Cottage, opposite Hugh Miller's birthplace. These restoration projects took much longer than envisaged but they all had their origins in ideas first mooted in the early 1960s.

The town council consistently promoted tourism in a number of ways – through the production of a revised Cromarty Guide in 1967, writing to those who might offer B&B, providing information on accommodation to prospective visitors through the town clerk, and trying to clamp down on the dumping of waste on the beach, from houses in the fishertown with no sanitation. The new guide promoted the town as the place 'for a carefree holiday' and noted that the fishertown had been described as 'a gem of Scottish Vernacular Architecture'.

When one group of holidaymakers left because the house they had rented, the Retreat, was in poor condition, the council attempted to use the sanitary inspector to prevent the property being offered for rent until the problems were resolved. They also attended meetings prior to the creation of area tourist boards and supported the establishment of a Black Isle & Mid Ross Tourist Association. By 1966 ideas were floated of converting the courthouse to a museum and employing a guide during the summer months to show visitors around the courthouse and the old parish church. They also reached agreement to have gates removed from the estate road to the South Sutor to allow easier access to this viewpoint.

Before the advent of cheap foreign holidays, local beaches and outdoor swimming facilities were of considerable importance. Invergordon, for example, opened an outdoor pool in the 1930s beside the shore. The annual Cromarty regatta was also a 'swimming gala' and the harbour was promoted as a bathing area, with a chute provided on its west face. In 1969 the council and the Amenities Association sought professional advice on building groynes to retain sand on the shore in front of the fishertown and in 1972 investigated reclamation of the west beach, in front of the Royal Hotel. The options considered included pumping sand ashore and bringing it from proposed works at Alness point, but the cost was too great despite the possibility of grant aid from the HIDB and the Countryside Commission. Lack of finance also ruled out plans for an improved caravan park, relocated to the playing field on the Victoria Park.

The council were also actively involved in attempts to attract craft business to Cromarty by offering house purchase loans, renovating property and assisting in finding business premises. In 1966 two craft businesses were established – by Ken Derby, a jeweller, and Alison and Alastair Dunn, potters who moved from Aultbea. The Dunns lived first in one of the empty buildings at the Sutor camp before a property at Shore Street was purchased and renovated, while Ken Derby was given the tenancy of a council house. The following year Kenneth and Janet Scott-Lodge moved from Cumbernauld to set up a woodworking business, making 'Swedish furniture'. There was also an approach from a blacksmith, Mr Yates, who wished to establish a business in wrought iron work, and a local woman made plans for dress-making on a commercial scale.

The Highlands and Islands Development Board was established in late 1965 by the Labour Government. Cromarty Town Council made immediate approaches to the new organisation and 'Daldon' Ross, Donald Matheson and the town clerk, Kenneth Sutherland, prepared a 'statistical survey of town'. The Board granted £500 for a study of the fishertown and its potential. The council had, however, cause for complaint when the Board advised two prospective entrepreneurs – Roddy and Jean MacBeath – against setting up a shop in Cromarty. The Board subsequently apologised and the MacBeaths had, in the event, ignored the advice – fortunately, since Mrs Macbeath went on to be an effective chair of the community council and chair of the trust which established a museum in the courthouse – but there were recurring problems for Cromarty of a negative image and adverse publicity. Although the *Press and Journal* had reported positively on 'New life for Cromarty' in 1963, in 1966 an ITV programme *This Week* was felt to have presented the town in a biased and distorted way, and the *Scotsman* criticised the HIDB's support of the Fishertown Survey the following year.

There was also negativity within the community. The predominant attitudes encountered by the Edinburgh College of Art students in 1962 were summed up in comments such as 'You're wasting your time up here!', 'Cromarty has no money' and 'We don't want to change. I just want to remain, just as I am, for the rest of my days.' This was also true on the town council, where there was a constant battle against the negative views of a number of members – who were always clear what they opposed, but were less forthcoming in ideas for progress.

Yet, despite pessimism and negativity, the town maintained its 'social capital' and people formed and joined a variety of local organisations. In the late 1940s the Literary Society had been re-established and Brownies, Guides, swimming and rifle clubs formed. A successful dramatic society was created in 1950 and a Gaelic Society in 1954. In 1962, the Edinburgh College of Arts' students found that, although the economic state of the town was depressed, Cromarty was an active community. The Urquhart Club (snooker) had thirty members, football was very popular, the swimming club was thriving and the tennis club had thirty members, mostly juniors. The bowling club, however, was not strong. The Dramatic Society had twenty members, the whist club twenty-eight and the Gaelic society forty; there were sixteen Brownies and eighty children attending Sunday school; and there was also the masonic lodge, the Women's Guild (thirty members) and the Territorial Army unit (twelve members).

Revival

By 1966 there was much greater optimism for the economy of the north, embodied in the HIDB's *Proplan Reports* of that year, which envisaged a major petrochemical complex at Invergordon and the development over twenty years of a 'linear city' stretching from Inverness along the A9 through Easter Ross. This required a major industrial development as a driver, particularly after a downturn in the market for whisky in the mid 1960s, and this took the form of the Invergordon aluminium smelter, brought to the north by preferential electricity prices offered to the company, British Aluminium. Planning approval for the smelter was given in 1968, following a public enquiry, nearly 2,000 were employed in the construction phase and the first aluminium was produced in 1971. As Marinell Ash has put it in her history of the Cromarty Firth, 'for the first time perhaps since the agricultural boom of the Napoleonic Wars, Easter Ross enjoyed full employment'.[40] In the same year, 1971, Highland Fabricators (Hifab), a company formed by the American Brown and Root and British-based George Wimpey, announced its plans for a platform construction yard at Nigg. In less than two years, 2,000 were employed and Cromarty Town Council supported the development 'without reservation'.

Lying on the other side of the firth from these major developments, Cromarty's greatest interest was in securing adequate ferry links, campaigning first for the Balblair–Invergordon link and then, with the coming of Hifab, for a regular ferry service to Nigg. This was successfully established, subsidised by Hifab, both as transport for workers and as a public service. This was expanded in 1986 with the purpose built two-car *Cromarty Rose*.

The employment available at Nigg allowed the town council to plan for a significant expansion of Cromarty through new house building. The poor state of existing housing was also apparent, as evidenced by the 1962 Edinburgh College of Art survey. Of the worst houses, in the fishertown, ten had neither water nor sanitation and a further ten had no running water.

In 1972 the planning authority, Ross & Cromarty County Council, had a target of twenty new houses over three years, but this was judged inadequate. The town council favoured fifty and within a few months the County approved one hundred. A leading figure in this was Duncan MacPherson, the tenant farmer at Cromarty Mains, who had been co-opted to the council in 1967 but had stood down in 1969 because of other commitments. He returned in 1972 as burgh treasurer and was appointed to represent Cromarty on a subcommittee of the County authority to consider future housing needs throughout the area. Three adjoining areas of land were identified at the west end – the Westerhaugh, the Station Field and part of Whitedykes.

In January 1973 Cllr MacPherson, seconded by Cathel Mackenzie, successfully moved that the town council proceed independently to erect a hundred council houses over a period of two years, and that Wimpeys be asked to proceed with preliminary work on the costings. Wimpeys indicated that 132 houses could be erected on the areas under consideration, but eighty-one houses were eventually built. The land at the west of the site was in the ownership of a Mr Cook, who had extant planning permission for the erection of chalets, and was unwilling to sell, so reducing the overall scope of the scheme. There had also been the problem of the former refuse dump, in the middle of the site, which belonged to the Cromarty estate and, in any case, was unsuitable for building.

Mr Pease, the County planning officer, had been unhappy with the design of Wimpeys' housing and felt that the proposed density was too high. He said that he appreciated Cromarty's 'special architectural importance' and that 'the average Council housing scheme would not do for Cromarty'. Some amendments were made and the Cromarty town clerk and master of works visited some of Wimpey's other developments, concluding that the standard and design were 'perfectly suitable'. It was finally agreed to phase the development – with sixty houses in phase I and twenty-two in phase II, one of which was deleted to resolve a dispute over access to the rear of the properties on Denny Road.

The scale and speed of the project was notable, carried out as it was by a small town council, with a clerk and master of works. The finances, over £800,000, were ultimately the responsibility of the burgh treasurer, Duncan MacPherson, and day-to-day supervision was entrusted to two of its members, councillors 'Alla' Macdonald and Cathel Mackenzie, both builders to trade. The only additional help employed was a typist, Jane MacAuley.

Houses were allocated in two batches – forty-one at the end of 1974 and the remainder in March 1975. Of the eighty-one properties, eight were two-apartment sheltered houses which went to single people from or closely connected with Cromarty, four houses were held back in reserve, and two were for the education authority, leaving sixty-seven for allocation. Of those allocated houses, twenty-six moved from addresses within the parish, ten of these from the earlier – and, as it turned out, much better built – council properties in Bayview Crescent, to which some of them later returned. A further twelve had close family connections with Cromarty and were included in the first batch of allocations, two were allocated to the Royal Hotel to accommodate their staff and a further three or four with weaker local connections were given houses in the second tranche. This left around thirty-three houses for incoming residents, almost all of whom already had temporary addresses in the Black Isle or Easter Ross, including a number in residential caravans and one from the 'floating hotel', the accommodation vessel *Highland Queen* anchored in the firth. Only a few of these became long-term residents but by 1981 the population had risen by 167 over the decade to 651.

No petrochemical complex was developed in the firth and, on Hogmanay 1981, the Invergordon smelter closed. However, the fabrication yard at Nigg continued to offer well-paid employment for a considerable number of Cromarty residents until the mid 1990s. This was undoubtedly the principal driver of the town's economy but attention was paid to other sectors, including tourism, in the knowledge that industries related to North Sea oil would eventually decline.

Conservation and development

In 1969 the Cromarty Fishertown was designated as conservation area but the town council resisted more stringent controls proposed under Article 4(1) of the Town & Country Planning (General Developments) (Scotland) Order 1950. In May of the same year the council considered the report on the Fishertown Survey, meeting 'in committee' to allow a frank expression of views. The council were generally supportive and adopted a policy of acquiring and building on gap sites to rehouse occupiers of existing properties, with the aim of then acquiring these properties for renovation.

After considerable debate and a vote it was agreed to acquire land and build four houses – two in Forsyth Place and two at the bottom of Big Vennel, on the west side. Plans were prepared for the Forsyth Place site but there were disputes about the quality of the design. The head teacher, Henry MacRae, who had been co-opted to the council in 1969 and was also secretary of the Development Committee, did not feel they were architecturally in keeping with the terms of the Fishertown Survey. Alternative plans were prepared but the council voted five to three in favour of the original. The proposals ground to a standstill as all energies became absorbed in promoting and overseeing the construction of Townlands Park. There were undoubtedly compromises between quality and the desire to build a substantial number of houses quickly and cheaply.

In 1972 the NTS began work to renovate Miller House but it was 1974 before the town council turned again to serious consideration of the fishertown, when the master of works, Mr Lowrie, outlined how it might be declared a Housing Treatment Area. In 1974 the Provost reported on a meeting with representatives of the Scottish Civic Trust and the County Planning Department. It was decided to extend the conservation area and have it declared an 'outstanding conservation area' to coincide with the European Architectural Heritage Year in 1975. This was a long way from the view, expressed in the Visitors' Guide of 1934, that Cromarty had 'few buildings of particular note'.

The process of restoration of the town's buildings was to last another thirty years. Some were the achievement of the local authorities (until 1996 Ross & Cromarty District Council and Highland Regional Council, thereafter the single-tier Highland Council), who repaired and upgraded the Hugh Miller Institute, converted most of the hemp factory buildings to houses, led in the restoration of the courthouse as a museum, and supported the rescue of the 1823 Masonic Lodge from dereliction. The Cromarty Arts Trust, established by Michael Nightingale, achieved major restorations of the Brewery and Stable Block, as part of a vision that they become an operating part of The Robert Gordon University, Aberdeen. Although this use was not, in the end, sustained the buildings have found other functions. Many private houses were restored with generous improvement grants in the 1980s and 1990s, with building preservation trusts stepping in to manage restoration projects in a few cases which required more extensive grant aid – such as the derelict house at the east end of the town, which had been built by the Cromarty merchant John Laing on the back of his exports of salt fish in the early eighteenth century.

There were some unfortunate losses. The Wrights and Coopers Lodge of the 1820s was demolished in 1971 after a long wrangle between interested (and uninterested) parties, and, in the following year, the north range of the factory buildings was removed by Col Ross to improve the view when the east range was converted to a bar and restaurant. When the queen visited Cromarty in 1964 some cottages in the fishertown were pulled down to 'improve' the appearance of the area. Yet thirty years later her son, Prince Charles, spent most of a day in Cromarty at the invitation of the Courthouse Museum, enjoying its now valued vernacular architecture.

Laird, vassals and ministers

For much of its history Cromarty was strongly influenced by its relationship with its lairds and by the role of its ministers. Both the feudal system and religious controversy cast surprisingly long shadows into the late twentieth century. In 1964 Michael Nightingale (1927–98) bought into the Cromarty estate, sharing the position of laird with Col 'Geordie' Ross until Ross's death in 1976, when Nightingale became sole proprietor. His thirty-four-year involvement with Cromarty was marked by a remarkable number of disagreements and disputes, but this was nothing unusual for a man whose obituary described him as already, at the age of sixteen, 'precocious, independent and intransigent'.

It was always an easier option to caricature Michael Nightingale than to attempt to understand him. The journalist George Rosie described his career as 'almost a parody of the upper-class Englishman's upbringing: educated at Winchester Public School, and Magdalen College Oxford ... a well-connected member of the Conservative party (who) like many British Conservatives ... believes firmly in the gracious way of life he lives, and works to maintain it.'[41] This was inaccurate on many counts, not least because it suggested a predictable and conventional man, motivated by his own self-interest. His obituary was, again, closer to the truth. Nightingale was an independent-minded man 'whose views were unfashionable, his methods frequently unconventional and his contribution to causes he espoused often significant'. These causes included environmental protection and, as mayor of Maidstone (Kent) he had one developer imprisoned for breach of a tree preservation order – the first use of the power in the UK. One long-term family friend described him as a man 'entirely devoted to doing good, but entirely on his own terms' – and here lay the problem for many in the community, who were used to more give and take in their relationship with the laird.

Nightingale believed in the feudal system and in exercising the rights he acquired with the superiority of the barony of Cromarty. His claim to ownership of the town's courthouse was successfully resisted by the district council but he used his right of pre-emption on a number of other properties which came onto the market, and in so doing generated much ill feeling in the community. He, however, perceived himself as acting to preserve the character of the historic town and he shared the dream of his seventeenth-century predecessor as laird – the eccentric Sir Thomas Urquhart – of turning Cromarty into a university town, in Nightingale's case by restoring and leasing buildings to Aberdeen and the Robert Gordon Universities.

There was also much controversy in the 1970s over a plan by the reclusive millionaire Daniel Ludwig to build a petrochemical complex at Nigg. Nightingale opposed the plan but eventually sold land to Ludwig, in the course of this falling out with both the proponents and opponents of the project. Money from the sale was used to establish the Cromarty Trust, a charitable body which would support restoration projects in the town and elsewhere. But even this altruistic gesture incensed his critics, who resented that fact that no local trustees were appointed and suspected that funds would be diverted to charitable purposes outwith the area. It is difficult to resist the conclusion that some inhabitants would, in fact, have preferred to deal with a landowner who was out to feather his own nest – and whose motivation they would have understood.

Relationships between the community and Nightingale were exacerbated by the parish minister, Robert Galloway, who also chaired the Community Council from its creation in 1976 and who took every opportunity to stir up resentment against Nightingale. Galloway's brand of religion, strong on anti-Catholicism and weak on toleration, was unsuited to the kind of place Cromarty had become. He rivalled Nightingale in his ability to alienate those who might have supported him and was removed from the Community Council in 1986. His congregation, increasingly ill at ease with his style and performance, declined dramatically to a few dozen before he finally left in 1998.

His successor, John Tallach, had unusually joined the Church of Scotland from the Free Presbyterian Church seeking, as he said at his induction to Cromarty in August 1999, 'a broader outlook and greater flexibility and understanding in his Ministry ... [which] he believes that he will achieve within the Church of Scotland'. He was attacked in print by some former colleagues.

> The Church of Scotland ... with its women ministers and elders (the Cromarty Session Clerk is a woman); its use of organs, hymns and paraphrases in public worship and its toleration within its ministry of men who deny the virgin birth and even the uniqueness of Christ as the alone Saviour of the lost. We ask ourselves: how can it be possible for anyone brought up within the bosom of the Free Presbyterian Church to feel at home in that environment?[42]

While this rhetoric would have been familiar to a congregation in the eighteenth or nineteenth century, it now had no resonance in Cromarty.

The place of the laird in local society had also changed. Michael Nightingale's death in 1998, the different approach of his son John, and the subsequent reform of the law of land tenure by the Scottish Parliament brought to an end almost 800 years of relationship between the community of Cromarty and a feudal superior.

Cromarty – to the Millennium and beyond

In 1982, after six years of construction, the Kessock Bridge was opened to provide a fixed link between the Black Isle and the growing town, now city, of Inverness. For the first time Cromarty was within an acceptable commuting time of a significant centre of population and, with the continuing benefit of over fifty local men still employed at Nigg, the revival of the town accelerated. During the next decade the town's population increased by 10 per cent to 720, many of them younger professionals willing to take on the restoration of the town's older houses.

Somewhat surprisingly, between 1991 and 2001 there was no growth in population. However, there was some turnover, with the characteristic that many of those who moved into the town had young children. They were attracted by the quality of the environment for families, by the education in local schools and by the availability of childcare, provided from the early 1990s by Cromarty Action for Young People in the renovated former hall of the old parish church. Unusually for a small community the primary school roll remained steady at just under ninety pupils and in 2001 almost 25 per cent of

FIGURE 16.7
Guide to Cromarty, 1980s – architecture becomes an asset.

the town's population were under-eighteens, as against Highland and Scottish averages of around 22 per cent. This success is a reminder that, for improved transport infrastructure to promote growth at the periphery, there must be something at both ends of the road – a reason to travel to, say, Inverness for work and a reason to live in, and contribute to, the community of the home. It is also important to note that, at the 2001 census, over 31 per cent of households in the town had no car. Although this was better than the Scottish average (34.2 per cent), it was a very high figure for an area poorly served by public transport and with few local services.

In the late 1990s there were further improvements in infrastructure, this time in telecommunications, with full broadband finally reaching Cromarty in 2005. The attractiveness of Cromarty, its historic buildings now almost entirely restored, led to the establishment of a number of small businesses, located in the town for reasons of 'life style'. This was, in a sense, the fulfilment of the 1960s vision of Cromarty as a 'craft village' – with the crafts being, not as expected, the traditional but instead the creative skills of multi-media design, software development and internet service provision.

There was also, as both Sir Thomas Urquhart and Michael Nightingale had desired, an academic community. Aberdeen University established a marine zoology field station, based in the Cromarty lighthouse buildings, for research and teaching on the ecology of seals, dolphins and other marine life. Aberdeen's Robert Gordon University also had a presence, creating a study centre in two restored buildings – the old brewery and the stable block of Cromarty House – and, although they abandoned this in 2004, it was taken on as a business venture by two Cromarty residents.

The restored town also became increasingly attractive to tourists, with access made easier by the road link to Inverness. The courthouse was renovated as an award-winning museum, which opened in 1991; the National Trust for Scotland extended their property in 2004 to include Miller House; and a successful eco-tourism business, Dolphin Ecosse, was built up focusing on the Moray Firth's resident population of 120 bottle-nosed dolphins. Cromarty remained off the beaten tourist track, which still drew most visitors to the 'bens and glens' of the west, but it evoked an enthusiastic response from those guide books favoured by the independent traveller. The French *Guide Routard* exclaimed 'Coup de coeur' (love at first sight) and for the *Rough Guide* it was 'a real treat ... a perfect example of an eighteenth-century Scottish seaport'.

The attraction of the fleet in the firth, promoted from the early twentieth century, was replicated by some new arrivals in these waters. The journalist, Charlie Connelly, visiting in the winter of 2002–3 noted both Cromarty's 'pleasant, welcoming demeanour' and its 'strong sense

TABLE 16.2 Employment according to the 2001 Census.

| Employment | 2001 Census | | | |
	Male	Female	Total	
Managers and senior officials	20	14	34	13%
Professional occupations	17	18	35	13%
Associate professional occupations	17	20	37	14%
Admin and secretarial	4	22	26	10%
Skilled trades	38	3	41	15%
Personal services	2	25	27	10%
Sales and customer services	5	10	15	6%
Machine operatives	18	4	22	8%
Elementary occupations	15	13	38	11%
Total	136	129	265	100%

of community', but he was also greeted, as he turned a corner after arriving on a winter's evening, by a sight 'among the most beautiful things I have ever seen' – this was the line of oil rigs anchored in the firth 'lit up with dazzling orange and white lights like an enormous birthday cake'.[43]

By 2001 the town's inhabitants were as a whole more highly educated and skilled, and better off financially, than at any time in its history. The population of 721 was similar to its level in 1950–1 (726) and the number employed, 265, was only slightly below the 274 of fifty years before. But the balance of employment was now almost evenly spread between males and females – 136:129 as compared with 196: 78 in 1951 – an added indication of the importance of childcare to the economy (Table 16.2).

In terms of its class structure, Cromarty had a lower proportion of inhabitants in social classes ABC1 than either Inverness or any other settlement on the Black Isle, and it retained a mix of population similar to both the Highland average and to towns like Dingwall and Tain. In the context of the Black Isle, the parish of Cromarty was the least dominated by the commuting, professional and skilled classes.

The 2001 census also revealed that Cromarty faced significant challenges. There was a very high level of male unemployment, 9.4 per cent of economically active males between the ages of 16 and 74. This, the third highest rate in the Highlands, may be explained by the lay-offs at the fabrication yard at Nigg that had taken place earlier in the year of the census. The rate of unemployment among economically active females in the age range (2.4 per cent) was similar to the Scottish average (2.7 per cent). Over 45 per cent of households had no adult in full time employment. This was higher than the Scottish average of 40 per cent and, perhaps, a matter for concern was the fact that 8.7 per cent of households had no adult in employment and had dependent children. This was, again, higher than the Scottish average (5.1 per cent). The number of lone parents with dependent children (10.4 per cent) was also above the national level (6.9 per cent).

This was undoubtedly a community divided by work, prospects and income. Cromarty had, however, long experience of containing and surviving divisions within the town – between Gaelic and English speakers, between the Free Kirk and the Old Kirk, between the town and fishertown – and the challenge would be to use its resources to overcome division. There were, and are, three aspects of Cromarty society which might contribute to healthy social interaction between sections of the community.

First, there is a continuing high level of social capital. In 2002 there were over twenty-five voluntary groups in the town, the Fourways Club for 'senior citizens' had over sixty members, all one hundred pupils in the primary school had taken part in a children's opera, commissioned to mark the bicentenary of Hugh Miller and featured on national television, and an average of one in five of the adult population were attending locally organised adult education classes.[44] Second, the physical heritage of the town means that most front doors open directly on to the street and, with no through traffic, this public space is a space for interaction. People acknowledge each other and greet strangers – and children play, with a freedom to range forgotten in many places.

And, finally, there is the less tangible, but vital, matter of self-confidence, the lack of which is seen by some, such as Carol Craig, author of *The Scots' Crisis of Confidence,* as Scotland's Achilles heel.[45] It is not a weakness that appears to afflict Cromarty. Charlie Connelly, in *Attention All Shipping,* summed up his impression of the town.

> It's known good years and bad, prosperity and penury, yet every time this small town on a remote headland has come up against another existence-threatening economic challenge, it has bounced back stronger. You can almost feel the sense of pride and satisfaction in the air. The people you pass in the street or who sell you a newspaper have a tangible air of confidence. There's a stubbornness about Cromarty that runs through the generations.[46]

Cromarty, since its decline in the 1840s, has spent more than 150 years seeking an appropriate way to portray itself to tourists and potential tourists. At the beginning of the twenty-first century the perception of Cromarty by visitors such as Charlie Connelly should be both a source of satisfaction and a spur to future development. Yet self-confidence alone will not protect the town from the greatest threat to its survival – the extreme weather events and rising sea levels which are already the almost inescapable consequence of changes in the earth's climate caused by high carbon emission. As a young boy, almost 200 years ago, Hugh Miller heard tales of an earlier Cromarty lost to the sea. Without a change of heart and behaviour, across the planet, the legend may become a reality.

Notes

1. Anon, *The Centenary of Hugh Miller* (Glasgow, 1902).
2. George Mackenzie, typescript account of Cromarty's housing and economy, 1913 (copy held by Cromarty Courthouse Museum).
3. *Invergordon Times*, 18 Mar 1908.
4. Isabella G. MacLean, *Your Father and I* (East Linton, 1998).
5. *Invergordon Times*, 29 May 1901.
6. *Invergordon Times*, 30 Dec 1903.
7. *Invergordon Times*, 22 Jan 1908; *Invergordon Times*, 17 Jan 1912.
8. Isabella G. MacLean, *Your Father and I* (East Linton, 1998), 96.
9. *Invergordon Times*, 6 Mar 1901.
10. *Invergordon Times*, 13 Jan 1906; 9 Jan 1909 .
11. Brian Short, *Land and Society in Edwardian Britain* (Cambridge, 1997).
12. George Mackenzie, typescript account of Cromarty's housing and economy, 1913 (copy held by Cromarty Courthouse Museum).
13. Isabella MacLean, *Your Father and I*, 123.
14. From information supplied by the late John Maclennan, Kinbeachie. James Livesey, who became an optician in Kilmarnock, died in 1972.
15. E. Alan Mackintosh, *War, The Liberator* (London, 1918), 126. Mackintosh appears in this piece under the pseudonym MacTaggart – but I have substituted 'Mr Mackintosh' in this quotation.
16. For an account of Mackintosh's work see Colin Campbell and Rosalind Green, *Can't shoot a man with a cold* (Glasgow, 2004).
17. *Ross-shire Journal*, 14 Feb 1919.
18. Eric H. Malcolm, *The Cromarty We Knew* (Cromarty, 2000).
19. Eric H. Malcolm, *The Cromarty & Dingwall Light Railway* (Cromarty, 1993).
20. *North Star*, 23 Jan 1920.
21. NAS AF15/14/2.
22. Peter Anson, *Fishing boats and fisher folk on the East Coast of Scotland* (London, 1930).
23. http://www.parliament.uk/commons/lib/research/rp99/rp99-020.pdf.
24. *Ross-shire Journal*, 5 Jan 1934.
25. *Ross-shire Journal*, 21 Aug 1931.
26. Robert D. Putnam, *Bowling Alone* (New York, 2000) is the most influential account of the role of social capital in economic history.
27. *North Star*, 12 & 19 June, 29 July, 29 Sep 1920.
28. Eric H. Malcolm, *The Cromarty We Knew* (Cromarty, 2000).
29. Isabella Maclean, *Your Father and I* (East Linton, 1998), 97.
30. Donald A. Mackenzie, 'Cromarty Dialects and folk lore', *Transactions of the Rymour Club*, 3 (1928), 75–82.
31. Jane Duncan, *My Friends the Miss Boyds* (London, 1959), 28.

32. Eric H. Malcolm in a talk to Cromarty History Society, November 1995.
33. *Ross-shire Journal*, 1 Apr 1949.
34. *Ross-shire Journal*, 21 Jan 1949.
35. From a talk given by Brian Shaw, manager of the Cromarty fish farm, to Cromarty History Society in 1996.
36. I am grateful to William (Ian) Ross, Golspie, whose father was head forester on the Black Isle, for the information in the preceding section.
37. This section is based on information from the town council minutes held in the Highland Council Archive.
38. *Press and Journal*, 27 July 1963.
39. Survey held in Cromarty Library.
40. Marinell Ash, *This Noble Harbour* (Edinburgh and Invergordon, 1991), 259.
41. George Rosie, *The Ludwig Initiative* (Edinburgh, 1978), 91.
42. From the website of the Free Presbyterian Church (designed so that it cannot be accessed on a Sunday).
43. Charlie Connelly, *Attention All Shipping* (London, 2004), 57.
44. Data from surveys conducted as part of the business plan for the development of Cromarty Victoria Hall.
45. Carol Craig, *The Scots' Crisis of Confidence* (Edinburgh, 2003).
46. Charlie Connelly, *Attention All Shipping*, 57.

Appendix

The seven tables in this appendix contain data not previously available in print. Tables 1–6 show the results of a study of corn and fish debentures, held in the National Archives of Scotland. Table 7 contains a series of fiars prices for Ross-shire from 1657 to 1740.

TABLE 1   Grain exported overseas from the customs precincts of Inverness and Caithness (in bolls).

Year	Total	Bear	Malt	Oatmeal	Rye	Wheat
1710–11	20,269	13,755	2,133	3,490	124	767
1711–12	13,469	5,581	3,300	3,957	160	471
1712–13	51,089	25,965	18,089	6,050	365	620
1713–14	40,938	27,811	4,478	8,211	0	438
Total	125,763	73,113	27,999	21,706	649	2,296

Source: Corn debentures in NAS, E508

TABLE 2   Corn debentures issued on exports of grain from Cromarty 1710–11 to 1713–14 (in bolls).

Year	For	From	Bere	Oatmeal	Wheat
1710–11	Drunton	Cromarty	768	16	
	Drunton	Cromarty & Portmahomack	540	200	
1711–12	Lisbon	Cromarty	885		149
	Lisbon	Cromarty & Inverness	810		
1712–13	Lisbon	Cromarty	2,100		
	Rotterdam	Cromarty	576		
1713–14	Rotterdam	Cromarty	1,028		
	Lisbon	Cromarty	1,176		
	Lisbon	Cromarty & Findhorn	1,490		169
	Cadiz	Cromarty	144		
Total			9,517	216	318

Source: Corn debentures in NAS, E508

TABLE 3   Exports of salt fish from Scotland from the Union to 15 July 1709.

Precinct	Barrels herring	Barrels salmon	Wet cod: Long hundreds	Dry cod: Long hundreds
Inverness	1,958	936	–	88
Kirkcaldy	27,776	42	77	128
Port Glasgow	6,384	98	–	295
Eyemouth	4,447	–	28	232
Leith	2,855	270	10	23
Aberdeen	446	2,448	111	1,615
Lewis	343	72	–	–
Prestonpans	286	286	–	–
Montrose	58	306	308	–
Dundee	1,938	12	17	–
Bo'ness	55	–	–	–
Ayr	–	10	–	–
Dumfries	–	32	–	–
Perth	–	–	–	–
Port Patrick	12	12	–	–
Campbeltown	216	–	–	–
Total	46,775	4,279	565	2,427

Source: NAS, RH2/4

TABLE 4   Exports of salt fish from the customs precinct of Inverness as recorded in fish debentures.

Year (June – May)	Barrels salmon	Barrels herring	Dried cod	No. of ships exporting
1707–9	935.5	1,958.5	10,560	not known
1709–10	121	392		5
1710–11	–	–	–	–
1711–12	–	–	–	–
1712–13	13.5	48		3
1713–14	1,477.75	6,523.5	57,996	22
1714–15	755	5460	94,631	25
1715–16	908	2,513.5	28,800	21
1716–17	539.75	9,084.2	32,300	36
1717–18	7.5	284	–	4
1718–19	310	950	5,700	10
1719–20	378.5	1272	116,001	10
1720–1	–	–	–	–
1721–2	–	1573	–	8
1722–3	314	5,083.5	55,200	19
1723–4	174	–	–	1
1724–5	–	–	–	–
1725–6	–	–	–	–
1726–7	–	–	–	–
1727–8	–	–	–	–
1728–9	814.5	10,987.5	16,800	28
1729–30	339	1629.5	64,700	11
1730–1	696.5	–		3
1731–2	145	–	1	
Total	6,994	45,800.7	472,128	207

Source: NAS, E508

TABLE 5   Value (rounded to nearest £ sterling) of fish debentures issued by customs precincts in Scotland 1714–15 to 1720–1.

Precinct	Total 1714–20	1714–15	1715–16	1716–17	1717–18	1718–19	1719–20	1720–1
Aberdeen	£2,893	£399	£345	£465	£565	£418	£694	£7
Ayr	£1,220	£244	£482	£222	£6	£17	£189	£60
Alloa	£57	–	£48	£5	–	£2	£2	–
Anstruther	£22,895	£432	£1,893	£6,477	£8,213	£3,380	£2,490	£10
Bo'ness	£730	–	£4	–	–	–	£726	–
Campbeltown	£832	£49	£60	£135	£163	£377	£14	£34
Crail	–	–	–	–	–	–	–	–
Dunbar	£1,057	£45	£345	£490	–	–	£9	£168
Dundee	£20	–	–	–	£16	–	–	£4
Port Glasgow	£692	–	£113	£303	£68	–	£197	£11
Greenock	£4,443	£1,388	£210	£968	£134	£653	£894	£196
Inverness	£15,330	£1,894	£1,945	£5,141	£2,901	£740	£2,456	£253
Irvine	£1,807	£797	£1	£20	£39	£195	£699	£56
Kerston	£183	–	–	–	–	–	£183	–
Kirkcaldy	£276	£58	£28	–	–	£190	–	–
Leith	£438	£28	£83	£308	–	–	–	£19
Lerwick	£6,184	£591	£589	£462	£3,229	£323	£542	£448
Montrose	£2,445	£91	–	£1,021	£541	£169	£599	£24
Prestonpans	£309	£19	£38	£5	£86	£151	£10	–
Stranraer	£36	–	£17	£19	–	–	–	–
Fort William	£118	–	–	–	–	£67	–	£51
Stornoway	£436	–	–	–	–	–	£341	£95
Thurso	£48	–	–	–	–	–	–	£48
Total	£59,734	£6,033	£6,202	£16,236	£13,056	£6,683	£10,042	£1,482

Source: NAS, E502

TABLE 6 Destination of exports of salt fish from the customs precinct of Inverness.

| Destination | 1709–10 to 1731–2 | | |
	Salmon	Herring	Cod
Mediterranean	77.21%	15.20%	7.00%
Baltic	–	45.60%	4.90%
North Sea ports*	9.00%	20.80%	20.10%
Le Havre	8.60%	.40%	–
North Atlantic coast	10.00%	5.50%	67.50%
America and W. Indies	–	5.40%	.50%
Ireland	.12%	3.40%	–
Not known	.07%	3.70%	–
	1713–14 to 1716–17		
Mediterranean	79.60%	24.60%	1.80%
Baltic	–	27.20%	5.10%
North Sea ports*	7.10%	26.00%	1.70%
Le Havre	5.80%	–	–
North Atlantic coast	7.10%	7.50%	91.40%
America and W. Indies	–	4.80%	–
Ireland	–	3.90%	–
Not known	.40%	6.00%	–
*Rotterdam, Amsterdam, Ostend and Hamburg.			

Source: NAS, E508

TABLE 7   Fiars (£ Scots) for Ross-shire (with Edinburgh fiars for comparison).

Year	Ross fiars	Edinburgh bere	Year	Ross fiars	Edinburgh bere
1658	£5.00		1687	£3.00	£5.75
1659	£6.66	£6.33	1688	£2.66	£5.70
1660	£5.66	36.33	1689	£3.00	£6.25
1661	£5.00	£9.00	1690	£4.00	£8.65
1662	£5.00	£7.50	1691	£3.00	£5.90
1663	£3.00	£7.00	1692	£3.33	£6.00
1664	£3.00	£5.66	1693	£3.66	£6.25
1665	£3.66	£5.66	1694	£4.00	£6.33
1666	£5.33	£6.00	1695	£4.33	£8.25
1667	£4.00	£6.50	1696	£5.00	£12.00
1668	£3.00	£6.00	1697	£5.66	£9.50
1669		£6.00			
1670		£6.00	1703	£3.66	£7.17
1671		£6.33	1704	£3.00	£6.75
1672	£4.00	£6.66	1705	£2.43	£6.60
1673	£4.00	£6.33			
1674	£8.00	£9.66	1711	£3.00	£7.33
1675	£6.00	£12.00	1712	£2.50	£6.33
1676	£4.33	£7.00			
1677	£4.00	£7.00	1734	£2.47	£6.25
1678	£3.66	35.60	1735	£2.47	£6.35
1679	£3.66	£6.66	1736	£3.27	£7.10
1680	£3.66	£6.00	1737	£3.13	£7.00
1681	£4.17	£6.00	1738	£2.47	£5.90
1682	£5.33	£8.66	1739		
1683	£5.00	£5.90	1740	£5.27	£10.60
1684	£4.66	£5.80			
1685	£3.66	£5.70			

Sources: Ross-shire fiars in William Macgill, *Old Ross-shire and Scotland as seen in the Tain and Balnagowan documents* (Inverness, 1909), ii. no. 432; and NAS, GD305/162/36. Other fiars from A. J. S. Gibson and T. C. Smout, *Prices, Food and Wages in Scotland 1550–1780* (Cambridge, 1995).

Select Bibliography

Manuscript sources

Bank of Scotland
British Linen Company records

Craigston Castle, Turiff
Urquhart family: deeds and papers (NRAS 0204)

Cromarty Courthouse Museum
Cromarty Estate Factors Accounts, 1803–11
Cromarty Kirk Session papers
History of the Bains of Newton
Survey of gravestones in Cromarty East Church kirkyard
Survey by Dr James Skinner of fishing settlements in Easter Ross
Survey of Sandilands House by Mary Washington College, Virginia &
    The Robert Gordon University, Aberdeen (1997)
Survey of Cromarty's housing and economy, George Mackenzie
    (1913)

Cromarty Harbour Trust
Minute books

Foulis Castle
Munro of Foulis papers

Guildhall Library, London
Sun Insurance Records (MS 11936/322)

Highland Council Archive, Inverness
Newhall estate papers
Minutes of Freeholders of County of Cromarty
Inverness Burgh Court records
Decreet of Division of the Church of Cromarty, 1756

Mackenzie of Scatwell v Magistrates of Fortrose, printed papers in the
    Fraser Macintosh Collection

Highland Council Libraries
Edinburgh College of Art, 'Burgh of Cromarty report' (1962)

Middleton Family, Rosefarm, Cromarty
Family papers

National Archives, Kew (NA) formerly Public Record Office (PRO)
Treasury papers (T1/123, 168 & 182)

National Archives of Scotland (NAS) formerly Scottish Record Office (SRO)
Agriculture and Fisheries Department for Scotland (AF)
Register of Testaments (CC8/8)
Inverness Outport and District Records (CE62)
Church of Scotland, Minutes of Presbytery of Chanonry (CH2/66/4)
    Cromarty Kirk Session (CH2/672)
Court of Session (CS)
Exchequer Records (E)
Gifts and Deposits (GD): Ross of Cromarty (GD1/481 & GD159);
    Warrand of Bught (GD23); Robertson of Kindeace (GD146); Ross
    of Pitcalnie (GD199); Mackenzie of Seaforth (GD 305); Sutherland
    Family of Rearquhar (GD347)
Heritors records (HR)
Inland Revenue (IRS)
Records of the Board of Trustees (NG)
English Customs Ledgers (RH4/157)
Papers of David Ross, Accountant to the GPO, Edinburgh
    (RH15/44)
Sheriff Court, Cromarty (SC24)
Tain (SC34)

National Library of Scotland (NLS)
Barkly papers (Ac 9907)
Sutherland papers (Dep313)
Edward Fraser of Reelig 'On Emigration from the Highlands and
    Islands of Scotland' (Ms9646)

Nightingale of Cromarty
David Aitken, 'Survey of the Cromarty Estate, 1763'
John Douglas, 'Cromarty estate plans, 1823'
Barony of Cromarty Cartulary

North of England Institute of Mining and Mechanical Engineers
Watson Collection, Colliery View Book (NRO 3410/Wat/2/10/47, 1
    Aug 1768)
Miscellaneous Collections, Borings and Sinkings (NRO 3410/ZA/12/
    57, 1 Aug 1768)

St Andrews University Archives
Diary of Alexander Oswald Brodie 1843 (MS TA140:B8E43)

Tain & District Museum
Cadboll Papers

Printed primary sources

GENERAL REFERENCE:
Calendar of Treasury Books
Calendar of Scottish Papers
Register of the Secret Seal
Fasti Ecclesiae Scoticanae: The Succession of Ministers in the Church
    of Scotland from the Reformation
Origines Parochiales Scotiae (Edinburgh, 1851–4)
Index to the Register of Sasines for the Sheriffdoms of Inverness,
    Ross, Cromarty and Sutherland (Edinburgh, 1966)

Anderson, G. and P., *Guide to the Highlands and Islands of Scotland*,
    (Edinburgh, 1834 & 1850 editions)
Anon, *The Jew Exile: A Pedestrian Tour and Residence in the Most*
    Remote and Untravelled Districts of the Highlands and Islands of
    Scotland, Under Persecution (London, 1828)
——*A Pastoral Apology on behalf of a Certain Flock in Ross-shire*

Bayne, Peter, *The Life and Letters of Hugh Miller* (Edinburgh, 1871)
Brodie, Alexander, *Diary of Alexander Brodie of Brodie, 1652–1680*
    and of his son James Brodie (Aberdeen, 1873)
Brown, Peter Hume, *Early Travellers in Scotland* (Edinburgh, 1891)
Burt, Edmund, *Letters from a Gentleman in the North of Scotland*
    (London, 1759). New edition (Edinburgh, 1998)

Carruthers, Robert, *The Highland Notebook; or, Sketches and*
    Anecdotes (Edinburgh, 1843)
Chalmers, Robert, *The Picture of Scotland* (Edinburgh, 1827)
Commissioners Appointed to Inquire into the State of Municipal
    Corporations in Scotland, *Report* (1835)
Commission for Inquiring into Administration of the Poor Laws,
    Report, PP 1844 XXXII–XXVI

Dalrymple, David (Viscount Stair), *Decisions of the Court of Session between 1666 and 1671*

Defoe, Daniel, *A Tour Through the Whole Island of Great Britain* (London, 1724–7). New edition 1985.

Dickson, N., *Cromarty: Being a Tourist's Visit to the Birthplace of Hugh Miller* (Glasgow, 1859)

Donaldson, James, *A General View of the Agriculture of the County of Elgin or Moray* (London, 1794)

—— *A General view of the agriculture of the county of Nairn* (London, 1795)

Dunbar, John G. (ed.), *Sir William Burrell's Northern Tour, 1758* (East Linton, 1997)

Forbes, Robert, *Journal of the Episcopal Visitation of the Right Rev. Robert Forbes M.A. of the diocese of Ross ... and a memoir of Bishop R Forbes* (London, 1886).

Forsyth, Robert, *The Beauties of Scotland* (Edinburgh, 1806)

Hall, J. N., *Travels in Scotland* (London, 1807)

Henderson, John, *A General View of the Agriculture of the County of Sutherland* (London, 1815)

—— *A General View of the Agriculture of the County of Caithness* (London, 1815)

Kennedy, John, *The Days of the Fathers in Ross-shire* (Inverness, 1895)

Leslie, William, *A General View of the Agriculture of the Counties of Moray and Nairn* (London, 1813)

Loch, David, *Essays on the trade, commerce, manufactures and fisheries of Scotland* (Edinburgh, 1775)

Macfarlane, Walter, *Geographical Collections* (Scottish History Society, 1906–08)

Macgill, William, *Old Ross-shire and Scotland* (Inverness, 1909)

Mackay, William (ed.), *The Letter Book of Bailie Steuart of Inverness* (Edinburgh, 1915)

Mackay, William and Boyd, Herbert Cameron (eds), *Records of Inverness*, II (Spalding Club, Aberdeen, 1911–24)

Mackenzie, M., *A View of the Salmon Fishery of Scotland* (London, 1834)

Mackenzie, George S., *A General Survey of the Counties of Ross & Cromarty* (London, 1810)

Maclean, J., *Reminiscences of Clachnacuddin* (Inverness, 1842)

Maxwell, R., *Select Transactions of the Honourable Society of Improvers in the Knowledge of Agriculture in Scotland* (Edinburgh, 1743)

Miller, Hugh, *My Schools and Schoolmaster* (Edinburgh, 1856). New edition 1993

Miller, Hugh, *Scenes and Legends of the North of Scotland* (Edinburgh, 1994)

—— *Tales and Sketches* (Edinburgh, 1863)

—— *Sketchbook of Popular Geology* (Edinburgh, 1870)

Miller, Hugh, in Michael Shortland (ed.), *From Stone Mason to Geologist: Hugh Miller's Memoir* (Edinburgh, 1995)

Miller, Lydia, *Passages in the Life of an English Heiress*

Munro, John Bennet, 'The First Dissenting Congregation in the Highlands' in *United Presbyterian Magazine* (Glasgow, 1865), New Series ix. 307–15, 354–60, 401–8

Pennant, Thomas, *A Tour in Scotland 1769* (London, 1790)

Pockocke, Richard, *Tours in Scotland 1747, 1750, 1760* (Scottish History Society, Edinburgh, 1887)

Robertson, James, *A General View of the Agriculture in the County of Inverness* (London, 1808)

Sinclair, John, *A general view of the northern counties and islands of Scotland* (London, 1795)

—— *The Statistical Account of Scotland* (1791–99)

Spalding, John, *The history of the troubles and memorable transactions in Scotland and England, from MDCXXIV to MDCXLV* (Edinburgh, 1828–9)

Stuart J. et al, *The Exchequer Rolls of Scotland* (Edinburgh, 1878–1908), 1882

Taylor, Louise B., *The Aberdeen Shore Work Accounts* (Aberdeen, 1972)

Telford, Thomas, *Survey and Report of the Coasts and Central Highlands of Scotland* (1802)

—— *Survey and Report of the Coasts and Central Highlands of Scotland*, 4th Report (1803)

Thom, William, 'Journal of a tour in the North of Scotland' in *New Agricultural and Commercial Magazine*, i. no 4 (1811)

Thomson, J., *The Value and Importance of the Scottish Fisheries* (London, 1849)

Urquhart, Thomas, of Cromarty, *Collected Works* (Edinburgh, 1834)

Wight, Andrew, *Present State of Husbandry in Scotland*, (Edinburgh, 1778–1784)

Wilson, J. M., *Imperial Gazetteer of Scotland* (1853)

Maps

Surveys by David Aitken
Estate of Tulloch, 1763 (NAS, RHP 1473)
Estate of Findon, 1769 (NAS, RHP 3513)
Estate of Novar, 1779 (NAS, RHP10671)
Estate of Drynie & Kilmuir, n.d. (Highland Council Archive, Inverness)
Estate of Brims, 1769 (NAS, RHP 1219)
Estates of Pulrossie & Skelbo, 1765 & 1788 (NLS, Dep 313/3587)
Estate of Tarradale, 1788 (Highland Council Archive, Inverness)
Estate of Cromarty, 1764 (Cromarty estate)

Surveys by Kirk
Kintradwell and Navidale (NLS, Dep 313/3582)
Loth (NLS, Dep 313/3583)

Surveys by John Hume
Golspie (NLS, Dep 313/3581)
Invergordon, in two sections, copies only, location of originals unknown [NAS, RHP 37985; Cromarty Courthouse Museum]

Others
Volume of Balnagowan Maps, 1808 (NAS, RHP 13229)
Plans of Cromarty Estate, John Douglas, 1823 (Cromarty estate)

Newspapers and periodicals

Cromarty News 1891–2
Invergordon Times
Inverness Advertiser
Inverness Courier
Inverness Journal
North Star
Northern Ensign
Ross-shire Journal
The Times
Transactions of the Highland Agricultural Society of Scotland (1877)

Secondary sources

Adams, Ian and Somerville, Meredyth, *Cargoes of Hope and Despair* (Edinburgh, 1993)
Allen, N., 'Highland Planned Villages' in *Highland Vernacular Building* (Edinburgh, 1989)

Alston, David, *Ross and Cromarty: A Historical Guide* (Edinburgh, 1999)

Anon, *The Centenary of Hugh Miller* (Glasgow, 1902)

Anson, Peter, *Fishing boats and fisher folk on the East Coast of Scotland* (London, 1930)

Ash, Marinell, *This Noble Harbour* (Invergordon & Edinburgh, 1991)

Bateson, Donald, *Coin Finds from Cromarty* (Cromarty, 1993)

Berg, Maxine, *The Age of Manufactures, 1700–1820* (London & New York, 1994)

Brown, Callum G., *Religion and Society in Scotland since 1707* (Edinburgh, 1997)

Brown, Thomas, *Annals of the Disruption* (Edinburgh, 1884)

Bruce, Steven, 'Social change and collective behaviour: the revival in eighteenth-century Ross-shire', *British Journal of Sociology*, 34 (1983)

Calder, Angus, 'The Disruption in Fiction' in S. J. Brown and M. Fry, *Scotland in the Age of the Disruption* (Edinburgh, 1993)

Campbell, Colin and Green, Rosalind, *Can't shoot a man with a cold* (Glasgow, 2004)

Campey, Lucille H., *'A Very Fine Class of Immigrants': Prince Edward Island's Scottish Pioneers 1770–1850* (Toronto, 2001)

——*Fast Sailing and Copper-bottomed: Aberdeen Sailing Ships and the Emigrant Scots they carried to Canada, 1774–1855* (Toronto, 2002)

Carter, Ian, *Farm Life in Northeast Scotland 1840–1914* (Edinburgh, 1979)

Clough, Monica, *Two Houses* (Aberdeen, 1990)

——'Early Fishery and Forestry Developments on the Cromartie estate of Coigach: 1600–1746' in John Baldwin (ed.), *Peoples and Settlement in North-west Ross* (Edinburgh, 1994)

Connelly, Charlie, *Attention All Shipping* (London, 2004)

Colley, Linda, *Britons: Forging the Nation 1707–1832* (London, 1994)

Coull, James, *The Sea Fisheries of Scotland* (Edinburgh, 1996)

Cragg, G. R., *The Church in the Age of Reason* (London, 1970)

Craig, Carol, *The Scots' Crisis of Confidence* (Edinburgh, 2003)

David, Elizabeth, *The Harvest of the Cold Months* (London, 1994)

Devine, Thomas M., *The Transformation of Rural Scotland* (Edinburgh, 1994)

——*From Clanship to Crofters' War* (Manchester, 1994)

——*Exploring the Scottish Past* (East Linton, 1995)

Dodgshon, Robert A., *From Chiefs to Landlords* (Edinburgh, 1998)

Dodgshon, Robert A., 'Budgeting for Survival: Nutrient Flow and Traditional Highland Farming' in S. Foster and T. C. Smout (eds), *The History of Soils and Field Systems* (Aberdeen, 1994)

Donnachie, Iain and Hewitt, G., *Historic New Lanark* (Edinburgh, 1993)

Drummond, A. L. and Bulloch, J., *The Scottish Church 1688–1843: The Age of the Moderates* (Edinburgh, 1973)

Duncan, Jane, *My Friends the Miss Boyds* (London, 1959)

Durie, Alasdair, 'Linen spinning in the north of Scotland, 1746–1773' in *Northern Scotland* (1974–77), ii, 13–36

—— *Scotland for the Holidays: Tourism in Scotland c.1780–1939* (East Linton, 2003)

Fenyõ, Krisztina, *Contempt, Sympathy and Romance: Lowland Perceptions of the Highlands and the Clearances during the Famine Years, 1845–1855* (East Linton, 2000)

Ferguson, William, 'The election system in the Scottish counties before 1832' in *Miscellany II*, Stair Society (Edinburgh, 1984)

—— 'The Urquharts of Cromarty' in *Scottish Genealogist*, vi. Part 2 (1959), 16–8

Flinn, Michael, *Scottish Population History* (Cambridge, 1977)

Fraser, William H., 'Social Class' in A. Cooke, I. Donnachie, A. MacSween and C. A. Whatley (eds), *Modern Scottish History 1707 to the Present, Volume I: The Transformation of Scotland, 1707–1850* (East Linton, 1998)

Fyfe, Janet, 'Cromarty Emigrants and Emigrant Ships' (Cromarty, 1997)

Gibson, A. J. S. and Smout, T. C., *Prices, food and wages in Scotland 1550–1780* (Cambridge, 1995)

—— 'Regional prices and market regions: the evolution of the early Scottish grain market' in *Economic History Review*, XLVIII, 2 (1995)

—— 'Scottish food and Scottish history 1500–1800' in R. A. Houston and I. Whyte (eds), *Scottish Society, 1500–1800* (Cambridge, 1989)

Graham, Eric J., 'The Scottish marine during the Dutch wars' in *Scottish Historical Review* (1982)

—— *Maritime History of Scotland 1650–1790* (East Linton, 2002)

Grant, W. and Murison, D. (eds), *The Scottish National Dictionary*, (Edinburgh, 1931)

Gray, Malcolm, *The Fishing Industries of Scotland 1790–1914* (Aberdeen, 1978)

Hancock, David, *Citizens of the World: London Merchants and the Integration of the British Atlantic Community, 1735–1785* (Cambridge, 1995)

Harper, Marjory, *Emigration from North-East Scotland, Volume 1: Willing Exiles* (Aberdeen, 1988)

Hillis, P. L. M., 'The Sociology of the Disruption' in S. J. Brown and M. Fry (eds), *Scotland in the Age of the Disruption* (Edinburgh, 1993)

Holderness, B. A., *Pre-Industrial Britain: Economy and Society 1500–1700* (London, 1976)

Hughes, Yseult, 'What Poyntzfield restoration in revealing' in *Clan Munro Magazine* 19 (1991), 7–12

Hunter, James, *The Making of the Crofting Community* (Edinburgh, 1976)

Hustwick, Iain, *Moray Firth Ships and Trade* (Aberdeen, 1994)

Lenman, Leah, *Living in Atholl* (Edinburgh, 1986)

Levitt, Ian and Smout, T. C., *The State of the Scottish Working Class in 1843* (Edinburgh, 1979)

Livingstone, A., *The Muster Roll of Prince Charles Edward Stewart's Army 1745–1746* (Aberdeen, 1984)

McDowell, Nicholas, 'Urquhart's Rabelais: Translation, Patronage, and Cultural Politics' in *English Literary Renaissance* (Oxford, 2006)

Macinnes, Allan, *Clanship, Commerce and the House of Stuart* (East Linton, 1996)

Mackenzie, Donald A., 'Cromarty Dialects and Folk-lore' in *Transactions of the Rymour Club* (Edinburgh, 1928)

Mackenzie, William Mackay 'Cromarty: its old chapels and parish church' in *Scottish Ecclesiological Society* (1905)

——'The old sheriffdom of Cromarty' in *Transactions of the Gaelic Society of Inverness* (Inverness, 1926), xxx, 289–335

——'The Royal Burgh of Cromarty and the Breaking of the Burgh' *in Transactions of the Gaelic Society of Inverness* (Inverness, 1927), xxxi, 374–91

——'The royal burgh of Cromarty and the breaking of the burgh' in *Transactions of the Gaelic Society of Inverness* (Inverness, 1927), xxxi, 374–91

Mackintosh, E. Alan, *War, The Liberator* (London, 1918)

MacLean, Isabella, *Your Father and I* (East Linton, 1998)

Macmillan, Mona, *Sir Henry Barkly: Mediator and Moderator* (Cape Town, 1970)

Macrae, A., *Revivals in the Highlands and Islands in the Nineteenth Century* (Stirling, n.d.)

Malcolm, Eric H., *The Cromarty & Dingwall Light Railway* (Cromarty, 1993)

——*The Cromarty We Knew* (Cromarty, 2000)

——*Heroes and Others* (Cromarty, 2003)

Martin, John, *Church Chronicles of Nigg* (1991)

Mowat, Ian R. M., *Easter Ross 1750–1850: The Double Frontier* (Edinburgh, 1981)

Munro, R. W. and J., *Tain Through the Centuries* (Tain, 1966)

Nenadic, Stena, 'Political reform and the Ordering of Middle-class Protest' in Thomas M. Devine (ed.), *Conflict and Stability in Scottish Society, 1700–1850* (Edinburgh, 1990)

——'Middle-Rank Consumers and Domestic Culture in Edinburgh and Glasgow 1720–1840' in *Past and Present* 145 (1994), 122–56

Oram, Richard D., *The Reign of Alexander II 1214–49* (Leiden, 2005)

Parker, Andrew W., *Scottish Highlanders in Colonial Georgia* (Georgia, 1997)

Putnam, Robert D., *Bowling Alone* (New York, 2000)

Randall, A., Charlesworth, A., Sheldon, R. and Walsh, D., 'Markets, Market Culture and Popular Protest in Eighteenth-century Britain and Ireland' in A. Randall and A. Charlesworth (eds), *Markets, Market Culture and Popular Protest in Eighteenth-century Britain and Ireland* (Liverpool, 1996)

Reid, F. N., *The Earls of Ross* (London, 1894)

Richards, Eric and Clough, Monica, *Cromartie: Highland Life: 1650–1914* (Aberdeen, 1991)

Robertson, Ian A., *The Tay Salmon Fisheries* (Glasgow, 1998)

Rose, Jonathan, *The Intellectual Life of the British Working Classes* (London, 2002)

Rosie, George, *The Ludwig Initiative* (Edinburgh, 1978)

Seton, B. G. and Arnot, J. G., *Jacobite Prisoners of the '45* (Scottish History Society, 1929)

Short, Brian, *Land and Society in Edwardian Britain* (Cambridge, 1997)

Slade, Harry Gordon, 'The biging on Allertown: a reconstruction of an 18th century farmhouse and steading in Cromarty' in *Proceeding of the Society of Antiquaries of Scotland* (1986), cxvi, 455–72

Smout, T. C., 'Peasant and Lord in Scotland: Institutions Controlling Scottish Rural Society, 1500–1800' in RA Houston & I Whyte (eds), *Scottish Society, 1500–1800* (Cambridge, 1989)

——*History of the Scottish People* (London, 1970)

Sprott, Gavin, 'Lowland Agriculture and Society' in Cooke, Donnachie, MacSween and Whatley (eds), *Modern Scottish History 1707 to the Present, Volume 2: The Modernisation of Scotland, 1850 to the Present* (East Linton, 1998)

Stell, Geoffrey, 'Architecture and Society in Easter Ross before 1707' in John Baldwin (ed.), *Firthlands of Ross & Cromarty* (Edinburgh, 1986)

Stevenson, David, *King or Covenant? Voices from the Civil War* (East Linton, 1996)

Tayler, Henrietta, *The Family of Urquhart* (Aberdeen, 1946)
Thompson, E. P., *Customs in Common* (London, 1991)
—— 'Which Britons?' in *Dissent* (Summer, 1993)
Thomson, William P. L., *History of Orkney* (Edinburgh, 1987)
Tyson, R. E., 'Famine in Aberdeenshire, 1696–1699: Anatomy of a Crisis' in D. Stevenson (ed.), *From Lairds to Louns* (Aberdeen, 1986)

Young, Alan, *Robert the Bruce's Rivals* (East Linton, 1997)

Walker, Bruce, 'Salmon Fishing' in G. Jackson and S. G. E. Lythe, *The Port of Montrose* (New York, 1993)
Walker, David, *A Legal History of Scotland* (Edinburgh, 1988)
Walsh, D., Randall, A., Sheldon, R. and Charlesworth, A., 'The Cider Tax, Popular Symbolism and Opposition in Mid-Hanoverian England' in A. Randall and A. Charlesworth (eds), *Markets, Market Culture and Popular Protest in Eighteenth-century Britain and Ireland* (Liverpool, 1996)
Whatley, Christopher A., *Scottish Society 1707–1830* (Manchester, 2000)
Whetstone, A. E., *Scottish County Government in the Eighteenth and Nineteenth Centuries* (Edinburgh, 1981)
Wilsher, Betty, *Understanding Scottish Graveyards* (Edinburgh, 1985)
Withers, Charles W J, *Urban Highlanders* (East Linton, 1998)

Theses

Campey, Lucille H., 'The Regional Characteristics of Scottish Emigration to British North America, 1784–1854' (University of Aberdeen, 1997)

Index